D1796622

Office Administration

for CSEC® Examinations

**Allison Trenfield-Newsome
and Colleen Walker**

CSEC® is a registered trade mark(s) of the **Caribbean Examinations Council (CXC).**
Office Administration for CSEC® Examinations is an independent publication and has not
been authorized, sponsored, or otherwise approved by CXC.

MACMILLAN

Macmillan Education Limited
4 Crinan Street
London N1 9XW
A division of Macmillan Education Limited
Companies and representatives throughout the world

www.macmillan-caribbean.com

ISBN: 978-0-230-02948-4

Text © Allison Trenfield-Newsome and Colleen Walker 2011
Design and illustration © Macmillan Education Limited 2011

All rights reserved; no part of this publication may be
reproduced, stored in a retrieval system, transmitted in any
form or by any means, electronic, mechanical, photocopying,
recording, or otherwise, without the prior written permission
of the publishers.

These materials may contain links for third party websites.
We have no control over, and are not responsible for, the
contents of such third party websites. Please use care
when accessing them.

Design by Jim Weaver
Illustrations by Peter Harper, TechType and Gary Wing
Typeset by J & D Glover Ltd.
Cover design by Cary Fielder at Clear 22
Cover photographs by Alamy, Getty, Macmillan Education Limited
/ Norman Livingston and Superstock

The authors and publishers would like to thank the following
for permission to reproduce their photographs:
AIR CANADA (screen grab used with kind consent of Air Canada,
information only correct as at February 2011);
Alamy pp100 (t), 146, 250(m), Alamy / Eye Ubiquitous p17 (t);
Brother UK Ltd (Images used with the kind consent of Brother UK Ltd)
pp18 (ml), 19(b), 250(t), 251(b);
Getty pp244, 264(t);
Image Source p15;
Konica Minolta (Images used with the kind consent of Konica /
Minolta Business Solutions UK) pp16, 17(b), 18(mr), 19(t);
Liat Airlines Ltd (Images used with kind consent of Liat Airlines Ltd)
p145(r)
neat (Images used with kind consent of the Neat Company) p114 (b);
NEC Corporation (Images used with kind consent of NEC Corporation)
p19 (m);
Photolibrary / Clear Image p15;
RIM (Images used with kind consent of Research in Motion / Blackberry)
p123;
Sanyo Electric Co Ltd (Images used with the kind consent of Sanyo
Electric Co Ltd) p20 (b);
Science and Society pp18 (t, b);
Superstock pp20 (tl, tr), 21(t), 100(b), 114(t, m), 117, 122, 250(m),
264(b), 266.

Commissioned photography by Norman Livingston pp61,145, 240.

Printed and bound by CPI Group (UK) Ltd, Croydon CR0 4YY
2022
10 9 8 7 6

Contents

List of figures and tables

Figures

Tables

Series Preface

This new series of textbooks for the Caribbean Examinations Council (CXC) General Proficiency examinations has been developed and written by teachers with many years' experience of CSEC examinations in Caribbean schools.

A textbook is used in different ways at different times. Readers might be starting a topic from scratch, and need to be led through a logical explanation one step at a time. Students with a working knowledge of a topic might need to clarify a detail, or reinforce their understanding. Or, they may simply need to believe that they do have a good grasp of the material being studied.

In this specially created format (the same for all of the books in the series) the pages are designed to allow study of the text, uninterrupted by anything but essential diagrams. Additional material, including references to unfamiliar technical terms, is placed where it can readily be consulted, in the side column. Examination-style questions are provided for each chapter, and short 'In-Text Questions' (with answers) are placed throughout the text, allowing students to check their grasp of the topic as they read.

Teachers throughout the region emphasize that inclusion of school-based assessment (SBA) material is of immense help and value. The CSEC syllabus explains the rationale for the SBA exercise, and explains its expected structure. The structure of the SBA component is explained in the last chapter of the text.

Dr Mike Taylor
Series Editor

About this book

This book isn't just words on a page. This one has some important features. Each will help you, in its own way, if you take advantage of it.

▶ There are TWO COLUMNS.
  • The bigger column has the text and some really large diagrams; you can read straight down it without interruption
  • The smaller column has other diagrams that are mentioned in the text. Look at them carefully, as you need them. You could find that a few seconds looking at a diagram is worth several minutes' reading.

▶ The first time that an important NEW WORD occurs, it is repeated in the smaller column. If you want to check what a word means, you can find it quickly.

▶ There are QUESTIONS called 'In-Text Questions' (ITQs). When you have read the nearby paragraph in the main column, try to answer the question in your head, or on paper, just as you wish. Some need a little thought; others may need you to recall what you have just read.
  • If you can, you're on the road to understanding
  • If you can't, just go back and read that bit again
  • Answers to the ITQs that are not pure recall are at the end of each chapter, so you can tell how accurate your answer was.

▶ For this examination you must submit a Project Report, based on a problem from one or more sections of the syllabus. For each year your teacher will help you to choose a suitable topic and will show you how the Report must be presented. There is a chapter giving the main points of the Report format at the end of the book.

▶ There is a detailed INDEX. Don't be afraid to use it to find what you want.

▶ At the end of each chapter, there are some EXAMINATION-STYLE QUESTIONS. Your teacher will suggest how you can best use them.

Office orientation

By the end of this chapter you should be able to:

- [x] describe the role of the office;
- [x] identify the activities of a modern office;
- [x] outline the major functions of the office in business activities;
- [x] describe the operations of the major functional areas/departments in a business;
- [x] describe the organizational structure of various sizes of businesses;
- [x] differentiate between centralization and decentralization of office activities;
- [x] distinguish between the traditional and the open-plan office;
- [x] explain the role of ergonomics in office efficiency;
- [x] describe the role of various types of equipment in office efficiency;
- [x] outline the required skills, attitudes and characteristics of office staff;
- [x] assess the importance of good human relationships with customers, colleagues and employees.

Concept map   Office orientation

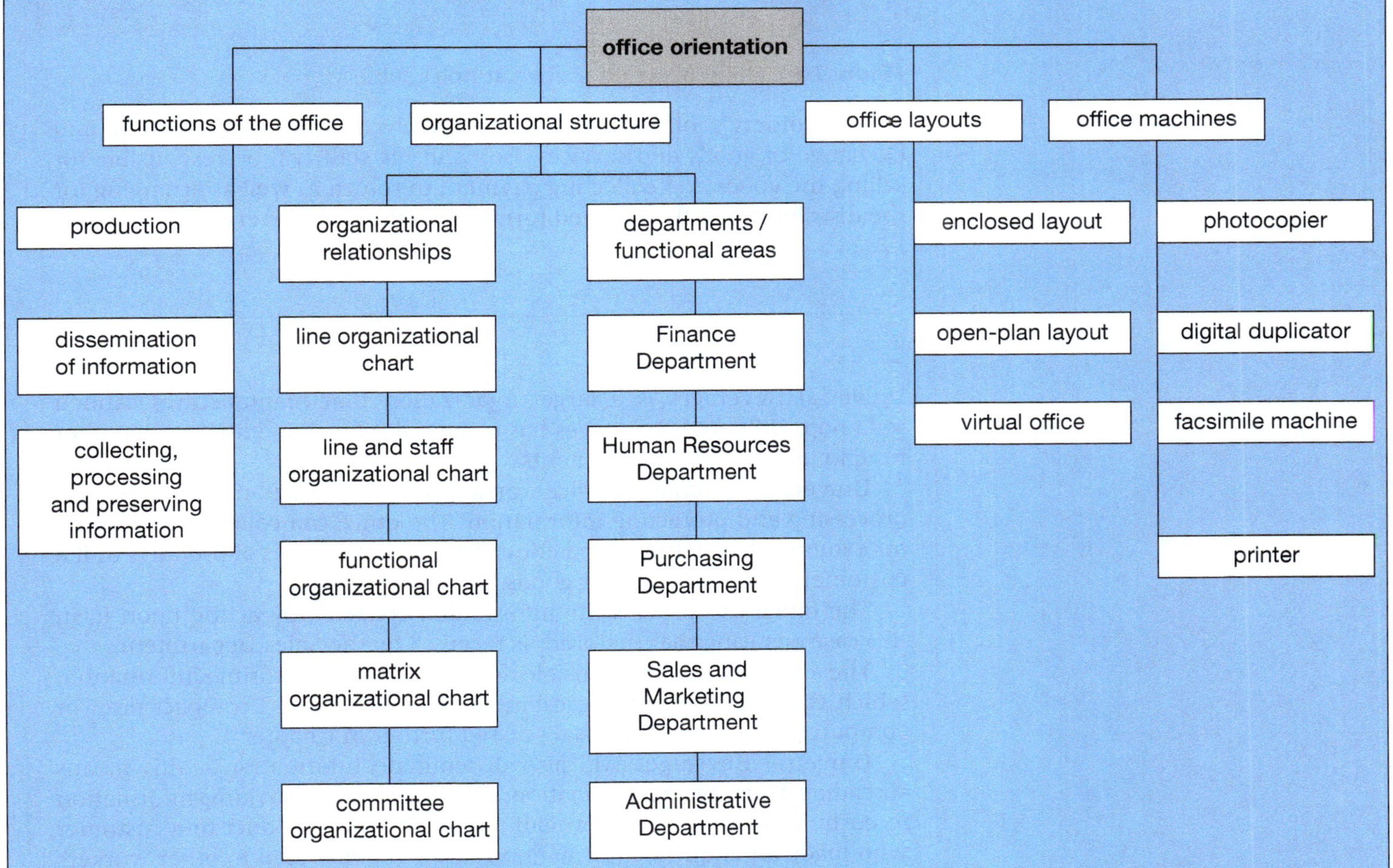

- office orientation
  - functions of the office
    - production
    - dissemination of information
    - collecting, processing and preserving information
  - organizational structure
    - organizational relationships
      - line organizational chart
      - line and staff organizational chart
      - functional organizational chart
      - matrix organizational chart
      - committee organizational chart
    - departments / functional areas
      - Finance Department
      - Human Resources Department
      - Purchasing Department
      - Sales and Marketing Department
      - Administrative Department
  - office layouts
    - enclosed layout
    - open-plan layout
    - virtual office
  - office machines
    - photocopier
    - digital duplicator
    - facsimile machine
    - printer

Functions of the office

office ▶

The office is considered as the centre of any business, whether large or small. It provides invaluable services to other members of the organization.

The functions of the office include:

- production;
- distribution and exchange of goods and services;
- collection, processing and preservation of information;

dissemination ▶

- dissemination of information;
- organizational and legal control.

Here are two examples:

Case 1: a small business

Bob's Joinery is a sole trader business owned by Bob Scarlett. Bob and his small staff of five employees produce furniture such as tables, chairs and dressers. All activities related to Bob's business are carried out at his workshop. The office at Bob's Joinery will carry out the function of production by creating the various types of furniture. The production process would look like the following:

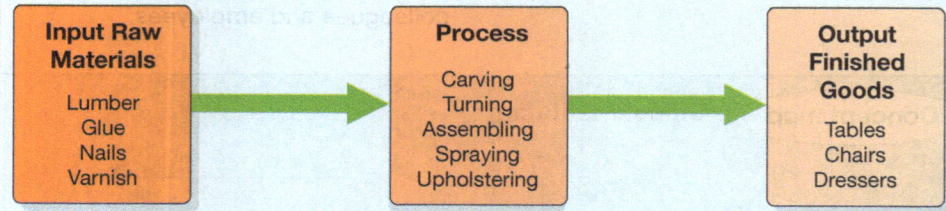

Figure 1.1   The production process at Bob's Joinery

The joinery's office will also be involved in the distribution and exchange of goods and services. Bob and his staff will be responsible for selling the goods and collecting payment in return as well as arranging for the distribution of the finished furniture to their customers.

Case 2: a large business

Universal Beverages is a large organization that manufactures canned soda pop. Universal Beverages has a general office in addition to its other functional areas and departments.

Universal Beverages' office carries out the functions of collecting, processing and protecting information. The office can collect information, for example if customers send enquiries about the prices of products or if a customer places an order for goods.

The office can process the information collected by acting upon it, in this case ensuring that the order is received by the Sales Department.

The office is also responsible for preserving or storing information, which can be done in filing cabinets, or on microfilm, compact discs or computer hard drives. This is discussed further in Chapter 4.

Universal Beverages will also disseminate information – this means spreading or giving out information. The office will be providing information to customers, for example providing the price of a product to a customer who made an enquiry. Information can also be provided to other workers within the organization.

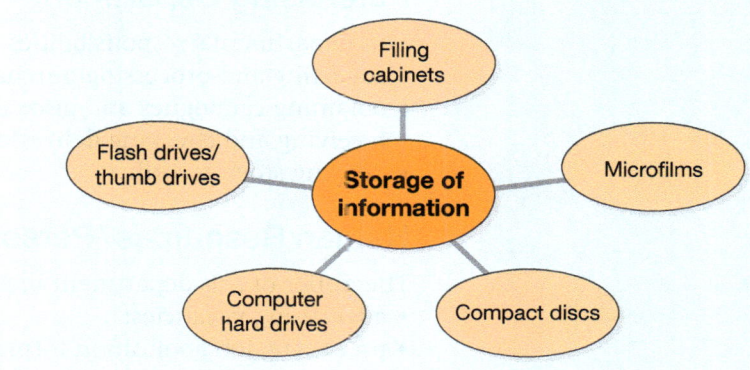

Figure 1.2 Methods of storing information

In large offices such as the one at Universal Beverages, an Office Manager might be put in charge of co-ordinating its activities, including carrying out organizational and legal control. The Office Manager's duties may include:

- supervising other office staff;
- monitoring the stock of office supplies;
- recording office expenditure and managing the budget;
- preparing reports;
- filing tax returns;
- performing clerical duties such as filing and typing.

The scope of the duties of the Office Manager will depend on the size and type of business.

Some common activities of today's modern offices include:

- protecting records, for example by filing;
- handling incoming and outgoing mail, including mail sent via the internet;
- making and receiving telephone calls;
- preparing written forms of communication such as letters, notices and memoranda;
- duplicating records;
- safeguarding assets, for example locking away valuables;
- receiving and directing visitors;
- making travel and meeting arrangements;
- faxing of documents.

outsourcing ▶ In today's modern business economy many firms, both small and large, have become involved in outsourcing. Outsourcing involves contracting with another firm to perform a function or service that the firm previously performed itself. Services and functions that are usually outsourced include making travel arrangements, data processing, advertising and preparing payroll.

Firms often outsource in order to reduce costs and to focus on their core functions and operations.

ITQ1
Outline **three** activities carried out in an office.

Functional areas and departments

functional areas ▶ Many medium-sized and large firms are organized based on functional areas or departments. Some common departments that exist in businesses are shown below.

3

Purchasing Department

This department's responsibilities include:
- collecting and processing purchase requisitions;
- obtaining catalogues and price lists from potential suppliers;
- receiving and checking deliveries;
- keeping stock records.

Human Resources / Personnel Department

The duties of this department include:
- advertising vacancies;
- processing job application forms;

interviews ▶
- arranging and conducting interviews;
- creating job descriptions and job specifications;
- keeping employee records up to date;
- addressing staff welfare issues, for example health and safety.

Finance / Accounts Department

This department is responsible for:
- preparing financial statements;
- preparing cheques for creditors;
- preparing payroll;
- preparing budget and final accounts, for example balance sheets.

Sales and Marketing Department

The duties of this department include:
- conducting market research;
- handling enquiries from potential customers;
- processing orders;
- preparing advertising and promotional material;
- handling customer complaints.

Administrative Department:

This department provides support services to the entire organization. This includes:
- desktop publishing;
- word processing;
- mail handling;
- clerical services;
- reprographics – making copies of an original document.

Computer Services/Information Technology Department

Because of the rise in the use of computers in businesses, many large firms, for example airlines, may find it necessary to have a Computer Services Department. The duties of this department include:
- managing the business's computer network;
- repairing hardware, software and network problems;
- training staff on the proper use of the software and hardware.

Many of these departments will be discussed in more detail later in this book.

Organization structure

organizational structure ▶
An organizational structure shows how the various tasks and individuals are coordinated in a formal way in order to achieve a common goal. The

organizational structure of the business will depend on the size of the business – a small sole trader business with just a few employees will have a much simpler chart than a large corporation with hundreds of employees.

An organizational chart is a graphical representation of a business's formal organizational structure. Organizational charts are able to illustrate the titles and responsibilities of workers, as well as to display the lines of authority, lines of responsibility, the chain of command and the span of control. The organizational chart will be able to identify how all the areas within the business are connected.

A good organizational chart should be simple and easy to understand. It should also be dated.

lines of authority ▶
lines of responsibility ▶
chain of command ▶
span of control ▶

> DEFINITION: **Authority** is the right of a superior to give orders and make decisions.

> DEFINITION: **Responsibility** is the obligation to accomplish set/prescribed goals.

> DEFINITION: **Chain of command** (also called **unity (line) of command**). This is the structure that shows where authority flows from top to bottom in an organizational structure.

> DEFINITION: **Span of control** is the concept that indicates the number of subordinates that a supervisor can manage effectively. A span of control may be described as 'narrow' or 'wide'. When a supervisor manages a small number of employees the span of control is said to be narrow, while if the supervisor manages a large number of employees the span of control is said to be wide.

The width of the span of control depends on:
- the abilities of the supervisors and workers – skilled workers will need less supervision. A skilful supervisor will also be able to manage large numbers of employees;
- the nature of the task – simple routine tasks will mean that workers may need less supervision which will allow for a wide span of control.
   Benefits of an organization chart include:
- it is a visual communication tool and makes it easier to understand the vast amount of information as a chart rather than as a list on paper;
- employees are able to verify their own position in the business;
- employees are able to see those staff members for whom they are responsible, as well as those to whom they report.
   Disadvantages of organization charts:
- if not reviewed regularly charts may become outdated, as, over time, employees may leave the business while new ones join;
- charts do not show the informal relationships that exist within the business;
- some workers may be unhappy with their status in the organization (perhaps they are shown as being at the bottom) and so may lose interest in their work, thus lowering productivity levels;
- charts do not show the leadership style used, for example democratic or autocratic.

Creating organizational charts has been made easier because of special software that will create a company's chart automatically, from the list of employees. This task will be made even easier if the employee names and their tasks are already in the business information technology database. Some types of software are also capable of inserting employees' photographs. Examples of organizational chart software include SmartDraw and Edraw Orgchart.

ITQ2
State **two** advantages of a narrow span of control and **two** advantages of a wide span of control.

A hierarchical structure of management would look like this:

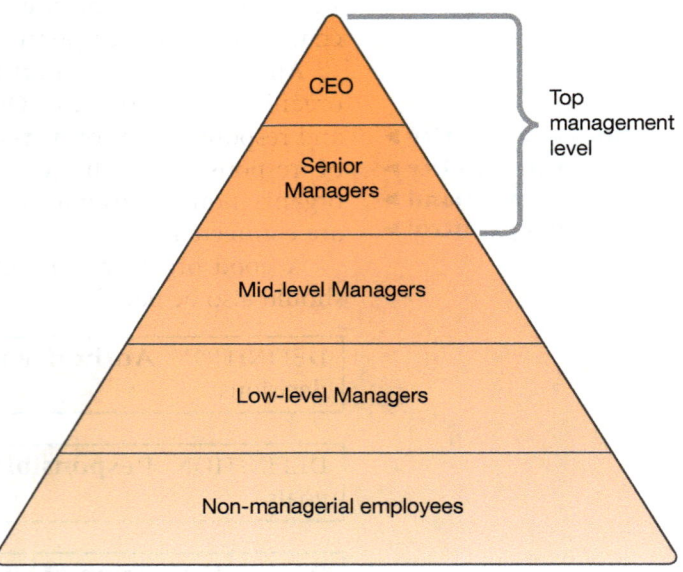

Figure 1.3 Hierarchical structure of management

top/executive management level ▶

The top/executive management level will include positions such as the CEO (Chief Executive Officer), Managing Director and Senior Managers such as the Financial Controller. This is the highest decision-making authority and is responsible for setting long-term goals for the organization.

middle management level ▶

The middle management level or mid-management level will include positions such as the Accounts Manager and the Advertising Manager. The middle managers assist the executive-level managers in implementing the business strategies set in order to achieve the organization's goals.

supervisory management level ▶

The supervisory management level, also known as 'First-level management' or 'Lower-level management', includes positions such as Accounts Supervisors. This level has the closest contact with employees and is responsible for putting the top and middle-level managers' plans into action. They also supervise workers to ensure that tasks are properly carried out.

At the bottom of the hierarchy are the non-managerial employees or the general workforce which makes up the bulk of the employees within most organizations.

The lower level has the highest number of managers, with fewer middle-level managers and the least number of managers at the top level.

Flat versus tall organizational structures

Organizational structures may be considered flat or tall, depending on the number of levels of management in the hierarchical structure.

flat organizational structure ▶

A flat organizational structure is typical of a small organization. It displays a few levels of management and a wider span of control.

Figure 1.4 Example of a flat organizational structure

In the flat structure shown in Figure 1.4, there exists only one management level – the owner, who is responsible for all the workers in the salon.

Over time, as small businesses grow into large businesses, the structure of the organization may change as new departments are added and more employees are hired. At this stage the larger firm might have a taller structure which is identified based on the many levels of management and a narrow span of control.

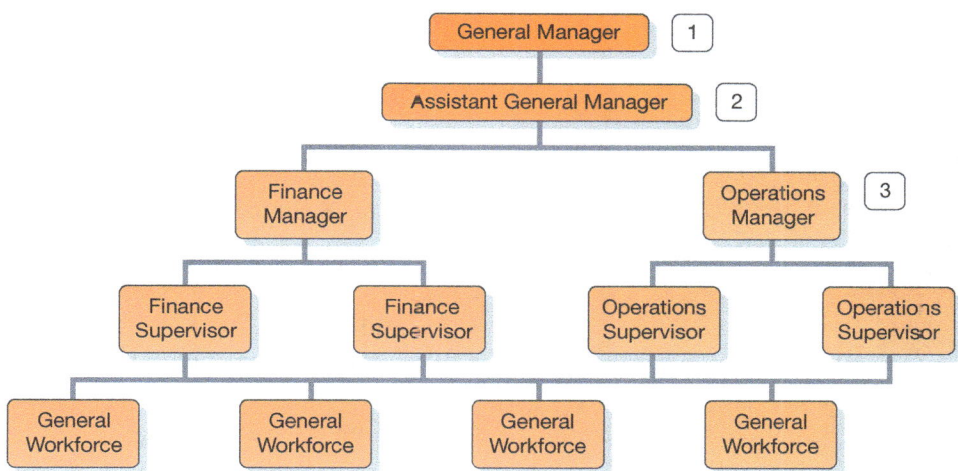

Figure 1.5 Example of a tall organizational structure

In the example in Figure 1.5, there are four levels of management.

Ways of presenting organizational charts

Organizational charts can be visually presented in three ways:

Vertical charts

Also known as the traditional method, having a vertical chart allows the chart to be read from top to bottom.

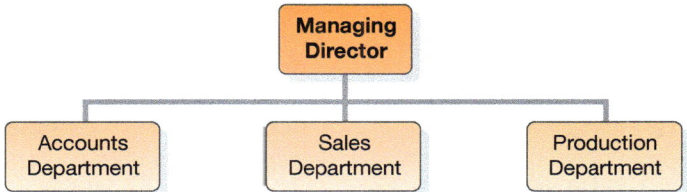

Figure 1.6 Example of a vertical chart

Horizontal charts

Horizontal charts allow the chart to be read from left to right.

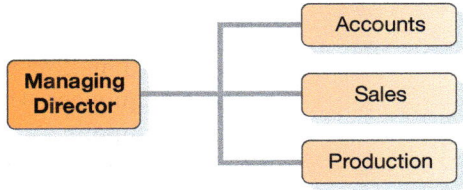

Figure 1.7 Example of a horizontal chart

Concentric charts

These are made up a series of circles, with the top management level located in the centre.

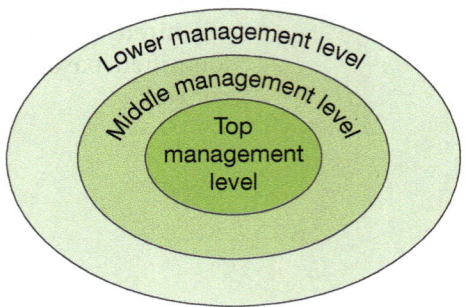

Figure 1.8 Example of a concentric chart

ITQ3

Explain the role of lower-level managers.

ITQ4

Differentiate between flat and tall organizational structures.

There are five basic types of organizational structure:
• line;
• line and staff;
• functional or departmental;
• matrix;
• committee.

Line organization structure

line organization structure ▶ The line organization structure shows a clear chain of command with a direct relationship between the supervisor and his/her subordinate. The line structure is common among small businesses, where employees may be on a first-name basis and the owner is usually directly responsible for carrying out most tasks in the business.

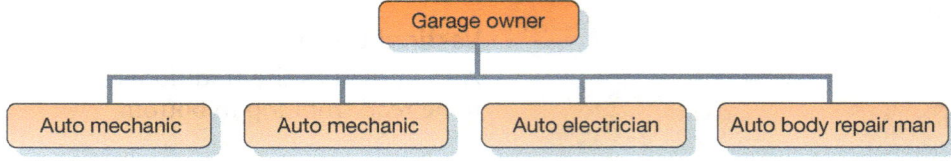

Figure 1.9 Example of a line organizational chart of a garage

A line relationship exists between the garage owner and the auto electrician, since the chain of command shows that the electrician reports directly to the garage owner.

lateral relationships ▶ Lateral relationships exist between employees who are on the same level, for example the auto mechanic and the auto electrician.

Line and staff organizational structure

line and staff structure ▶ The line and staff structure includes a regular line structure as shown in Figure 1.2, but also employs a staff function. The staff function includes persons who are hired to advise and support the line functions in areas such as public relations, janitorial services and legal services. The staff function's authority is limited to making recommendations – it has no authority over line managers or their employees. The line and staff structure is usually used by medium-sized to large companies.

In Figure 1.10, the example of a staff relationship is the Marketing Advisor. This individual provides marketing advice to the line managers but has no authority over them.

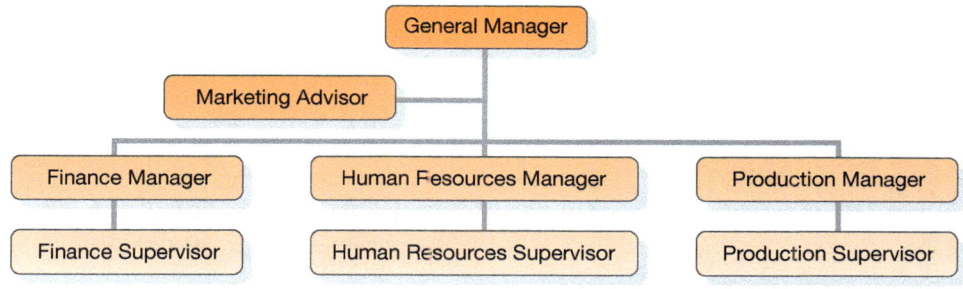

Figure 1.10   Example of a line and staff organizational structure

Functional or departmental organizational structure

functional organization structure ▶

The functional organization structure focuses on grouping similar tasks. Most structure therefore is divided into functional areas or departments. For example, all the marketing tasks will be done in the Marketing Department, which is staffed with specialists in the field of marketing. This can lead to greater efficiencies within each department, since each functional area is manned by specialists. Many small as well as large businesses use the functional organizational structure to outline their solid chain of command and the specialist units.

Figure 1.11   Example of a functional organizational structure

Matrix organizational structure

matrix organizational structure ▶

The matrix organizational structure allows employees who are members of a specific functional area or department to come together temporarily to form teams to work on special projects. This will mean that these employees will report to both their functional manager as well as their project manager. While the dual accountability may lead to some degree of confusion and contradiction, the matrix structure is ideal for obtaining creative and diverse ideas from across the various departments of the organization.

The matrix structure would be suitable in a case where a company is trying to create a design for a new product and would like input from specialists in the various departments.

Figure 1.12 shows that each departmental group reports not only to its line managers but also to the project manager.

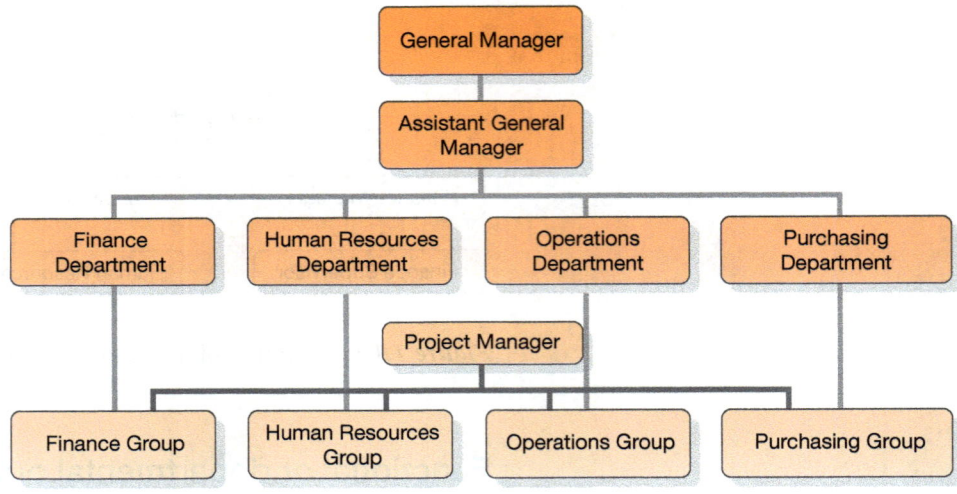

Figure 1.12 Example of a matrix organizational structure

committee organizational
structure ▶

Committee organizational structure

The committee organizational structure facilitates the creation of various committees within the organization. Committees are usually established to carry out specific tasks such as making decisions and planning events. Committees may be standing committees, which are permanent in nature, or ad hoc committees, which are temporary committees that are created to perform a specific function and then disbanded.

A committee is usually made up of representatives from various groups in the organization. This creates a diverse pool of talents and expertise and so the committee is likely to make more informed decisions and suggestions.

ITQ5

Use the following list to prepare a line organizational chart:
- Accounts Manager;
- Payroll Clerk;
- Marketing Manager;
- Sales Associate;
- Accounts Clerk;
- Sales Representative;
- General Manager;
- Human Resources Manager;
- Human Resources Clerk.

ITQ6

Explain the term 'lateral relationship'.

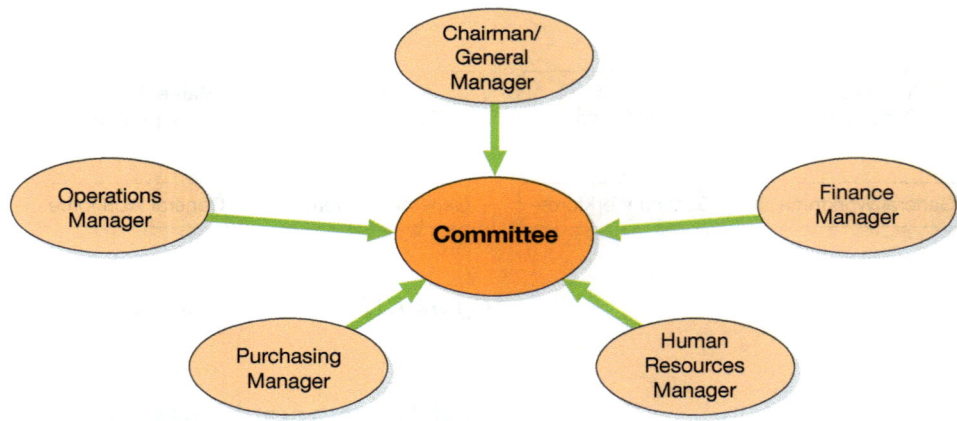

Figure 1.13 Example of a committee organizational chart

Centralization and decentralization

centralization ▶

Centralization occurs when certain office activities/services are concentrated in one department. For example, if the office activity of filing is centralized this will mean that all filing matters are dealt with in one location, usually under the supervision of someone who is a specialist in filing. All other departments in the organization would need to go to this centralized filing office to deal with all their filing needs.

centralized filing ▶

decentralization ▶
decentralized ▶

Decentralization occurs when office activities are carried out in each individual department. For example, if filing is decentralized this will mean that each department within the business will have its own filing system accessible to its staff.

Examples of office activities that will be centralized or decentralized include:

- duplicating/reprographics – the process of making copies from an original document;
- filing;
- typing and word processing;
- mailing;
- legal services;
- recruiting.

The decision to centralize or decentralize activities will depend on the size of the business as well as the nature of the tasks being done. Small firms usually have one general office and may not be divided into departments. However, medium-sized and large firms which are divided into departments are better able to make decisions regarding centralization and decentralization. Businesses may also be able to use both centralization and decentralization – for example, a firm may centralize filing and legal services because of their sensitive nature, while it may decentralize duplicating and word processing.

Advantages of centralization

- The staff will be specially trained to carry out their functions and will be able to operate relevant equipment correctly.
- Noisy equipment will be housed in one place.
- Supervision of the task will be improved and accountability maintained.
- The tasks performed will be standardized.
- Costs will be minimized – for example, instead of purchasing photocopiers for each department, a few copiers may be bought for one duplicating/reprographics office.

Disadvantages of centralization

- There may be a delay in work, for example if duplicating is centralized, when a worker from the Sales Department needs to make copies of a document they will have to go to the Duplicating Office which could be far away.
- The staff may find their jobs repetitive and boring.

Advantages of decentralization

- Work can be carried out quickly, as equipment needed is close by.
- It allows for the maintenance of privacy.

Disadvantages of decentralization

- There may be a duplication of work throughout the various departments.
- Costs may be increased as equipment will need to be provided for the various departments.

Office layout

office layout ▶

open-plan layout ▶

enclosed layout ▶

The office layout looks at the amount of space provided in the work environment as well as how desks, chairs and furniture and resources are placed in the office.

The two main forms of office layout are the open-plan layout and the enclosed layout.

The enclosed layout is also referred to as a traditional or cellular layout. It includes rooms where employees work by themselves or in small groups. The enclosed layout will be enclosed by walls and accessible by a door.

The open-plan layout is a large open area where employees work together in one integrated office. In the open-plan layout there is no privacy and workers are able to see and communicate with each other freely. In order to create some privacy in an open-plan layout, sound-proof screens or dividers can be used to separate the employees.

Factors determining the choice of office layout

There are a number of factors that help to determine whether a business will choose to use an open-plan or enclosed layout:
- the number of employees in the organization – a business with a large number of employees may choose to use an open-plan layout;
- the amount of space that is available;
- the type of work to be done – for example, companies which have to discuss sensitive information may choose to use an enclosed layout while an advertising agency might choose an open-plan layout in order to facilitate creativity;
- the amount of money available.

Advantages of the enclosed layout

- Allows employees to have greater levels of privacy, for example to meet with clients.
- Employees are able to work in peace and quiet and concentrate on their tasks without interruption.
- The office may be locked, providing security for confidential information as well as valuable possessions.
- Employees within the enclosed layout can organize the office the way they want – for example, they can choose where to place their desk.
- Employees will also be able to personalize their space – for example, with family photographs

Disadvantages of the enclosed layout

- This layout does not encourage teamwork.
- Workers may feel isolated.
- Security devices, such as panic buttons, may need to be installed to protect the occupant of the office, who may be alone most of the time.
- There is poor utilization of space, as walls take up space that could have been efficiently organized into an open-plan layout to hold more people.
- Increased supervision is needed to ensure that workers are actually doing their jobs behind the closed door.
- There will be increased maintenance costs because of elements such as separate air-conditioning and lighting to run the enclosed office.

Advantages of the open-plan layout

- Communication is easier as all the workers are in one area – feedback will be immediate.
- Teamwork is encouraged and friendships are developed.
- Workers are easily supervised as they are all in one area.
- The open-plan layout is more cost effective in terms of bills such as cooling and lighting. For example, one large room being centrally cooled by air conditioning will be cheaper than having to place air-conditioning units in several offices.
- The layout can be re-arranged, if needed, quickly and with little effort.

Disadvantages of the open-plan layout

- Lack of privacy – confidential calls or conversations may be jeopardized.
- Open-plan offices tend to be noisy and chaotic, and prevent workers from concentrating on their tasks.
- Sicknesses and infection can spread easily in an open environment.
- The constant traffic of employees may be distracting and lead to lower productivity and efficiency.
- It will be difficult to cater for all employees in the provision of heating, lighting and air conditioning. Some employees may find the air conditioning too cold, while others may think it's not cold enough.

Virtual office (e-workplace)

virtual office ▶

Unlike traditional office layouts, such as enclosed and open-ended, the virtual office is a company that does not have a physical location and whose employees work remotely by computer e-mail, groupware software, and other communications technology. Many employees in a virtual office work from home, however, the virtual office can be accessed from anywhere, including a hotel or a car. Working from home via telecommunications is known as telecommuting.

telecommuting ▶

If necessary, a virtual office can rent a Post Office (PO) box if it needs items to be delivered to it. Conference rooms can also be rented in cases where meetings need to be held.

Virtual receptionists can also be hired when needed, to carry out tasks such as screening and forwarding telephone calls.

Advantages	Disadvantages
1. it is cost effective – costs such as rent and electricity will be eliminated;	1. the lack of face-to-face communication may lead to miscommunication;
2. it increases the firm's flexibility;	2. workers may lack team spirit, because of feelings of separation and isolation;
3. employees can be hired irrespective of their physical location.	3. workers may experience technical difficulties with their equipment

Table 1.1 Advantages and disadvantages of the virtual office

Other variations of the traditional office are hoteling and hot-desking.

hoteling ▶

Hoteling is a work arrangement where the office includes providing unassigned desks or cubicles which employees who work from home (telecommuters) can reserve for specific periods of time when needed.

hot desking ▶

Hot desking is a work arrangement where employees are not given their own desks, but instead there are specific sets of desks or cubicles that are fully equipped, with computers connected to the firm's network and telephones, which will be used when needed. Hot desking is suitable for workers who travel a lot and do not visit the office often, such as journalists and sales representatives. Hot desking is similar to hoteling except that reservations do not need to be made.

Define the term 'office layout'.

State two advantages of an enclosed layout.

State two advantages of an open layout.

Ergonomics

ergonomics ▶

Ergonomics is the science of work area interaction. Ergonomics looks at how the working environment, including furniture, equipment, temperature and lighting, affects the performance of the employees.

If ergonomics is improved it will lead to:

- increased productivity and efficiency;
- a decrease in accidents and injuries;
- a decrease in illnesses and absence because of illness;
- improved morale and reduced stress levels.

Lighting

In order for there to be efficiency in the workplace there needs to be adequate lighting. Too much light, too little light, glare and flickering are all lighting problems that can affect employees. These problems can lead to eyestrain, headaches and errors on the job, especially in cases where accuracy and precision are essential.

Lighting problems can be solved by methods such as replacing light bulbs regularly and using localized lighting, for example using a task lamp.

Temperature

Ideally, the temperature in the office should be between 21.1°C (70°F) and 25°C (77°F). The office should not be too hot or too cold. Either extreme will make employees uncomfortable and less efficient, as they will be prone to making more mistakes.

Furniture

Well-designed office furniture helps to enhance the health of the workers as well as improving the efficiency of the office. Furniture such as desks and chairs should be ergonomically designed to suit the needs of the workers.

Figure 1.14   The proper way to sit or stand at a computer desk

Desk

A desk should not be cluttered and only things frequently used should be kept close by, such as the mouse. The desk should not be too low or too high: the ideal height is 20–28 inches. There should also be adequate leg room underneath. The space under the desk should not be used for storage, for example for books.

Chair

An ergonomically designed chair should follow the sitter as he or she changes position. The chair should have an adjustable seat so that the user's feet can touch the floor. If, even after adjusting the seat, the sitter's feet do not touch the floor, a footrest should be used. The chair should also have adjustable arm rests. Chairs should also be cushioned to provide comfort for the sitter. The chair should support the lower back to prevent poor posture and back pain.

Monitor

The monitor should be of the flat-panel type (they are not as reflective as other monitors), with high resolution for optimum clarity. It should be positioned away from direct light in order to avoid glare and should be placed directly in front of the user to prevent excessive twisting of the neck.

Keyboard

The keyboard should be at elbow level, while the upper arms should be relaxed at the typist's side to prevent strain on the wrists. When the user is typing, the hand and wrist should be 'floating' above the keyboard instead of resting on the keyboard or desk. Modern ergonomical keyboards are designed to increase the comfort of the user.

Figure 1.15   An ergonomically designed mouse and keyboard

Mouse

The mouse should be held lightly and not tightly gripped. It should be used by moving the elbow instead of the wrist. Ergonomic mouse devices are available, to help to reduce repetitive motion disorders.

Some illnesses caused by a poorly organized office include:

Repetitive motion disorder (RMD) or cumulative trauma disorder (CTD)

This is a medical condition caused by carrying out repetitive work, holding one position for too long or from vibration of power tools such as jack hammers or drills. Signs of CTDs include aching, burning, persistent pain, numbness and tingling in areas such as fingers, wrists and elbows. Examples of RMDs include tendonitis.

> DEFINITION: **Tendonitis** is the inflammation of a tendon, for example at the wrist joint.

Repetitive motion disorder can be prevented by:
- taking frequent breaks from the work station;
- changing the sitting position at regular intervals;
- doing regular stretches or exercises, for example rotating the wrist or stretching forward and backward at the desk;
- using ergonomically designed equipment.

Eyestrain

This illness is usually manifested by burning, blurred vision, watering, pain, tightness and headaches. These conditions may be caused by too much or too little light provided to work with, glare on the computer screen or not enough distance between the eye and the computer screen.

In order to prevent some of these problems occurring, the employee should:
- prevent computer glare by adjusting the monitor or using an anti-glare flare;
- take frequent breaks and shift focus from near to far regularly.

ITQ10
Explain **three** aspects of ergonomics and how they lead to office efficiency.

Equipment used in the office

Office equipment is necessary in order to increase the level of productivity within the office as well as to improve the efficiency of the office staff. Equipment commonly found in offices includes photocopiers, digital duplicators, shredders, scanners, LCD projectors and paper cutters.

Photocopiers

photocopier ▶

The photocopier – or simply copier – has become a standard piece of office equipment that both small and large businesses are able to own. The main function of the copier is to provide an exact copy of a document. Many desktop copiers are multifunction machines that are able not only to copy but also to print, scan and fax.

Figure 1.16 Photocopier

Features to look for when buying a copier

- Paper capacity – how much paper can the machine store? The ideal paper capacity is at least 250 sheets.

duplexing ▶
- Duplexing – this is the ability to print on both sides of the paper.
- Whether the copier can copy in black and white or colour – colour copiers are usually more expensive and slower than black and white copiers.
- Copy speed – ideally, a black and white copier should copy at least 16 pages per minute (ppm) and a colour copier at least 12 ppm.

- Duty cycle – this is the number of copies that can be made per month, efficiently.
- Other features such as collating, which is arranging documents in a specific order, as well as stapling the documents.

Digital duplicators

digital duplicator ▶ The digital duplicator is essential for a business that handles a large volume of copying, for example of fliers and brochures. Digital duplicators produce high-quality output at speeds of between 60 and 180 pages per minute. They are also able to print on different surfaces such as postcards and file folders. Modern digital duplicators are able to connect to computers and can be used as printers. The digital duplicator is more economical than a copier because of the high volume of copies (one master stencil can make up to 5,000 copies).

How the digital duplicator works

An original document is sent from a computer or placed on a glass surface, like that of a copier. The document is then scanned onto a master stencil; the master stencil is wrapped around a cylinder. As the cylinder rotates, a roller presses paper against it and ink is forced through the openings in the master stencil and onto the paper as a copy.

Figure 1.17 Digital duplicator

The Risograph, commonly referred to as the Riso Printer-Duplicator, is a popular example of a digital duplicator.

Shredders

shredder ▶ A shredder is a mechanical device used to cut paper into small strips or unrecognizable particles. The shredder is usually used to maintain a certain amount of security regarding documents, and as such is a piece of equipment from which both large and small businesses can benefit. Confidential documents that are no longer required will be shredded, but only after the document retention period has been verified. The document retention period is that period of time during which all documents must be kept – when the period expires, the documents can be destroyed. For example, if a firm sets its document retention period for all invoices at two years, this means that all invoices are kept for two years, after which time they can be destroyed.

Figure 1.18 Shredder

Most shredders cut paper into long, narrow strips, known as a 'strip cut'; other shredders do a 'cross cut', which involves cutting the paper both horizontally and vertically.

When buying a shredder, a business should look at the model's cutting ability, for example the ability to shred staples, paper clips, CDs and credit cards. It is also important to be aware of the sheet capacity, which is the number of sheets of paper that can be shredded at one time. General office shredders have a sheet capacity of up to 30 sheets, while some heavy-duty shredders have a sheet capacity of up to 450 sheets.

Paper cutters/guillotines

paper cutters ▶ Paper cutters are designed to cut documents accurately or to cut a large amount of paper at the same time. Small economy cutters suitable for a small business are able to cut up to 10 sheets at a time. On the other hand, there are larger guillotine cutters, more suitable for large businesses, that are able to cut up to 800 sheets at a time. There are automated cutters that will automatically adjust and cut paper based on dimensions provided by the operator.

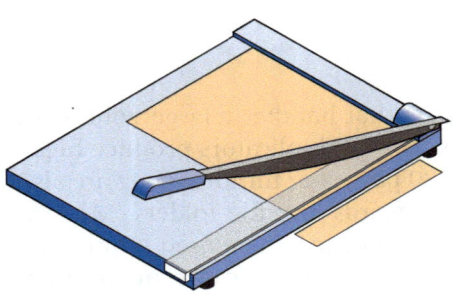

Figure 1.19   Paper cutter

Printers

printer ▶ A printer is an output device that produces text and graphic on paper. The most common types of printers used in offices include laser printers, inkjet printers, dot-matrix (impact) printers and plotters.

Figure 1.20   Guillotine

Laser printers

These use laser beams to create an electronically charged image of the document, which then attracts powdered ink (toner) to the paper.

Laser printers are:
- very fast;
- ideal for high-volume printing;
- available in black and white and in colour;
- expensive.

LED (light emitting diode) printers

LED printers are not very common in most offices. They use light instead of laser to create images on the paper. They are:
- safer to use, since some laser printers release particles which can cause respiratory problems;
- capable of producing high-quality prints.

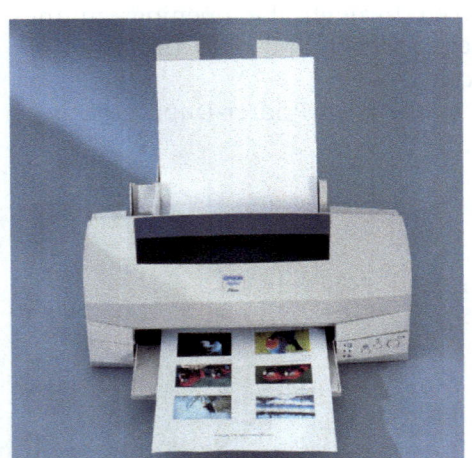

Figure 1.21   Laser printer

Inkjet (bubblejet) printers

These spray drops of ink through a nozzle on to a page to create an image. Inkjet printers:
- produce high-quality print;
- are quiet;
- are relatively fast;
- are low cost.

Figure 1.23   Dot-matrix printer

Dot-matrix (impact) printers

In the dot-matrix printer a print head moves across the page. Tiny pins on the print head hit a ribbon which then hits the paper and creates tiny dots which make up the image, whether graphics or characters (letters, numbers or symbols). Dot-matrix printers:
- print up to 500 characters per second;
- are used to print receipts, labels and so on;
- print multiple-part documents such as invoices;
- are able to use continuous paper.

Figure 1.22   Inkjet printer

Plotters

Plotters are large-scale graphic printers typically used by architects, engineers and graphic designers to create technical drawings (such as plans for houses) and computer–assisted design (such as the design plan for a car). There are two types of plotters:

Figure 1.24 Plotter

- a flatbed plotter – has a flat surface where pens or pencils move across the surface of paper to create an image;
- a drum plotter – the pen moves up and down while the paper moves beneath it on a large roll or drum.

  Plotters:
- create large drawings;
- can draw in colour;
- are very accurate;
- are slow.

Digital projectors

Figure 1.25 Digital projector

digital projectors ▶

Digital projectors are used to project digital images, usually from a computer onto a screen. Projectors have become very popular in meeting rooms where various types of visual presentations are made. For example, the Marketing Department might make a presentation showing a new advertisement or the Accounting Department might make a presentation showing the financial statements of a business.

   Features to look for when buying a projector include:
- the resolution – which looks at the sharpness and clarity of the image projected on the screen;
- the brightness – this looks at the projector's light output – ideally at least 1000 lumens;
- the weight – the lighter the projector, the more expensive it is. Typically, projectors weighing less than 7 pounds are good buys;
- the ability to connect to several computers at the same time.

Facsimile machines

Facsimile (or fax) machines ▶

Facsimile (or fax) machines send and receive documents through a telephone line.

How a fax machine works
- The machine converts the document to a digital image.
- The fax machine prepares to send the document by converting the digital image to a special sound/tone that can be understood by another fax machine.
- The receiving fax machine responds with a special tone known as the line acceptance tone.
- When the sending and receiving fax machines are linked to one another, the sending machine sends the fax as a series of tones while the receiving machine converts these tones into a digital image which is then printed or stored.

Figure 1.26 Fax machine

- Some sending machines will print a report to confirm that the fax transmission was successfully sent.

The internet is fast replacing the facsimile machine. Many documents are being sent as attachments in electronic mail. There is also online faxing provided via the internet by various firms such as FaxZero and PamFax. Online faxes are cheaper than traditional faxing and are easier to use and more secure. Online faxes can be saved as e-mails and so the user needs to print only what is needed – thereby saving paper.

Computers

Figure 1.27   Personal computer (PC)

Figure 1.28   Laptop computer

The computer has become commonplace in even the smallest of businesses. The computer helps all offices to carry out their regular daily activities such as:
- word processing – to prepare letters, reports, and other forms of written communication;
- filing clients' or suppliers' information;
- facilitating various software so that tasks such as accounting, including preparing cheques and calculating payroll, can be done easily.

Features to look for when buying a computer:
- Hard drive space (where all information, such as documents and photos, is stored) – this should be at least 500 GB (gigabytes).
- Processor clock speed (determines how fast the computer processes the information). This should be 2–3 GHz (gigahertz).
- Random Access Memory (RAM) – should be at least 2 GB (gigabytes).
- Monitor type and size – a 19-inch or 22-inch LCD flat screen should be a good buy.
- The computer should be able to network with other computers.

Voice recorders

Voice recorders are handheld devices used to record sound. Digital voice recorders are used to record notes, meetings, interviews, dictations and personal reminders. Modern digital voice recorders have long recording times – in some cases up to 540 hours. Many are also able to transfer files to a computer.

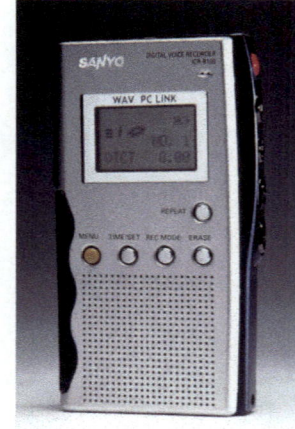

Figure 1.29   Voice recorder

Laminators

Laminating involves applying a plastic film to either one or both sides of a document. Laminators are used to:
- protect documents from water, fingerprints, dust etc;
- provide stability to documents, allowing them to stand upright, for example menus;
- add gloss to documents such as posters and maps.

Figure 1.30 Laminator

Binding machines

Binding machines align, punch and bind documents. Binding gives documents a professional look and make them easier to use, as in many cases they can be laid flat. Some binding styles allow the document to be re-opened and pages added or removed. Many offices will bind company reports, proposals and training manuals. Binding machines may be manual or electronic and many are small enough to hold on the top of a desk.

Types of binding styles include:
- Comb – this allows the document to be edited (it can be re-opened) and holds over 400 sheets.
- Wire – can be used for brochures and calendars. It can also be laid flat, but it cannot be edited.
- Coil or spiral – is like a spiral notebook that can be laid flat.
- Velo – this allows the document to be edited and can bind documents up to 3 inches thick.
- Thermal or Perfect – the pages in the document are glued together. Documents up to 500 pages can be bound using this method.

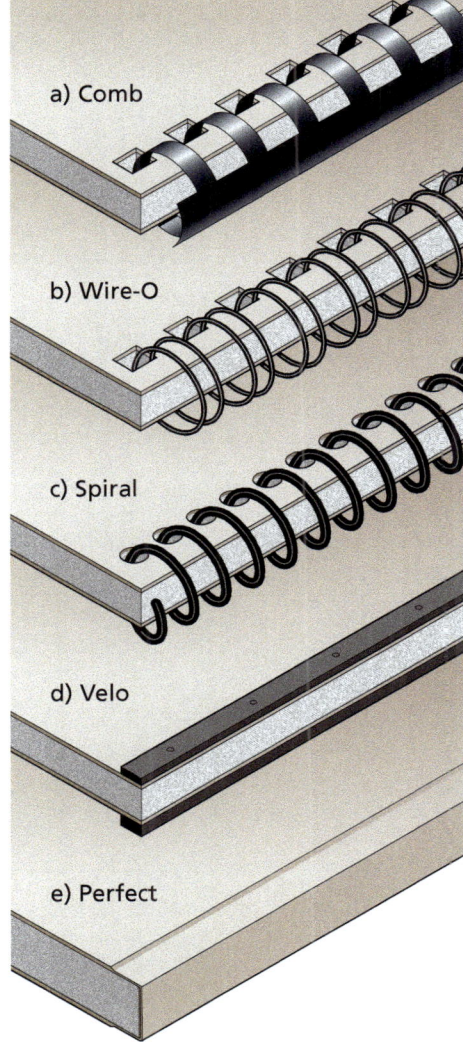

Figure 1.31 Binding styles

Human relationships

human relations ▶

In order to maintain and improve office efficiency, positive relationships need to exist with supervisors, colleagues and customers. Human relations involves creating a work environment that will motivate employees to work together in harmony. Practising good human relations is a skill that needs to be continued once you enter the world of work.

Relationships with supervisors

Having a good relationship with your supervisor is necessary in order to reduce stress and conflicts in the workplace, as well as to motivate employees to improve their performance.

Some ways of maintaining a positive relationship with a boss are:
- maintaining a professional attitude – know your boundaries, even if the boss is your close friend. When you are at work the relationship should be strictly about business;
- showing respect – treat your supervisor with the respect that his/her position deserves;
- carry out your duties – the supervisor will appreciate the fact that you are working to the best of your ability;
- seek clarification if you do not understand something that your boss said. Poor communication is one of the greatest sources of conflicts between employers and employees, so try to keep the communication lines clear.

Relationships with colleagues

Maintaining a good human relationship with your colleagues is extremely important. Having bad relationships with your co-workers can cause you to be less productive and efficient; it can also turn your work life into a nightmare. On the other hand, a good relationship with your co-workers can cause you to be find your job enjoyable, thus increasing your levels of productivity and efficiency.

Some ways of maintaining a positive relationship with your colleagues are:
- show respect for your colleagues – in the same way as you would expect them to be respectful to you;
- be professional – for example, do not spread gossip or belittle your colleagues;
- practise good manners and office etiquette – for example, do not engage in loud conversations on your cell phone that may disturb other workers around you.

Relationships with customers

Employees need to display good customer service in order to send a positive image of the business to its customers. Customers who experience good customer service will no doubt return with their business to that organization.

Ways of maintaining a good relationship with customers include:
- treating them with respect;
- being a good listener and trying to identify and satisfy their needs;
- allowing the customer to feel important and appreciated, for example by using their name and speaking in a sincere manner;
- trying to deal with the customer's problems as quickly as possible.

Entry-level positions

entry-level positions ▶

Entry-level positions are usually non-managerial positions that require minimum experience and as such are usually geared towards high school and college graduates. Entry-level positions jobs are good starting points for moving up the 'corporate ladder'.

A few examples of entry-level positions are shown in Table 1.2 below, along with some examples of duties, skills, attributes and attitudes that they require.

Entry-level jobs	Duties and responsibilities	Skills	Attitudes	Attributes
Sales Associate	Maintain excellent customer service. Assist in cashing and bagging merchandise. Aid customers in locating merchandise. Assist in merchandizing and display maintenance.	Good verbal and written communication skills. Good interpersonal skills. Proficiency in the use of computers. Numeracy skills.	Team-spirit. Co-operation. Tolerance. Socially responsible. Safety conscious.	Courteous. Sociable. Patient. Confident.
Payroll Clerk	Process time cards. Prepare and maintain payroll reports. Compute wages and salaries payments,	Good verbal and written communication skills. Numeracy skills. Computer literacy. Analytical and problem-solving skills.	Sensitivity to social responsibility. Commitment to lifelong learning. Tolerance	Honesty. Integrity. Trustworthiness. Sound judgement.
Accounts Clerk	Post journal, ledger and other records. Save and file documents. Prepare invoices and other statements.	Numeracy skills. Good verbal and written communication. Numeracy skills. Computer literacy – knowledge of accounting software.	Inter-personal skills. Analytical skills. Problem-solving skills. Computer skills.	Honesty. Integrity. Trustworthiness. Loyalty.
Administrative Assistant	Perform clerical duties including answering the telephone. Co-ordinate meetings and conferences.	Excellent verbal and written communication skills. Inter-personal skills. Analytical skills. Problem-solving skills.	Cultural awareness. Group interaction. Acceptance of diversity. Sensitivity to social responsibility.	Diplomatic and tactful. Polite and courteous. Patient. Confident.
General Clerk	Perform routine clerical tasks, such as answering the telephone.	Good verbal and written communication skills. Inter-personal skills. Analytical skills. Problem-solving skills.	Cultural awareness. Group interaction. Acceptance of diversity. Sensitivity to social responsibility.	Diplomatic and tactful. Polite and courteous. Patient. Confident.
Mail Clerk	Receive incoming mail; open, sort and deliver mail. Collect outgoing mail and use scales and franking machines to weigh and affix postage.	Computer literate. Ability to multi-task. Time-management skills. Good communication skills.	Cultural awareness. Group interaction. Acceptance of diversity. Sensitivity to social responsibility.	Sociable. Dedicated. Flexible. Organized.
Secretary	Typing or word processing. Maintain files, sort mail and receive visitors. Answer and route calls. Schedule appointments. Operate office equipment.	Excellent verbal and written communication skills. Inter-personal skills. Analytical skills. Problem-solving skills. Computer skills.	Cultural awareness. Group interaction. Acceptance of diversity. Sensitivity to social responsibility.	Diplomatic and tactful. Polite and courteous. Patient. Confident.

Table 1.2 Examples of entry-level positions and their requirements

Human Resources Clerk	Maintain files and records. Process employment applications. Assist employees with forms and procedures.	Excellent verbal and written communication skills. Resourceful. Analytical and problem-solving skills. Computer literate,	Sensitivity to social responsibility. Acceptance of diversity. Co-operation.	Diplomatic and tactful. Courteous. Flexible. Willingness.
Purchasing Assistant	Prepare, transport and deliver documents. Complete reports of purchasing activities and costs. Verify deliveries.	Resourceful. Ability to multi-task. Time management skills. Computer-literate.	Aware of environmental responsibility. Sensitivity to social responsibility. Team spirit.	Honesty. Fairness. Positive work ethic. Sociable.
Quality Assurance Technician	Test manufactured parts to certify quality and adherence to specifications. Record results of testing procedures.	Numeracy skills. Analytical skills. Good communication skills. Computer literacy skills.	Aware of environmental responsibility. Sensitivity to social responsibility. Team spirit.	Honesty. Fairness. Positive work ethic. Sociable.
Legal Assistant	Assist with preparation of legal documents. Research background information on legal issues. Maintain files.	Good research skills. Organizational skills. Ability to multi-task. Excellent communication skills.	Aware of environmental responsibility. Sensitivity to social responsibility. Team spirit.	Honesty. Fairness. Positive work ethic. Sociable.
Computer Programmer	Assist with encoding, testing, debugging and documenting small programs.	Critical thinking skills. Attention to detail. Good communication skills. Analytical and problem-solving skills.	Aware of environmental responsibility. Sensitivity to social responsibility. Team spirit. Safety conscious.	Punctuality. Flexibility. Patience. Dedication.
Receptionist	Answer the telephone. Greet and welcome visitors. Answer visitors' queries.	Excellent communication skills. Inter-personal skills. Analytical skills. Problem-solving skills. Computer literacy skills.	Cultural awareness. Group interaction. Acceptance of diversity. Sensitivity to social responsibility.	Confidence. Willingness. Regularity and punctuality. Professional deportment.

Table 1.2   (continued)

deployment ▶   After being in an entry-level position for some time, workers may be deployed to other departments in the organization. Deployment involves positioning employees within the organization in a strategic manner so as to improve the overall efficiency of the organization. A deployment may be a promotion (where a worker is moved to a higher position) or it may be a lateral move (on the same level but to another department). The Human Resources Department should ensure that each person is matched with the right job. For example, an employee with a Bachelor's degree in marketing would be placed in the Marketing Department where his/her knowledge and skills would be best utilized.

Summary

The office is the 'hub' of every office and is responsible for tasks such as duplicating records and handling mail.

- Major functional areas/departments within a business include Marketing, Finance, Human Resources and Production.
- Types of organizational structure include line, line and staff, functional and matrix.
- Organizational charts are able to show the chain of command and span of control within a business.
- Two main forms of office layout are open-plan layout and enclosed layout.
- Aspects of ergonomics include lighting, temperature and furniture.
- Machines used in the modern office include photocopiers, digital duplicators, shredders and facsimile machines.
- Humans relations involves maintaining good relationships with employers, colleagues and customers.
- Entry-level positions include Administrative Clerks, Sales Associates and Accounts Clerks.

Answers to ITQs

1 Activities carried out in an office include:
- making and receiving telephone calls;
- duplicating/photocopying records;
- filing;
- faxing documents.

2 Two advantages of a narrow span of control:
- managers can communicate quickly to subordinates;
- greater supervision reduces the chances of errors.

Two advantages of a wide span of control:
- quicker decision making;
- it is more cost effective as fewer managers need to be hired.

3 The role of lower-level managers is to provide direct supervision to the general workforce.

4 A flat organizational structure has a few levels of management and a wider span of control while a tall organizational structure has many levels of management and a narrow span of control.

5 Organizational chart:

Figure 1.32 An organizational chart

6 A 'lateral relationship' is the relationship between workers on the same level in the organization.

7 'Office layout' is the arrangement or design of furniture, equipment and employees in an office.

8 An enclosed layout allows for privacy in conducting business activities; there are fewer distractions.

9 An open layout is easy to re-arrange; it is more economical.

10 • Lighting – proper lighting can improve the workers' levels of accuracy and precision and it will also prevent eyestrain and headaches.
• Furniture – properly designed furniture, such as desks and chairs, can impact on the workers' comfort levels. The more comfortable a worker is, the more efficient and productive he or she is likely to be. Properly designed furniture also supports the worker's posture to prevent aches and strains.
• Monitors – should be properly placed so as to avoid glares and strain on the user's neck. When workers are comfortable around the monitor, their level of productivity is likely to be increased.

Examination-style questions

Multiple choice questions

1 The chain of command within an organization can be shown on a/an:
a organizational chart
b matrix
c line graph
d office layout.

2 Which machine is suitable for making 2000 copies of a coloured document?
a facsimile machine
b photocopier
c scanner
d digital duplicator.

3 The science of work area interaction is known as:
a human relations
b ergonomics
c office layout
d organizational structure.

4 Which type of organizational structure includes persons hired to support and advise members?
a matrix
b line
c line and staff
d functional.

5 The type of organizational structure most suited for creating project teams is the:
a matrix
b line
c line and staff
d functional.

6 Which department is responsible for tasks such as preparing payroll, budgets and final accounts?
a Purchasing
b Human Resources
c Production
d Finance.

7   Which management level has the greatest interaction with the non-managerial staff?
    a   executive level
    b   supervisory level
    c   middle level
    d   top level.

8   A flat organizational structure tends to display:
    a   a few levels of management and a narrow span of control
    b   many levels of management and a narrow span of control
    c   a few levels of management and a wide span of control
    d   many levels of management and a wide span of control.

9   The concept which outlines the number of people a manager can supervise effectively is called:
    a   span of control
    b   chain of command
    c   line of authority
    d   organization structure.

10   Which of the following are functions of the Human Resources Department?
    I   advertising vacancies
    II   maintaining employee records
    III   preparing payroll
    IV   organizing training.
    a   I and II only
    b   II and III only
    c   I, II and IV only
    d   I, II, III and IV.

Structured questions

1   a   State **three** duties which an Office Manager would be expected to perform. [3]
    b   Identify **two** pieces of office equipment from the following list and explain how each contributes to office efficiency:
        • facsimile machine
        • photocopier
        • digital duplicator
        • computer. [4]
    c   Figure 1.33 is an organizational chart of the Finance Department of CG's Chemicals Ltd.

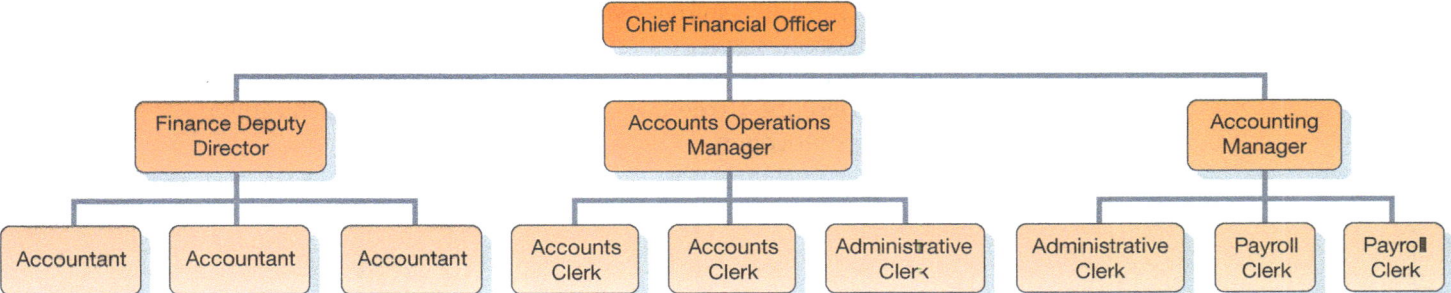

Figure 1.33   Organizational chart of the Finance Department of CG's Chemicals Ltd

Use Figure 1.33 to answer the following questions:
i   Who does the Finance Director report to?   [1]
ii State the relationship between the Administrative Clerk and the
    Accounts Clerk.   [1]
iii How many levels are depicted on the chart?   [1]
iv Identify **two** advantages and **two** disadvantages of
    organizational charts.   [4]

2 a State **two** ways in which good human relationships between
      employees and employers can contribute to office efficiency.   [4]
   b Outline **three** ways in which the general office contributes to
      the smooth running of an organization.   [6]
   c Use the following staff list to create the organizational chart of
      Bowling Ltd.
      • Wanda Davis, Chief Accountant
      • Camille Williams, Sales Manager
      • Larry Perry, Sales Representative
      • Elizabeth Anderson, Payroll Clerk
      • Jean Hawthorn, Clerk/typist
      • Lorna Sawyer, General Manager
      • Andrea Gillette, Sales Clerk
      • Bob Porter, Production Manager
      • Danielle Smith, Chairman/CEO
      • April Chung, Production Clerk
      • Sharon Crawford, Accounts Clerk
      • Peter Smith, Stock Control Clerk
      • Debra James, Office Manager
      • Mary Johnson, Clerical Assistant
      • Megan Deans, Advertising Manager.   [15]

3 In the office where you work, management has decided to
   centralize the functions of duplicating and reprographics.
   a Outline **three** benefits which will result from this decision.   [3]
   b State **three** office activities that may be centralized or
      decentralized in a general office.   [3]
   c State **three** ergonomic factors present in a general office and
      tell how each contributes to workers' satisfaction.   [6]

4 a Differentiate between the following terms:
      line organizational structure
      line and staff organizational structure
      functional organizational structure
      matrix organizational structure
      hoteling   hot-desking.   [3]
   b Identify **three** responsibilities of the following departments:
      Finance
      Human Resources
      Purchasing
      Administration.   [12]
   c Describe **three** factors to consider when purchasing a
      photocopier.   [3]

2 Communication

By the end of this chapter you should be able to:

- ☑ list the various means and channels of communications used in offices;
- ☑ identify factors affecting the selection of communication media;
- ☑ select the appropriate channel to be used in a given situation;
- ☑ identify common barriers to effective communication;
- ☑ communicate information in writing, using different formats (letters, memos, reports etc.);
- ☑ prepare meeting documents (notice, agenda, minutes);
- ☑ select appropriate paper for different documents;
- ☑ select relevant sources for reference documents;
- ☑ describe the proper techniques for receiving and relaying telephone messages;
- ☑ outline services provided by telephone companies;
- ☑ describe the services available for despatching mail;
- ☑ outline procedures for sending and receiving parcels;
- ☑ outline procedures for dealing with incoming and outgoing mail in large and small offices.

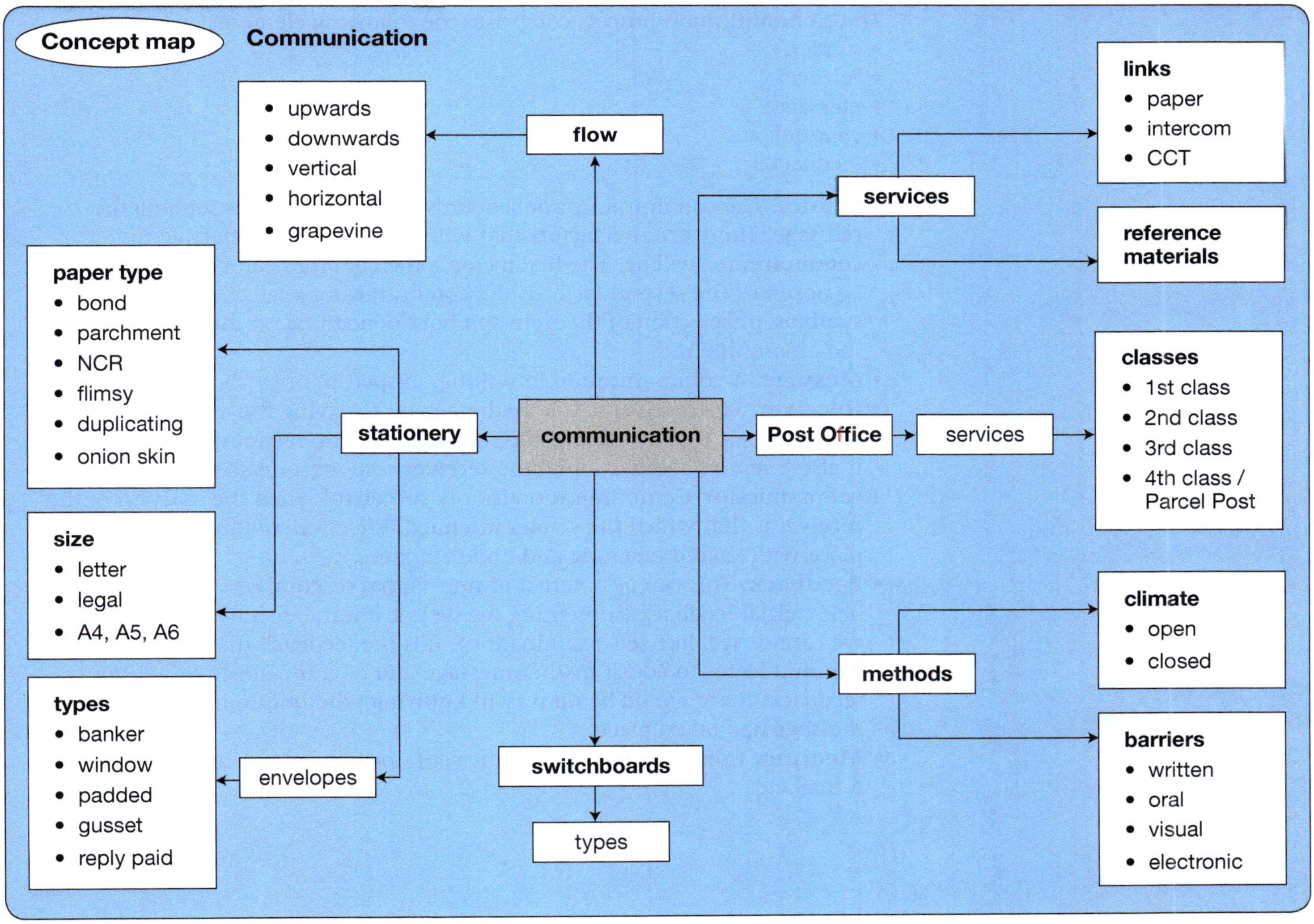

Concept map — Communication

flow
- upwards
- downwards
- vertical
- horizontal
- grapevine

services

links
- paper
- intercom
- CCT

reference materials

paper type
- bond
- parchment
- NCR
- flimsy
- duplicating
- onion skin

stationery ← **communication**

size
- letter
- legal
- A4, A5, A6

types
- banker
- window
- padded
- gusset
- reply paid

envelopes

Post Office → services

classes
- 1st class
- 2nd class
- 3rd class
- 4th class / Parcel Post

methods

climate
- open
- closed

barriers
- written
- oral
- visual
- electronic

switchboards

types

The importance of communication

communication ▶ Communication is the most important way to stay ahead in the world.

However, communication can be difficult sometimes. There are many reasons for this, one of which is cultural differences. Stella Ting-Toomey, a communication specialist, has identified three cultural barriers that impede effective communication. Knowing these barriers can help you avoid them.

What is communication?

> Communicating with others is an essential skill in business dealings, family affairs, and romantic relationships.

Communication takes place between individuals and can be said to be the conveying of ideas from the mind of one person to the mind of another. Effective communication is essential to life itself and imperative if businesses are to prosper and survive in a competitive environment.

Within an organization, communication of information is what the work of offices is all about and a variety of communication media will be required for both internal and external purposes.

The communication process

The communication process comprises the following elements:
- sender;
- receiver;
- message;
- channel; and
- feedback.

- **Sender.** The communicator or sender is the person who is sending the message. There are two factors that will determine how effective the communicator will be. The first factor is the communicator's attitude. It must be positive. The second factor is the communicator's selection of meaningful symbols, or selection of the right symbols, depending on the audience and the environment.
- **Message.** A communication in writing, in speech, or by signals.
- **Receiver.** The receiver is simply the person receiving the message, making sense of it, or understanding and translating it into meaning. The receiver is also a sender because when the receiver responds, he/she is then the communicator. Communication is only successful when the reaction of the receiver is that which the sender intended. Effective communication takes place with shared meaning and understanding.
- **Feedback.** This can be a verbal or non-verbal reaction or response. It can be external feedback (something we see) or internal feedback (something we cannot see, like self-examination). It is the feedback that allows the communicator to adjust his/her message and be more effective. Without feedback, there would be no way of knowing whether understanding of the message had taken place.
- **Medium.** How the message is being sent, for example by letter, memo, e-mail etc.

Characteristics of good communication

The essential features of effective communication are key for productive communication. The chief principles or characteristics of an effective communication system are as follows:

- Clearness and integrity of message to be conveyed.
- Adequate briefing of the recipient.
- Reliability and uniformity of the message.
- Knowing the main purpose of the message.
- Proper response or feedback.
- Correct timing.
- Use of appropriate medium to convey the message properly.
- Appropriate spelling and punctuation.
- Relevant, with no use of jargon

Barriers to effective communication

communication barrier ▶

internal barriers ▶

external barriers ▶

At any point in the process a communication barrier can occur. Barriers keep us from understanding each other's ideas and thoughts. There are two types of barriers – internal and external. Examples of internal barriers are fatigue, poor listening skills, attitude toward the sender or the information, and emotions. Examples of external barriers include noise, distractions, e-mail not working, bad phone connections, time of day, and environment. Barriers keep the message from getting through.

Other factors which acts as barriers include:
- pre-judging an issue;
- previous experience;
- vocabulary, for example language too technical;
- body language;
- stereotyping etc.

 ITQ1

List the elements of the communication process.

Methods of communication

The methods of communication can be divided into four broad categories: written, oral, visual and electronic. Table 2.1 shows various channels that may fall under each method of communication.

Written	Oral	Visual	Electronic
Letter	Radio	Sign language	Tele-conferencing
Memo	Telephone	Chart	Video-conferencing
Agenda	Meeting	Pictogram	Electronic mail
Notice	Conference	Year planner	Tele-messaging
Minutes	Interview	Pie chart	Paging
Itineraries	Intercom	Bar graph	Telephone
Report	Face-to-face	Signals	Facsimile
Press release	Voicemail	Body language	World Wide Web
Questionnaire	Television	Pictures	

Table 2.1   Methods of communication

ITQ2

Look at the following types of communication and place a tick under the heading to show whether they are visual, written or oral.

	Visual	Written	Oral
E-mail			
Telephone			
Forms			
Gesture			
Radio			
Reports			
Meeting			
Poster			
Agenda			
Pie chart			

Factors affecting the selection of communication channels

There are many factors that influence the choice of communication channel/media, but essentially the final decision is whether to use some form of oral, written, visual or electronic communication. There are, however, many other possibilities which can also be used. The first factor to consider in deciding which method to use will be to consider 'Who needs to ask what of whom?'.

The method of communication used will depend upon a number of factors. It is important to remember that sometimes a combination of several of these factors will influence the choice of communication method selected. For instance, it may be necessary to communicate the same message to a large number of persons (for example, inviting all parents of students at your school to attend a Parent–Teacher Association (PTA) meeting). The telephone could be used in this situation, but making several calls might be too expensive and not every parent may have a telephone. Therefore, the best channel of communication would be issuing circular letters, which would also be a less expensive alternative method. It will also be necessary to take account of the following.

- **Urgency.** Think about how important the message is and which channel would transfer the message to the receiver as quickly as possible – for example, telephone, e-mail, fax etc.
- **Privacy.** Think about how confidential the message is, then decide on which of the channels will allow the message to remain private. A sealed letter addressed to a named person suggests confidentiality and therefore such a letter should not be opened by anyone else but the person to whom it is addressed.
- **Need to reach a large audience.** How many people the message should be sent to must also be considered. If the principal at your school wished to address all students, it would not be in his/her best interests to walk around and speak to each student on a one-to-one basis. The best form of communication would be a public address system which would allow all students to hear the principal's address at the same time.
- **Distance.** The distance that a message has to travel also influences the method chosen. For example, if the person receiving the message is in the next room to the sender, it may be easy to deliver the message personally. However, if the receiver is in another country, another method, such as the telephone or e-mail, would have to be used.
- **Cost.** The cost of using a particular method of communication will have an influence on the channel chosen. There is no point in using a particular method if it is expensive and the need does not justify the cost involved.

- **The need for permanent records.** Sometimes it is necessary to communicate in written form, as there may be a need to keep a record of the message. For example, the ordering of goods could be done by telephone; however, a written order must be sent so that there is a permanent record on file.
- **Time zone.** When communicating, one must remember that the time may be different in the country of receipt. For example, it may not be wise to try to place a business telephone call to England at 5.00 pm Jamaican time, as England is five hours ahead of Jamaica and most business places will have closed by that time.
- **Efficiency.** Whether the communication is meant for internal or external purposes must be considered – for example, a memorandum is an internal form of communication while a letter is usually used externally.
- **Effectiveness.** Is the message good or bad news? The sender must be especially sensitive when communicating anything that might be considered bad news and should use an appropriate channel of communication.

The above may seem like a lot of factors to bear in mind when trying to communicate but due consideration to such points will help to ensure effectiveness.

ITQ3

List **four** factors to be considered when deciding on the channel of communication to be used.

ITQ4

For each of the following, state the factors you would consider before selecting the channel of communication to be used:
- an urgent request for a catalogue;
- asking 1200 parents to attend a Parent–Teacher Association meeting;
- sending 100 books to an overseas destination;
- sending a fax message to a remote location.

agenda ▶

Channels of communication	Uses
Meetings	A group of people coming together to discuss specific matters
Telephone	For internal and external oral communication
Minutes	A brief record of what was discussed at a meeting
Memorandum	Used for internal communication within a firm
Agenda	A list of items to be discussed at a meeting
Telegrams	A service for transmitting urgent written information
Facsimile	For transmitting replicas of documents.
Voicemail	A computerized mailbox recording messages
Line chart	For presenting information by using straight lines
Pictogram	Symbols are used to represent elements

Table 2.2 Some channels of communication and their uses

Communication flow

communication flow ▶

The communication flow may be:

Vertical communication

vertical communication ▶

Vertical communication consists of communication up (upward) and down (downward) the organization's chain of command.

hierarchy ▶

- **Upward communication** is the process of information flowing from subordinates (the lower levels) of a hierarchy to the superiors (the upper levels). Communication usually concerns employees' reports, their comments on policies and any ideas they wish to communicate. The main function of upward communication is to supply information to the upper levels about what is happening at the lower levels. This type of communication includes progress reports, suggestions, explanations and requests for aid or decisions. Upward communication is very good for employees because they feel that they are being noticed in the organization. Managers also benefit from this because they learn more about the organization.

- **Downward communication** is where information flows from the top of the organizational management hierarchy to subordinates. Communication starts with top management and flows down through management levels to line workers and non-supervisory personnel. The major purposes of downward communication are to advise staff on new company policies, inform on changes, direct and instruct employees on carrying out specific tasks, to evaluate employees and to provide organization members with information about organizational goals and policies.

Horizontal communication

horizontal communication ▶

Horizontal communication is the flow of information across functional areas at a given level of an organization. With this system, people at the same level are permitted to communicate directly without going through several levels of the organization. This way of communicating allows workers to assist with solving problems quickly, and better coordination between departments or groups helps the organization to remain effective.

Grapevine/informal communication

grapevine ▶

Grapevine communication, sometimes referred to as the 'jungle telegraph', is an informal channel of communication within the organization. The grapevine stretches throughout the organization in all directions and is used as a source of information there. Sometimes the information is merely rumour and it exists more at the lower levels of the organization.

Grapevine communication may be developed for the following reasons:
- low profit margin which leads to employees sensing uncertainty for their jobs;
- management's preferential treatment of some employees;
- poor communication between management and workers.

Advantages	Disadvantages
Information is spread quickly	Information may be based on rumours
Managers get feedback on issues	Information may not be trustworthy
Employees feels a sense of unity among themselves	It is an informal way of communicating

Table 2.3   Advantages and disadvantages of grapevine communication

Communication climate

communication climate ▶

The communication climate may be:

Closed

closed communication ▶

Closed communication is where the message is limited to a set number of people because of the nature of the message. For example, accounting information on payroll is restricted so that confidential information can be accessed by authorized workers only.

Open

open communication ▶

Open communication means that anyone working in equal conditions can gain access to and share information within the organization – for example, newsletters, or information placed on the notice board.

Types of communication barrier

communication barrier ▶

A communication barrier is anything that impedes the communication process. Communication barriers complicate the communication process and, while they cannot be totally avoided, the sender and the receiver can work to minimize them. Barriers will be caused by a number of factors – these could include:

Perceptual bias

perceptual bias ▶

Perceptual bias means bias against or for something based on the sensory inputs (sight, hearing, smell, taste, touch). If one person has biases against the topic under discussion, anything said in the conversation will be affected by that perceptual factor.

stereotyping ▶

Stereotyping is one of the most common examples. This is when we assume that the other person has certain characteristics, based on the group to which they belong, without verifying that they in fact have these characteristics.

Semantics

semantics ▶

Semantics is the study of the meaning of a sign to achieve a desired effect on an audience, especially through the use of words with double meanings. Within this view, sounds, facial expressions and body language have semantic (meaningful) content. Someone might say in an argument 'That's just semantics', implying that the point bears no relationship to anything in the real world. For example, there are figures of speech that in their entirety do not mean what each word means literally: 'Raining cats and dogs' does not mean that cats and dogs are actually falling from clouds. Communication problems occur when people use either the same word in different ways, or different words in the same way.

Language

Inability to converse in a language that is known by both the sender and receiver is the greatest barrier to effective communication. When a person uses different language, vocabulary, inappropriate words, accent or dialect while conversing or writing, it could lead to misunderstanding between the sender and the receiver. On the other hand, the same word can have different meanings for different people because of their background and cultural differences. Using words that have different meanings to those used by others does not pose a problem: the problem is that we assume that other people interpret the words with the same meaning as we do.

Lack of subject knowledge

If the sender lacks subject knowledge then he/she may not be able to convey the message clearly and the receiver is likely to receive an unclear or mixed message. This could well be a barrier to effective communication.

Organizational barriers

These include poor organizational culture or climate, stringent rules, regulations, status, relationship, complexity, inadequate facilities/opportunities for growth and improvement, the nature of the internal and external environment (such as large working areas being physically separated from others), poor lighting, staff shortages, outdated equipment and background noise.

Individual barriers

Individual barriers may be the result of an individual's perceptual and personal discomfort. Even when two people have experienced the same event, their mental perception may or may not be identical, which then acts as a barrier. Halo effect, poor attention and retention, defensiveness, closed-mindedness and insufficient filtration are personal barriers.

Interpersonal barriers

interpersonal barriers ▶

Interpersonal barriers are those between individuals in an organization. Those coming from employers are:
- lack of trust in employees;
- lack of knowledge about non-verbal clues such as facial expression, body language, gestures, postures and eye contact;
- different experiences;
- shortage of time for employees;
- no consideration for employees' needs;
- a wish to capture authority;
- fear of losing control of power; and
- bypassing and informational overloading.

Barriers coming from employees include:
- lack of motivation;
- lack of co-operation;
- lack of trust;
- fear of penalty; and
- poor relationships with the employer.

By knowing the barriers to effective communication, steps can be taken to lower them. Though it is not at all easy to eliminate all the barriers, for a variety of reasons, knowing more about them is always better for all concerned.

Decision-making business structures

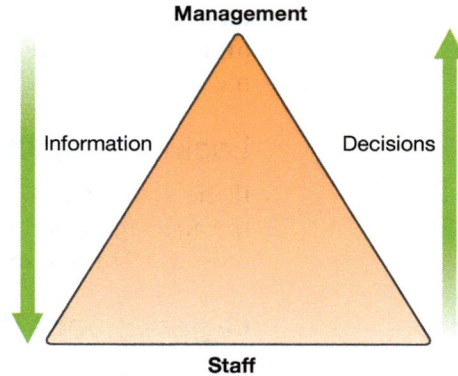

Figure 2.1   Traditional view of organizations

Decisions pass down formal channels from managers to staff (on the right). Information flows up formal channels from staff to management (on the left).

A business structure can be:
- centralized – decisions are made centrally;

entrepreneurial ▶
- entrepreneurial;
- decentralized;

pyramid ▶
- pyramid – staff have a role; there is shared decision making; specialization is possible;

matrix ▶

- matrix – staff with specific skills join project teams, and individuals have responsibility;
- independent – seen in professions where the organization provides support systems.

Matrix (or project-based) organizations

matrix ▶

A matrix structure organization contains teams of people drawn from various sections of the business. These teams will be established for the purposes of a specific project and will be led by a project manager. Often the team will only exist for the duration of the project and matrix structures are usually deployed to develop new products and services.

Advantages	Disadvantages
Project managers are given deadlines and budget	Individuals may suffer if both bosses make heavy demands on them
Uses variety of skills and expertise	Communication and control are more likely to become confused
Project groups are dynamic and have different approaches	May be difficult to understand

Table 2.4   Advantages and disadvantages of matrix organizations

Written communication

Written communication can take many forms and will range from the informal note made to pass on a message to a colleague, to the formal report prepared for submission to shareholders and perhaps publication in the press. It also includes the accurate completion of letters and a vast array of business documentation necessary for the completion of a business transaction.

Written communication has the following advantages and disadvantages:

Advantages	Disadvantages
Information transmitted in a uniform manner	Costly and time consuming to prepare
Provides a permanent record for future reference	Feedback may not be instant
Can be used as legal evidence in case of any disputes	May be difficult to maintain privacy

Table 2.5   Advantages and disadvantages of written communication

Business letters

Many types of letters are required to suit a wide variety of business purposes, ranging from those providing information or confirming details of some kind to those making a complaint, offering an apology or conveying thanks. Additionally, letters are required for more specialist purposes such as checking creditworthiness or advertising goods and services, while it should not be overlooked that certain occasions require letters of a personal kind, for example extending congratulations or expressing sympathy. The writer must always bear in mind the purpose of the letter and the person to whom it is being written.

The style should reflect the tone of the letter and should be chosen with the intention of conveying the message to effect. Remember that a letter is a written record and as such must be carefully worded and logically presented to avoid any misunderstanding or possible ambiguity.

Information found on a business letterhead

business letterhead ▶ On most business stationery there is a printed business letterhead. The main aim of this letterhead is to give information about the firm. Many firms include their letter heading in their computer software, so that it is automatically incorporated into their letters as they are created. This, of course, saves them the costs related to printing letter-headed stationery.

Some pieces of information that can be found on a firm's printed letterhead are:

- company's logo;
- name of the company;
- telephone number(s);
- fax number(s);
- our reference/your reference
- e-mail address;
- names of directors.

Parts of a business letter	Information
Date	The date will usually be typed in order of year, month and day, e.g. '2010/10/15', however, alternative forms are: '2010 October 15'; 'October 15, 2010'; or '15 October 2010'.
Reference	The reference is useful in helping to identify a particular letter in a filing system. There are many ways of arranging reference numbers, one of which is a combination of the dictator's and the typist's initials along with the number of the letter, e.g. 'SR/OP/10'.
Inside name and address	This is the name and address of the addressee. The addressee is the person to whom the letter is being sent.
Salutation	This is the writer's greeting. The type of greeting is dictated by the relationship between the sender and the receiver of the correspondence. The usual salutations for business correspondence are 'Dear Sir/s', 'Dear Madam' or 'Dear Mrs Black'.
Subject heading	This tells the reader of the letter exactly what the letter is about. NOTE: not all letters will carry a subject heading.
Body of the letter	The opening sentence in the body of the letter should refer directly to what the writer wishes to convey to the receiver of the letter. The sentences and paragraphs in the body must be arranged so that they appear in a logical sequence so that each aspect is dealt with in a separate paragraph.
Complimentary close	This is the closing complimentary remark in a letter and is again governed by the relationship existing between the sender and the receiver and by the salutation used. The most common forms of complimentary close used today are 'Yours faithfully' with 'Dear Sir/s' and 'Yours sincerely' with, e.g., 'Dear Mrs Black'.
Description of signatory	In a business letter the name of the business may be typed immediately under the subscription and the name of the writer and his position in the business are typed below this, leaving space for the signature, e.g. 'Yours faithfully SMART CLOTHING A McCarthy Managing Director'

Table 2.6 Parts of a business letter

ITQ5

Write the complimentary close that goes with each of the following salutations:
- Dear Sir;
- Dear Pat;
- Dear Mr Small.

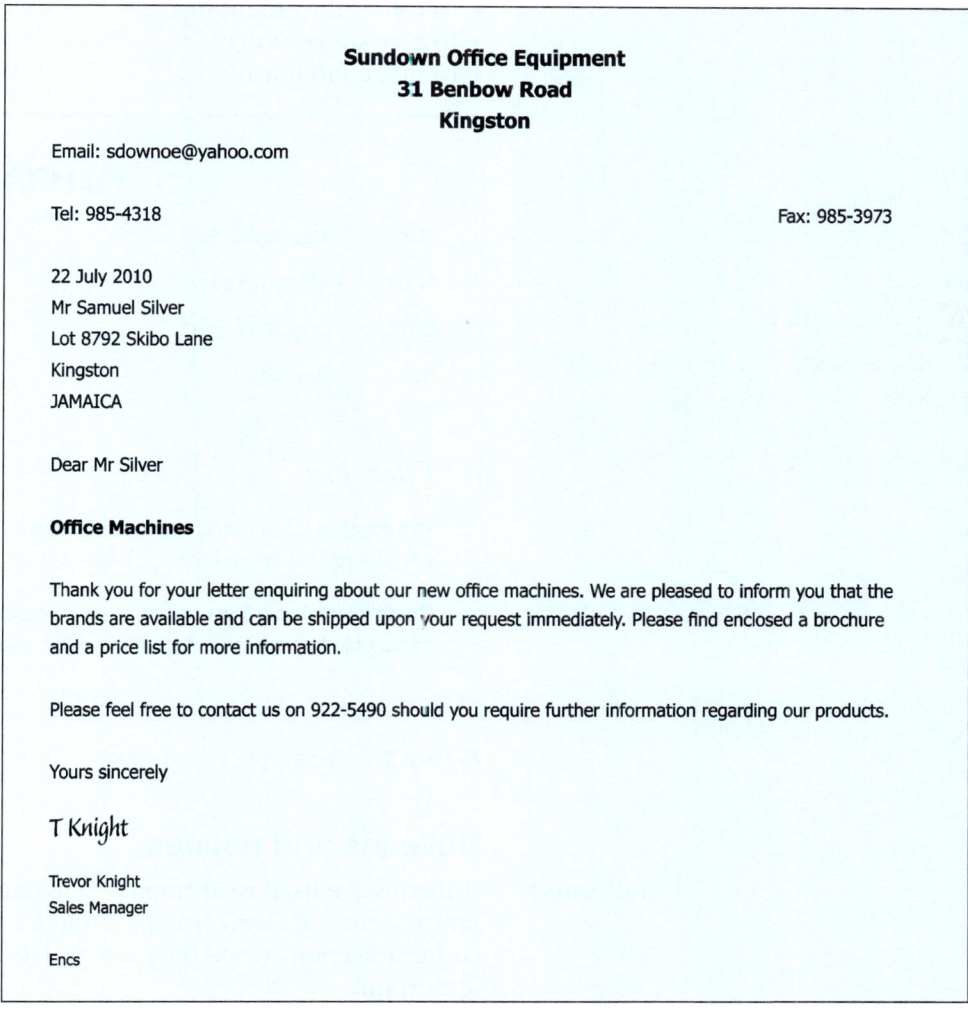

Sundown Office Equipment
31 Benbow Road
Kingston

Email: sdownoe@yahoo.com

Tel: 985-4318   Fax: 985-3973

22 July 2010
Mr Samuel Silver
Lot 8792 Skibo Lane
Kingston
JAMAICA

Dear Mr Silver

Office Machines

Thank you for your letter enquiring about our new office machines. We are pleased to inform you that the brands are available and can be shipped upon your request immediately. Please find enclosed a brochure and a price list for more information.

Please feel free to contact us on 922-5490 should you require further information regarding our products.

Yours sincerely

T Knight

Trevor Knight
Sales Manager

Encs

Figure 2.2 Example of a business letter

Memoranda

memoranda ▶ Memoranda or memos are the most common channels of communication used within any organization. Memos are usually short and deal with one or two specific points. They differ from letters in style and content, depending upon the status of the originator and that of the recipient, the content of the message and the degree of urgency attached to it. Memos are usually handwritten or typewritten on pre-printed forms. They usually contain the following headings:
- to;
- from;
- date;
- reference;
- subject.

Currently, many organizations have network systems where all computers are linked or have internet capabilities: this results in paper memoranda being replaced by e-mail. E-mail memoranda are the most common form of communication within many organizations.

Uses of memoranda
- To seek information.
- To outline policies.
- To outline progress.

- To clarify information.
- To give suggestions.
- To make modifications.

ITQ6

State the differences between a letter and a memorandum.

MEMORANDUM

TO: Mrs Francis Finn

FROM: Ms Betty Finlay

DATE: August 18, 2011

REF.:   fmw120

Client List

The attached list of clients who have utilized our services at least once in the last six months will give you the information you requested for your semi-annual report.

Please let me know if you still need additional client information for your report. You may contact me by telephone at extension 6754 or by e-mail at Btty_lay@yahoo.com.

Figure 2.3   Example of a memo

Bulletins and notices

bulletins ▶ Bulletins are used to announce upcoming events, changes in policies and other matters to all concerned. Bulletins and notices are effective forms of communication. Once they are received by persons, the content is considered important.

Bulletins are often several pages long and can refer to several topics, whereas notices are normally much shorter and refer to one matter.

Circulation slips

circulation slip ▶ A circulation slip, sometimes called a distribution slip or a routing slip, is attached to a document that has to be read by a number of employees in turn. It consists of a list of names of persons who should read the attached document and then sign their names to it. The document, along with the circulation slip, is then passed on to the next person listed. Finally, the document is sent back to the original sender.

Magazines on Human Resources Involvement in strategy formulation

Please read and pass on in order shown below:

NAME	DEPT	INITIAL/DATE
George Harvey	Human Resources	
Lorraine Samuels	Production	
Olive Parchment	Accounts	

Please return to: William James

By: September 11, 2011

Figure 2.4   Example of a circulation slip

Compliments slips

compliments slips ▶

DEE BEE'S PRINTING COMPANY

15 James Boulevard
Kingston, Jamaica   Tel: 933-0541
Debpr12@yahoo.com   Fax: 933-0542

WITH COMPLIMENTS

Figure 2.5   A compliments slip

Compliments slips contain the name and address of the firm together with telephone and other contact numbers. The words 'With compliments' are printed, leaving just sufficient space for a brief message, or the sender's own name and title to be added. Compliments slips can be used for enclosing with anything which is being sent by post, where a letter is not necessary but where the recipient must know the name and address of the sender. They save typing letters and are used by many firms whose outgoing mail includes items for which the recipient is not expected to pay – the word 'complimentary' means 'given free'.

Types of paper

The most commonly used sizes of business stationery are as follows:

Bond paper

bond paper ▶

Bond paper is a good-quality paper used for headed paper and 'top-copy' work.

Flimsy

flimsy ▶

Flimsy paper is used for making carbon copies. This paper is usually lighter.

Duplicating

duplicating ▶

Duplicating paper is used for stencil duplicating.

Parchment paper

parchment paper ▶

Parchment paper is elegant stationery, ideal for a special handwritten letter, wedding invitations and other special occasions. This type of stationery can also be used in an inkjet or laser printer to enhance the look and impact of printed documents.

Onion skin paper

onion skin paper ▶

Onion skin paper is a type of very lightweight, almost translucent, paper which somewhat resembles the outer skins of an onion. It is also relatively durable, given how lightweight it is, because it usually contains a high percentage of cotton fibres, which make for stronger paper. There are numerous practical applications for onion skin paper, including airmail stationery, Bibles and other situations where lightweight, strong paper is needed. Along with other specialized papers, onion skin paper is available from paper supply stores and companies in varying sizes to meet differing needs.

Onion skin paper can be used for art tracing. It can also be used as an interleaving material in books with colour plates which have the potential to be damaged.

ITQ7

State the uses of the following types of paper:

Types of paper	Uses
Flimsy	
Bond	
Parchment	
Onion skin	

NCR (No carbon required)

This is a multiple-part paper form that does not use carbon paper. The ink is adhered to the reverse side of the previous sheet. When typed or written on, a copy is made automatically on the other sheets behind the original. This type of stationery is also called 'carbonless paper'. It is used for sets of forms such as school reports, invoices and so on.

Name	Dimension	Use
A3	29.7 cm x 42 cm	Legal documents, balance sheets and financial statements
A4	21 cm x 29.7 cm	Letters, reports, minutes, agendas, estimates, invoices, etc.
A5	14.8 cm x 21 cm	Short letters, memos, invoices, message pads, statements
A6	14.8 cm x 10.5 cm	Compliments slips, petty cash vouchers, index cards, invitations, etc.
A7	74 mm x 105 mm	Labels

Table 2.7   Paper names, dimensions and uses

Paper quantities

ream ▶
quire ▶

Typing paper is usually sold by the ream. One ream of paper contains 500 sheets and 25 sheets of paper are equal to one quire.

Types of envelope

- **Banker** – envelopes with the opening on the longer side.
- **Window** – contain a transparent 'window' opening, so that the name and address do not need to be typed on the envelope.

pocket envelope ▶
- **Pocket envelope** – an envelope with the opening on the shorter side, used for documents and reports.

padded envelope ▶
- **Padded envelope** – used for sending fragile articles.

gusset envelope ▶
- **Gusset envelope** – these will take more bulky materials and are used for sending thick documents, for example books, pictures or picture frames.

reply-paid envelope ▶
- **Reply-paid envelope** – enables client to reply to an organization without paying postage.

Format	Size	Contents
C4	324 mm × 229 mm	A4 letters, unfolded
C5	162 mm x 229 mm	A4 letters, folded once
DL	110 mm x 220 mm	A4 letters folded twice = 1/3 A4
B5	176 × 250 mm	C5 envelope
B6	125 × 176 mm	C6 envelope

Table 2.8   Envelope formats

Sources of information

On a daily basis, office staff need to source information about aspects of their jobs. As a result, they must be aware of the types of reference books available and also how to locate the information in these books.

Names	Information contained
Hansard	Parliamentary verbatim report
Dictionary	Words and their spellings, meanings, derivations and pronunciations
Ready reckoner	Volume of calculations already worked out to save time
Post Office Guide	Postal services – inland and overseas postal information
Roget's Thesaurus	Words and phrases – listing all words of similar meaning or related meanings (synonyms and antonyms)
Whitaker's Almanack	Contains statistics and information on every country, for example names of government officials, population and so on
Telephone directories	Names, address and telephone numbers of persons
Official Gazette	Lists all Acts of Parliament and statutory instruments
Trade journals	List names of companies and products offered
Internet	Information on any topic the searcher cares to research
Maps	Self-explanatory
Schedules	Self-explanatory

Hansard ▶

ready reckoner ▶

Roget's Thesaurus ▶

Whitaker's Almanack ▶

Table 2.9   Reference material

Oral communication

Oral communication is the most common way of passing on information within an organization. This involves using the telephone, speaking to people face to face and holding meetings.

Oral communication falls largely into three categories. These are:

- person to person;
- meeting situations;
- telephone.

Advantages	Disadvantages
This is a direct means of communication	Lacks the security of the written word
It is faster	No record of conversation
There is instant feedback	Difficulty in discussion where many people are involved

Table 2.10   Advantages and disadvantages of oral communication

The telephone

The telephone is the primary method of communication used by businesses today, due to its speed. The telephone provides immediate feedback and can be inexpensive if properly used. Extensions are used in organizations to facilitate communication between different departments.

Employees becomes the 'voice' of the organization when they use the telephone to communicate to others. Each time employees speak over the telephone, they create an impression of the organization in the minds of the people with whom they are communicating. By employing some specific techniques when using the telephone, employees will be able to influence positively the impressions people have of the organization.

Answering the telephone

When an employee answers an incoming telephone call, they represent their organization by the way in which the call is handled. The telephone should be answered with a pleasant and businesslike attitude. Remember that the caller relies on the answerer's tone, therefore, the answerer should always put a 'smile' in his/her voice.

Telephone etiquette

The telephone is an important means of communication in business organizations and should be treated as such. It is important that the company's image be maintained. As a result, suitable persons should be employed to handle incoming calls at the switchboard. Other office employees must also answer the telephone when calls are transferred to various designated extensions, so the following points must be considered when answering the telephone:

- **Identifying yourself on the phone.** Gently pick up the receiver and identify the company's name, and if necessary the department or section, as well as your own name. For example 'Belmont High School, good morning'; 'Good afternoon, Science Department, Florence Yen speaking'. When answering someone else's telephone, say, for example, 'Mrs Sinclair's office, Florence Yen speaking', so that the caller knows immediately which office or department has been reached. Include your name so that the caller knows who is answering the phone. An enormous amount of time can be saved by answering in this way.
- **Responding to the telephone quickly.** When you receive a telephone call, try to answer by the second or third ring. Most voice messaging takes over on the third or fourth ring. Avoid picking up the receiver and merely saying 'Hello'. This response gives no information about the company and wastes time since the caller is likely to follow by asking for the company, department or person.
- **Attending to the caller.** The caller deserves your full, courteous attention. If you are speaking with a staff member in your office when the phone rings, say 'Excuse me, please' to the staff member and pick up the phone. If the call is confidential, politely ask the staff member to return in a few minutes. If that is not possible, ask the caller whether you can return the call in a short time.
- **If there is a problem in locating the person or information,** do not leave the caller 'holding on' for a long time. Either:
  - ask the caller whether they would like to leave a message;
  - ask whether someone else could help;
  - offer to call back with the information requested; or
  - ask the person whether they are willing to hold the line while the person or information is found.

Always be calm and courteous throughout, even if the caller has an annoying complaint.

Recording telephone messages

When answering the telephone, you must be ready to take a message in case the call is for another person in your office. Your options include keeping a message pad or notebook handy for writing down messages; using your computer to key the information directly into an e-mail message form; or forwarding the call to the intended receiver's voice mailbox.

When recording telephone messages for another person, care must be taken that a pen or pencil is readily available to record accurate and complete information.

The following list includes the types of key information that need to be included in a message:
- date and time of call;
- name of caller, with title;
- name of business;
- telephone number of caller;
- the message itself;
- best time to return call;
- signature of person taking message (this is useful for reference).

MESSAGE FOR

Mr/s ....

WHILE YOU WERE OUT

Mr/Mrs/Ms: ....

Of: ....   Tel. No.: ....

....

- ☐ Telephone   ☐ Please return call
- ☐ Called to see you ☐ Will call again
- ☐ Please call   ☐ Returned your call
- ☐ Urgent

MESSAGE:

....

....

Date: ....   Time: ....

Taken by: ....

Figure 2.6   Example of a telephone message form

Delivering messages

When you are taking another person's calls and recording messages, be sure to deliver them to that person promptly. If you write the messages on message forms, place them in a designated mailbox or location so that the person can access them easily. Telephone messages recorded in the form of e-mail messages should be sent to the individual immediately so that they will be available next time that person opens his/her e-mail.

Making telephone calls

Making a telephone call requires thought and careful planning to facilitate effective communication. The objective of the message to be sent must be ascertained; the information needed for the discussion must be available; the recipient's response must be anticipated; and you must determine how to respond.

Having thought about these factors, you need to:
- determine what type of call is to be made – local or overseas;
- ascertain the correct telephone number and the name of the person to be telephoned;
- ascertain whether the person would be available to speak at the time the call is to be made (remembering time differences in other countries);
- ensure that information to be given is ready;

- write down any specific questions you want to be sure to ask during the conversation;
- dial the person's number;
- when the call is answered, identify yourself immediately to the person who answers. Then ask for the person to whom you wish to speak, for example: 'May I please speak to Tommy Smith?';
- if you are not sure to whom you need to speak, give the reason for your call so that the call can be transferred more quickly and easily to the appropriate person.

Voice messages

voicemail message ▶ You may be able to leave a voicemail message if the person you are calling is not in. A voicemail system stores messages digitally. Using suitable etiquette is very important when leaving voicemail messages. Instead of someone answering the telephone in person, you will hear a recording with directions for leaving a message; or the recording will put you through several steps (using a touch-tone phone) until finally you are connected with an office, a person or a voicemail system.

Advantages	Disadvantages
• Easier to send and receive messages	• Receiver may not be aware that a message is waiting unless they check
• Messages may be sent and received 24/7 anywhere in the world	• Voice mailboxes must be accessed regularly so that important messages are not missed

Table 2.11   Advantages and disadvantages of voicemail systems

Using telephone directories

Administrative professionals find telephone directories helpful in locating such information as telephone numbers, areas codes, addresses and website information. The telephone directory is divided into many sections:

White Pages ▶
- The alphabetic listing of all telephone numbers assigned within a given city or area is included in the *White Pages*. These numbers are only those that are available as listed numbers of businesses, individuals and government agencies. Unlisted telephone numbers are private numbers not available to the general public in a telephone directory.

Yellow Pages ▶
- The *Yellow Pages* are used when you wish to find out quickly where to obtain a particular product or service. The names, addresses, e-mail addresses and telephone numbers of business subscribers are listed in alphabetical order under the name of the products or services. To use the *Yellow Pages*, find the main heading then the specific name of the company needed. For example, to find RB Caterers, first go to the heading 'Restaurant' then search alphabetically for RB Caterers.

Types of switchboard

When you look in the telephone directory for the name and address of a company, you will probably find one or two numbers, even though the company employs hundreds of people, and is divided into many different departments. If you dial the number given, the switchboard operator will answer you. The switchboard acts as a main telephone, and all the other telephone sets in the building are numbered extensions connected to the switchboard.

Private Manual Branch Exchange (PMBX)

Private Manual Branch Exchange ▶

A Private Manual Branch Exchange is the oldest kind of switchboard and is no longer widely used. All calls into and out of the organization must go through the switchboard operator. If an employee needs to make an outside call he/she lifts the receiver, dials the switchboard operator and gives the operator the telephone number of the person who is needed. The operator will either connect him/her to the number or give him/her an outside line – that is, connection to the public telephone circuit – in which case the caller can dial the number him/herself as soon as the dialling tone is heard.

Private Automatic Branch Exchange (PABX)

Private Automatic Branch Exchange ▶

With a Private Automatic Branch Exchange type of switchboard, calls can be made from one extension to another, and external calls can be made without contacting the switchboard operator. To telephone a colleague in another department, you would pick up the receiver and dial the extension number. Incoming calls go through the telephone operator.

Central Exchange (also called Centrex) (CBX)

These are computerized switchboards. The essential features are the direct dialling facility and access to a number of extensions. Whereas with the PBX systems the switching equipment is usually installed on the customer's premises, with the modern or computerized PABXs or CBXs, the switching equipment is installed on the premises of the telephone company.

Private Branch Exchange

Small companies usually use these switchboards. They facilitate the receipt and transfer of calls, but the operator handles the making of calls. The system does not allow for many outside lines to be at a caller's disposal, as with the PABX system. As a result, the operator is required to dial the majority of outgoing calls.

Effects of time zone on long-distance calls

It is important to remember time zone differences when placing long-distance or international calls. For example, the UK is five hours ahead of Jamaica, and Barbados is one hour ahead of Jamaica, therefore, if it is 8.00 am in Jamaica it is 1.00 pm in England; if it is 6.00 am in Jamaica it is 7.00 am in Barbados. As a result of these time differences, business calls placed too early in the day from one country to another are not likely to be answered as employees in the other country may not be at work. For a map of time zones, see Figure 7.6 on page 149.

In the UK during the Summer months, clocks are moved forwards by one hour so that daylight ends at a later time. There is a proposal (2011) that this be increased to two hours in the future, to fit in with Central European Time.

(Whenever it is noon EST (Eastern Standard Time) in Jamaica)	
Country	**Time**
Antigua	1.00 pm
Bahamas	12.00 pm
Barbados	1.00 pm
Denmark	6.00 pm
Iraq	8.00 pm
Nicaragua	11.00 am
Philippines	1.00 am
UK	5.00 pm

Table 2.12 Time in some countries around the world

The 12- and 24-hour clocks (see also pages 151 and 152)

ante meridiem ▶
post meridiem ▶

The 12-hour clock is a time-keeping convention in which the 24 hours of the day are divided into two periods, called ante meridiem ('am' or 'before noon') and post meridiem ('pm' or 'after noon'). Each period consists of 12 hours numbered 12 (acting as zero), 1, 2, 3, 4, 5, 6, 7, 8, 9, 10 and 11. The indication of noon and midnight in the 12-hour system is disputed.

	Time AM		Time PM	
12-hour clock	**24-hour clock**	**12-hour clock**	**24-hour clock**	
midnight 12.00 am	0000	12.00 noon	1200	
1.00 am	0100	1.00 pm	1300	
2.00 am	0200	2.00 pm	1400	
3.00 am	0300	3.00 pm	1500	
4.00 am	0400	4.00 pm	1600	
5.00 am	0500	5.00 pm	1700	
6.00 am	0600	6.00 pm	1800	
7.00 am	0700	7.00 pm	1900	
8.00 am	0800	8.00 pm	2000	
9.00 am	0900	9.00 pm	2100	
10.00 am	1000	10.00 pm	2200	
11.00 am	1100	11.00 pm	2300	

Table 2.13   12- and 24-hour clocks

ITQ8

Convert the following to 24-hour clock time:

	12-hour	24-hour
a	5.30 am	
b	8.15 pm	
c	10.00 pm	
d	10.30 am	
e	12.00 midnight	
f	3.40 pm	

Telephone features

- **An extension.** This allows calls to be made and received in all departments of a firm. This is a piece of telephone equipment connected to the main telephone.
- **The engaged tone.** A short single note repeated at regular intervals usually means the number being called is in use but it can also mean that the exchange equipment is engaged. In either case you should replace the telephone receiver and try again later.
- subscriber ▶ **Subscriber.** A subscriber is a person who rents a telephone line from the telephone companies. Private subscribers are people who have rented sets for use in their own homes. Business subscribers are organizations which have telephones installed in their offices.
- **Direct inward dialling.** This allows an incoming call to reach a specific extension without assistance from the telephone operator.
- hunting ▶ **Hunting.** The hunting service routes a call to an idle extension number in a prearranged group, when the extension number needed is busy.
- **Call transfer.** This service allows an extension user on any two-party calls to hold the existing call and originate another call to a third party.

call override ▶
- **Call override.** Call override service enables an extension user, after reaching a busy number, to override the busy condition and enter the existing conversation on a bridge basis, preceded by a warning tone.

call forwarding ▶
- **Call forwarding.** Call forwarding service automatically routes incoming calls to an extension. An executive who has to see a colleague elsewhere in the building can route all his calls to the extension concerned.
- **Call waiting.** This feature allows the subscriber to be alerted, by a beep, to another call waiting to be answered.
- **Speed dialling.** This allows the telephone user to dial telephone numbers being stored in a speed dialling register. The register is automatically sorted after each call – the telephone numbers are always in an order which is determined by how frequently they are dialled. The most frequently dialled number is always at the top. By pressing step/skip buttons, the caller can easily scan such an adaptable register. The method is advantageously applied in mobile telephones, in particular car radiophones.
- **Cellular phones.** The cellular phone, also called mobile phone or wireless, is a short-range, portable electronic device for mobile voice or data communication over a network of specialized base stations known as cell sites.

Telephone services

- **Advice of duration and charge (ADC) calls.** This type of call is also referred to as a 'time and charge call'. This is made through a telephone operator by a caller who may need to know how much the call will cost and the duration of the call. The operator is then asked to ring back at the end of the call to tell the caller the cost of the call.

collect call ▶
- **Collect calls.** If a person does not have money to pay for long-distance service but needs to make a long-distance call, he/she can hope that the person he/she is calling will pay for the call. This can be done by calling the operator and telling him/her that the caller would like to make a collect call. When the operator tries to connect the call, he/she will ask the person answering whether they would like to receive a collect call. Keep in mind that collect calls cost a fair amount more than if the recipient were to call back long distance, so that person may not want to accept the call.
- **Station-to-station calls.** The concept of a station-to-station call is that the caller will speak to anyone who answers the telephone. In some Caribbean territories the direct distance dialling (DDD) facility, which results from modern technological development, is not available and so subscribers and other telephone users must route calls through the operator. Since the caller can speak to anyone who answers the telephone, the cost of this type of call is less because the operator does not have to wait for a particular person to answer the telephone. The first three minutes attract the lowest rate.
- **Person-to-person calls:** These are operator-assisted calls charged to the caller. The charge is made only if the person being called is able to come to the phone. A person-to-person call allows the caller to specify the person he/she wishes to speak to, by either name, department or reference number. Person-to-person calls are charged at a higher rate than station-to-station calls, however, a fee is payable whether or not the call is connected.

conference call ▶
- **Conference calls.** A manager may wish to speak to a number of overseas dealers at the same time. This can be done via a conference call. The long-distance telephone operator will be given the names, addresses and telephone numbers of the persons who will be in dialogue. The operator then arranges to have a network of connecting telephone circuits to allow each person to speak and to hear others speaking. This facility aids the decision-making process. Conference calls costs are usually high, but the alternatives may be less suitable: letters do take time to reach their overseas

destinations and business travel is extremely expensive, as well as time-consuming for busy executives.

- **Local calls.** These are calls made to another telephone number within the local exchange area.
- **Overseas calls.** A consumer can make overseas calls from a home phone or cell phone. Currently, these calls can be made for essentially local rates, or even less.
- **Direct-distance dialling (DDD).** This is used to place a long-distance call to another telephone number without the help of the telephone operator. A long-distance access (1), plus an area code, plus the number of the party with whom you wish to speak, must all be dialled. This type of call results in a station-to-station call.
- **Card calls.** These allow the caller to charge the service to a specific account number. The card company assigns personal identification numbers (PINs) so that the account number can be verified before the card call is completed and the account charged.

Internal communication links

- **Pager.** This is a device for contacting people when they are away from their office, using bleeps to alert them to a telephone call or using a two-way speech system.

closed-circuit television ▶
- **Closed-circuit televisions.** Unlike ordinary television, a closed-circuit television (CCTV) is a video magnification system consisting of a video screen interfaced with a video camera. It does not broadcast, but there is a link between the camera and the television screen. These systems are used so that managers can see what is happening in remote parts of factories or to detect thieves in supermarkets and department stores.

public address system ▶
- **Public address system.** A public address system is commonly found in factories, airports, department stores, supermarkets and schools. If there is a message for anyone in the area, this will be announced over the loudspeaker and the person called will go to the nearest telephone and identify himself to the switchboard operator. A disadvantage of this system is that if there is too much background noise the announcement may not be heard.

intercom ▶
- **Intercom.** An intercom device enables communication to take place between two or more persons. A small microphone and a loudspeaker enable communication to take place.

Telecommunication media

There are a wide range of other important telecommunication services which you should be aware of, including electronic mail, facsimile transaction (fax), telex and telemessage.

Electronic mail

This involves the use of computer terminals linked via the telephone network. Subscribers must have a password to enter the system and are then able to send messages to a 'mailbox', where they are stored until retrieved by the receiver.

Facsimile

Figure 2.7 Facsimile machine

The word 'facsimile' means 'extra copy'. The word is abbreviated to 'fax' which is used to refer to the machine, the document transmitted or received and the act of sending documents over telephone lines so that they can be received at the same time they are sent.

A fax machine may be linked to a telephone or may have its own integral telephone including dial. The person wishing to send a fax dials the fax number of the addressee. When the callback signal is received, the document is fed into the machine which scans the print and converts the 'shapes' – that is, letters, drawings and so on – into signals which can travel along a telephone line. The receiving machine converts the signals back into 'shapes' which are then printed on paper stored in the machine.

It is important that the original document is of good-quality print. If it is of uneven density (darkness of print) or smudged, the copy printed by the receiving fax machine may be illegible.

Radiophone

radiophone ▶

The radiophone can be used in cars or boats for calls anywhere in the world. Calls from a radiophone are dialled in the usual way and incoming calls can be received. It is more expensive than the regular telephone service but is useful for businessmen such as sales representatives whose job involves a great deal of travelling, and who need to keep in touch with their firms. The latest developments have a small microphone above the windscreen and receiver via a loudspeaker, so that the driver does not have to take a hand away from the steering wheel when taking or making a call.

Telemessage

telemessage ▶

A telemessage is accepted by telephone and kept, then delivered the next day by first-class mail.

Tele- and video conferencing

This service links individuals or group of people from different places by sound and vision. Persons who cannot be physically present at a meeting can join the meeting from a distance using this service.

Electronic transfer

electronic funds transfer ▶

Electronic funds transfer refers to the computer-based systems used to perform financial transactions electronically.

The term is used for a number of different concepts:

• cardholder-initiated transactions, where a cardholder makes use of a payment card;
• direct deposit – payroll payments for a business to its employees via a bank;
• direct debit payments from customer to business, where the transaction is initiated by the business, with customer permission;
• electronic bill payment in online banking;
• wire transfer via an international banking network (generally carries a higher fee).

Visual communication

'Seeing is believing'– seeing something usually has a more lasting impact than hearing the same thing described. Therefore, if information is important to a large number of people, it is better to present it to them where they can see it rather than simply tell it to them. Offices usually use charts and graphs to display information so that information will not be overlooked.

Sign language

This is mainly used by hearing-impaired persons. They use body movements, especially their hands, to get their message across to the receiver.

Pie charts

These are often used to illustrate relative quantities, proportions or percentages. Pie charts are usually used for information purposes rather than comparison. A circle is divided into proportional segments, expressed usually in percentage terms. The circle can also be shown using different colours to represent different areas.

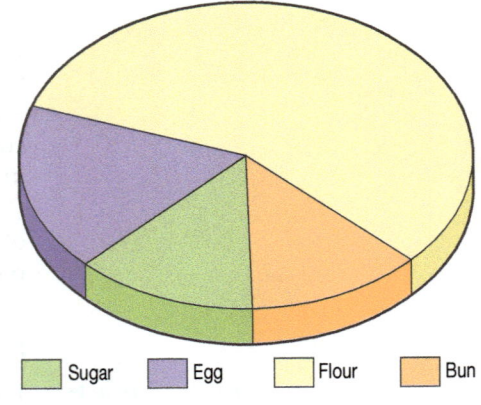

Figure 2.8 Pie chart

Bar graphs

These may be presented either vertically or horizontally. They are very effective where information about one item is to be compared and contrasted with information about another.

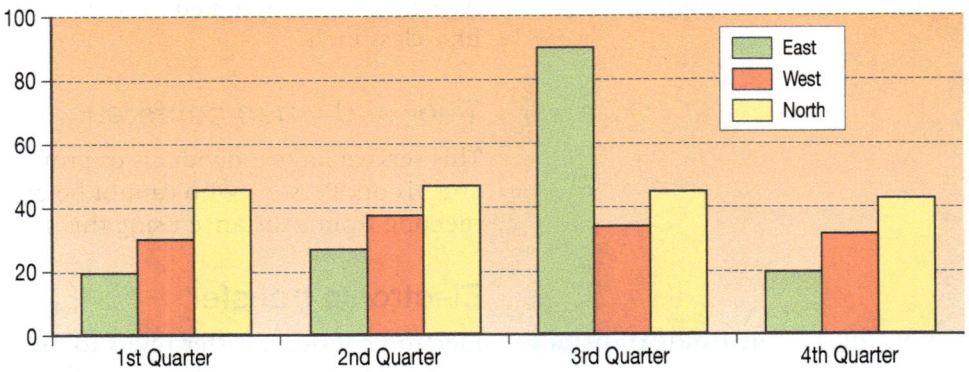

Figure 2.9 Bar chart

Post Office

Office employees who are responsible for handling the incoming and outgoing mail should have a sound knowledge of the postal services available and they should also be familiar with all rules governing the despatching of mail and parcels.

Postal guides and any current postal service regulations giving the cost of stamps and packages can be obtained from the Post Office.

Services offered by the Post Office

Inland / local mail

'Local mail' refers to letters, packets and parcels posted to destinations within the country. These mails can be sent by first- or second-class mail. Sending first-class mail is usually more expensive than second-class mail.

International / overseas mail

'Overseas mail' refers to letters, parcels and packets posted to overseas destinations.

Public letter boxes

Public letter boxes are metal boxes that are placed at strategic points on the sidewalks of major thoroughfares to enable members of the general public to mail their letters without having to go to the Post Office. Postal workers who take the contents to the nearest Post Office for processing will clear these boxes at specific times of the day.

Private letter boxes

Private letter boxes are rented from the Post Office, by applying to the Postmaster General. At the time of the rental transaction two keys are assigned – one is given to the subscriber and the other kept by the Post Office. All incoming mail for the subscriber, except registered letters and parcels, is placed in these boxes. A major advantage of this service is that letters can be collected at any time of the day or night.

Registered mail

registered mail ▶

When anything valuable has to be sent by post, it should be sent by registered mail. Letters and parcels sent by registered mail are handled by the Post Office with special security measures and separately from ordinary mail. If these letters are lost, limited compensation can be collected. All outgoing registered mail must be handed to a postal clerk and the necessary fees paid.

An advice slip is sent by the Post Office to the receiver of the registered mail who must then visit the Post Office with a valid identification card in order to claim the mail.

Recorded delivery

recorded delivery ▶

Any inland postal packet, except a parcel, can be sent by recorded delivery service, which provides proof of posting and of delivery. Letters and packets for recorded delivery must be taken to the Post Office. A fee, additional to the postage, is payable. The name of the addressee must be written on the recorded delivery receipt. The receiver of a recorded delivery packet must sign a receipt. If the sender completes an advice of delivery form and pays an additional fee, he will be notified when the packet has been delivered. Recorded delivery packets must not contain bank notes, coins or jewellery.

Freepost

A firm that wishes to obtain a reply from a customer without putting him to the expense of paying postage may include in its address the word 'FREEPOST'. The reply bearing this word can then be posted in the ordinary way but without the need for a stamp. The firm sending the letters pays the postage to the Post Office. The replies will be sent by second-class post only.

Business reply service

business reply service ▶

Business reply service is used by firms who wish to obtain replies from customers without putting then to the expense of paying postage. Business reply forms may be in the form of a postcard, an envelope or a gummed label.

Poste restante

Poste restante ▶

Poste restante service is used by visitors and travellers. These persons can collect their mail at the nearest Post Office to where they are staying. The mail is addressed to the Post Office and the person to whom the letter belongs will visit the Post Office and present an identification card before receiving the letter.

Figure 2.10   *Poste restante* address

Priority mail

This is a fast, two-day service for documents and packages. It offers one of the best values in shipping, with competitive, economical prices.

Express delivery

This is a fast delivery service where the sender pays an extra fee for delivery of parcels or letters.

Courier services

courier services ▶

Some companies use courier services extensively. There are several private companies which offer fast and effective mail services – for example, Federal Express (FedEx) and United Parcel Services (UPS). FedEx offers services worldwide, including overnight service and international services with delivery within one to three days.

Franking machine

franking machine ▶

A franking machine may be purchased or hired from the manufacturers. A licence to use the machine must first be obtained from the Post Office.

Electronic mail

electronic mail ▶

The use of electronic mail is being found as an efficient way to distribute messages from the sender to a receiver in the same organization. However, if the sender and receiver also have an internet address and the ability to access the internet, electronic messages can be sent between individuals regardless of their location throughout the world.

Mail room

Large firms tend to have a mail room where incoming and outgoing letters and parcels are taken so that they can be sorted and distributed efficiently.

Handling incoming mail

Incoming mail must be dealt with efficiently and in a systematic order. This is so that the mail can be distributed to the addressees as quickly as possible, so that office staff will be able to carry out their duties without delays.

In some large firms mail room staff usually arrive early so that the distribution of mail to the various departments is done before the other office staff arrive.

Sometimes there are letters, which arrive in the mailbags, which should not be opened by the Mail Room Clerk. Only the person to whom it is addressed should open this type of letter. These are letters marked 'private', 'confidential' or 'personal'. Such letters should be put aside and delivered only to the persons to whom they are addressed.

Handling outgoing mail

Outgoing mail may arrive at the mail room throughout the day, however, most mail tends to arrive there in the afternoon. To ensure that mail is dealt with promptly so that important documents are not delayed, some companies employ the following:

- each department is given trays marked 'Outgoing mail' and at regular intervals the messenger from the mail room will collect the mail so that it can be dealt with promptly;
- the mail room may also be given a cut-off time after which no mail will be collected for that day.

In some firms, outgoing mail is sent to the mail room already folded and inserted into envelopes, with a pencilled '1' or '2' in the top right-hand corner, to show whether the letter should go by first- or second-class post. It is necessary to weigh a letter if it is bulky or seems heavier than the maximum weight allowed by the Post Office for minimum first-class or second-class postage.

Other letters which must be weighed are letters going abroad, whether by airmail or 'surface' mail. At the Post Office an airmail letter form is available which is the cheapest way to send letters by air. This form is called an 'aerogramme'.

Surface mail is carried by train, ship or van, and is cheaper than airmail but slower.

In many firms, letters and other documents are sent to the mail room accompanied by correctly typed envelopes, and the Mail Room Clerk's job is to fold and insert the letters into the envelopes. While he/she is doing this, he/she should:

- check, by looking at the letter, to see whether there should be an enclosure. If the enclosure is missing, the letter should be placed on one side and later returned to the sender;
- check that enclosures are attached to letters by stapling or by using a paper clip;
- check that the letter has been signed;
- ensure that the inside address is the same as that on the accompanying envelope – if not, the sender should be consulted;
- fold the letter so that it fits into the envelope properly;
- place the letter into the correct size of envelope and seal it;
- weigh the letter, especially if it is addressed to an overseas destination; affix the correct stamps and place the letter into one of the following three categories:

- inland – anywhere within the sending country;
- overseas – both airmail and surface mail;
- registered post or recorded delivery – for which a receipt has to be obtained from the Post Office. Such letters cannot be posted in a letter box.

Opening the incoming mail

Before opening the mail the following steps should be followed:
- place all envelopes facing up;
- put aside all envelopes marked 'private', 'confidential' or 'personal' – these must be opened only by the person whose name appears on the envelope;
- open the remaining letters using a letter opener or letter-opening machine;
- remove the contents – if there are enclosures, remove these and attach them to the letter;
- if the letter contains money, remove and record the method of payment and the amount in a remittance book then pass it to the cashier for signing;
- if you open an envelope marked 'personal' by mistake, seal the letter with tape and write 'opened in error' and sign your name;
- stamp each letter with a date stamp indicating the date of receipt.

Date	Sender	Remittance	Amount	Signature
200-				
Dec 1	Denise Small	Money order	500.00	*Anne Brown*
Dec 3	Anthony McCarthy	Cash	210.00	*Anne Brown*
Dec 5	Tijean Miller	Postal order	250.00	*Anne Brown*
Dec 10	Pauline Little	Cheque	1230.00	*Anne Brown*

Figure 2.11   Example of a page from a remittance book

Handling mail

In a large office

In a large organization all mail is dealt with in the mail room. The incoming mail is opened, sorted and distributed throughout the firm by messengers who at the same time take the outgoing mail to the mail room to be prepared for posting.

In a small office

In a small firm, one person (perhaps the secretary/receptionist) will deal with all facets of mail handling. Sorting may be done on the desk or sorting trays may be used. In this situation the incoming mail is usually opened, stamped with a date stamp then distributed by hand.

Outgoing mail is collected, weighed, stamped and sent to the Post Office for posting, while incoming mail involves receipt, sorting and internal distribution.

Parcel post

Parcel post is another service offered by the Post Office for the sending of parcels through the post, at home, or to another business, anywhere in the world. It is generally one of the less expensive ways to ship packages that are too heavy to be sent by regular letter post but is usually a slower method of transportation.

Packaging of parcels

It is important that suitable packaging material be used to package items for mailing. Parcels should be clearly addressed and the name and address of the sender should appear on the outside as well as on the inside of a parcel.

Fragile items should be clearly marked and the correct cushioning material used to protect the items. The Post Office Guide outlines all the rules which should be followed when packaging items as well as other services offered.

List of prohibited items

Various types of prohibitions apply to items sent by post. The sender is held responsible for non-compliant mail.

The items listed below are prohibited regardless of the chosen destination:

- perishable biological materials, infectious or non-infectious;
- items that, due to their nature or packaging, are hazardous to postal workers or may spoil or damage other mail or postal facilities;
- illegal drugs and psychotropic substances;
- live animals;
- obscene or immoral items;
- counterfeit goods;
- explosives and inflammable products, for example alcohol, radioactive materials;
- jewels, precious metals, banknotes, money and other items of value unless sent by registered mail.

Compensation fee

Compensation can be collected from the Post Office for damages or losses caused to packages handled there. The amount of compensation paid is determined by the amount of fee paid. However, there are instances where the Post Office refuses to make compensation. The following are some reasons:

- packages left unclaimed for long period of time;
- damages or losses caused by natural disaster, for example hurricane;
- packages which contain prohibited articles, for example guns or ammunition;
- packages for which no documentary proof can be established that the Post Office did handle them.

Mail room equipment

Franking machine

A franking machine prints in red the value of a stamp on an envelope, postcard or label, as well as the date and time of posting, the place of posting, licence number of the machine and an advertising slogan, if required. It saves the time spent on keeping a record of stamps used, as well as the trouble of sticking stamps on envelopes, parcels and packages.

Franking machines may be purchased or hired from the manufacturers. A licence to use the machine must first be obtained from the Post Office. The Post Office sets the meter on a franking machine in accordance with the amount of money paid to it and then seals the meter. Each time an envelope, postcard or label is franked, this meter deducts the amount used and shows the balance remaining.

Franked mail, or 'metered mail' as it is also called, can by-pass the Post Office queue and cancelling in the Post Office sorting office and often catches earlier trains and aircraft as a result. Because such mail saves the Post Office time, it has to be posted in a special way – handed in over the counter of a Post Office, tied in bundles and 'faced' or posted in a letter box in a special envelope for franked mail.

Addressing machine

An addressing machine may be linked to folding and inserting equipment, or used on its own. Firms who regularly send out a great deal of mail to the same people, for example mail order firms and charitable organizations, use addressing machines.

The mail room staff prepare address plates with the names and addresses of all the people on the mailing list. The plates are kept in alphabetical order and when needed are stacked in the addressing machine. As each envelope passes through the machine, one plate descends on to it, printing a name and address.

Collating and inserting machine

Where a large series of documents, brochures or other items is to be sent to a large number of people, these have to be sorted into sets and put into envelopes. The mail room staff can do this either by hand or by using a collating machine.

Letter opener

Sealed letters should be opened, either with a paper knife or with a letter-opening machine. This machine shaves off a very tiny strip of paper from the edge of an envelope so that the contents may be removed.

Classifications of mail service offered by the Post Office

Mail sent through the post falls into either first-, second-, third- or fourth-class mail service. Mail is charged based on the class it falls into. Therefore it is important that all classes of mail be understood.

First-class mail

Any item weighing 13 ounces or less that is mailable may be sent as first-class mail. This includes: personal correspondence, postcards, business reply mail or any document that is sealed in an envelope.

Second-class mail

Second-class mail carries a lower postage rate than first-class mail. Periodicals and newspapers are usually sent using this class. No piece of first-class mail should be included in this category. If first-class mail is found among second-class mail then the first-class rate will be applied.

Third-class mail

This is mail consisting mainly of printed materials such as newspapers, books or brochures weighing less than one pound. Third-class mail must be clearly stated on the package.

Fourth-class mail/parcel post

This class of mail is also called 'parcel post'. It includes domestic parcel post, bound printed matter and films weighing up to 70 pounds with a combined length and girth of 108 inches or less. It is generally one of the less expensive ways to ship packages that are too heavy to be sent by other classes of mail.

Summary

- Communication is essential to everyday life.
- Communication may be visual, oral, electronic or written, formal or informal, open or restricted, internal or external.
- The main verbal methods of communication are face to face, interviews, meetings, conferences or by telephone.
- The main types of written communication are letters, memos, agendas and reports.
- The main types of visual communications are charts, flyers, posters and bar graphs.
- The main types of electronic communication are teleconferencing, internet and electronic mail.
- Memorandums are usually sent within an organization.
- Letters are mainly used for external communication.
- There are many barriers to communication, such as noise, personal attitudes and physical factors.
- To save time when making a telephone call, collect all necessary information or documents needed beforehand.
- Put a 'smile' in your voice – let the caller feel welcome and appreciated.
- Answer the telephone by the second or third ring.
- When taking telephone messages, ensure that all relevant information is noted.
- There are a number of reference books which may be used in business organizations.

Answers to

1
- sender;
- receiver;
- message;
- channel;
- feedback.

2

	Visual	Written	Oral
E-mail		√	
Telephone			√
Forms		√	
Gesture	√		
Radio			√
Reports		√	
Meeting			√
Poster	√		
Agenda		√	
Pie chart	√		

3
- cost;
- urgency;
- time/distance;
- need to reach a large audience.

4
- urgency;
- cost and the need to reach a large audience;
- cost and time;
- confidentiality and whether the receiver has the equipment to receive the fax.

5
- Yours faithfully;
- Yours truly;
- Yours sincerely.

6 The letter is a more formal means of communication; it has a complimentary close, addresses and salutation. The memorandum is used internally and is less formal; it has no address, salutation or complimentary close.

7

Types of paper	Uses
Flimsy	Used to make extra copies
Bond	To prepare top-copy business documents
Parchment	Wedding invitations, handwritten letters etc.
Onion skin	Tracing

8

	12-hour	24-hour
a	5.30 am	0530 hrs
b	8.15 pm	2015 hrs
c	10.00 pm	2200 hrs
d	10.30 am	1030 hrs
e	12.00 midnight	0000 hrs
f	3.40 pm	1540 hrs

Examination-style questions

Multiple choice questions

1 Which of the following should be included on a memo?
  a salutation
  b date of communication
  c telephone number
  d complimentary close.

2 Which of the following would provide the quickest delivery of an urgent message?
  a memo
  b letter post
  c fax
  d telemessage.

3 A written communication between two departments of a company would be made by:
  a letter
  b memo
  c intercom
  d Viewdata.

4 Which is the most suitable form for communicating information to a large number of persons?
  a intercom
  b voicemail
  c tannoy
  d loudspeaking telephone.

5 Which of the following pieces of information would you expect to hear on an answering machine?
   a firm's name
   b time
   c date
   d receptionist's name.

6 Which of the following tasks are carried out in the Personnel Department?
   a designing advertisements
   b recruiting staff
   c secretarial services
   d induction of new employees.

7 An organization chart shows:
   a how the organization works
   b the structure of the organization
   c the most important people in the organization
   d the people working in the organization.

8 The message waiting facility is usually indicated by:
   a a buzzer
   b a message on a register
   c a light
   d a beep.

9 A block paragraph is one:
   a with a justified right margin
   b with every line indented from the margin
   c where all lines begin at left
   d printed in a different type and style.

Structured questions

1 Explain the difference between a memorandum and a letter, stating two differences. [4]

2 Write the complimentary close that goes with each of the following salutations:

SALUTATION	COMPLIMENTARY CLOSE
Dear Sir or Dear Madam	
Dear Mr Green	
Dear Frederick	

[3]

3 State how you would indicate that there is an enclosure to a letter. [2]

4 List **six** pieces of information that may be found on a company's letterhead. [6]

5 List and explain **four** factors which should be considered before selecting the channel of communication to be used in any given situation. [6]

6 Complete the table below:

DOCUMENT	SIZE OF PAPER TO BE USED
A letter	
An invoice	
An invitation card	
A compliments slip	

[4]

7 Explain the difference between a window envelope and a banker envelope. [3]

8 Use the following information to address an envelope:

Jasmine Young, 1278 Frills Street, Kingston, Jamaica. [3]

9 Write a professional word or phrase for each of the unprofessional words or phrases listed in the table below:

UNPROFESSIONAL	PROFESSIONAL
Hello, Hi	
Who?	
What?	
Hold on	
He's out	
What do you want?	
Thanks	

[7]

10 Digital telephone systems have many facilities. Briefly explain each of the facilities listed below:
- call waiting;
- call override;
- call transfer. [6]

11 Write the most appropriate channel of communication for the following:
- An urgent order from the buying department to a firm in New York

  _____

- A request for a transfer from one branch to another

  _____

- A confidential discussion between the President and the General Manager _____
- A detailed financial document to be delivered the same day to the representative in St Lucia

  _____

[4]

3 Recruitment and orientation

By the end of
this chapter
you should be
able to:

- ☑ identify sources of information on job opportunities;
- ☑ outline factors to be considered when seeking employment;
- ☑ prepare an application for a job;
- ☑ prepare a résumé;
- ☑ prepare various types of follow-up letters;
- ☑ explain factors to be considered when preparing for an interview;
- ☑ demonstrate knowledge of the requirements of the work environment;
- ☑ develop a portfolio;
- ☑ outline labour laws.

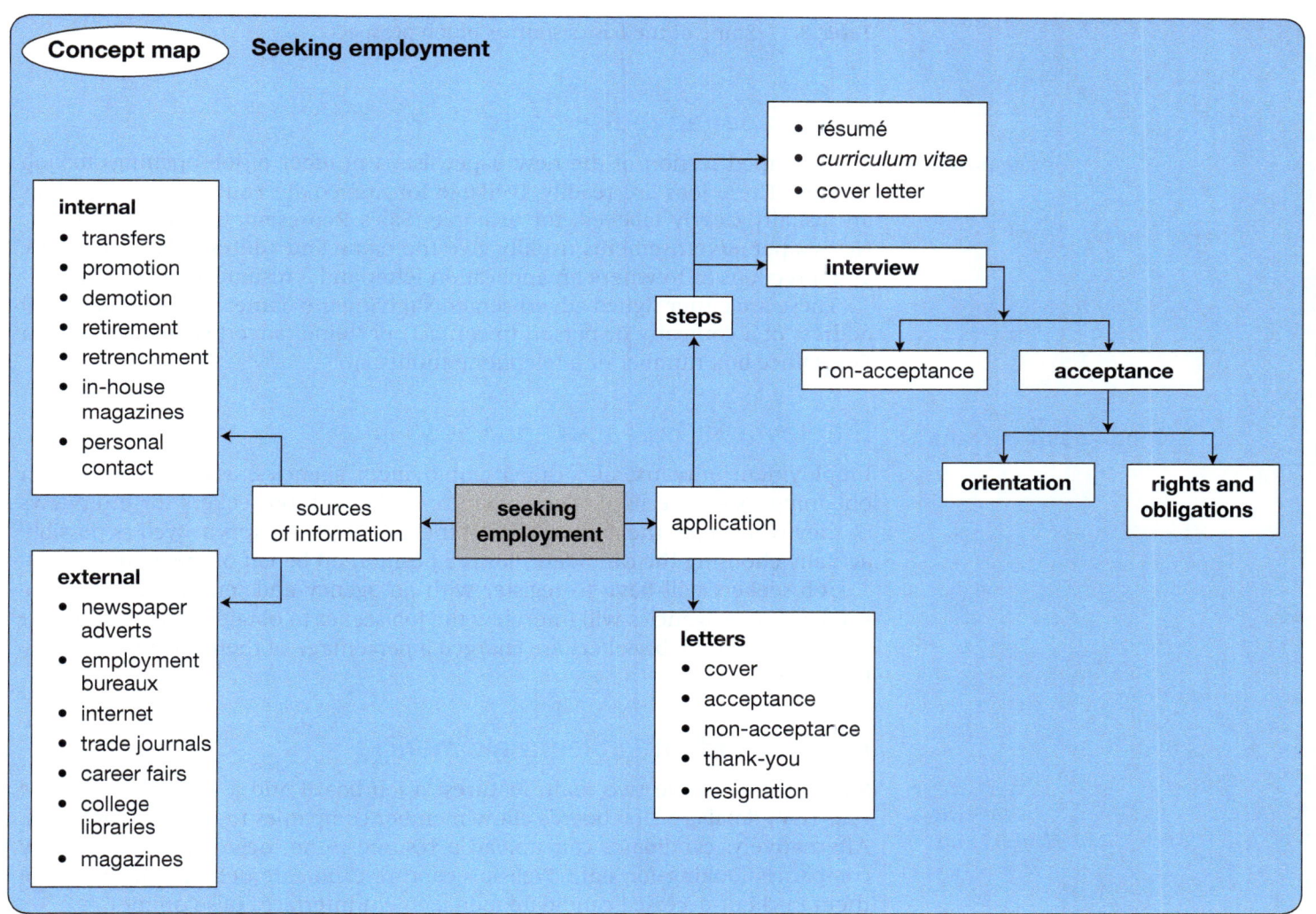

Concept map   **Seeking employment**

internal
- transfers
- promotion
- demotion
- retirement
- retrenchment
- in-house magazines
- personal contact

external
- newspaper adverts
- employment bureaux
- internet
- trade journals
- career fairs
- college libraries
- magazines

sources of information

seeking employment

application

letters
- cover
- acceptance
- non-acceptance
- thank-you
- resignation

steps

- résumé
- *curriculum vitae*
- cover letter

interview

non-acceptance

acceptance

orientation

rights and obligations

Sources of job information

There is a wide range of potential sources of job advertisements. The rule of thumb here is – leave no stone unturned! Note that job seekers need to register online in order to use some of the websites of newspapers, journals and online job seekers' services.

Internal sources	External sources
Transfers	Newspaper advertisements
Promotions	Employment bureaux
Demotions	Internet/electronic media
Retired employees	Trade journals/magazines
Retrenched employees	College libraries
In-house magazines	Careers fairs

Table 3.1   Some of the basics sources of job prospects

Newspaper advertisements

newspaper ▶
The classified section of the newspaper lists a number of job openings for job seekers. These jobs are readily available for immediate employment. The jobs are usually clearly labelled, for example 'Sales Representative' or 'Secretary'. Newspaper advertisements usually give the name and address of the company and directions as to where an application letter and a résumé should be sent.

These are either signed advertisements (giving the name, address and e-mail address of a company or person to contact) or 'blind' advertisements (giving a Post Office box number or a telephone number).

Employment bureaux/agencies

employment bureaux ▶
Employment bureaux, also called employment agencies, assist job seekers in obtaining jobs advertised. These agencies will send job seekers for interviews or they will supply the employer with the CVs of job seekers as well as possibly actually choosing the candidates for the position on behalf of the employer.

Job seekers will have to register with an agency and send their CV to the agency. Some agencies will interview the job seeker to obtain an idea of his/her skills. Successful job seekers are charged a percentage of their starting salary by the agency.

Internet and other electronic media

websites ▶
résumé ▶
***curriculum vitae* ▶**
Such websites have two main features: a job board and a résumé/*curriculum vitae* (CV) database. Job boards allow member companies to post job vacancies. Alternatively, candidates can upload a résumé to be included in searches by companies looking for staff. Websites capture candidate details and then pool them in client-accessed candidate management interfaces (also online).

Online recruitment websites can be very helpful in finding candidates who are very actively looking for work and posting their résumés online, but they will not attract 'passive' candidates who might respond favourably to an opportunity that is presented to them through other means.

Personal contact

One of the best resources of job information can be your friends and family. They may not be able directly to get a job for you but they can point you in the right direction by introducing you to prospective employers.

Trade journals

trade journal ▶ A trade journal, also called a trade magazine, is a publication that is targeted to people in a very specific industry. For example, people in the industry may use the trade journal to keep up on developments in the industry, connect with potential employers and network with suppliers. Such journals also generally contain industry-specific job notices; this is highly accepted by readers.

Company newsletters

company newsletter ▶ A company newsletter is used to bring an organization's image before the public. Newsletters are usually attractively designed and will deliver the message of the company to the right people. As a result, they are a very good recruiting tool. Job seekers will find reliable information on job opportunities in these newsletters.

Libraries and career centres

libraries ▶ Libraries offer a great deal of information about careers and job training. Begin by searching the catalogue under 'vocations' or 'careers' and then look under specific fields of work that match areas of interest.

career centres ▶ Career centres are where people and jobs connect. These centres are an integrated source of career opportunities for individuals and talent for employers. They provide career information and facilitate employment connections for job seekers through internet access, workshops and online talent banks in addition to recruitment and training.

University careers services

careers service ▶ Your university or college careers service is a useful source of job vacancy information. Some universities have an online vacancy service for students and graduates. Once registered, users can search for graduate job vacancies.

Careers fairs

careers fairs ▶ Graduate recruitment careers fairs are a good source of information about employers and the types of jobs they have on offer. Here, a number of employers will be invited to attend a college or university to interview members of the graduating class for vacant positions in their organizations.

ITQ1

In the table below, tick True or False to indicate your answer:

Items	Statements	True	False
1	A job search is the same as a strategic job search.		
2	I may utilize resources such as the Career Development Centre, executive search firms or placement services in my job search, but ultimately it is my responsibility to plan, maintain and conclude my job search.		
3	When it comes to job search skills, either you have them or you don't.		
4	The purpose of a well-structured résumé and a good cover letter is to land a job.		
5	External factors are an important consideration in which job I get.		
6	Positions offered through on-campus recruiting are rarely advertised elsewhere.		

Seeking employment

When you are looking for a job, there are several factors to bear in mind. The following are a few you should consider.

Career interest

advertisement ▶
- The **advertisement**. Read the advertisement for a vacant position carefully to decide whether you are interested in the type of job advertised.
- **Job description**. You should read the job description, which gives the title of the job, and outlines the main duties and responsibilities. It may also state the department in which the job is located. Read it carefully to decide whether this is the type of job you want.

Personal taste

personal taste ▶
The types of jobs that are appealing to you, i.e. that are to your personal taste, will influence the type of job you will apply for. For example:
- What type of work am I most interested in?
- What skills do I have that I enjoy using?
- Am I a team player or do I prefer working alone?
- What are my long-term goals?

Job satisfaction

job satisfaction ▶
Job satisfaction has to do with how enjoyable you find the work you do. Sometimes the satisfaction of the work you do is more essential for your wellbeing than money alone.

Training and qualifications

Most job seekers are rightly concerned with the training opportunities which exist in an organization. Job seekers know that in the long run they will benefit tremendously from their skills and perhaps bring them better qualifications, which no doubt will help them in the future.

Career advancement

career advancement ▶
Career advancement is an incentive to job seekers. Job seekers also look at the promotional opportunities existing in an organization. If there are opportunities for promotion, they will want to place an application for the job advertised.

Salary and fringe benefits

fringe benefits ▶
The salary is the amount you will be rewarded for the work you will do and the responsibility you will have. Some jobs offer fringe benefits, that is, extra rewards that are not part of the normal salary. The following are some fringe benefits:
- subsidized meals (reduced-cost);
- free or subsidized health care;
- use of company vehicle;
- pension schemes;
- good holiday entitlement;
- provision of work clothing;
- life assurance;
- company products at discount prices.

Hours of employment and vacations

The hours you are expected to work will also be important and will influence the type of job you take. For example, if you have to work shifts this means that you will have to adjust to working at different times.

Many organizations operate a vacation roster whereby employees take turns in going on paid vacation. Other organizations operate a shutdown period, when the firm does not operate at all and all employees take their vacation at the same time.

Location of employment

You need to consider the location of the job. If you have to travel long distances to and from work, the cost and time involved can be a problem. Job seekers tend to seek employment closer to home, as the cost of transportation can be very expensive. They also are able to arrive at work early.

Image of the organization

You may prefer working with firms you consider prestigious. This gives a sense of satisfaction from working for a large, well-known organization. This is because people like to be a part of success, and like to be associated with people or organizations that are well known and popular.

ITQ2
How do you decide what kind of a job to look for?

Making applications

Very often, an applicant's first contact with prospective employers is by means of the cover letter, *curriculum vitae* or application form. Prepare these carefully – these are your selling tools!

Résumés

application form ▶

A résumé is a summary of an applicant's employment history, educational background and skills. Sending a résumé and filling out an application form are two ways to provide employers with written evidence of your qualifications. This is the basic information that is usually included in a résumé:

- name, address, e-mail address, and telephone number;
- employment objective – state the type of work or specific job you are seeking;
- education, including school name and address, dates of attendance, major, and highest grade completed or degree awarded. Consider including any courses or areas of focus that might be relevant to the position;
- experience, both paid and volunteered. For each job, include the job title, name and location of employer, and dates of employment. Briefly describe your job duties;
- special skills, computer skills, proficiency in foreign languages, achievements, and membership of organizations;
- references, only when requested;
- keep it short – only one page for less experienced applicants.

Résumé

THOMASA ANDERSON
3b Sunset Boulevard
Kingston 6
Jamaica
Tele: 876-960-4513 email: Andersont_@yahoo.com

Objective: To achieve a leadership sales position with a world-class and high-integrity food products company.

| EDUCATION: | 2003–2009 | Bellofield High School |
| | 1997–2003 | Ainsley Smith Primary School |

QUALIFICATION: **2009 CSEC General proficiency:**

English Language	(II)
Mathematics	(II)
Principles of Accounts	(II)
Principles of Business	(II)
EDPM	(III)
Social Studies	(III)

EXPERIENCE: Summer 2009 – Sales Clerk at Marks Carpeting Manufacturing Ltd. Duties included: filing, word processing and answering the telephone.

Summer 2008 – Clerk at Latro Tyre Manufacturing Ltd. Duties included: filing, word processing and answering the telephone.

PERSONAL DATA:

AGE:	17 years
DATE OF BIRTH:	February 15, 1994
INTERESTS:	Reading, dancing, collecting stamps and meeting new people.
REFERENCE:	Principal
	Excelsior High School
	137 Mountain View Avenue
	Kingston 3

Figure 3.1   Example of a résumé

ITQ3

Why should your résumé relay the significance of your accomplishments?

ITQ4

Should you include in your résumé personal information such as age, marital status and hobbies?

ITQ5

In your résumé, should you state your reasons for leaving each employer?

Curriculum vitae

curriculum vitae ▶   A *curriculum vitae* presents in-depth and structured information about the experience and qualification of a person. This document is usually two to three pages long.

Name: DEVLYN BENTLEY

Vision:
To increase the shareholder value and maximizing profit by improving the operational efficiencies and maximum utilization for the available resources.

Keys of success:
- Integrity and Ethics
- Training
- Leadership
- Recognition
- Teamwork
- Communication

CONTACT INFORMATION

45 Drewey Drive	Phone: 875 6527 878 (Home)
St Ann's Bay	Mobile 876 9810 9899
St Ann	E-mail: king_910@hotmail.com

CAREER OBJECTIVE
To find a challenging position to meet my competencies, capabilities, skills, education and experience.

PROFESSIONAL EXPERIENCE

September 2005 – Present:

Production Manager.
Suzie's Restaurant & Pastries
31 Red Hills Road, Kingston

1. Establishes production standards of efficiency, minimum wastages and maximum utilization of resources (machines, raw material and manpower).
2. Supervises production processes to ensure implementation of company standards.
3. Prepares annual production plans and obtains approval of Director of Production.

EDUCATION

December 2004: **University of Technology**, Jamaica, Masters, MBS by Distance Learning

May 2004: **National Inspection and Technical Testing Co Ltd**, Jamaica Certification/Diploma

SKILLS

Skill	Level	Years practised
MS Word, MS Excell, PowerPoint,	Intermediate	More than 9 years

REFERENCES Available upon request

ITQ6

Should you use the personal pronouns 'I', 'me' and 'my' in your *curriculum vitae*?

ITQ7

How should you choose your references?

Figure 3.2 Example of a *curriculum vitae*

Letters of application

letter of application ▶

A letter of application (also referred to as a **cover letter**) introduces you to the employer, outlines why you are the best candidate for the job, and encourages the employer to find out more about you. Therefore, you will need a well-written cover letter to display your qualifications to their best advantage. It is likely to pay off handsomely in helping you to secure future earnings. This letter is usually sent with a résumé or an application form.

Currently, job seekers have the opportunity to e-mail or fax their letter of application, however, the original should still be delivered to the firm. When preparing the letter of application, care must be taken with spelling, grammar and presentation.

Your opening paragraph must attract favourable attention and make the interviewer interested enough to read on. You can begin by:
- identifying the type of position you are applying for and telling how you learned about the opening; then
- summarize your qualifications for a specific kind of position; and
- express support for the kind of work the organization performs. This type of opening shows the employer that you are aware of the needs of the industry.

Always try to give a convincing presentation of your qualifications. The qualifications must be related to the work you are applying for. Use a strong closing, with a request for action. The closing paragraph provides a smooth transition from a description of your qualifications to a specific request for an interview. Figure 3.3 shows a sample letter of application:

1867 Terrain Close
Kingston 11
JAMAICA

16 November 2011

Human Resources Manager
Mrs Debra Logan
Tyre Plus Distributors
20 Kings Road
St Ann

Dear Mrs Logan

I am applying for the position of Sales Representative advertised in the *Sunday Observer* dated 10 November 2011.

I am 17 years old and will be leaving Smith High School in July of this year. Early this year I sat the following subjects in the CSEC examinations: English Language, Mathematics, Principles of Accounts, Principles of Business, Information Technology and Religious Studies. I await the results.

I am particularly interest in working as a Sales Representative as last year I spent two months in the summer working at Auto Parts Guaranteed as a Sales Representative and found that I greatly enjoyed the work.

I am available for an interview at a time convenient to you. I can furnish letters of recommendation on request.

Yours sincerely

Michelle McIntyre

Michelle McIntyre

Figure 3.3 Example of a letter of application

Application form

Businesses and other organizations design their application forms in the manner that suits them best, although they all contain some basic requirements such as personal details, education, experience and reference. Some application forms are more complex than others and require more information. Preferably, an application form should be completed using black ink. The way you complete the employment application tells the interviewer the following:

- how well you can follow written instructions;
- whether your work habits are neat or sloppy;
- how accurately you can complete a task.

When completing an application form, be careful not to include any false information. Remember that your credibility and trustworthiness will be questioned and if it is revealed that you had included false information, that company will not hire you and, if you were already hired, your employment will be terminated. If the application form contains illegal questions, such as ones on age or marital status, you can choose either to answer the questions or to fill in the blank with the letters 'N/A' for 'not applicable' or draw a dash across the response blank.

HIPRO GARMENT DESIGNERS, INC

APPLICATION FOR EMPLOYMENT
PERSONAL

Name: _____   Phone Number: _____

Last _____   First _____   Middle _____

Present Address

_____

_____

_____

_____

TRN No: _____   **NIS No:** _____

Are you authorized to work in this country?   Yes ☐   No ☐

Contact person in case of emergency: _____

Name (Relationship) _____

Type of employment you are seeking:
Full-time ☐   Part-time ☐   Seasonal ☐   Temporary ☐

Position applied for: _____

Date available to start: _____

Have you ever applied to this company before?   Yes ☐   No ☐

Have you ever worked for this company before?   Yes ☐   No ☐

How did you learn of this company and/or position?: _____

EDUCATION:

Name and address of school	Course of study	Numbers of years completed	Did you graduate?	Diploma or degree received
College/University				
High School				
Others				

Name and address of previous employer: _____

_____

Special skills: _____

Applicant's name: _____

Signature: _____   Date: _____

Figure 3.4 Example of an application form

Interview

interview panel ▶

A typical job interview has a single candidate meeting with between one and three persons representing the employer; the potential supervisor of the employee is usually involved in the interview process. A larger interview panel will often include a specialized Human Resources worker. While the meeting can be over in as little as 15 minutes, job interviews usually last less than two hours.

The job interview will entail the interviewers asking the candidate questions about his/her job history, personality, work style and other factors relevant to the job. For instance, a common interview question is 'What are your strengths and weaknesses?'.

The candidate will usually be given a chance to ask any questions at the end of the interview. These questions are strongly encouraged since they allow the interviewee to acquire more information about the job and the company, but they can also demonstrate the candidate's strong interest in them.

The purpose of interviewing is to select and appoint the best candidate for the job, based solely on merit and suitability. To achieve this, employers must ensure that the interviewing process is fair, thorough, unbiased and based on objective and job-related criteria.

At the interview, each candidate should be treated consistently. To achieve this, the panel should:
- ask the same initial questions of each candidate;
- try to understand the candidate's responses by using follow-up questions where necessary;
- be consistent in allowing access to presentation material, notes and so on;
- not allow any discriminatory questions, harassment, or any other conduct which breaches the labour laws related to code of conduct;

labour laws ▶

- ensure that disabled candidates are treated according to the labour laws.

Common mistakes made by applicants

ITQ8

How should you respond to questions in an interview?

Some of the most common mistakes made by applicants during their interviews are:
- arriving late for the interview;
- showing a lack of confidence;
- dressing inappropriately;
- giving inappropriate answers to questions asked by the interviewer.

Preparation for an interview

You should do adequate preparation before an interview. Proper preparation will show how interested you are in the job, thus increasing your confidence and ultimately your chance of getting the job.

Before the interview:
- **Find out as much as possible about the firm.** It is important to learn as much as possible about the firm to which you are going for the interview. Knowing about the firm will help you to converse with more ease and to ask relevant questions. If the interviewer feels that you do not know much about the firm, he/she may feel that you are not interested in the job. The following information on the firm should be researched before the interview:
  - the products and services offered;
  - number of employees;
  - length of time the firm has been in existence;
  - how the firm operates.
- **Ensure that you know the place for the interview.** Visit the location for the interview before the day if you are not sure of the location. This will save valuable time on the day of the interview, as you will not have to be searching for the location, especially if you are running late.

- **Be prepared to answer questions.** The interviewer(s) will ask a number of questions and you are expected to answer by using your own words. The interviewer will expect you to explain your job objective and why you feel you are qualified. Be prepared to speak with the interviewer about yourself without hesitation. You could try to anticipate questions the interviewer will ask and prepare to answer them.

Consider your responses to the following questions which may be asked at the interview:

  - **Why do you wish to work for this company?** Be prepared to answer this question based on the results of your research of the organization. You may wish to mention something about the organization's product or service. Relate your skills or interests directly to the company features that you selected.
  - **Why did your leave your previous job?** When asking this question, the interviewer is looking for a response that will or will not support the position for which you are applying. In answering this question, avoid being critical of your former company.
  - **Why do you think you are the best candidate for this job?** Outline your qualifications and experiences directly to the requirements for the position.
  - **What do you know about our organization?** You can really be impressive with your answer to this question if you have done your research. Pick out the major achievements of the company to illustrate your knowledge of its products, community involvements, size, successes or other factors.
  - **What are some your accomplishments on your last job?** To answer this question, you should have two or three solid major accomplishments to discuss.

On the day of the interview

Guidelines for dressing appropriately include the following:

- clean, well-ironed and conservative clothing;
- clean, neat and work-related hair style;
- keep jewellery to a minimum and avoid flashy jewellery;
- shoes should complement clothing;
- nails should be neatly cut.

- **Dress neatly and tidily.** Ensure that you dress appropriately. Your clothing should indicate to the interviewer how you would look if you were employed at that firm. Do not wear clothing that is too tight or not fitting properly, as you may then lack the confidence needed for the interview.
- **Arrive promptly.** Arriving late for an interview will cause the interviewers to feel that you are not really interested in the job and that should you be employed you are likely to turn up late for work. Try to arrive at least 10–15 minutes before the start of the interview, as this will give you enough time to be relaxed before entering the interviewing room.
- **Speak clearly and answer questions fully.** You will be asked a number of questions and you are expected to give an answer or discuss a situation. You should look the interviewer in the eyes and answer all questions frankly. Ensure that you listen to the interviewer's question, so that you are able to give the required answer. Avoid giving 'yes' and 'no' answers but instead answer using a sentence. If you do not understand a question, ask for clarification.
- **Have some questions to ask about the organization.** Usually, at the end of an interview, the interviewer will ask you whether you have any questions you wish to ask. Be prepared to ask questions. Interviewers are happy when you do so, as they feel that you are showing interest in the organization. A candidate who asks questions tends to earn a few points above those candidates who do not. Be sure to ask questions specific to the position you are been interviewed for, such as:
  - What are the opportunities for advancement in the position?
  - Is the position permanent or not?
  - What skills are needed for the position?
  - What training will I be given?

ITQ9

Read the questions in the table opposite and use a tick to indicate whether the interview question should or should not be asked at an interview.

Items	Questions	Interview legal questions	Interview illegal questions
1	Have you ever been arrested?		
2	How did you learn about this job?		
3	Do you have any credit problems?		
4	What are your strengths?		
5	Do you smoke?		
6	Why do you wish to work with this company?		
7	What religion are you?		
8	What is your marital status?		

Types of letter

These may include the following:
- thank-you letters to interviewers;

letters of job acceptance ▶
- letters of job acceptance;
- letters of non-acceptance of job;
- letters of resignation;

letters applying for leave ▶
- letters applying for leave;

letters of acknowledgement ▶
- letters of acknowledgement.

Thank-you letter to an interviewer

After completing your interview you should correspond with the interviewer by writing a thank-you letter. Employers like conscientious employees and, by sending such a thank-you letter, you are also keeping your name and your qualifications on the interviewer's mind.

109 Bayles Avenue
Kingston 6
Jamaica

22 June 2011

The Human Resources Manager
Quality Fabric Manufacturer
314 Nelson Street
Kingston 11

Dear Mr Smith

Thank you for offering me the opportunity to discuss the opening at Quality Fabric Manufacturer as a member of the administrative staff. I have a very positive feeling about your organization and my ability to work effectively with you.

You mentioned that the decision on those who would be called would be made by July 11. I look forward to hearing from you. Please call me at 985-9908.

Yours sincerely

Andrew Williams

Figure 3.5 Example of a thank-you letter to an interviewer

Resignation letter

letter of resignation ▶ When you decide to change jobs, you should prepare a letter of resignation. You should always notify your supervisor or employer of the changes in writing, even if you communicate your decision orally. You should give at least two weeks' notice.

Although you may be dissatisfied when you resign, avoid the temptation to write an emotionally charged letter. Remember that this letter will become a permanent part of your file.

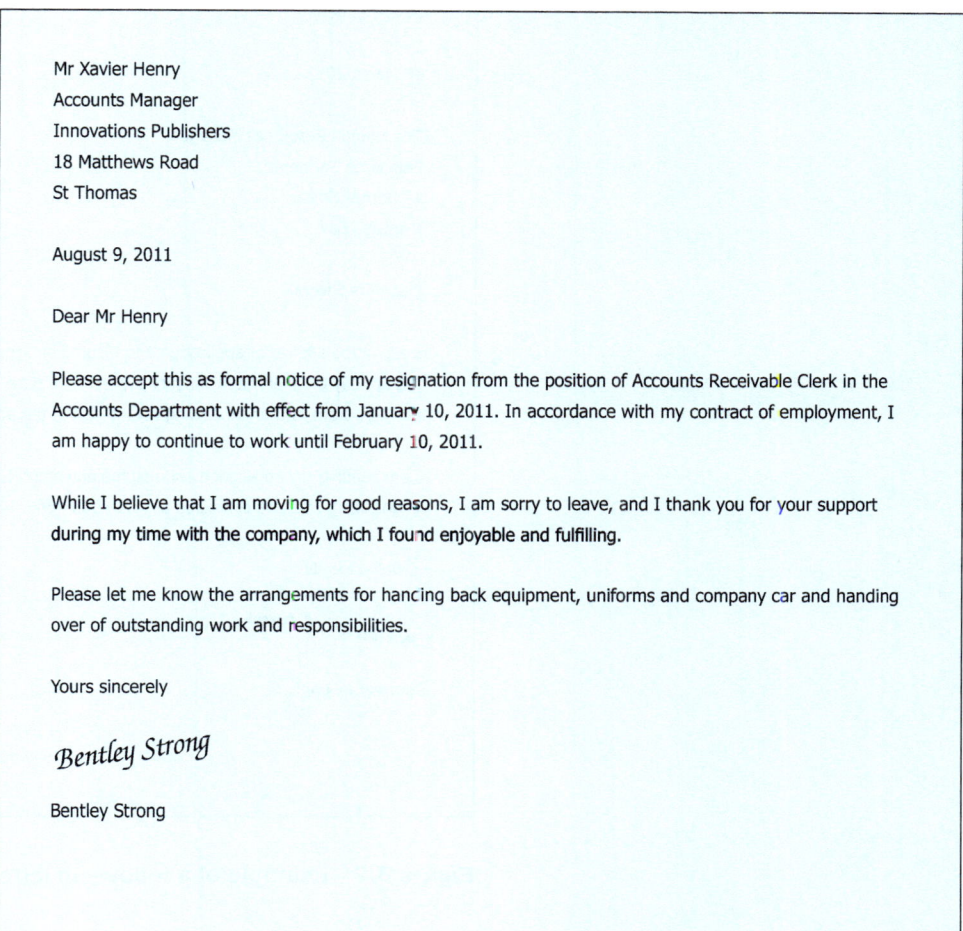

Mr Xavier Henry
Accounts Manager
Innovations Publishers
18 Matthews Road
St Thomas

August 9, 2011

Dear Mr Henry

Please accept this as formal notice of my resignation from the position of Accounts Receivable Clerk in the Accounts Department with effect from January 10, 2011. In accordance with my contract of employment, I am happy to continue to work until February 10, 2011.

While I believe that I am moving for good reasons, I am sorry to leave, and I thank you for your support during my time with the company, which I found enjoyable and fulfilling.

Please let me know the arrangements for handing back equipment, uniforms and company car and handing over of outstanding work and responsibilities.

Yours sincerely

Bentley Strong

Bentley Strong

Figure 3.6 Example of a letter of resignation

No reply received to application

Sometimes an applicant may send out application letters and after waiting for a period of time receive no response to the application. The applicant may choose to send a follow-up letter to the company.

34 Braemar Street
Spanish Town
St Catherine

10 March 2011

The Human Resources Manager
Plus Sizes Garments
11 Barrett Street
Montego Bay

Dear Mrs Silvera

I submitted a letter of application and résumé on January 21, 2011 for the Sales position advertised in the Sunday Gleaner dated January 17, 2011. To date, I have not heard from your company regarding the position. I am further expressing my interest in the position.

I am sending my application and résumé again and I am willing to provide any further information you might need. I can be contacted at (876) 985-1645. I look forward to hearing from you soon.

Yours sincerely

Andrew Adams

Andrew Adams

Figure 3.7 Example of a follow-up letter if no response to application

Letter of non-acceptance

non-acceptance letter ▶ A non-acceptance letter is a form of communication indicating the refusal of a job position.

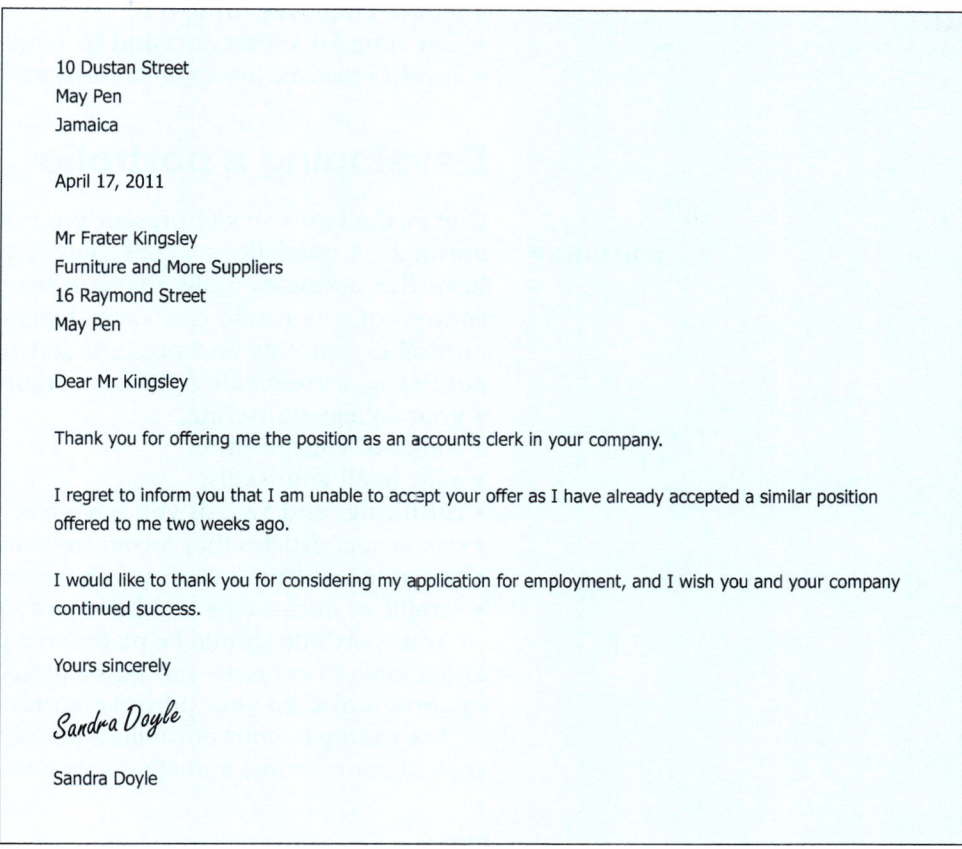

10 Dustan Street
May Pen
Jamaica

April 17, 2011

Mr Frater Kingsley
Furniture and More Suppliers
16 Raymond Street
May Pen

Dear Mr Kingsley

Thank you for offering me the position as an accounts clerk in your company.

I regret to inform you that I am unable to accept your offer as I have already accepted a similar position offered to me two weeks ago.

I would like to thank you for considering my application for employment, and I wish you and your company continued success.

Yours sincerely

Sandra Doyle

Sandra Doyle

Figure 3.8 Example of a non-acceptance letter

Orientation

After the interviewing process is completed and the employer decides on the candidate to be selected for the position, a letter, telephone call or e-mail will be sent to the successful candidate. offering the position. The candidate may or may not accept the position. However, should the position be accepted by the candidate a contract will be drafted and the candidate will be called in for an orientation session.

orientation ▶ Staff orientation, also called job-specific orientation, is the process that is used to help employees fit in quickly with their new position. A good orientation will make a significant difference in how quickly employees become productive. Orientation is usually conducted by the supervisor or manager in the section or department in which the new recruit will be working. The following are some areas that are outlined at a recruitment session:
- duties and responsibilities of the employee;
- employer's expectations of the employee;
- organizational function;
- rules and regulations of the organization;
- policies and procedures to be followed;
- training on operating equipment;
- introduction to co-workers.

Purposes of orientation

These are to:
- reduce anxiety;
- reduce start-up costs;
- reduce employee turnover;*
- save time for supervisors and co-workers;
- develop realistic job expectations, positive attitudes and job satisfaction.

ITQ10

Who should participate in the orientation programme?

Developing a portfolio

portfolio ▶

One of the best ways to present your qualifications and talents is to develop a portfolio. A portfolio is a collection of your work that serves as proof that you have the necessary skills that are needed in the working environment. The content of a portfolio can vary, depending on the type of job you seek. The portfolio's contents and presentation may also vary, based upon the kind of position you are seeking. Here are some possible contents for your portfolio:
- your college transcript;
- copies of your résumé;
- a list of all your skills;
- certificates and awards you have received;
- newspaper articles that recognize your achievements or promotions;
- programmes from events you have planned;
- sample of documents you have written.

Your portfolio should be placed in a professional-looking binder. A title page and a table of contents should be placed at the beginning of the portfolio. It is important to keep your portfolio current even after obtaining a job.

For example, your portfolio may include several examples of your writing, a copy of your résumé and, if you are a photographer, examples of pictures taken.

The work environment

A work environment is the place where you work. Workers should have a comfortable work environment as this will help facilitate higher production, staff morale and a reduction in absenteeism. Labour laws have been established to govern the working environment.

A good work environment should focus on the following:
- **Noise.** Noise is usually caused by loud machines – as a result, these should be placed away from the general staff population. Employees who use these machines should be provided with hearing protection devices.

ventilation ▶
- **Ventilation.** Fresh air facilitates respiration and helps in the removal of excess heat and the dilution of odour. There should be proper windows to facilitate adequate ventilation.
- **Lighting.** Proper lighting is important in the work environment, as it helps to prevent eyestrain.

Labour laws

Labour laws define the legal rights and obligations of working people and their organizations. Such laws generally cover:
- the right to freedom of association – that is, the right to join a certified union of workers;
- the right to collective bargaining whereby the trade union negotiates with the employer on behalf of the workers;
- workplace health and safety;
- employment standards, including general holidays, annual vacations,

working hours, unjust dismissals, minimum wage, layoff procedures and severance pay.

- Information about job vacancies can be located in many places, including the internet, newspaper advertisements, newsletters, friends and family, magazines, libraries, employment bureaux, careers fairs and trade journals.
- Applying for a job includes preparing a résumé or *curriculum vitae*, writing an application letter and completing an application form.
- A résumé is a tool used to market a job seeker and as such should be carefully prepared, including employment history, educational background, experience, special skills and abilities.
- A résumé differs from a *curriculum vitae* in that it is usually prepared on one page while a *curriculum vitae* usually has two or more pages.
- The main purpose of a cover letter is to obtain an interview.
- There are many factors that should be considered when seeking employment: these include personal taste, career interest, and location of the job as well as the image of the firm.
- There are many types of letters that a prospective or current employee may need to prepare relating to employment at a firm. These include: letters of resignation and letters applying for leave.
- Follow-up letters include: thank-you letters, enquiries, job acceptance and job refusal letters.
- A letter of resignation is prepared when an employee has decided to leave their place of employment.
- Interviews enable employers to assess the suitability of candidates, who themselves will be able to learn more about the organization.
- Preparing for an interview includes:
  - finding out about the prospective organization;
  - selecting appropriate dress;
  - asking questions at the interview;
  - answering questions.
- A portfolio is a collection of your work that serves as proof that you have the necessary skills that are needed in the working environment.
- Labour laws define the legal rights and obligations of working people and their organizations.

Answers to 

1

Items	True	False
1		√
2	√	
3		√
4		√
5	√	
6	√	

2 By carefully evaluating my skills, interests and goals I can target a profession that would allow me to achieve my goals and keep me interested over a long period of time.

3 When you provide quantifiable accomplishments, employers understand the impact of your job performance and can predict your chance of future success.

4 Your résumé will be more effective if it focuses on work-related credentials, rather than including details about your personal life.

5 No, these should not be stated because the résumé is a marketing tool.

6 The pronouns 'I' and 'my' should be used only in the objective statement. Always use an implied first-person voice – without the use of personal pronouns – throughout your résumé.

7 I should think about who I have worked for and where I got job experience that relates to the job I am looking for. Then, I call the former employers I have selected as references and ask them if they would be willing to speak about me. Finally, if they agree to be one of my references, I send them a copy of my résumé and a letter telling them the type of work I am looking for.

8 Listen carefully and take time to think about each question before offering a response, making sure to highlight my strengths in the answers given.

9

Items	Interview legal questions	Interview illegal questions
1		√
2	√	
3		√
4	√	
5		√
6	√	
7		√
8		√

10 Every new employee needs some type of orientation program.

Examination-style questions

Multiple choice questions

1 What body language and presentation skills will serve you well in an interview?
  a Firm handshake.
  b Speaking clearly.
  c Maintaining eye contact.
  d All of the above.

2 When asked vague questions, what should you do?
  a Respond with specific examples, keeping to your goals.
  b Respond with vague answers.
  c Say 'I don't know'.
  d Ask for a drink of water so that you can buy some time.

3 How should you handle illegal questions at an interview?
  a Tell the interviewer that what he / she just asked is illegal.
  b Refuse to answer.
  c Recognize the underlying issue and redirect your response.
  d Get up and leave the room.

4 When the interview is completed, what should you do?
  a Go home and wait by the phone for an acceptance call.
  b Go home and write a thank-you follow-up letter.
  c Go home, call the interviewer right away and ask more questions.
  d All of the above.

5 What will boost your confidence, and hone your interviewing skills?
 a Reading about the industry.
 b Talking to people who know the environment.
 c Practice, practice, practice.
 d A deep breath before meeting the interviewer.

6 When should you arrive at your interview?
 a Right on time.
 b 10 minutes early.
 c 30 minutes early.
 d One hour early.

7 The best way to dress for success is to:
 a dress comfortably
 b wear a formal suit
 c bring a sport coat, in case you need it
 d be trendy.

8 How long does it normally take for the interviewer to determine whether you are a good match for the company?
 a 5 minutes.
 b 20 minutes.
 c 30 minutes.
 d At the conclusion of the interview.

9 What should you **not** do to prepare for an interview?
 a Research the company.
 b Learn the company's concerns and challenges.
 c Practise top interview questions and answers.
 d Memorize key answers to interview questions.

Structured questions

1 List **four** sources of job information. [4]

2 Outline the steps to be taken when preparing for an interview. [6]

3 Write **five** questions that you could ask at an interview. [5]

4 Write **five** questions that you would expect the interviewer to ask of you. [5]

5 Identify **two** factors to be considered when seeking employment. [2]

6 Assume that you are Thomas Harlington of 19 Summerset Way, Kingston, and that you are employed with a large firm. You are offered a better opportunity in another company. Write a letter of resignation to your company. [7]

7 List **two** differences between the school culture and the organization culture. [4]

8 Explain two labour laws in place for employees' protection. [4]

9 Assume that you wrote a cover letter to Mrs Clover Daley, Brimax Auto Supplies, 2190 Princess Street, Kingston, and that you were interviewed yesterday for a position as a Customer Service Representative in the Customer Service Department. At the end of the interview you were not offered the job but instead were told that you would hear from them within a few weeks' time. Write a thank-you letter to Mrs Daley, Human Resources Manager. [7]

10   Assume that you had sent your résumé and cover letter to Trendy Fashion Manufacturers, 37 Barnett Street, Montego Bay, St James, in response to a position advertised about four weeks ago in your daily newspaper. You have not received a response from the organization. Write a follow-up letter enquiring about the status of the opening. [7]

11   List at least **six** ways in which a job could be advertised. [6]

12   Outline the importance of a portfolio, giving examples of documents that should be included in it. [6]

13   Imagine that you read the classified section of the newspaper and realize that there is a job posting seeking a qualified Accounts Clerk. You realize that you are a likely candidate for the job. Prepare the following to be sent to the company:
   • your résumé; [8]
   • a cover letter. [7]

4 Records and information management

By the end of this chapter you should be able to:

- ☑ explain the importance of a records management system;
- ☑ classify documents;
- ☑ list characteristics of an information management system;
- ☑ list duties and responsibilities of a File Clerk;
- ☑ describe the steps for preparing documents to be filed;
- ☑ outline the classifications of records management;
- ☑ apply basic alphabetical filing rules;
- ☑ explain procedures for dealing with inactive files;
- ☑ describe the main legal stipulation governing access to the retention of documents;
- ☑ describe filing supplies and equipment;
- ☑ differentiate between centralized and departmental filing.

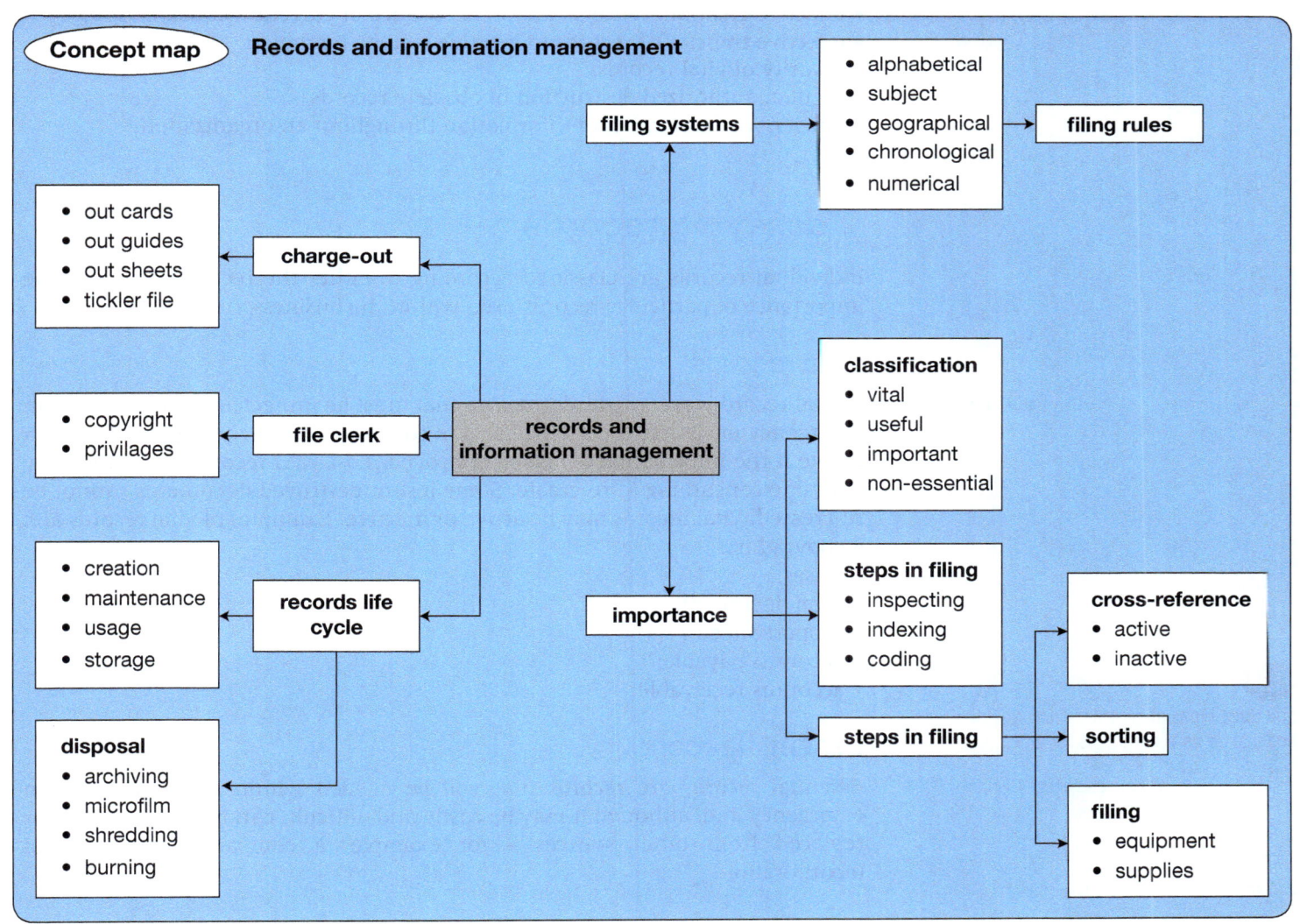

What is records management?

Records management is important to institutions, corporations and governments, no matter what their size. Records management is the systematic planning, controlling, organizing and training involved in the maintenance of the records of an organization – from their creation to their ultimate disposal. This may include classifying, storing, securing and ultimate destruction of records.

Figure 4.1 A clerk filing

Importance of records management

Records management helps an organization, institution or government ensure:
- retention of records needed to meet administrative and operational requirements;
- permanent retention of vital records;
- effective creation, retrieval and maintenance of current records;
- effective transfer of records to inactive storage (archive);
- security of vital records;
- regular, authorized destruction of obsolete records;
- efficient dissemination of information throughout an organization.

Classifying records

Individual records are classified according to either the record activity or the importance of particular records used within the business, or both.

Vital records

vital record ▶ A vital record is recorded information that must be protected in the event of an emergency or disaster because of severe consequences to the organization as a whole if the information is lost or destroyed. Lost vital records are both costly and time consuming to re-create. Some lost or destroyed documents cannot be re-created. Vital records may be active or inactive. Examples of vital records are:
- copyrights;
- leases;
- legal documents;
- property deeds;
- accounts payable;
- accounts receivable.

ITQ1
List three types of records which would be considered as vital records for an organization.

Essential records

essential records ▶ Essential records are records that will be needed within 72 hours after an emergency and, although it may be costly and difficult, **can** be reconstructed or replaced from other sources – for example, a company's certificate of incorporation.

Useful records

useful records ▶

Useful records are records used in the operation of the organization. In the event of a disaster, loss of these records would not prevent routine operation. Examples are:
• business reports;
• letters of enquiry;
• letters of complaint.

Non-essential records

non-essential records ▶

Non-essential records are records that are not needed for the survival of the business and therefore have little or no predictable value to it. Examples are:
• stores' catalogues;
• brochures;
• telephone messages;
• newspapers.

Important records

Important records contribute to the smooth operation of an organization. These documents can be replaced if lost or damaged but with considerable expenditure of time and money. Examples are:
• customer orders;
• case files;
• tax records;
• some legal records, for example divorce certificates.

ITQ2

Complete the table below by writing the correct records classification in the right-hand column.

Records	Classification
Copyright	
Tax records	
Letter of enquiry	
Catalogue	

Records lifecycle

records lifecycle ▶

A basic concept in records management is the records lifecycle. The life of a record goes through phases starting from when it is created or received by the agency, through to its use, maintenance and temporary storage before finally being destroyed or archived permanently.

Creation

The first phase of the records lifecycle involves records being created, collected or received through the daily transactions of the business. These include letters, reports, e-mails, company policies and so on.

Maintenance

This is the next stage of the records lifecycle and involves filing, retrieving, use, duplication, printing, dissemination release or exchange of the information in the record.

Disposition

At the disposition phase, records are examined to determine their retention value, using the records retention schedule set up by the company. This will lead to either the preservation or the destruction of the record.

Preservation

archiving ▶

When a record has been determined to be of permanent value to the company it is transferred to long-term storage for permanent archiving.

Permanent storage and destruction

If a record still has ongoing value to the company it will be stored temporarily, either onsite at the company or offsite. When the retention date of these records is reached, permission will be sought from the company for their destruction.

ITQ3

1 During which of these phases in the records and information lifecycle might a record be destroyed?
   a disposition;
   b storage;
   c creation;
   d maintenance.

2 The second phase of the records and information lifecycle is:
   a creation;
   b disposition;
   c distribution;
   d maintenance.

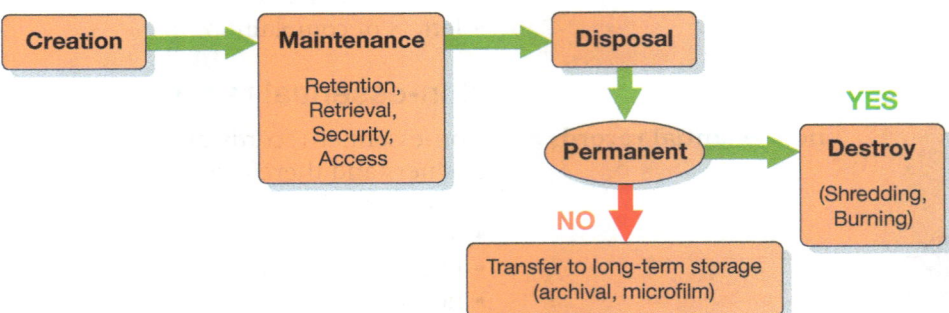

Figure 4.2   Records management lifecycle

A records management system usually includes hardware, software, information, data, applications, communications and people.

ITQ4

In the table below, place a tick in the column indicating whether the statements are true or false.

Items	Statements	T	F
1	When a government employee leaves his/her position, the records created by him/her during employment should be shredded.		
2	Routing is part of the records lifecycle.		
3	Misfiling resulting in lost records or slow retrieval is usually a result of poor filing procedures.		

Characteristics	Means that the system should…
Reliability	Provide easy access to records and organize records appropriately.
Confidentiality	Prevent unauthorized access.
Cost-effectiveness	Reduce costs in each stage of the records cycle.
Fixity	Store records in ways that mean they cannot be tampered with, deleted inappropriately or altered.
Accessibility	Allow easy access to records by all authorized users.
Protection of document	Prevent destruction, alteration or removal of records.
Accountability	Ensure that all records can be found.
Flexibility of system	Allow for expansion and contraction of system.
Comprehensiveness	Manage all records resulting from the business activities that are documented or managed by the system.

Table 4.1   Characteristics of a good records management system

The File Clerk

File Clerks are also called Record, Information, or Record Centre Clerks. There are a number of duties which must be performed by File Clerks to ensure the smooth operation of the records and information management system. Some of these duties include:

• collection of records to be filed;
• pre-sorting – checking for release symbols;
• placing papers in the correct file, with the latest paper on top;
• retrieving documents needed by authorized persons and lending records only when a record of the borrower has been correctly completed;
• completing cross-reference sheets for any files on which names have been changed;

- arranging miscellaneous files for single papers that cannot be filed until four or five documents have been received from the same firm;
- filing as frequently as possible – preferably several times per day.

Filing procedures

There are seven steps that must be followed to prepare documents for filing so that they can be retrieved when required. The steps are as follows:

1. Collecting	Collect documents for filing.
2. Inspecting and releasing	Inspect all documents to ensure that they have been released for filing. A release mark indicates that a document is ready for filing. Release marks could be a check mark, a stamp with the word 'file' or initials.
3. Indexing	Determining the key word or number under which a record will be filed. Careful indexing is the key to success in finding documents.
4. Coding	After determining how a document should be filed, the indexing caption should be marked on the document.
5. Cross-referencing	This must be done if a document can be called for under more than one heading. For example, a company that has changed its name or a person who has changed their name either by marriage or by deed poll.
6. Sorting	Rearranging the document in the same order in which they will be filed. This will help the file clerk to file more easily.
7. Filing	Here, the documents are actually placed in the paper folder.

indexing ▶

coding ▶

cross-referencing ▶

Table 4.2   Steps in filing

Classifications of records management systems

An important component of the records management system is the filing system that is used. The filing system involves systematically classifying, coding, arranging and placing records in storage and facilitating their quick and easy retrieval when requested by a user.

Two basic filing methods are in existence – these are the alphabetical and non-alphabetical methods. The alphabetical method consists of three specialized indexing systems – filing by name, subject or geographic area. The non-alphabetical method consists of numerical and chronological indexing systems. The filing classification system selected by an organization should be based on the kind of information to be stored, as well as the retrieval procedure in the future.

- Filing by subject / category.
- Filing in alphabetical order.
- Filing by numbers / numerical order.
- Filing by places / geographical order.
- Filing by dates / chronological order.

classification ▶

These methods of filing are called classification and mean organizing things that are similar together. You can, however, combine some of these methods. For example, files that are kept together according to what they are about we say

subject filing ▶

are subject filing but inside each file the documents could be filed according to date order.

Alphabetical filing

alphabetical filing ▶

Alphabetical filing is the most common filing system used by business organizations. The names of individuals, businesses, institutions, government agencies, subject, topics or locations determine the location of the files. This system is known as 'direct filing' as records can be located without consulting a reference. Documents are stored according to the first letter of the name. If the first letters of names are the same then you simply move to the next letter until you reach a different letter to determine which record should be placed first.

Advantages	Disadvantages
Simple to use and understand	Difficult to estimate space requirements
Indexing is required	Common names may cause confusion
It is a direct filing method	Cross-referencing is necessary
Less costly to install and maintain	Confidentiality cannot be guaranteed

Table 4.3 Advantages and disadvantages of alphabetical filing

Rules governing alphabetical filing

Alphabetical filing rules are standard rules which must be applied each time filing is done so that documents and material may be found quickly when needed. These common rules will determine the indexing, as well as the coding (determining the heading under which records are to be filed) which is outlined below.

The rules are based on filing names on a unit-by-unit basis, in which each part of the name is considered a separate unit. The individual filing units of each name must be compared letter by letter in order to place the names in proper alphabetic sequence.

It is very important that the File Clerk master all rules governing alphabetical filing, as this is an integral role in all the other filing methods.

Individual people

Rule 1: All personal names should be indexed so that the last name (surname) is placed first, the first name is placed second, and the middle name or initial is placed last.

NAME AS GIVEN	INDEXING	UNIT 1	UNIT 2	UNIT 3
Beverley O Smith	Smith, Beverley O	Smith	Beverley	O

Rule 2: An initial in a name is indexed and coded so that it appears before a name that begins with the same letter. This is commonly referred to as the 'nothing comes before something' rule.

NAME AS GIVEN	INDEXING	UNIT 1	UNIT 2	UNIT 3
S R Williams	Williams, S R	Williams	S	R

Rule 3: If surnames are the same, the first name must be used to determine the filing order. If, however, the first and surnames are the same, the middle name determines the alphabetic order. If middle names are the same, the street names of the individual or date of birth may be used.

NAME AS GIVEN	INDEXING	UNIT 1	UNIT 2	UNIT 3
Richard N Bonner St James	Bonner, Richard N St James	Bonner	Richard	N
Richard N Bonner Kingston	Bonner, Richard N Kingston	Bonner	Richard	N

Rule 4: Some surnames have prefixes and are indexed and coded in terms of the first letter of the prefix. A last name with a prefix is considered as one indexing unit. The common prefixes include: 'D', 'De', 'La', 'Mac', 'Mc', 'O', 'Van', 'Von' and 'Vander'. Spacing before the prefix or capitalization of the prefix makes no difference when indexing.

NAME AS GIVEN	INDEXING	UNIT 1	UNIT 2	UNIT 3
Moffat de la Vega	de la Vega, Moffat	de la Vega	Moffat	
Paula V McBride	McBride, Paula V	McBride	Paula	V

Rule 5: Surnames that are hyphenated are treated as one filing unit.

NAME AS GIVEN	INDEXING	UNIT 1	UNIT 2	UNIT 3
Tricia Panton-Black	Panton-Black, Tricia	Panton-Black	Tricia	

Rule 6: Personal titles, such as 'Sir', 'Rev' and 'Hon', and professional titles, such as 'Dr', 'PhD' and 'MD', should be placed at the end of the name, in brackets. The name is then indexed according to the relevant rules.

NAME AS GIVEN	INDEXING	UNIT 1	UNIT 2	UNIT 3
Rev Tom Adams	Adams, Tom (Rev)	Adams	Tom (Rev)	
Sir Andrew C Coley	Coley, Andrew C (Sir)	Coley	Andrew	C (Sir)

Rule 7: Titles such as 'Jr', 'Sr', '2nd' and 'III' are considered separate indexing units. The titles 'Jr' and 'Sr' are indexed alphabetically. In numerical designations, arabic numerals are placed before roman numerals and are then indexed numerically in ascending order.

NAME AS GIVEN	INDEXING	UNIT 1	UNIT 2	UNIT 3
Thomas Matthew 2nd	Matthew, Thomas 2nd	Matthew	Thomas	2
Thomas Matthew 3rd	Matthew, Thomas 3rd	Matthew	Thomas	3
Thomas Matthew III	Matthew, Thomas III	Matthew	Thomas	III
Peter Mark, Jr	Mark, Peter Jr	Mark	Peter	Jr
Peter Mark, Sr	Mark, Peter Sr	Mark	Peter	Sr

Rule 8: Academic degrees and other professional designations written with a name are ignored when indexing and placed at the end.

NAME AS GIVEN	INDEXING	UNIT 1	UNIT 2	UNIT 3
Sandra P Wilkins, MSc	Wilkins, Sandra P MSc	Wilkins	Sandra	P MSc
Roy Van-Black, PhD	Van-Black, Roy PhD	Van-Black	Roy	PhD

Rule 9: Religious titles followed by a first name only should be filed as given.

NAME AS GIVEN	INDEXING	UNIT 1	UNIT 2	UNIT 3
Sister Martha	Sister Martha	Sister	Martha	
Father Matthew	Father Matthew	Father	Matthew	

Companies

As a general rule, names of some companies remain as given. However, there are some exceptions.

Rule 10: The articles ('a', 'an', 'the'); prepositions ('in', 'by', 'from', 'for', 'of', 'on' and 'at'); and conjunctions ('and', 'ampersand' (&) and 'or') are not considered when filing but should be placed at the end, in brackets.

NAME AS GIVEN	INDEXING	UNIT 1	UNIT 2	UNIT 3
Blue & Black Auto	Blue & Black Auto	Blue	Black	Auto (&)
The Club Hut	Club Hut (The)	Club	Hut	(The)
Sunny & Bunny Co	Sunny (and) Bunny Co	Sunny (and)	Bunny	Company

ITQ5

Index and place the following in the correct alphabetical order:
- Audley Thomas 1st;
- Susan Vassel, MSc;
- Troy John Jr;
- Rev Howard Howell;
- Audley Thomas 3rd;
- Troy John Sr;
- Father Stephens;
- Trevor Williams PhD;
- Mrs D A Wilson;
- Delores Hinds;
- Mr Sydney Daley;
- Audley Thomas III;
- Mrs S Daley;
- Sister Jacqueline.

Rule 11: Consider each part of the hyphenated business name as a separate indexing unit.

Compare this with Rule 5

NAME AS GIVEN	INDEXING	UNIT 1	UNIT 2	UNIT 3
Brimax-Tyle Printing Co	Brimax-Tyler Printing Co	Brimax	Tyler	Printing Company

Rule 12: Compound names, which are formed by joining two words or a prefix and a word, are indexed as one unit. Disregard the hyphen that is usually in such names.

NAME AS GIVEN	INDEXING	UNIT 1	UNIT 2	UNIT 3
South-West Shipping Co	South-West Shipping Co	South-West	Shipping	Company

Rule 13: If a firm's name is made up of single letters, then each letter must be considered a separate unit. Firms' names made up of single letters are filed before words beginning with the same letter because of the 'nothing before something' rule.

NAME AS GIVEN	INDEXING	UNIT 1	UNIT 2	UNIT 3
A A Auto	A A Auto	A	A	Auto
A D Printers	A D Printers	A	D	Printers

Rule 14: Names of companies beginning with numerals should be indexed as though they were spelled out. If the numbers appearing at the beginning of the name are spelled out, they are indexed and filed according to the alphabetical rules. The entire number. when spelled out, should be treated as one filing unit.

NAME AS GIVEN	INDEXING	UNIT 1	UNIT 2	UNIT 3
2000 Century Printer	2000 Century Printer	2000	Century	Printer
Three Hundred Pub	Three Hundred Pub	Three Hundred	Pub	

ITQ6

Index and place the following in the correct filing order:
- The Forbidden Pub;
- An Apple Spot;
- Zenith-Bell Car Wash;
- North-East Restaurant;
- N P Flower Shop;
- A R Caterers;
- Delroy Nelson Printery;
- N L Daley Autos;
- 21st Century Bakers;
- Roberts & Roberts Funeral Home.

Rule 15: If a firm's name includes a full name, the person's last name is considered as the first indexing unit. then the first name, then the middle name and the rest of the firm's name.

NAME AS GIVEN	INDEXING	UNIT 1	UNIT 2	UNIT 3
Chin Lee Supplies	Lee, Chin Supplies	Lee	Chin	Supplies
Grace Samms Pepper	Samms, Grace Pepper	Samms	Grace	Pepper

Government agencies

Rule 16: Index names of government institutions so that the key part of the name appears first.

NAME AS GIVEN	INDEXING	UNIT 1	UNIT 2	UNIT 3
Ministry of Health	Health, Ministry of	Health	Ministry	of

ITQ7

Index and place the following business names in the correct alphabetical order:
- Jamestown Public Hospital;
- University of Montpelier;
- Excelsior High School;
- National Mineral Bank;
- Bogle Educational Institution;
- Black River Primary School.

Institutional names

Rule 17: Institutions include hospitals, financial institutions, schools, colleges, and universities.

Names of hospitals are filed as written, followed by the city and state names.

NAME AS GIVEN	INDEXING	UNIT 1	UNIT 2	UNIT 3
Kingston Public Hospital	Kingston Public Hospital	Kingston	Public	Hospital
National Caribbean Bank	National Caribbean Bank	National	Caribbean	Bank
Garvey High School	Garvey High School	Garvey	Marcus	High School

Geographical filing

geographical filing ▶

Geographical filing involves arranging records alphabetically, according to the names of geographic locations. A company that operates throughout a country may divide its files first by county, then city or town, and then by names of correspondent. A company with several offices within a single city may require a geographical system that is divided by districts of the city, and then by street names. Geographical filing is an indirect method of locating folders for individual correspondents. It is slower to operate since paper must be sorted up to three times.

Advantages	Disadvantages
• Convenient to use, especially for companies who have customers worldwide	• A poor knowledge of geography can lead to misfiling
• Allows for direct filing if location is known	• Indexing may be necessary if location is not known
• Useful for collecting statistics for comparative purposes	• More work on the part of the File Clerk, as documents must be sorted by counties then by towns and so on

Table 4.4 Advantages and disadvantages of geographical filing

Examples

> Kingston
>> **Cross Roads**
>>> Samuels Bun Company
>>> Victory Delights Sweets
>> **Half-Way-Tree**
>>> Tamms Fabric Store
>>> Twenty-four Hour Coffee

Numerical filing

numerical filing ▶

With the numerical filing method, each name, document or folder is given a number in exact numerical sequence. For example, the first document is assigned '1', the second '2' and so on. This system is widely used by government departments, for example hospitals, banks, credit card accounts, sales and purchase orders.

It is impossible to recall the file number of business organization, thus, an alphabetical card index is maintained by name in alphabetical order. The numeric filing systems are indirect in finding a file since reference must be made to the alphabetical card index before a document can be found.

alphabetical card index ▶

There are four main parts to the numerical filing system.

1 The **alphabetical card index** in which names or subject titles are arranged alphabetically.

2 The **numerical file** itself, which consists of individual documents or folders for active correspondence and is given a number.

miscellaneous file ▶

3 The **miscellaneous file**, which contains inactive correspondence.

accession book ▶

4 An **accession book** or register in which records of assigned numbers are kept.

Advantages	Disadvantages
• Confidentiality can be maintained easily	• Indirect filing method
• Files numbers can be used as reference numbers	• More costly in materials and time taken to maintain the system
• Unlimited expansion	• High possibility of transposing figures, for example '184' may be written as '148'.

Table 4.5 Advantages and disadvantages of numerical filing

Example

Auto Stores	300
Butter Auto Company	301
Calvary Auto Supplies	302
Schools	200
Anderson Beauty School	201
Ascott High School	202

Subject filing

Subject filing is a system where documents are arranged, usually in alphabetical order, according to the subject matter – for example, telephone, salary or fuel. One difficulty in operating any subject filing system is the problem of deciding under which subject heading an item may be filed.

A subject filing classification system requires the use of an index. This is a list, in alphabetic order, of all the topic names that are used in the system. Use of the index can significantly reduce the chance of a record being incorrectly filed.

Advantages	Disadvantages
• All documents referring to a particular subject matter are kept together	• Extensive cross-referencing is necessary
• Direct access to file, as no index is necessary	• Difficulty to estimate space requirements
• Unlimited expansion	• Subject title may become cumbersome, with too many files.

Table 4.6 Advantages and disadvantages of subject filing

Chronological filing

◀ **chronological filing**

In chronological filing documents are arranged according to the date. The system is usually used as a back-up to a main filing system. It is important to note that documents are arranged in chronological order within a folder, which is filed in some other methods of classification.

Advantages	Disadvantages
• Easy to set up	• Retrieval speed can be slow
• Copies of documents can be stored	• Cannot act as a standalone system

Table 4.7 Advantages and disadvantages of chronological filing

Electronic filing

◀ **electronic filing**

Electronic filing allows for the filing of data on special equipment, which can store and retrieve information faster than any other equipment. When information is required from the computer it may be printed on sheets or be shown on visual display units

Advantages	Disadvantages
• Increases speed of filing and retrieval	• Costly to set up and maintain
• Reduces the need for paper	• Specialist will be needed
• Accurate filing of records	• Reader equipment is needed

Table 4.8 Advantages and disadvantages of electronic filing

Cross-referencing

Companies often merge or change their names. Sometimes people change their names, especially women who become married, and other persons change their names via deed poll. Also, there may be several surnames in the name of a company. When these situations occur, cross-reference sheets must be filled out

◀ **cross-reference sheets**

ITQ8

1 A system that enables users to compose, transmit, receive and manage electronic documents and images across networks is:
a electronic imaging;
b a podcast;
c electronic mail or e-mail;
d a collection of web pages.

2 In cases where records are physically located in the departments where they are kept and used, the records program is said to be:
a centralized;
b remote;
c decentralized;
d specialized.

to ensure that the correct file can be found quickly when needed. To ensure that documents can be retrieved without delay, the File Clerk should file the documents according to the indexing of the name that it is most likely to be requested. A reference should be filed using a cross-reference sheet or a copy of the document could be filed under the other name.

CROSS-REFERENCE SHEET
For correspondence for: **Knight, Barbara**
PLEASE SEE
Anderson-Knight, Barbara

Figure 4.3 A cross-reference sheet

Although cross-referencing is important for locating filed information quickly, one must note that too much cross-referencing takes up a lot of time and space. On the other hand, too little cross-referencing will result in costly delays when locating information

File charge-out systems and follow-up procedures

charge-out system ▶
active files ▶

When setting up a records management system a charge-out system must be included. This is a set of steps taken to ensure adequate tracking of active files and documents removed from the filing system.

A charge-out or tracking process must be in place for any documents that have been borrowed from the filing system. When this process is in place, a record will be made every time a file is removed from the system. This allows the Records Clerk to know where all the files in the system are at all times; makes it easier to respond to another user's need for the files; and also help to monitor how active files are.

Charge-out records will be used to keep track of:
• the file that was taken;
• the name of the person or department borrowing the record or file;
• the date on which it was removed;
• the date on which it should be returned;
• the location in the filing station where the file belongs.

Types of charge-out systems

There are different ways to set up a charge-out system. This can be done by using charge-out cards, charge-out guides or charge-out sheets.

Charge-out cards

charge-out card ▶

A charge-out card or 'out card' is used to record information on a file when it is taken from the filing system. For example, the card will list the file number, file title or date of the file. There is also space available to record the name of the borrower as well as the date the file was borrowed and the return date.

| | | | | **OUT** |
Date	Name/number of document	Name of borrower	Department	Return Date

Figure 4.4 An out card

Charge-out guides

charge-out guides ▶

Charge-out guides or 'out guides' are similar to charge-out cards except that a guide is always placed in the filing system to hold the spot for the file that is removed. This prevents the files from closing ranks which could then result in misfiling. Some out guides have pockets that allow the Records Clerk to place documents that came in while the file was out. Once the file is returned these documents will be removed from the out guide and placed in the file.

Charge-out sheets

charge-out sheets ▶

Charge-out sheets are larger and thicker than letter-size paper and are therefore conspicuous in the files. Most out sheets are colour coded which alerts the Records Clerk to the fact that documents are out. Out sheets are placed in the exact location when a document is removed.

Tickler system

tickler system ▶

The tickler system is used to remind, or 'tickle' the memory of, the Records Management Clerk that action needs to be taken at a particular time. It provides a method of securing not only the return of files but also other regular check-up procedures. For example, the Sales Manager may wish to review a particular file on June 10, 2009. This request would be recorded in the tickler system on that date so that the file can be sent off.

The tickler system consists of two sets of cards – 12 monthly primary guides cards labelled January–December and a set of 1–31 daily cards. This system enables notes on records to be recorded on cards and placed behind the appropriate month and day guide where action is to be taken. By creating a tickler file system and checking it daily, the File Clerk will have a fail-proof reminder system.

Colours as indicators

colour indicators ▶

Colour indicators are one of a number of ways that can be used to draw attention to information. In filing, coloured sheets can be used to indicate that a document is out of a file. Also, an out or absent card could be coloured to show that the entire file is on loan. The colours are usually shown on the tab of the document, however, it is not unusual to see the entire document coloured. The following list highlights ways in which colour can be used in filing:
- to differentiate various types of files;
- to differentiate similar types of records that belong to various departments;
- to identify records that were temporarily removed from files.

Retention periods

retention period ▶

Some records must be kept permanently, while others are useful for a short period of time and are kept for a year or more and some records are disposed of immediately after use. A record retention period outlines for how long documents should be kept. Records kept for more than a year will be removed and placed in long-term storage. The length of time for which a record should be kept will be outlined by management. There are three major factors that determine this:
1 The nature of an organization's business operations.
2 Statutes of limitation.
3 Government regulations.

Types of records	Retention period
inventory records	2 years
Petty cash vouchers	3 years
Employees' records	6–7 years
Contracts	6 years after expiration
Tax matters, titles, annual reports	Indefinitely

Figure 4.5 Example of a record retention chart

ITQ9

1 In determining a retention period, which one of the following is not a factor?
   a administrative value;
   b historical value;
   c legal value;
   d type of paper the record is on.

2 Usually, records are used and retained because:
   a they serve as the 'memory' of a business;
   b they have administrative, legal or historical value to a firm;
   c they document the information needed for complying with regulations and the transactions of an organization;
   d all of the above answers are correct.

ITQ10

For how long should you keep records?

Before setting up a retention policy, the following should be considered:
- How valuable is the document?
- Do copies exist elsewhere?
- How often are they requested?
- Is their retention a statutory obligation?
- Is it possible to keep them in another format?

Long-term storage

archive ▶

Inactive files are no longer used by the firm, if they belong to customers who no longer purchase goods or services from your organization or staff who no longer work for the firm, and so on. Once the Office Manager is satisfied that such files will not be needed, they can be removed and stored in long-term storage called an archive and later removed and destroyed.

Disposal of files

Outdated files are called 'dead' files. Dead files are usually destroyed. The most efficient way of doing so is by burning or by shredding the files, using a shredding machine – this helps to protect confidential information. The shredded paper that is produced can be used as cushioning material for packages.

Archiving

This is a facility used to store records being retained for research, historical value or for future use. An accession register is used to identify records in an archive.

Microfilm

microfilm ▶

Due to increasing information needs, many organizations are using microfilm as one solution to information challenges. This is a filing process using photographic methods to copy material in reduced form for storing. Microfilm is used for storing inactive files. Text on microfilm cannot be seen by the naked eye, thus a machine called a reader-printer is used. This machine magnifies the microfilm text.

Advantages	Disadvantages
There are savings in terms of filing and floor space.	Films cannot be viewed without reader equipment
Storing original documents can ensure safety	It is difficult and costly to update
Films have longer lasting qualities than paper	Sometimes there is difficulty in locating the required information

Table 4.9 Advantages and disadvantages of microfilm

Laws governing access to and retention of documents

freedom of information ▶

There has been a tremendous increase in the number of countries adopting freedom of information legislation. The main reasons are due to:

- the rise of new democracies, with constitutional guarantees of the right to information;
- an increased involvement of International Bodies (Commonwealth, OAS, etc.) in the promotion of this type of law;
- a growing push on the part of international lending agencies (IMF, World Bank, etc.) towards the promotion of improved government accountability globally.

The Access to Information Act gives one a general right of access to official government information, which would otherwise be inaccessible. Further, under the Act, certain information will not be subject to disclosure in order to protect essential public interests and private rights.

The Act aims to reinforce fundamental democratic principles vital to:

- improved, more transparent government;
- greater accountability of government to its people;
- increased public influence on and participation in national decision making;
- knowledge of the functions of government.

Legislation on access to information (ATI), or freedom of information (FIO) as it is called in some jurisdictions, has existed since 1776 and is in force in many countries such as the United States, Australia, Canada and most of Europe, Trinidad and Tobago and Belize.

Infringement of copyright

copyright infringement ▶

Copyright infringement is the unauthorized or illegal use of material that is covered by copyright law. Under the Copyright Act 1968, owners have certain rights and reproducing materials without the owner's permission violates his/her rights. There are, though, certain exceptions to the infringement that allows some uses of copyright material without permission, free of cost. However, there may be cases where copying may require payment. These include:

Copying that is free

- **Fair dealing for the purpose of research or study.** Copying 10 per cent of one chapter of a published literary, dramatic or musical work of ten pages or more, and one article from a periodical, is deemed to be fair.
- **Fair dealing for the purpose of criticism or review.** Allows reviewers to use copyright material as long as they acknowledge the work.
- **Library provision.** General non-profit libraries and archives have the right to reproduce or communicate copyright work for clients; for inclusion in the collection of another library; and for the purpose of preservation.

Copying that requires payment

statutory licences ▶

Statutory licences allow educational institutions, institutions assisting people with disabilities and governments to copy protected material for defined purposes, without the need to obtain the copyright owner's permission.

Defamation

defamation ▶

In law, defamation is the communication of a statement that makes a false claim, expressly stated or implied to be factual, that may give an individual, business, product, group, government or nation a negative image. 'Slander' refers to a malicious, false and defamatory statement or report, while 'libel' refers to any other form of communication such as written words or images. Most jurisdictions allow legal actions, civil and/or criminal, to deter various kinds of defamation and retaliate against groundless criticism. Related to defamation is public disclosure of private facts, which arises where one person reveals information which is not of public concern and the release of which would offend a reasonable person.

Breach of confidence

breach of confidence ▶

A common law protects private, secret or commercially valuable information that is conveyed in confidence. The action for breach of confidence protects confidential information by preventing persons, to whom the information has been divulged in confidence, from using that information to obtain an unfair benefit for them.

Parliamentary privilege

parliamentary privilege ▶

Parliamentary privilege, also known as absolute privilege, is a legal mechanism employed by the legislative bodies of countries. These privileges are those that are necessary in order to allow Members of the House of Commons to perform their parliamentary functions. These rights are enjoyed both by individual Members of Parliament – because the House cannot perform its functions without its Members – and by the House, as a whole, for the protection of its Members as well as its own authority and dignity.

Privileges that are protected may be grouped under the following headings:
- **Freedom of speech.** This privilege allows Members of Parliament to speak freely in Parliament without fear of legal action on the basis of defamation.
- **Freedom from arrest in civil actions.** While a member is within the grounds of Parliament he/she cannot be arrested on civil matters.
- Exemption from **jury duty**.
- Exemption from being *subpoenaed* to attend court.

Note: The two most important collective privileges or powers of the House of Commons are its disciplinary powers and its exclusive right to regulate its own internal affairs.

Secrecy provisions

Protected information is personal information that a person obtains while performing their duties under, or in relation to, the child support legislation. Any personal information gathered by employees and contractors, and other government agencies for the purposes of administering the child support legislation, is protected information.

secrecy provisions ▶

The secrecy provisions of the child support legislation apply to all people occupying positions where they may obtain protected information about customer in the course of their duties under, or in relation to, the child support legislation.

Filing equipment and supplies

Vertical filing equipment

vertical filing equipment ▶

Of the various types of vertical filing equipment, standard four-, five- and six-drawer file cabinets continue to be the most widely used. Document folders are placed one behind the other, usually in a traditional file cabinet drawer, which will often be fitted with suspension pockets.

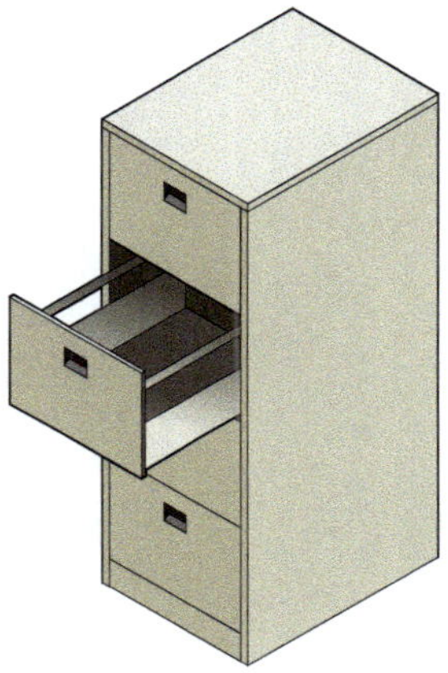

Figure 4.6 A four-drawer file cabinet

One advantage of the standard file cabinet is the ease with which it may be moved with its contents intact. However, in time, the space-wasting feature of the drawer cabinets will probably make them obsolete for storage of large accumulations of records.

Advantages	Disadvantages
Suitable for small records	Only one person at a time can retrieve files
Requires little space and is not costly	Costly
Easy to transport	More floor space is required

Table 4.10   Advantages and disadvantages of vertical filing equipment

Lateral filing equipment

lateral filing equipment ▶ Lateral filing equipment uses lateral pull-out drawers that require considerably less space than standard file cabinets. Files are arranged side by side, like books on a shelf. The word 'lateral' means 'from the sides'. Lateral filing cupboards can also be extended upwards towards the ceiling, but it will be essential to have a safe means of reaching the top shelves.

Horizontal filing equipment

This type of filing equipment is used mainly to store documents that need to remain flat until needed. Some of these documents are: large paper, such as plans, artwork, large maps, photographs and so on.

Microfilm

Microfilm is a filing process, using photographic methods to copy materials in reduced form for storing. Microfilm is used for storing inactive files. The microfilm rolls are stored in cylindrical containers and then placed in labelled boxes or drawers.

Text on microfilm cannot be seen by the naked eye, thus, a machine card reader-printer is used. This machine magnifies the microfilm text.

For the advantages and disadvantages of microfilm as a filing process, see page 97.

Figure 4.7   A microfilm reader-printer

Flash drive

flash drives ▶ Flash drives are small hand-held removable and rewritable media devices that plug into the USB port of a computer and are much smaller than a floppy disk. They are made up of a small circuit board protected in a plastic, metal or rubberized case. The case protects the board from harm and

Figure 4.8   A flash drive

makes it easy to carry in pocket or purse. Flash drives were meant to be portable, and users can purchase cases as well as lanyards to wear them on. As the units are compact, data stored there is safer than on most portable media devices twice their size. Most flash drives will work between different operating systems, such as Windows and Linux.

Advantages	Disadvantages
Flash drives are scratch proof compared with the floppy drive	Most USB drives do not have a write-protect system
Compact and durable	Increased risk of computer virus attacks
Fast, reliable and portable	Lacks confidentiality if lost

Table 4.11   Advantages and disadvantages of flash drives

Optical disc drive (ODD)

An optical disc drive is a disc drive that uses laser light to read and write information on a disc. Some discs can read and record information.

Filing accessories

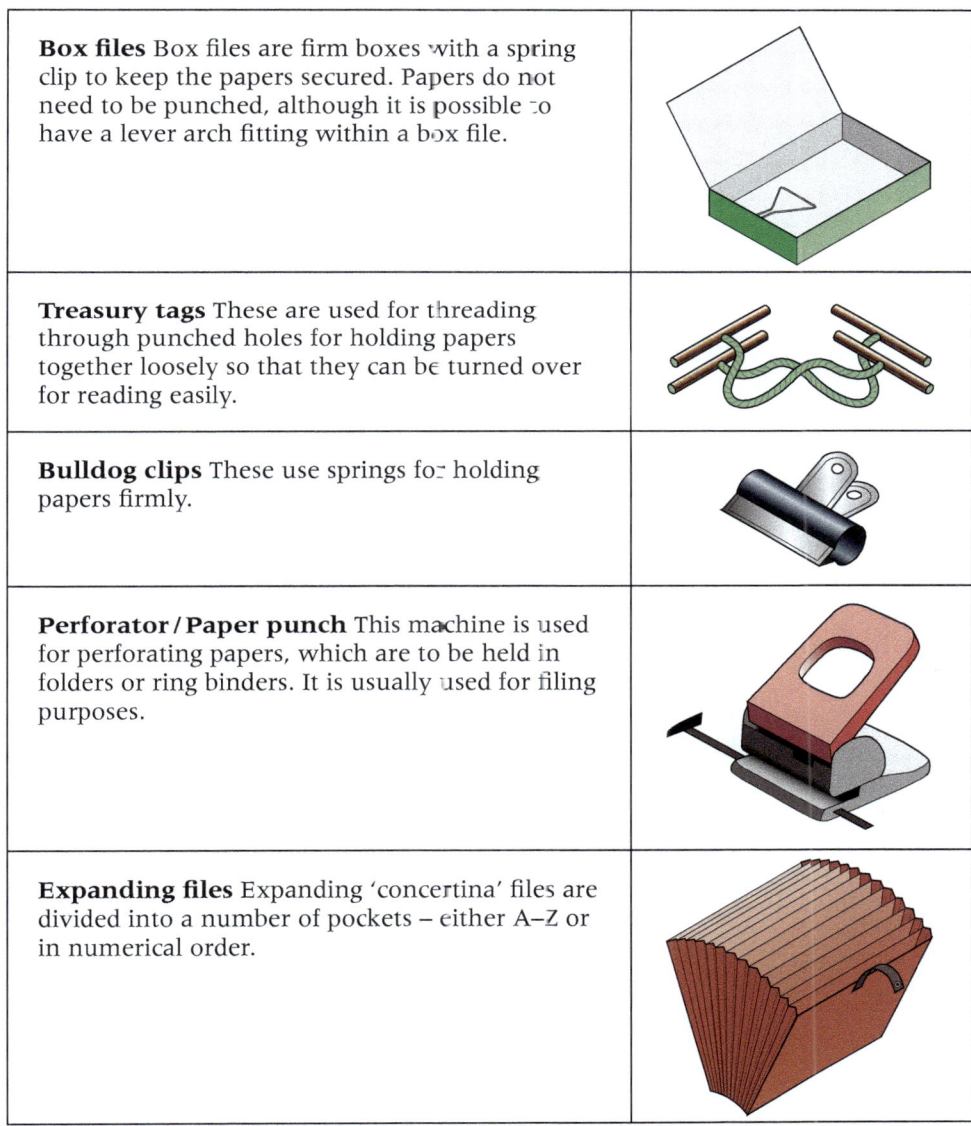

Box files Box files are firm boxes with a spring clip to keep the papers secured. Papers do not need to be punched, although it is possible to have a lever arch fitting within a box file.	
Treasury tags These are used for threading through punched holes for holding papers together loosely so that they can be turned over for reading easily.	
Bulldog clips These use springs for holding papers firmly.	
Perforator / Paper punch This machine is used for perforating papers, which are to be held in folders or ring binders. It is usually used for filing purposes.	
Expanding files Expanding 'concertina' files are divided into a number of pockets – either A–Z or in numerical order.	

Figure 4.9   Some common filing accessories

Lever arch files Paper needs to be punched, and then the documents are secured on two arch-shaped metal rods which are opened and closed via a lever.	
Diskettes This is a data storage medium that is composed of a disc of thin, flexible ('floppy') magnetic storage enclosed in a square or rectangular plastic case. Floppy discs are read and written by a floppy disc drive.	
Compact discs (CDs) Compact discs, often referred to as 'CDs', are used as a medium for storing and distributing large quantities of information in a reliable package.	
Clips and clipboards These are used for papers which have to be (or have been) dealt with in a particular sequence. Worksheets for mechanics in a garage are sometimes handled in this way.	
Card index Information about each customer or each member of staff is written on a card, usually a little smaller than a postcard. The cards are then kept in alphabetical order in a box. If a customer stops placing orders, or a staff member leaves, that card can be removed without affecting the filing order.	
Flash drive This is a small storage device that can be used to transport files from one computer to another. They can be kept on a key chain, carried around the neck or attached to a book bag.	
Labels There are two main types of labels – folder and drawer labels. Drawer labels are small strips placed on drawers to identify the contents of each file drawer. Folder labels are placed or written on the edge of each folder for easy identification of the files.	

Figure 4.9 (continued)

Folder A folder is made of a sheet of heavy paper. It is folded in half and is used to hold documents for filing.	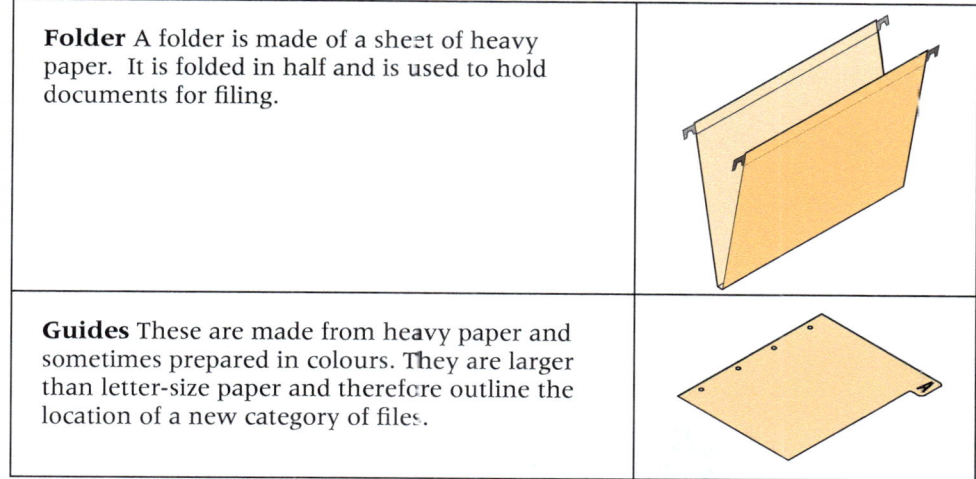
Guides These are made from heavy paper and sometimes prepared in colours. They are larger than letter-size paper and therefore outline the location of a new category of files.	

Figure 4.9 (continued)

Centralized control and decentralized control

When setting up a records management programme, one must first decide whether a centralized or decentralized system should be used. This refers both to where hard-copy records are to be stored and also to how the records are to be managed.

Centralized filing system

When a records management programme uses centralized control, the overall authority and responsibility for the programme is under the control of one individual – usually the File Clerk

Advantages	Disadvantages
Eliminates the need for storing duplicate copies of documents	Not being able to obtain records immediately may result in inconvenience
Records relating to a particular subject are stored in one place	Records may be too distant from staff for adequate service
Trained employees are used	Transporting frequently used records to and from central storage may delay their use
Improved control and security over records	Records may be more vulnerable as they are stored in one central location

Table 4.12 Advantages and disadvantages of centralized filing

Decentralized filing system

Decentralized control means that records are kept within the various departments of an organization until the time has arrived for their destruction or transfer to low-cost storage areas. The following are advantages and disadvantages of decentralized storage:

Advantages	Disadvantages
Does not require full-time staffing	**Lack of uniformity or consistency**
Confidential documents are stored in each department throughout the organization	Filing equipment may not be used efficiently, as some departments may need few drawers of a filing cabinet
Time is not wasted walking to and fro to collect documents	Duplicate filing equipment will be required, as each department will need its own storage

Table 4.13   Advantages and disadvantages of decentralized filing

Summary

- The filing and records system is the nerve centre of any firm.
- There are four main classifications of filing, namely: alphabetical, numerical, subject and geographical.
- A number of rules are outlined to ensure correct filing of records.
- The filing steps are: inspecting, indexing, coding, cross-referencing, sorting and filing.
- Filing supplies include guides, labels, folders and treasury tags.
- Cross-referencing is an integral part of each filing system since some documents may be referred to under more than one heading.
- Cross-reference sheets may be colour coded as this increases the speed and accuracy of locating files.
- There are three ways in which files may be organized: centralized, decentralized and electronic or automated.
- A centralized filing system has all the files located in one area.
- A decentralized filing system has files located in different areas or departments.
- An electronic or automated filing system electronically stores files and records.
- The categories of files are: vital, essential, non-essential and important.
- Before a file can be removed from the system, a requisition form must be filled out by the borrower. giving the name or department, file name or file number and the expected return date. This is to facilitate tracing and monitoring.
- Three main methods are used to trace files: out cards, out sheets and out guides.
- Every document has a lifecycle and lives only as long as it serves its purpose.
- A retention schedule should be set up, listing the files and their lifecycle. Records retention is the time period during which records must be maintained by an organization because they may be needed for legal, operational, historical or other purposes.
- When the file's retention period has expired, the file and its contents should be removed from the active filing system and stored in an inactive records facility or destroyed.
- Inactive records are seldom needed for the business of an office. Inactive records are usually stored in filing cabinets, storage boxes outside the main storage area or on microfilm.
- A shredder machine is used to destroy some inactive files and the end product can be used as cushioning material for packages.
- Currently, documents can be stored using flash drives or CDs, among other modern storage devices.
- An optical drive is a disc that uses laser light to read and write information to disc.

Answers to

1
- copyrights;
- property titles;
- insurance certificates.

2

Records	Classification
Copyrights	Vital
Tax records	Important
Letter of enquiry	Useful
Business report	Non-essential

3 **1** a
  2 c.

4

Items	T	F
1		√
2		√
3	√	

5

Order	Correct filing
1	Daley, S (Mrs)
2	Daley, Sidney (Mr)
3	Father Stephens
4	Hinds, Delores
5	Howell, Howard Rev
6	John, Troy Jr
7	John, Troy Sr
8	Sister Jacqueline
9	Thomas, Audley 1st
10	Thomas, Audley 3rd
11	Thomas, Audley III
12	Vassel, Susan
13	Williams, Trevor PhD
14	Wilson, D A (Mrs)

6

Correct filing
A R Caterers
Apple Spot (An)
Daley N L Autos
Forbidden Pub (The)
N P Flower Shop
Nelson Delroy Printery
North-East Restaurant
Roberts & Roberts Funeral Home
21st Century Bakers
Zenith-Bell Car Wash

7

Correct filing
Excelsior High School
Black River Primary School
Bogle Educational Institution
National Mineral Bank
Jamestown Public Hospital
University of Montpelier

8 **1** c;

2 c.

9 **1** d;

2 c.

10 It depends on what type of record it is and whether I created it.

Examination-style questions

Multiple choice questions

1 The systematic control of records from their creation to final disposal is called:
  a records life cycle
  b indexing
  c document preparation
  d microfilm.

2 Which of the following business documents would be classified as a vital record?
  a copyright for a piece of software
  b catalogue
  c bank statement
  d tax records for the previous year.

3 The process of marking the units of the filing name (or segment) by which the record is to be stored is called:
  a cross-referencing
  b inspecting
  c indexing
  d coding.

4 Which of the following filing classification systems allows for direct access to records?
  a an alphabetical system
  b a numerical system
  c a chronological system
  d a geographical system.

5 In which of the following situations would the numerical filing system **not** be useful?
  a Law firms that assign a case number to each client.
  b Utility companies where street names and numbers are of primary importance.
  c Warehouses that stock by part numbers.
  d Insurance companies that keep records according to policy number.

6 Microfilm technology enables retrieved documents to be viewed if:
   a a reader-printer is available
   b the microfilm is stored in an internal system
   c no special micro-graphics equipment is available
   d the microfilm is housed in self-contained equipment.

7 Which of the following records are essential to the effective, continued operation of an organization and should never be destroyed?
   a vital records
   b useful records
   c non-essential records
   d important records.

8 A records retention schedule specifies:
   a the period of time for which a record should be kept before destruction
   b the time for collection of dead files
   c the period of time for which documents should be kept before filing
   d the time for retrieval of active files.

9 Which of the following is used to replace an entire file when it is removed from the filing cabinet?
   a out guide
   b out sheet
   c cross-reference sheet
   d index card.

10 Which of the following filing systems ensures greater confidentiality of documents?
   a numerical filing
   b subject filing
   c geographical filing
   d alphabetical filing.

Structured questions

1 **a** State **two** types of record which are vital to the survival of a business. [2]
   b Outline **three** advantages and three disadvantages of alphabetical filing. [6]

2 Imagine that you are a new File Clerk and the following list of names is sent to you for filing. Index and place them in the correct alphabetical order.
   - Mr S Daley;
   - Mr Sidney Daley;
   - Aubrey Thomas 1st;
   - Father Stephens;
   - Troy John Snr;
   - Delores Hinds;
   - Rev Howard Howell;
   - The University of Neptune;
   - Troy John Jr;
   - Sister Jacqueline;
   - Audley Thomas 1st;
   - Susan Vassel MSc;
   - Trevor Williams PhD;
   - Mrs D A Wilson;
   - Mrs Pamela Harvey;
   - J M Dillon;
   - Martha Daley Beauty Shop;
   - 12 Hour Pizza Shop. [18]

3 a State the purpose of the following equipment used in the Records Management Department:
- microfilming equipment;
- vertical filing cabinet;
- computer. [6]

b List **three** filing supplies used in records management. [3]

c List **three** supplies used to facilitate storage of data. [3]

d Outline **six** characteristics of an efficient filing system. [6]

4 a What are the benefits of a records management programme? [3]

b Explain the importance of an effective records management programme. [3]

c Outline the purposes of a records retention schedule. [4]

d Briefly explain **three** methods used by companies when dealing with inactive files. [6]

5 a What types of records would be considered as vital records for an organization? [4]

b List the steps involved in determining the retention period for records. [5]

c As a summer worker assigned to the Sales Department, you are handed the following files for new clients. Arrange the files in the correct indexing order and then place them in the correct filing order.
- St Michael's Primary School;
- Sandra Pamela Anderson;
- Sunlight Hotel;
- Peter Jones Grocery;
- The Price Right Wholesale;
- Dianne Patricia O'Brian;
- Peters & Peters Bakery;
- Dr Amerila McIntosh, [8]

d State the differences between a flash drive and an optical disc drive. [3]

6 a List **three** duties of a Records Management Clerk. [3]

b State the filing system most suitable for each of the following:
- hospital records for patients;
- a company with branches nationwide;
- an auto parts shop;
- an insurance company. [4]

7 a Some companies store records off-site: what are the reasons for this practice? [3]

b What are the legal implications associated with a records management programme? [4]

c Outline the factors that should be considered when determining the appropriate retention periods for records. [6]

d List **three** types of records which would be considered as vital to the survival of any organization. [3]

5 Reception and hospitality

By the end of this chapter you should be able to:

- ☑ discuss the role of the reception area;
- ☑ identify the items to be found in a reception area;
- ☑ state the attributes and skills of good receptionist;
- ☑ outline the procedures for dealing with expected and unexpected visitors;
- ☑ describe the procedures for introducing people to each other;
- ☑ identify the records kept by the receptionist;
- ☑ explain the receptionist's role in managing appointments;
- ☑ outline the importance of reminder systems.

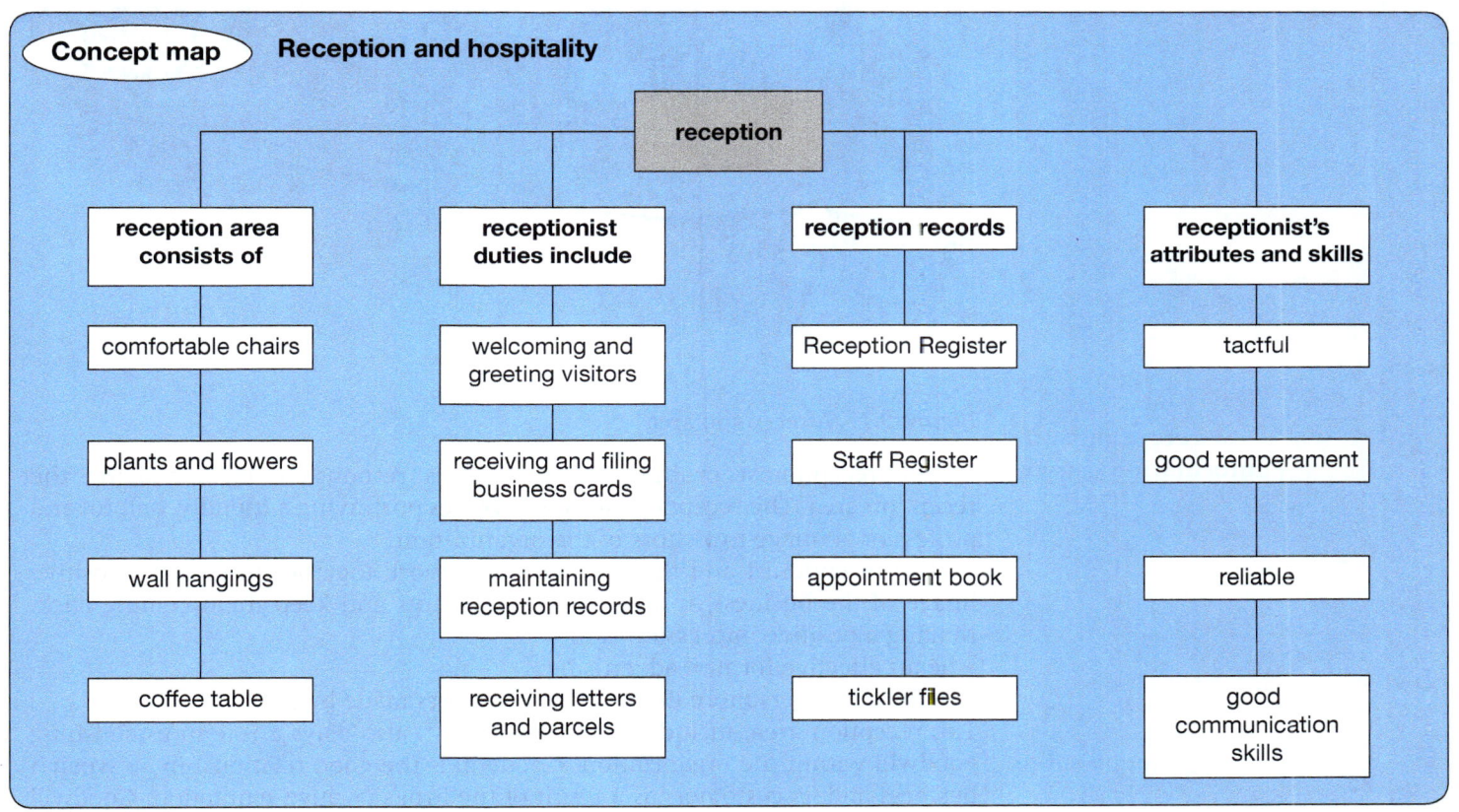

Concept map — **Reception and hospitality**

reception

reception area consists of	receptionist duties include	reception records	receptionist's attributes and skills
comfortable chairs	welcoming and greeting visitors	Reception Register	tactful
plants and flowers	receiving and filing business cards	Staff Register	good temperament
wall hangings	maintaining reception records	appointment book	reliable
coffee table	receiving letters and parcels	tickler files	good communication skills

The reception area

This is that section just inside the entrance of an office or commercial building where visitors are received and enquiries from members of the public are dealt with. The reception area may also be referred to as the hospitality desk, the information desk or the foyer.

The reception area is the first room that visitors will see and so it is important to make a good first impression. Customers or visitors tend to make judgements on the quality of service and level of professionalism they will receive based on the appearance of the reception area. It should therefore be a warm and friendly room that is clean, tidy and well laid out.

The layout of the reception area will depend largely on the size of the area as well as the type of business being conducted. For example, a hotel reception area is likely to be a very large, open space with a relaxed feel.

Figure 5.1 A reception area

receptionist or information clerk ▶

The receptionist or information clerk is responsible for managing the reception area. The receptionist's role involves portraying a friendly, helpful and professional image to visitors of the organization.

The receptionist and the reception area work together to create a positive image of the business in order to attract clients and keep them coming back. Making a positive impression can:
- be an effective form of advertising;
- make customers more likely to forgive errors made by the firm.

goodwill ▶

The reception area, including the receptionist, also plays a role in establishing goodwill within the organization. Goodwill is the good relationship between a business and its customers as a result of the firm's positive reputation. Goodwill may also be referred to as an intangible asset which adds value to a business.

What makes a good reception area?

Items that may be found in a reception area include:
- Comfortable chairs, in an adequate number – these may be laid out in rows or arranged informally.
- Plants and flowers – these improve the aesthetic appeal of the environment, as well as helping with air circulation. Green plants absorb carbon dioxide and give off oxygen, and so help to improve the quality of the air in the room.
- Refreshment – this may be in the form of a water dispenser or a beverage station which may provide, for example, coffee or tea. Vending machines are also popular in some reception areas.

- Wall hangings – which may include:
  - photographs of owners or managers, recognized staff, for example Employee of the Year;
  - mission statement – which is the general outline of the organization's goals;
  - organization chart – which is a pictorial representation of the structure of the company;
  - paintings or artwork;
  - newspaper clippings of the company's achievements.
- A coffee table with items such as magazines, company brochures, newspapers and the organization's reports, for example its audited financial statements.
- Television or light music piped through speakers.
- Discreet security cameras and closed-circuit television (CCTV). CCTV involves the use of video cameras that provide signals to specific monitors within the organization – usually used to deter theft and to monitor employees' activities.
- Computer – used to maintain an electronic diary and online 'tickler' system (discussed later in the chapter). The computer is also used for filing information and preparing documents such as letters and memoranda.

Attention must also be paid to the colour of the walls in the reception area. Colours such as light shades of blue and green, as well as shades of yellow and beige, tend to have a calming effect on people and would be suitable for a reception area which is heavily used.

Figure 5.2 Colour schemes are important in reception areas

There should also be adequate lighting and ventilation within the reception area.

The room should be at a comfortable temperature, ideally between 72°F and 77°F (22–25°C). Therefore fans, air conditioners and heaters may have to be provided to maintain such a temperature.

ITQ1

Identify **three** pieces of equipment and furniture which may be found in a reception area.

Attributes and qualities of a good receptionist

- Smart personal appearance – this includes:
  - maintaining an erect posture when sitting, standing or walking;
  - practising proper hygiene and grooming standards, for example keeping nails clean and wearing clean shoes;
  - ensuring that clothes are well laundered and free from flaws.

- Good temperament – this includes being bold and reactive, pleasant, confident and alert.
- Tact – dealing with others in a sensitive and discreet manner.
- Attentive to detail.
- Willingness to use initiative – acting independently in order to solve a problem.
- Trustworthiness – should be loyal and reliable.

A receptionist should:
- have good verbal and written communication skills;
- be able to use office machines such as the photocopier, the facsimile and the telephone switchboard;
- practise proper time management;
- be able to multi-task.

ITQ2

State two negative effects that an unprofessional receptionist can have on a business.

Duties of the receptionist

The duties of receptionists will vary, depending on the type of organization in which they are employed – for example, a medical receptionist in a doctor's office would be responsible for:
- activating patients' files;
- assisting patient check-in

whereas a hotel receptionist would be responsible for:
- greeting guests and dealing with check-in;
- forwarding incoming mail and messages to guests;
- controlling advance bookings.

Some of the core duties of the receptionist are as follows:

Welcoming and screening visitors

All visitors to the organization must be warmly greeted by the receptionist. Common courtesies, such as saying 'Good morning, Sir', must be observed. If the visitor's name is known, it should be used – for example, 'Good afternoon, Mrs Barnaby'. Any less usual title such as 'Dr' should be used. The greeting must be accompanied by a smile and good eye contact. In some cases a handshake may be appropriate. As soon as a visitor enters the reception area, the receptionist must politely ascertain the reason for his/her visit and his/her name.

There are three types of visitors that the receptionist will have to deal with:

1 expected visitors – these are visitors who have appointments;
2 unexpected visitors – these are visitors without appointments;
3 regular visitors – these are persons who do not need appointments, for example courier service delivery men and cleaners.

Procedures for dealing with expected visitors
- Greet the visitor, find out his / her name and take their business card, if they have one.
- Refer to the appointment book to confirm the appointment.
- Ask the visitor to sign the Reception Register.
- Issue a visitor's pass, if applicable.
- Inform the member of staff who is expecting the visitor of his / her presence.
- If the staff member is delayed, inform the visitor and find out whether they are able to wait. Offer magazines and refreshment while the visitor waits.
- If the staff member is available, bring or direct the visitor to his/her desk or office. A representative may also be sent to escort the visitor.

Procedures for dealing with unexpected visitors

- Greet the visitor, find out his/her name and take their business card, if they have one.
- Find out who he/she wishes to see.
- Ask the visitor to sign the Reception Register.
- Find out whether the staff member requested will be able to see the visitor.
- If the staff member is available, issue a visitor's pass, if applicable.
- Bring or direct the visitor to the staff member's desk or office.
- If the staff member is unavailable, find out whether anyone else can help or ask the visitor to make an appointment for another time.

Dealing with difficult visitors

There will be times when visitors to an organization become angry or rude. However, the receptionist must always remain calm and polite.

- Recognize that the visitor is angry with a situation and not at you.
- Never argue with or embarrass the visitor.
- Apply effective listening skills, such as maintaining eye contact.
- Empathize with the visitor – this will help in dissipating any anger.
- If you cannot solve the visitor's problem, turn over the issue to your supervisor or someone in authority.
- Thank the visitor for being patient and request his/her future patronage.

All visitors will form an opinion about the business, based on the way in which they are treated by the receptionist. Therefore it is important that the receptionist makes a good first impression.

ITQ3

An unsatisfied customer walks into a reception area, sounding very loud and angry. What are the steps that the receptionist should use to resolve the customer's problem?

Receiving and filing business cards

Many visitors who possess business cards will readily present them to the receptionist upon being welcomed. The business card will contain information such as:

- the name of the visitor;
- the visitor's job title;
- the name of the company the visitor represents and its address;
- contact information such as telephone number and e-mail address;
- the products or services offered.

PATTON HARRISON & DEES
Corporate Law

MATT THOMLINSON
Partner, Trinidad
Equity Capital Markets

m.thomlinson@phdees.com
Tel: (868) 600-2212
Fax: (868) 603-5765

92 Harris Promenade
San Fernando
Trinidad, West Indies

GRACE BARNES
photographer

weddings ✦ portraits ✦ landscape ✦ stock ✦ photos

www.gracesphotography.com

**72 LOWER BANK HALL MAIN ROAD
ST MICHAEL, BARBADOS**

TEL: 1 (246) 229-2866
EMAIL: gracebarnes@gracesphotography.com

St Elizabeth Taxi Co-op Society Ltd

24 Hour Taxi Service

Ian Palmer

Cell: +1 876 4782044   Email: palmer.Ian_taxi@hotmail.com

Figure 5.3 Business cards

Figure 5.4   A business card book

The receptionist is responsible for filing the numerous business cards received in order to keep the reception area tidy and also to be able to find the business card easily in the future.

Business cards may be filed using a number of different devices, such as rotary files, which can hold up to 400 cards and provide easy access to the cards.

Business cards can also be filed in mini filing cabinets or card books. Some mini cabinets can hold as many as 800 cards.

Business card information may also be filed on computer. Computer files may be organized based on the company's name, the person's name or by category of product or service, for example plumbing or insurance.

An easy way to transfer information from a business card to a computer is by using a card scanner using special software that allows it to be connected to the computer. The business card is inserted into a slot and the scan button is selected on the device. The information on the card is then automatically uploaded into the computer.

Figure 5.5   A rotary file

ITQ4

State **three** items of information that may be found on a business card.

Figure 5.6   A card scanner

Introducing people to each other

- When introducing persons to each other, 'rank' is very important. The main rule is that a lower-ranking person must be presented to a higher-ranking person, regardless of gender. So, you would introduce a supervisor to a Managing Director. Say the name of the person with the higher rank first, while maintaining eye contact with him/her. It is also important that, whenever possible, you should stand when making introductions. You should say, for example, 'Mr High, may I introduce Mr Low?'.

- A client or visitor to the organization is given a higher rank than the employees within the organization. So, the employee must be introduced to the visitor. For example, 'Mr Visitor, may I introduce Mr Employee?'.

- When introducing people of equal rank, for example a Marketing Manager and an Accounts Manager, the person outside of the department is given a higher rank. If both persons of equal rank are from the same department or both persons are visitors to the firm, the introductions may be done based on age. The younger person would be presented to the older person. For example, 'Ms Older, I would like to introduce Ms Younger'.

- If possible, use both first and last names, as well as official titles, for example 'Doctor' or 'Professor'. The person's preferred name should be used – for example, James Campbell may prefer to be introduced as 'J C Campbell'. The person's job title should also be included in the introduction. For example, 'Professor Ann Brown, I would like introduce Mr Donald Seymour, Marketing Director of Workers Bank Ltd'.

- Introduce an individual to a group first and then the group to the individual. For example, Mrs Pearson, may I present my colleagues Ann Parker, Stacy Harris and Tim Porter? Everyone, this is Janice Pearson'.

- If you forget a name or title, it is acceptable and good manners to apologize and acknowledge that you have forgotten. People like to be remembered, so try to fix a visitor's name in your mind. One way is to use their name in subsequent sentences, for example 'May I offer you a chair, Mr Brown?' or, when they leave, 'Goodbye, Mr Brown'.

Figure 5.7 Making an introduction

Maintaining reception records

A number of records will be handled by the receptionist, including the Reception Register and the Staff Register.

Reception Register

Reception Register or Visitors Book ▶

The Reception Register or Visitors Book is a record of all visitors to an organization. In a large organization, all visitors are required to sign the Reception Register. The register will show the name of the visitor, the name of the organization he/she represents, if applicable, the date, the name of the person they want to see, the time of arrival and the time of departure.

Reception Register					
Date	Name of visitor	Organization	Name of person/department referred to	Arrival time	Departure time
Sept 5	Elaine Palmer	Pearson's Insurance Co	Willard Smith, Human Resources Manager	10.26 am	11.40 am
	Marissa Palmer	ABC Stationery Supplies	Danae Panton, Sales Manager	10.45 am	

Figure 5.8 Excerpt from a Reception Register

The Reception Register allows the business to be able to know all the persons who were in the premises at a particular time. In the event of an emergency, the Reception Register will show how many persons were inside the building and give their names.

In many large, modern offices the Reception Register is kept electronically, using a computer. The receptionist will be responsible for completing the electronic register once the visitors are received into the organization.

In some organizations the Reception Register or Visitors Book is kept by a security guard outside the reception area.

Staff Register or Staff In or Out Book

Staff Register ▶

The Staff Register is used for monitoring the movement of employees and acts as a record of attendance. When members of staff arrive at work they must sign their name and the time they arrived. Staff members who leave work during office hours should state their reason for doing so in the Staff Register, along with their time of departure and return time.

Some offices use the time card system for monitoring staff movement and attendance. Each employee is assigned a time card which is kept next to a time clock. When the employee arrives for work he/she will insert the time card into a slot in the time clock which prints the exact time of arrival on the card. At the end of the day the employee will once again place the time card in the time clock to record the time of departure.

Some modern offices require that staff members 'sign in' using computers, which may be kept in the reception area or in the various departments in the case of large companies. Employees will log on to the computer system using a unique password or code; the computer system will automatically record the time that the employee logs in as the arrival time. At the end of the day the employee will log off the system and the time will be recorded as the departure time.

Staff Register						
Number	Name	Arrival time	Departure time	Arrival time	Departure time	Remarks
27	John Tate	8.51 am	11.20 am			Gone to the bank
5	Emily Bernard	8.59 am				

Figure 5.9 Excerpt from a Staff Register

The receptionist can use the Staff Register to ascertain those employees who are in the building at a specific time.

Operating a telephone switchboard

Telephone switchboards allow for connections within the business via extensions, as well as connections to outside lines. The receptionist should have at hand an internal directory, showing the list of extensions within the office, so that callers will be promptly transferred to the person or department requested. The receptionist should also have a telephone message pad at hand to write messages in case the person requested by the caller is unavailable.

Figure 5.10 A typical PABX

Many telephone switchboards can be fitted with a headset. This will increase the receptionist's efficiency by keeping both hands free to handle tasks such as taking messages and using the computer.

Extension	
21	Unit Manager, James Blair
22	Accountant, Manda Samuels
34	Accountant, Keisha Laird
24	Accounts Clerk, Bert Salmon

Figure 5.11 Extract from an internal directory

Figure 5.12 A receptionist operating a telephone switchboard

117

Receiving letters and parcels

Procedures for the handling of mail will differ, depending on the size of the organization. Large organizations usually have a mail room dedicated to dealing with all mail that comes in or goes out of the organization. In a small organization, specific staff members, such as the receptionist will be responsible for handling any incoming or outgoing mail. Mail may be sent by post, courier service, facsimile (fax) transmission or electronic mail (e-mail).

The receptionist would be responsible for identifying, recording and reporting any damaged or suspicious mail that comes into the organization. Suspicious mail will include envelopes that appear to be resealed and contents that make a noise.

All mail received should be promptly delivered to the relevant staff member. If there is only one receptionist, in order to not leave the area unmanned, a representative from the relevant department will be asked to retrieve the mail.

In some small companies there may be instances where the receptionist will be required to receive goods on behalf of the organization. In such cases the receptionist may be asked to sign a delivery note or consignment note or complete a goods received note.

delivery note ▶ The delivery note shows the quantity, description and sometimes the cost of the goods being delivered. The driver of the delivery vehicle must obtain the buyer's signature on a copy of the delivery note as evidence of delivery.

consignment note ▶ A consignment note accompanies goods being delivered. It is used when the seller hires an external carrier to make the delivery. The consignment note is signed by the buyer as evidence that the goods have been received.

goods received note ▶ The goods received note is used to record the entry of goods received into the organization. The goods received note details the quantity of items received, the quantity ordered and any discrepancies or faults.

Before signing for any goods, the receptionist must check that:
- the items delivered have indeed been ordered by someone in the organization;
- the items delivered match the information on the delivery note;
- the items are in good condition, and not damaged.

If satisfied, the receptionist can sign for the goods. If the receptionist is unable to check the goods, the documents can be signed with the notation 'Goods received but not checked'.

Goods Received Note					
Supplier: Mid-Town Stationery	GRN No: 5 Delivery Note No: 26 Checker's Name: Charmaine Brooks				
Order #	**Quantity Ordered**	**Quantity Delivered**	**Quantity Rejected**	**Description of Goods**	**Detail of Discrepancies**
16	50	50	1	Hardcover note books	The cover of one book was missing

Figure 5.13 Goods received note

Managing appointments

The receptionist may be responsible for making, rescheduling and cancelling appointments. When making appointments on behalf of an employee, the receptionist needs to be aware of his/her schedule so that a suitable time can be selected for both the employee and the client. When appointments are made, both the client and the employee should be clear regarding the time, place and date of the appointment. It is also the responsibility of the receptionist to confirm the appointment with both parties, perhaps a day before the scheduled meeting.

appointment book ▶   An appointment book is used to record future appointments and allows the receptionist to know which visitors are expected and those who arrive without appointments. Appointment books can be maintained manually or electronically.

Manual appointment books are cost effective and easy to use. They can be purchased at stationery stores and will provide adequate pages for each day of the year.

One drawback of this manual system is that in an office with several executives it will become difficult to manage all the appointments, as each executive may have a separate appointment book.

DATE: Monday, March 8		
9 AM	:00	
	:15	Pete Samuels of Mid-Town Pharmacy
	:30	
	:45	
10 AM	:00	
	:15	
	:30	Appointment with Sarah Scott from Prime Real Estate Co
	:45	
11 AM	:00	
	:15	
	:30	
	:45	
12 PM	:00	
	:15	
	:40	Staff Meeting in Conference Room 2
	:45	
1 PM	:00	
	:15	
	:30	
	:45	
2 PM	:00	
	:15	
	:30	
	:45	Vera Wallace from Island Pharmaceuticals
3 PM	:00	
	:15	
	:30	
	:45	
4 PM	:00	Rotary Club meeting at the Starfish Hotel Ballroom. Bring donation for their sponsored activities
	:15	
	:30	
	:45	
5 PM	:00	
	:15	
	:30	
	:45	

Figure 5.14   Example of a page from an appointment book

The receptionist can also facilitate the scheduling and management of appointments electronically. Various appointment-scheduling software programs are available to provide effective and speedy management of appointments using the computer. Examples are Power Notes Lite and Schedule View. Some scheduling software is also built into Microsoft Windows, which employees may use.

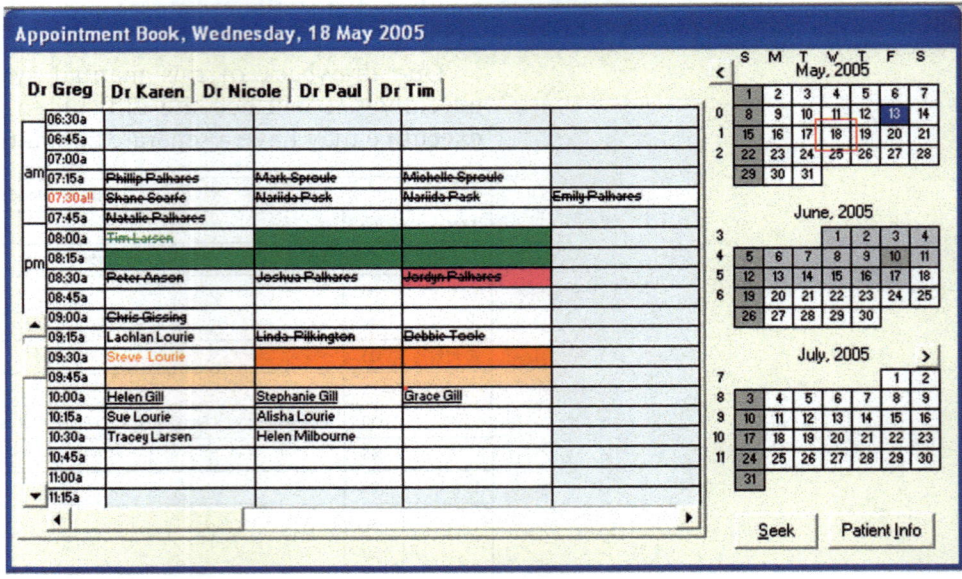

Figure 5.15 Appointment-scheduling software

Benefits of electronic scheduling

- Allows the receptionist to keep track of multiple appointments.
- Allows customer information to be organized in one place.
- The software automatically finds the next available appointment time.

Online appointment scheduling can also be used. This requires special software plus access to the internet. Examples of online scheduling software are Appointment Plus and Appointment Quest.

Benefits of online scheduling

- Customers are able to make their own appointments online at any time, day or night.
- The online system sends automatic notifications to the receptionist of all new appointments made.
- The online system sends automatic reminders, via text or e-mail, to clients of their appointments.
- A master calendar coordinates appointments made online with those made by phone or in person.

Whenever appointments need to be rescheduled or cancelled the receptionist needs to notify the client immediately, by the quickest method available – for example, by telephone or e-mail. The receptionist should apologize to the client and, if possible, give a reason for the cancellation and provide possible dates for rescheduling.

ITQ5

Explain how you would treat a client who is half an hour late for his appointment.

Maintaining reminder systems

The receptionist will be responsible for maintaining a number of reminder systems, such as:

- tickler file;
- diary;
- calendar.

tickler file system ▶ The tickler file system is an organizational tool that helps keep track of events, tasks and deadlines. The tickler file is also able to keep track of important documents such as bills.

Steps in creating a tickler file system

- Select 12 file folders (one for each month) and label them 'January', 'February' and so on through to 'December'.
- Select 31 file folders (one for each day in a month) and label them '1', '2', '3' and so on through to '31'.
- Arrange the monthly file folders starting with the current month and followed by the subsequent months.
- Arrange the daily file folders beginning with the current date – for example, if today is March 6, the first folder in the tickler file would be March. Behind the March folder would be the daily file folder beginning with 6, then 7 all the way to 31. The April folder would have daily file folders 1 through 5. When March 6 has passed, the number 6 daily folder will be moved to the April folder.
- Any item that will require attention should be placed in the folder of the relevant date. The receptionist should make a habit of checking the day's folder each morning to ensure that any action that is to be taken that day is done so in a timely manner.

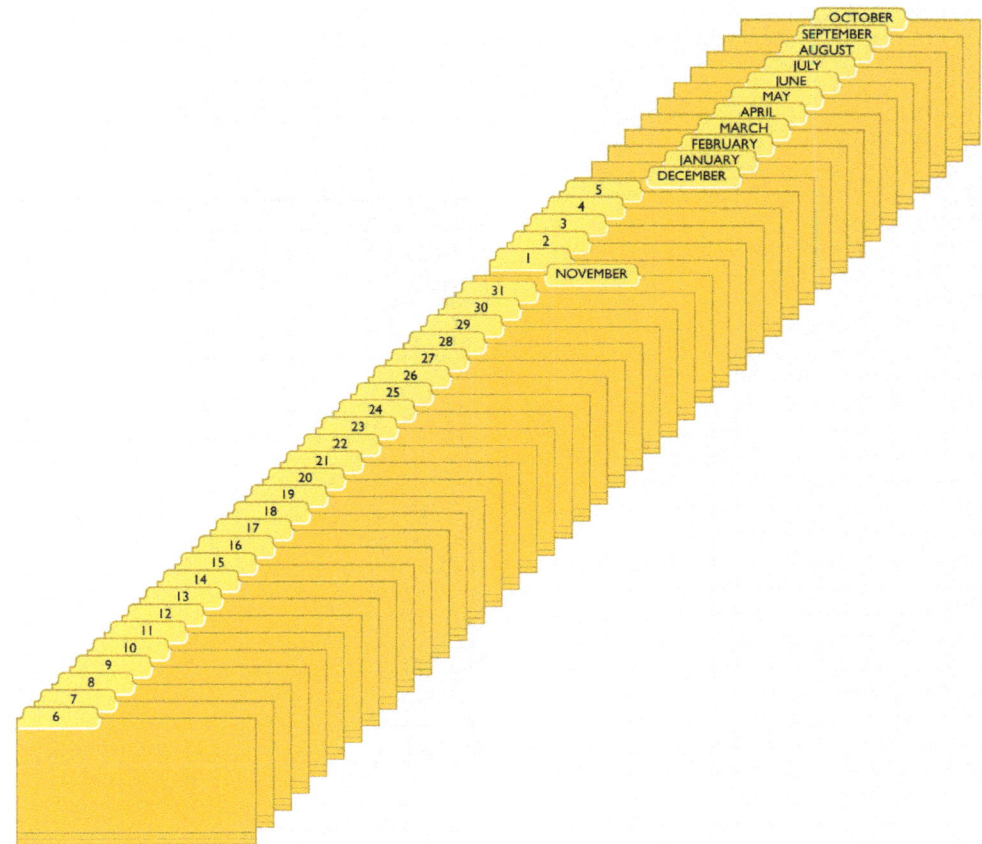

Figure 5.16   A tickler file system

Instead of having to create your own tickler system, ready-made systems are available, which will prevent the user from having to purchase folders and label them.

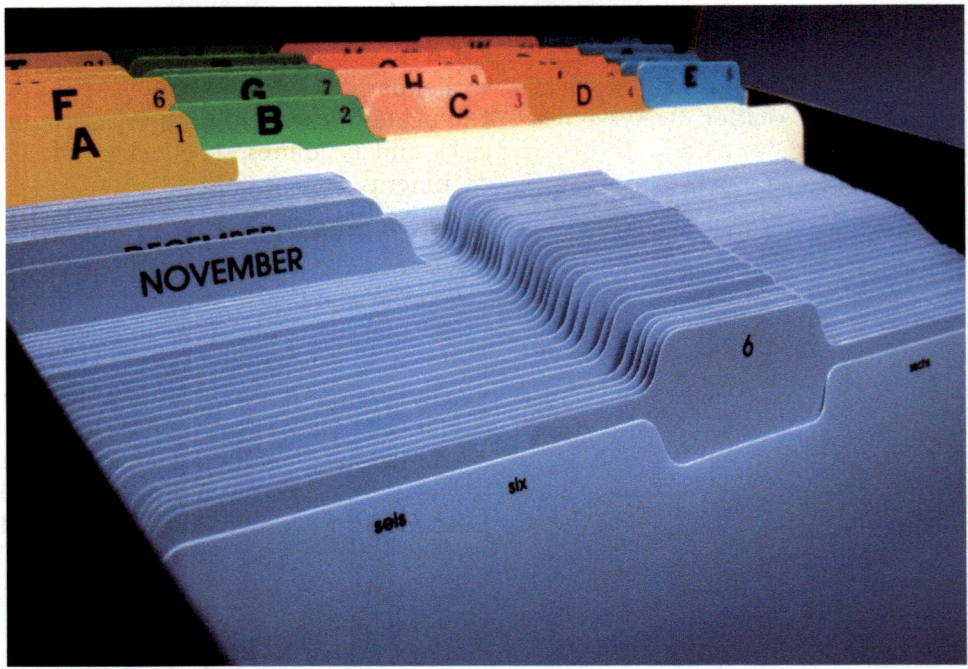

Figure 5.17   The GTD tickler file system

Diary

diary ▶   The diary is a book used to record daily activities and to act as a reminder for future events and appointments.

Figure 5.18   A typical business diary

electronic diaries ▶   Some modern offices are able to use electronic diaries. These are a way of keeping a copy of a diary on a computer.

Benefits of an electronic diary

- It automatically adds pages when needed.
- Information is able to be shared over a computer network.
- It shows when staff are free.
- It makes booking meetings with staff easier.

Calendars

calendars ▶

Calendars are charts which outline the days, weeks and months in a particular year. Calendars will allow the receptionist to record reminders for future activities and appointments. Desk calendars, which are calendars which cover the top of desks, are popular in many offices.

Some modern offices utilize online calendar organizers. Specialized software, for example Kirby Alarm Pro Task Scheduler, can be purchased in order to facilitate online organization of events and appointments.

Benefits of online calendars:

- Keep your schedule online and allow it to be accessed from any computer.
- Event reminders can be received via e-mail.
- Allows for the coordination of activities and appointments.

Personal Digital Assistants (PDAs)

Personal Digital Assistants ▶

Personal Digital Assistants are small, lightweight computers that are able to fit in the palm of one's hand. Many modern PDA devices include built-in software for calendar, reminders and scheduling capabilities. Many high-tech cellular phones are able to carry out similar, and even more advanced, features than the PDA. Some large organizations may provide their executives as well as other employees with PDAs and cellular phones.

These reminder systems allow you to work more efficiently and improve your time and resource management. They allow you to set up reminders for important meetings and occasions.

Figure 5.19   A typical PDA

Maintaining the reception area

The receptionist is also responsible for managing and maintaining the reception area, by keeping it tidy and well organized. This involves:

- straightening magazines;
- watering plants;
- making sure that there is adequate water and also enough cups at the water cooler;
- updating notice boards.

Security

The receptionist may also be responsible for dealing with some aspects of security. Based on the security concerns of the organization, some reception areas may contain barriers that limit the access of visitors to the reception staff. Other considerations include:

- the receptionist area should always be manned. If the receptionist has to leave the desk, a relief receptionist should be used;
- paperwork on the reception desk and the contents of the computer screen should be kept out of the view of visitors;
- the receptionist should be aware of emergency numbers including police, fire and ambulance;
- the use of a door-entry system, which will require the visitor to ring a buzzer. When the buzzer is pressed the receptionist can use the telephone to speak to the person at the door as well as unlock the door.

Clerical duties

The receptionist will also be responsible for carrying out certain clerical functions such as:

- typing – preparing letters and other documents for members of the organization;
- filing – storing documents for later use;
- taking messages from callers/visitors and passing these messages on to the relevant individuals;
- receiving and sending information by facsimile transmission and electronic mail;
- receiving payments and writing receipts;
- the receptionist will also be responsible for handling enquiries from the public and providing them with information about the business as well as the products/services it provides. The receptionist will need to be knowledgeable about matters such as:
  - history of the business;
  - names of its officials;
  - location of other branches;
  - types of goods or services available;
  - cost of goods or services available.

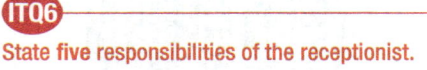

ITQ6

State **five responsibilities** of the receptionist.

Summary

- The reception area is that section at the front of an office where visitors are received.
- Items found in the reception area include chairs, tables, plants and water dispensers.
- Attributes of a receptionist include having a good temperament, paying attention to detail, being tactful and practising proper hygiene.
- Duties of a receptionist include welcoming and screening visitors; receiving and filing business cards; managing appointments; maintaining the reception area; and maintaining reminder systems.
- Types of visitors include expected visitors, unexpected visitors and regular visitors.
- Records kept by the receptionist include the Reception Register, the Staff Register and the appointment book.
- Reminder systems include tickler files, diaries and calendars.

Answers to 

1 computer; coffee table; filing cabinet; television.

2 • Loss of sales and profit.
   • A poor reputation will be developed.

3 • Try to find out what the problem is.
   • Empathize with the visitor.
   • Try to solve the problem – if you cannot, find someone who can.
   • Thank the visitor for his patience.

4 Name of the business; address; telephone number; type of service or product provided.

5 Find out whether the person he wanted is still available:
   • if the employee is unavailable, find out whether someone else can help;
   • if not, make a new appointment.

6 • Handling enquiries.
   • Managing appointments.
   • Maintaining reminder systems.
   • Operating a switchboard.
   • Receiving letters and parcels.

Examination-style questions

Multiple choice questions

1 Which document is used to record all visitors to an organization?
   a diary
   b Staff Register
   c tickler file
   d Reception Register.

2 Mr Jarrett, a very important client, visits the office without an appointment and wishes to see the General Manager. What action should the receptionist take?
   a Explain to Mr Jarrett that he must have an appointment.
   b Find out whether the General Manager is able to see him.
   c Allow Mr Jarrett to speak with the General Manager over the telephone.
   d Offer Mr Jarrett a drink and tell him to wait.

3 What is the purpose of a tickler file?
   a To act as a reminder.
   b To store business cards.
   c To keep permanent records.
   d To maintain the office files.

4 What information should a receptionist know before setting up appointments for his/her supervisor?
   a The reason for the appointment.
   b The supervisor's schedule.
   c The length of the visit
   d The supervisor's job description.

5 Which group of items is **not** likely to be found in a reception area?
   a Television, security camera, coffee table.
   b Security camera, filing cabinets, plants.
   c Coffee table, telephone, computer.
   d Dining table, computer, filing cabinet.

125

6 How should the receptionist carry out introductions between the Finance Manager, Mr Grant, and the General Manager, Mr Phillips.
   a Mr Grant, may I present Mr Phillips?
   b Mr Grant, I would like to introduce the General Manager.
   c Mr Phillips, may I introduce Mr Grant?
   d Mr Phillips, I would like to introduce you to the Finance Manager.

7 Which of the following shows the correct sequence of dealing with an expected visitor?
   i   Greet the visitor.
   ii   Issue a visitor's pass.
   iii Inform the staff member that the visitor has arrived.
   iv   Refer to the appointment book.
   a i, ii, iii, iv
   b ii, i, iv, iii
   c i, iv, iii, ii
   d iii, iv, i, ii.

8 Which of the following is the **primary** responsibility of a receptionist?
   a Welcoming and screening visitors.
   b Typing letters and memos.
   c Coordinating departmental meetings.
   d Assisting the General Manager with decision making.

9 Which of the following is **not** a duty of the receptionist?
   a Scheduling appointments.
   b Welcoming employees.
   c Answering the telephone.
   d Receiving goods.

10 'Goodwill' refers to:
   a the positive relationship between a business and its customers
   b products manufactured by the firm
   c the goods received note
   d tangible assets owned by a business.

Structured questions

1 You are the receptionist at High Rise Ltd. Show how you would deal with the following situations:
   a At 3 pm your executive asks you to reschedule his 3.30 pm appointment because of a family emergency. [3]
   b A visitor without an appointment requests to see the Purchasing Manager. [3]
   c Ms Lacey is on time for her appointment with the Sales Manager, Mr Foxx. Mr Foxx, however, just called to say he will be an hour late. [3]
   d An angry visitor walks into the reception area and in a loud voice complains that he has not received his goods that he ordered three weeks ago. [3]

2   Rule up a Reception Register and record the following visitors to
    your office on June 12, 2012:

    1030   Stacy Richie of Rams Ltd. Referred to the Purchasing
           Manager. She left at 1120.
    1145   Kerry Lee of Japs Printery to see the Sales Manager.
           She left at 1235.
    1310   Casey Bernard to see the Human Resources Manager.
           Left at 1440.
    1630   Brenton Campbell of National Insurance to see Jon Skeeter,
           Human Resources Manager.   [10]

3   Draw a plan or layout of a typical reception area.   [10]

4   Your friend wants to be a receptionist. Tell her of **four** attributes
    and **four** skills needed to carry out the job.   [8]

5   While you were out the relief receptionist scheduled an appointment
    with a visitor but failed to record it in the appointment book. What
    do you do when the visitor turns up for his appointment?   [3]

6   **a** State **three** ways in which the receptionist can portray a
           positive image of the firm.   [3]
    b Describe the **three** categories of visitors to a business. [3]

Meetings

By the end of this chapter you should be able to:

- ☑ list the various types of meetings;
- ☑ list reasons why meeting are held;
- ☑ identify documents used in meetings;
- ☑ define terms associated with meetings;
- ☑ organize different types of meetings;
- ☑ state basic legal requirements of annual general meetings;
- ☑ outline follow-up procedures related to decisions made at meetings.

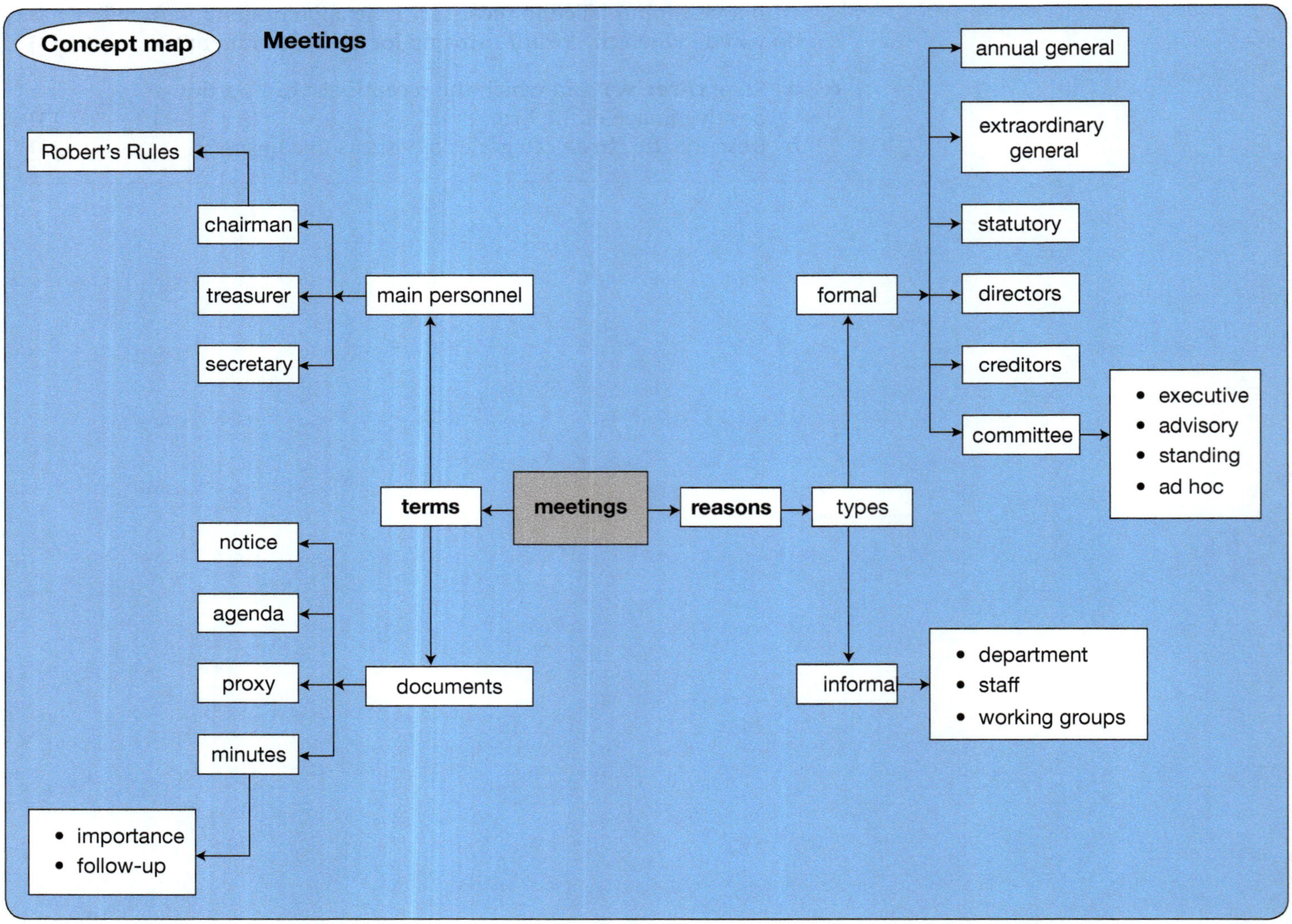

Concept map   **Meetings**

- Robert's Rules
- chairman
- treasurer ← main personnel
- secretary
- **terms** ← **meetings** → **reasons** → types
- notice
- agenda
- proxy ← documents
- minutes
  - importance
  - follow-up

- formal
  - annual general
  - extraordinary general
  - statutory
  - directors
  - creditors
  - committee
    - executive
    - advisory
    - standing
    - ad hoc
- informa
  - department
  - staff
  - working groups

Reasons for holding meetings

meetings ▶

Meetings are held when a group of persons come together to discuss matters of mutual interest. Meetings give members the opportunity to exchange ideas and try to find acceptable solutions to problems.

Meetings are held for various reasons. The chairperson decides on the reason and informs the members. Typical reasons are:

- to make decisions;
- to discuss matters relating to the firm;
- to pass on information;
- to plan activities that will help the company (for example, a workshop session);
- to collect ideas from members that will be beneficial to the success of the business;
- to give or receive feedback on matters;
- to find acceptable solution to problems;
- to decide on strategies needed to succeed;
- team-building/motivation.

Types of meeting

There are two main types of meeting: formal and informal.

informal meetings ▶

minutes ▶

In large organizations most formal meetings are held 21 clear days after giving notice to members. However, in smaller organizations the number of days needed may be fewer. Informal meetings are called at short notice to discuss matters which have arisen suddenly. When these meetings are called minutes are usually taken but there may be no agenda. These meetings are called by word of mouth or by informing members by means of a note.

Formal meetings

Annual general meetings

annual general meeting ▶

An annual general meeting, commonly referred to as an AGM or annual meeting, is a formal meeting which is held once a year. This type of meeting is a legal requirement for charities, large companies or voluntary organizations that have company status. An AGM is held every year after giving 21 days' clear notice. This type of meeting deals with issues such as the election of committee or board members and reviewing the annual accounts. Members are also informed of the company's previous activities and its successes and failures over the past year, as well as future activities

Extraordinary general meetings

extraordinary general meeting ▶

An extraordinary general meeting, commonly abbreviated as EGM and in some cases known as an emergency general meeting, is a meeting of members of an organization, shareholders of a company, or employees of an official body, which occurs when needed. These meetings are held where an issue arises which requires the input of the entire membership and is too serious or urgent to wait until the next AGM – for example, there is a fire in the organization's premises and members must meet to decide the next step for the company.

Board of directors meetings

board of directors meetings ▶ Board of directors meetings are management meetings of members of the board of directors of a company. These members are responsible for management, and usually have power to make decisions and act on behalf of the company.

Meetings of creditors

meetings of creditors ▶ Meetings of creditors are held when a group of persons to whom money is owed meet to decide on a common course of action in order to recover their money or part of the money owed to them. At these meetings creditors may also decide to offer new terms of payment.

Statutory meetings

statutory meetings ▶ Every public limited company having a share capital must hold a general meeting of its members within a period of not less then one month and not later than six months from the date on which the company is entitled to commence business. These statutory meetings are required by law to ensure open communication between directors and shareholders.

Committee meetings

committee meetings ▶ Committee meetings are held either to give advice or to make recommendations to management. Members are appointed or elected according to requirements. One special type of member is the *ex-officio* member, who is appointed because of the official position or office they hold. For example, the CEO may be designated as an *ex-officio* member on all committees. There are several types of committees and they convene meetings for varying purposes.

Types of committee meetings

Executive committee

executive committee ▶ An executive committee carries out the actual management of an organization. It has the power to make decisions on the organization's behalf.

Standing committee

standing committee ▶ A standing committee is set up to deal with recurrent matters that have been assigned to it, for example education. This committee will act on its own but within the framework of the powers conferred upon it and will report to the executive committee.

Advisory committee

advisory committee ▶ An advisory committee gives advice to the executive committee on matters regarding the firm. The advisory committee may form a sub-committee that will investigate matters and report to it based on the findings. It will give advice to the executive committee.

Ad hoc committee

ad hoc committee ▶ An ad hoc committee is a short-lived committee, which is set up for a particular purpose. For example, a committee may be set up to plan an event; at the end of the event, the committee no longer exists. Some meetings may be held '*in camera*'. This is when the meeting takes placed behind closed doors because of the sensitive or confidential nature of the information being discussed.

ITQ1
List **three** terms used in meetings.

Informal meetings

Departmental meetings

departmental meetings ▶

Departmental meetings are informal meetings called by heads of the departments or divisions to discuss the progress of the departments, to make plans or even to give instructions.

Staff meetings

staff meetings ▶

Staff meetings are those held between a manager and those who report to the manager. They are seen by many organizations as an important venue for communicating with workers directly and efficiently. Some staff meetings encourage an open exchange of dialogue with staff, while others are conducted as more of an 'in-person memo', wherein management retains the majority of the floor.

ITQ2
If not enough members are present at a meeting to constitute a quorum, what can the chairperson do?

Articles of association

article of association ▶

An article of association is an official document governing the internal regulations and by-laws covering procedure, shares, meetings, directors and other administrative issues of a company, that is placed with the Registrar of Companies. The articles of association constitute a contract between the company and its members. The article of association set out:
• voting rights of stockholders;
• conduct of stockholders' and directors' meetings;
• details of the powers of management of the company.

Functions of main personnel at a meeting

Chairperson

chairperson ▶

The chairperson is responsible for controlling the meeting. One of the main ways in which the chairperson maintains control is by the convention of speaking 'through the chair', which means that members address the meeting via the chairperson.

The chairperson's duties are generally as follows:

• to open the meeting at the time at which the assembly is to meet, by taking the chair and calling the members to order;
• to announce the business before the assembly, in the order in which it is to be acted upon;
• to recognize members entitled to the floor;
• to put matters which come up in the meeting to a vote;
• to announce the result of the vote;
• to protect the assembly from disruption.

The chairperson also has a casting vote. This is a deciding vote in the event of a tie.

When conducting a meeting it is the chairperson's responsibility to ensure that the rules of the company are followed. For example, there must be a

quorum ▶

quorum before a meeting can begin. A quorumn is the minimum number of memebers who must attend a meeting for business of that meeting to be valid. Each member of the meeting must be given the opportunity to vote once on any issue. In the event of a tied vote, the chairperson has the **casting vote**. This is a second vote cast by the chairperson to decide the issue.

ITQ3
What steps should be taken if the chairperson has resigned before the end of his term of office?

Secretary

secretary ▶ The secretary is responsible for recording the business of a meeting. In addition to keeping the records of the minutes of the meetings, it is the duty of the secretary to keep a register of the members; to notify officers, committees and delegates of their appointment; and to furnish committees with all papers referred to them, and to sign with the president all orders on the treasurer authorized by the society, unless otherwise specified in the by-laws. The secretary is also responsible to send out proper notices of all called meetings to members and to conduct the correspondence of the organization.

After a meeting, the secretary is responsible for presenting a draft of the minutes to the chairperson to be signed and then copies circulated to members.

Treasurer

treasurer ▶ The treasurer acts as a banker for the organization or the meeting body, either by keeping the funds deposited with him/her or, where the funds are large sums, in a bank account. Funds may then be paid out on the order of the society, signed by the president and the secretary.

ITQ4

Does a treasurer's report need to have a motion of approval?

The treasurer is always required to make an annual report, and in many societies a quarterly report too. The treasurer must maintain adequate cash flow, prepare financial statements and deal with any financial matters for the committee.

ITQ5

How should a member of a meeting address the chairperson?

Robert's Rules of Order

Robert's Rules of Order ▶ Robert's Rules of Order are intended to provide a basic background in meeting procedure in order to conduct business in as efficient and orderly a manner as possible.

The purpose of the chairperson is to preserve order during meetings, to restrain the members engaged in debate, and to serve the will of the majority of the meeting participants while permitting the minority (viewpoints) a reasonable opportunity to be heard.

Addressing the chair

addressing the chair ▶ All meetings should be conducted 'from the chair'. Members addressing the chair should refer to the presiding officer as 'Mr Chairperson' or 'Madam Chairperson'.

Obtaining the floor

motion ▶ A motion is a formal proposal put forward at a meeting for decision and consideration.

Before a member may make a motion or speak in debate, he/she must 'obtain the floor'. To do this, a member raises his/her hand and waits to be 'recognized' by the chair. The chair will recognize the member by announcing his/her name or title. This member will then put forward his/her argument.

While a motion is open to debate, there are two important cases where the floor should be assigned to a person who may not have been the first to rise and address the chair. These cases are:

• If the member who made the motion claims the floor and has not already spoken on the question, he/she is entitled to be recognized in preference to other members.
• No one is entitled to the floor for a second time as long as any other member who has not yet spoken to the pending motion requests the floor.

Making a motion

- First, a member makes a motion. When a motion is made, the word 'move' must be used to make the motion (for example: 'I move that … ').
- Another member seconds the motion by saying 'I second it' or simply 'Second'. It should be noted that a second by a member merely implies that the motion should come before the meeting and not that he/she necessarily favours the motion. A member may second a motion because he/she would like to see the assembly go on record as rejecting the proposal, if he/she believes a vote on the motion would have such a result.
- The chair then states the 'question' on the motion. Neither the making nor the seconding of a motion places it before the council; only the chair can do that by this step (stating the question). When the chair has stated the question, the motion is pending and is then open to debate (providing that it is a debatable motion). If the council decides to do what a motion proposes, it 'adopts' a motion or it is 'carried'. If it decides against the motion, it is 'rejected', "dropped' or 'lost'.

ITQ6

If a motion has been defeated, can it be brought up again at the next meeting?

Amending a motion

motion to amend ▶

A formal proposal can be put forward to alter the wording of a motion. The motion to amend is intended to modify the wording (within certain limits) of a pending motion before it is acted upon. An amendment must be closely related to or have some bearing on the subject of the motion to be amended.

A motion to amend is handled in the same way as a main motion and requires a second to be considered. An amendment is adopted by a majority vote even in cases where the motion to be amended requires a two-thirds vote for adoption.

A member may propose that a motion be allowed to lie on the table. This means that a decision on that matter is temporarily laid aside. It the proposal is accepted the matter is said to '**lie on the table**'.

approval of the minutes ▶

Approval of the minutes

At the beginning of regularly scheduled meetings, copies of minutes of the previous meeting will be distributed to members; in most cases minutes are sent out with the agenda for them to read and corrections made before the meeting. This saves time during the meeting as members will quickly be able to point out errors identified. The chair then asks 'Are there any corrections to the minutes?' and pauses then says 'If there are no corrections' (or 'no further corrections') the minutes stand approved (or 'approved as corrected').

Seating arrangements

Seating arrangements are usually left to chance, but where meeting participants sit in some meetings may suggest authority, position or how much members intend to participate in the meeting. Seating arrangements can influence overall meeting effectiveness. The seat next to the chairperson may mean that the person sitting there is the deputy chairperson. The secretary is usually seated close to the chairperson.

Place a tick in the correct box on the right of the table to indicate whether the statement is true or false.

Items	Questions	True	False
1	A meeting should involve as many people as possible, even if the topic does not directly concern them.		
2	A meeting should not start until all participants are present and quiet.		
3	Participants should be notified of meetings at the last minute so that they do not try to get out of them.		
4	The person conducting the meeting should also take notes on the meeting.		
5	Side discussions are acceptable during meetings, as long as they are kept quiet.		

Before the meeting	On the day of the meeting	After the meeting
Secure a room for the meeting	Ensure that the room is properly ventilated	Prepare a draft of the minutes for the chairman to review
Send out notice	Have stationery for members	Ensure that there is a follow-up on matters discussed at the meeting
Prepare minutes of past meeting	Place 'meeting in progress' sign on the door	Ensure that the room is left in order
Organize refreshments	Ensure that members sign the attendance register	Remove signs
Collect reports	Write the minutes of the meeting	Distribute minutes of meeting
Arrange for audio-visual aids	Assist the chairperson	

Table 6.1 Things that must be done before, during and after a meeting

Requisites of a valid meeting

To ensure that the business transacted at a meeting is valid, the following must be considered:
- The meeting must be properly convened – this means that notice, in a legally acceptable manner, must be given to every person entitled to attend.
- quorum ▶ A quorum must be present before a meeting can commence – a quorum is the minimum number of persons who should be in attendance of a meeting by law.
- The rules and regulations of the particular organization must be followed – rules and regulations governing the conduct of meetings are set out in a company's articles of association.

Place a tick in the respective columns to indicate when the following activities should be done:

Activities	Before the meeting	Day of the meeting	After the meeting
Sign the attendance register			
Book a room for the meeting			
Prepare a draft of the minutes for the chairman			
Book audio visual aids			
Send out minutes of meeting			

Meeting documents

Notice of a meeting

notice ▶   A notice is used to inform members that there will be a meeting and also to let them know the date, time and venue of the meeting. Note that a notice sent out too early will be ineffective, as the details can be forgotten. The amount of lead time for sending out notice is determined by the type of meeting to be called. For example, an annual general meeting notice requires 21 days while a department meeting notice may require only one or two days.

Information needed to prepare a notice

When writing a notice, use 'who, what, when, where and why' as guides. The information that would be needed to prepare the notice and agenda of a meeting and to ensure that all persons concerned are notified is:

- date and day of meeting;
- where the meeting will be held;
- time of the meeting;
- topic to be discussed;
- names of members;
- addresses of members.

> ***NOTICE OF MEETING***
>
> **MASTER STITCHER CARPETING COMPANY**
>
> NOTICE IS HEREBY GIVEN THAT THE ANNUAL GENERAL MEETING of Master Stitch Carpeting Company will be held in the Boardroom on April 20, 2011 at 3.30 pm.

Figure 6.1   Notice of a meeting

Agenda

An agenda is a list of items to be discussed during a meeting. It can be said to be the tool or instrument used to control the meeting. An agenda is usually included with the notice and is sent to all members to allow them to attend the meeting prepared to participate in the discussions. An agenda usually begins with apologies for absence and minutes of the last meeting. The agenda usually ends with an item in which the date and time of the next meeting are set. If no date is set for the next meeting it is said to be adjourned ***sine die***. Below is an example of an agenda:

> ### MASTER STITCHER CARPETING COMPANY
>
> ANNUAL GENERAL MEETING
>
> **AGENDA**
>
> 1. Apologies for absence
> 2. Minutes of the last annual general meeting
> 3. Matters arising from the minutes
> 4. Chairperson's report for the year end
> 5. Financial accounts for the past year
> 6. Election of officers
> 7. Any other business
> 8. Date and time for next meeting.

Figure 6.2   Agenda for a meeting

Chairperson's agenda

chairperson's agenda ▶

A chairperson's agenda contains more information than the ordinary agenda. A wide space is usually provided on the right-hand side of the paper for the chairperson to make notes which will assist him/her in the conduct of an effective meeting.

Chairperson's Agenda	
MASTER STITCHER CARPETING COMPANY	
ANNUAL GENERAL MEETING	
AGENDA	
	NOTES
1. Apologies for absence	1.
2. Minutes of the last annual general meeting	2.
3. Matters arising from the minutes	3.
4. Chairperson's report for the year end	4.
5. Financial accounts for the past year	5.
6. Election of officers	6.
7. Any other business	7.
8. Date and time for next meeting.	8.

Figure 6.3 Chairperson's agenda

ITQ9

Assume that you are the assistant secretary for your dance club. A meeting is scheduled to be held on October 23, 2011 at 3.45 pm at the Community Centre, to discuss upcoming performances. Prepare a notice for the meeting, to be sent to all concerned.

Minutes of meeting

'Minutes of a meeting' is the term given to the written record of business discussed at a meeting. The minutes must be a true record of what had taken place at a meeting and be capable of being called upon for future reference. Minutes serve as a legal paper trail in case of litigation and as a record of the factors considered in decision making. They also serve as internal documentation to help provide information to new directors, as a reminder to members of deliberations and actions, and as an update for members unable to attend. Finally, the minutes provide documentation for managers' follow-up.

After the meeting, type the notes and circulate them straight away; send a copy to all attendees, including the date of the next meeting if applicable, and also to anyone else who should see the notes. The minutes should be brief or people won't read them, but they must still be precise and clear. Include relevant facts, figures, accountabilities, actions and timescales.

Minutes are always written in the past tense, using reported speech, for example: 'The Treasurer raised the question of ...'. Minutes must be a precise, unambiguous account of what actually happen at a meeting. The minute must be understandable to someone who was absent from the meeting. Figure 6.4 shows an example of a set of minutes.

Importance of the contents of the minutes

Minutes are important as they provide a record of actions points decided at the last meeting and of agreements made. The minutes of a meeting can be used to clarify many issues and also to inform persons who were absent. After the meeting the minutes should be checked with the chairperson to confirm accuracy and then circulated to all members of the meeting, both those who attended and those who were absent.

Minutes are required in order to:
• confirm any decisions made;
• record any agreed actions to be taken;

- record who has been allocated any tasks or responsibilities;
- prompt action from any relevant attendees;
- provide details of the meeting to anyone unable to attend;
- serve as a record of the meeting's procedure and outcome.

MINUTES OF MEETING:

A monthly meeting of Master Stitcher Carpeting Company was held in the Board Room on January 10, 2011 at 2.30 pm.

PRESENT:	Mr B Gayle (Chairperson) Mrs Pamela James (Secretary) Miss Victoria Knight (Treasurer) Ms Leshawn Thomas Mrs Portia Knight Mr Oliver Lucas
APOLOGIES:	Apologies for absence were received from Mr Jim Smith, Mr Andrew Young and Miss Della Yen
MINUTES:	The minutes of the last meeting were read and **confirmed**.
MATTERS ARISING:	Renovation to the old building is complete and the relocation of the Sales Department will commence within two weeks' time.
NEW BUSINESS:	Painting of the entire organization. Introduction of a new product. [...]
ANY OTHER BUSINESS:	There was no other business.
DATE OF NEXT MEETING:	It was decided to hold the next departmental meeting on Monday, April 20, 2010 at 5.30 pm.

Figure 6.4 Example of minutes of a meeting

ITQ10

List **two** important reasons for recording the minutes of a meeting.

Importance of circulating minutes of meeting

For some companies, minutes may be circulated on the day of the meeting, however, it is important to circulate minutes of meeting before the next meeting as this will give members a chance to read and make any correction to the last minutes before the upcoming meeting. Also, this saves valuable time at the meeting as the secretary will not have to concentrate on reading the minutes of the last meeting but concentrate only on making the corrections noted by members of the meeting.

Minute books

minute books ▶

Some organizations use bound minute books to record minutes, while others use loose-leaf books. Using a minute book will ensure that minutes are not lost and that they are always in the correct order, while the leaves of a loose-leaf binder may become misplaced or lost. Currently, most organizations are using electronic filing, also referred to as 'e-filing'. This is a method of filing documents that uses an electronic format rather than a traditional paper format. Electronic filing reduces copying fees; use of paper, and staff time, E-filing can be a tremendous cost saving.

Whichever method is used to record the minutes, the following must be done to ensure their safety:

- sheets must be numbered;
- the book/leaves must be kept in a fireproof safe (or electronic file secured);
- the chairperson must initial each sheet at the time of signing the minutes.

Voting at a meeting

co-opted ▶

All members at a meeting have the right to cast a vote unless they are co-opted. Co-opted members are those appointed to the meeting to fulfil specific needs which have been identified. They have the same status, rights and privileges as committee members but may not serve as chairperson or vice-president. When a decision must be made at a meeting – for example, there is a 'no confidence' motion in the chair – it will be necessary for members to vote. When voting, if there are equal votes for or against the motion then the chairperson may have the 'deciding vote'. Voting may be done at a meeting in several ways.

Proxy

proxy ▶

A member of a meeting may be appointed to vote by proxy. A proxy is someone who is appointed to attend a meeting and cast a vote on behalf of the absent member.

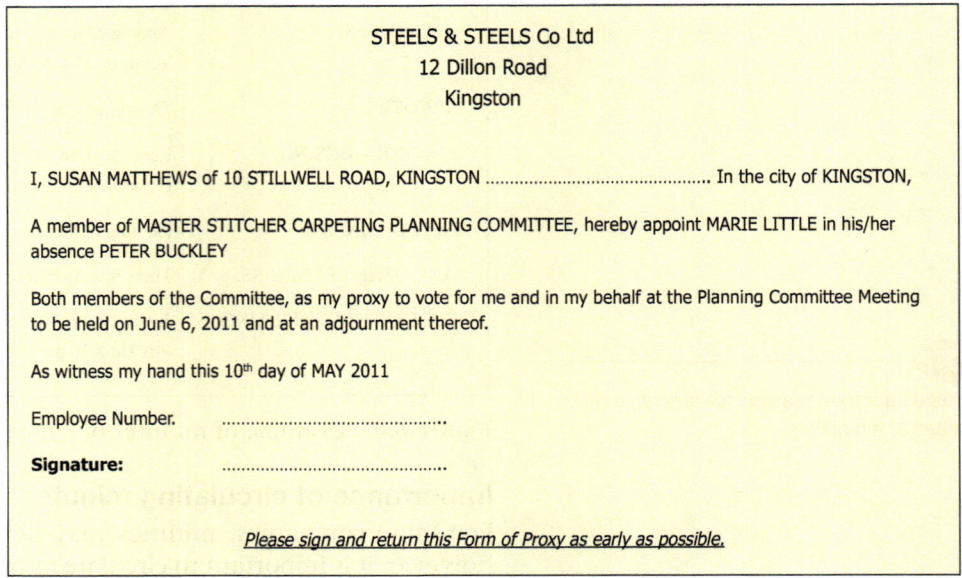

STEELS & STEELS Co Ltd
12 Dillon Road
Kingston

I, SUSAN MATTHEWS of 10 STILLWELL ROAD, KINGSTON …………………………………….. In the city of KINGSTON,

A member of MASTER STITCHER CARPETING PLANNING COMMITTEE, hereby appoint MARIE LITTLE in his/her absence PETER BUCKLEY

Both members of the Committee, as my proxy to vote for me and in my behalf at the Planning Committee Meeting to be held on June 6, 2011 and at an adjournment thereof.

As witness my hand this 10th day of MAY 2011

Employee Number. …………………………………...

Signature: …………………………………...

Please sign and return this Form of Proxy as early as possible.

Figure 6.5 Proxy form

Secret ballot

secret ballot ▶

A secret ballot takes place where the voters mark votes anonymously on a slip of paper and then deposit them into a box for counting.

Show of hands

Hands are raised and counted 'for' or 'against' a motion.

By standing

At large meetings members may be asked to stand and be counted.

ITQ11

How many votes is the chairman entitled to at a meeting?

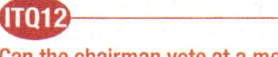

ITQ12

Can the chairman vote at a meeting?

Follow-up procedures related to decisions

Follow-up on the agreed action is the final crucial element of a meeting. If you run a successful meeting, issue helpful notes but then fail to ensure that the actions are completed, all is lost – not least your credibility. You must follow up agreed actions and hold people to them. If you don't, they will very soon learn that they can ignore these agreements every time. Not following up on actions can result in failure in team management and results. Following up agreed actions, at future meetings particularly, will result in better performance and response from members. These are some of the follow-up matters that will need attention:

- **Filing and indexing minutes.** At the end of a meeting the secretary must draft the minutes and allow the chairperson to sign, indicating that it was a true summary of the proceeding of the meeting. The secretary will then type and circulate the minutes to members. A copy of the minutes must also be filed for future reference after the minutes are corrected at the next meeting. Some companies also maintain a register that indicates the serial number of the minutes of each meeting.
- **Acting on decisions taken at the meeting.** All decisions taken during the meeting must be followed up. The secretary is responsible for ensuring that these decisions are carried out. A report will be presented to the members at the next meeting, under the title 'matters arising', provided that there was an agenda.
- **Circulation of action sheet.** The action sheet is usually circulated to advise members of the tasks they are expected to carry out.
- **Circulation of minutes.** After the chairperson signs the minute, the secretary must copy and circulate the minutes to all members.

ITQ13

Why is it important to follow up after a meeting?

Summary

- A meeting is held when a group of persons come together to discuss issues.
- There are many terms associated with business meetings, for example 'agenda', 'motion', 'proxy' and 'ex-officio'.
- There are two main types of meeting – formal and informal meetings.
- Formal meetings include: annual general meetings, extraordinary general meetings, board and committee meetings as well as statutory meetings and meetings of creditors.
- Annual general meetings are held yearly. as the name suggests.
- Extraordinary general meetings are held when there is a matter to be discussed and it cannot wait until the next AGM.
- Informal meetings include staff meetings and departmental meetings.
- Meetings are held for a number of reasons – for example, to make decisions or to solve problems.
- Before a meeting can be held a notice must be prepared and sent to members, informing them of the date, place and time for the meeting.
- An agenda is the instrument which guides a meeting – this must be prepared for the day of the meeting.
- Voting can be done in many ways at a meeting – some of these are: by standing, by show of hands, by using ballot paper or by proxy.
- A proxy is a person who is authorized by an absent member to attend a meeting and vote on the absent member's behalf.
- The person responsible for planning the meeting must ensure that all equipment and supplies needed for the meeting are available on the day itself.
- There are a number of activities which must be completed before, during and after a meeting.
- Minutes are a brief written record of what was discussed at a meeting.
- They are important as they provide a record of action points decided at the last meeting and of agreements made.
- The minutes must be typed and given to the chairman for vetting before they are printed and distributed to members.
- All follow-up activities must be carried out after the meeting.

1 Motion; quorum; proxy.

2 The chairperson could employ any of the following:

   a Wait until enough members arrive, if time permits.

   b Postpone the meeting until a later date.

3 The vice-chairperson automatically becomes the chairperson for the remainder of the term of office.

4 No motion is needed. A treasurer's report is simply 'received' as it is given and no motion should be made to 'adopt', 'accept' or 'approve' it. However, an annual auditors' report is 'accepted' or 'adopted', but not the treasurer's financial report itself.

5 'Madam Chairperson' if the person is female or 'Mr Chairperson' if the person is male.

6 Yes, if the meeting is a different session, which is the normal situation in other legislative bodies.

7

Items	True	False
1		√
2		√
3		√
4		√
5		√

8

Activities	Before meeting	Day of meeting	After meeting
Sign the attendance register		√	
Book a room for the meeting	√		
Prepare a draft of the minutes for the chairman			√
Book audio-visual aids	√		
Send out minutes of meeting			√

9

> **NOTICE OF MEETING**
>
> **COMMUNITY DANCE GROUP**
>
> A meeting with all Dance Members will be held at the
> Community Centre on October 23, 2011 at 3.45 pm.

10 Two important reasons for recording minutes of a meeting are:
   • They provide details of the meeting to absent team members who will be able to read the minutes.
   • They are legal records that document actions and approve business decisions made by members at the meeting.

11 The chair can vote twice – once as a member and then again in his/her capacity as presiding officer.

12 As a member, the chairperson has the right to vote, and does so on small boards of not more than about a dozen members present. In larger assemblies, the chairperson may vote when his/her vote would affect the outcome: to make or break a tie or to make or prevent a two-thirds vote; or when the vote is by ballot (at the same time as everybody else).

13 Meeting follow-up is the action made after a gathering discussion. Business meetings are the best tool for a company as they provide crucial information about the company's progress or weaknesses. As a result, it is important to follow up after a meeting to ensure that any strategies planned are implemented successfully or any weaknesses identified are effectively eliminated to ensure the continued success of the company.

Examination-style questions

Multiple choice questions

1 What is the main reason for sending out adequate notice for an Annual General Meeting?
   a To ensure that the meeting is properly constituted.
   b To ensure sufficient time to arrange documentation.
   c To allow members to respond to the notice.
   d To give members time to prepare for the meeting.

2 An 'ad hoc committee' is best described as a committee which:
   a supervises the work of other committees
   b is set up to deal with a specific matter
   c is set up to select shareholders
   d is set up to decide on the profit margin of the company.

3 Members who cannot attend a meeting at which officers will be elected, but who wish to vote, can do so by:
   a poll
   b order
   c ballot
   d proxy.

4 For which of the following reasons should a meeting be postponed?
   a The chairperson is absent.
   b Minutes of the last meeting have not been prepared.
   c Too few members are present.
   d The agenda for the meeting was not mailed to members.

5 Which of the following should be present before a meeting is called to order?
   a panel
   b committee
   c quorum
   d proxy.

6 A formal proposal put forward at a meeting is known as a/an:
   a motion
   b resolution
   c adjournment
   d minute.

7 A poll is:
   a A secret vote by ballot.
   b A vote of no confidence.
   c Voting by a show of hands.
   d Voting by standing.

Structured questions

1 **a** List **six** possible reasons why meetings are held. [3]
   b Outline the reasons for the room and the equipment being important to the success of a meeting. [4]
   c List **three** activities that must be performed on the day of the meeting to ensure that the meeting is successful. [3]

2 **a** What is meant by the term 'quorum'? [2]
   b Assume that you are the chairperson at your committee meeting. Before you begin the meeting you realize that there are insufficient people present to start the meeting. List **two** actions you could take in this situation. [2]
   c Select any **two** of the following types of meeting and explain them:
      i   statutory meetings
      ii meetings of creditors
      iii annual general meetings
      iv executive committee meetings. [6]

3 **a** List and briefly describe **three** types of committee meeting. [6]
   b Assume that you are asked to prepare the notice of a meeting and ensure that all members are informed of the meeting. List the information you would need in order to prepare the notice and also to ensure that members are informed of the meeting. [6]
   c List and explain **four** important reasons for taking minutes at a meeting. [4]

4 **a** Explain the following terms:
      i   agenda
      ii proxy
      iii *sine die*
      iv minutes. [4]
   b Explain what is meant by Robert's Rules of Order governing meetings. [3]
   c Outline **two** of the rules which govern meetings. [4]
   d List the main personnel at a meeting. [3]

5 **a** List **three** reasons for distributing minutes of a meeting to members before the start of the next meeting. [3]
   b Imagine you are the secretary for your school's Netball Club. A meeting is scheduled to be held on July 16, 2011 at 2.30 pm in the Drama Room, to discuss matches to be played off campus. Prepare a notice for the meeting, to be sent to all concerned. [4]
   c Based on the information outlined in question 5b, prepare an agenda for the meeting. [5]

6 **a** Explain what is meant by follow-up duties after a meeting. [3]
   b You are responsible for the planning of Master Stitcher Carpeting Company's committee meeting. List **four** types of equipment that you may need to acquire in preparation for the meeting. [4]
   c Define the following meeting terms:
      i   proxy
      ii resolution
      iii lie on the table
      iv *ex-officio*. [4]

7 Travel arrangements

By the end of this chapter you should be able to:

- ☑ outline the role of travel agencies;
- ☑ describe the process of making air travel arrangements;
- ☑ outline the process of making car rental and hotel arrangements;
- ☑ prepare itineraries;
- ☑ prepare travel folders;
- ☑ identify time zones in relation to the Coordinated Universal Time;
- ☑ express time in 12-hour and 24-hour formats;
- ☑ interpret travel schedules;
- ☑ describe at least four documents required for travel;
- ☑ identify monetary instruments used when travelling.

Concept map   **Travel arrangements**

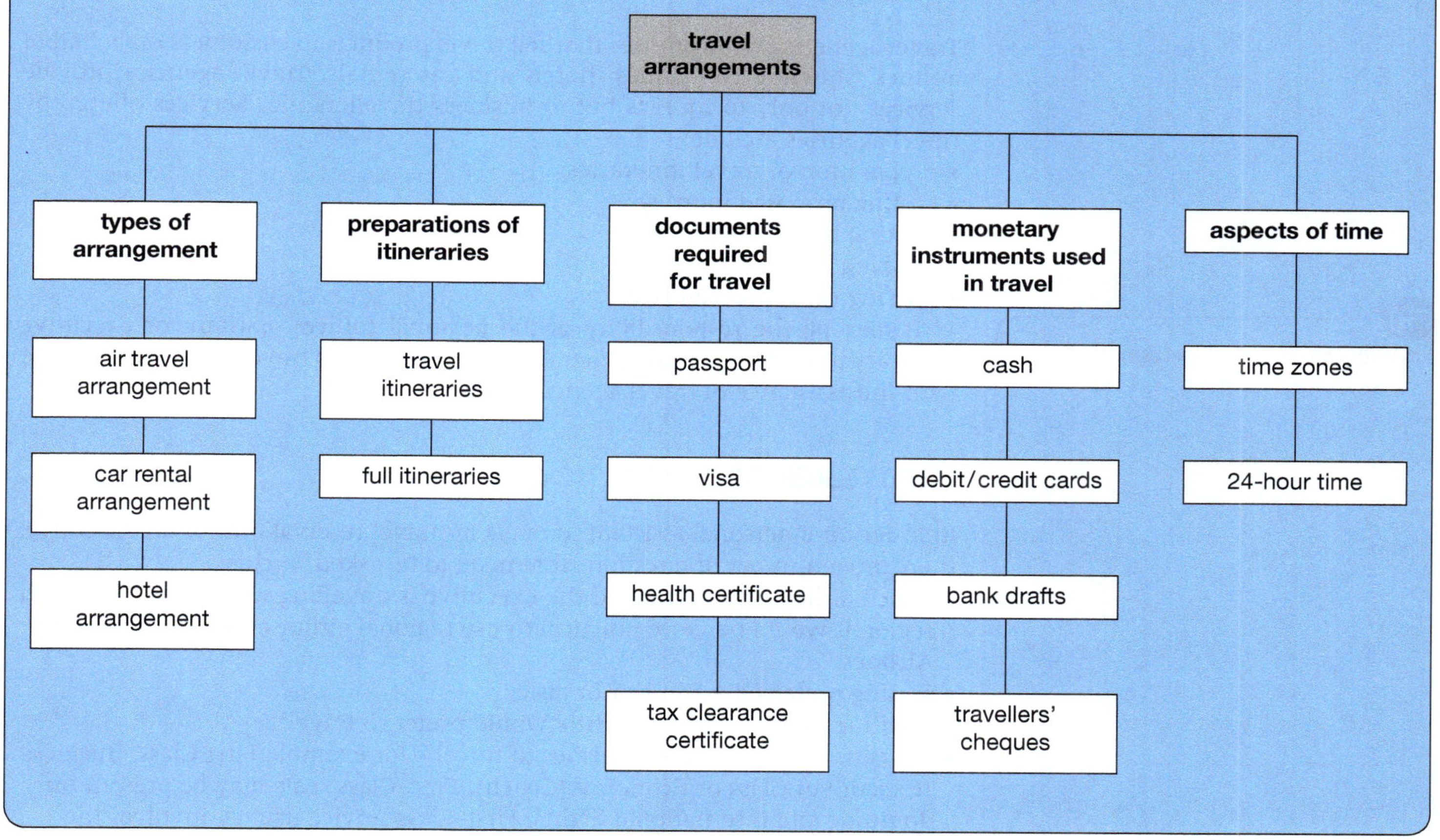

```
                          travel
                        arrangements
  ┌──────────────┬──────────────┬──────────────┬──────────────┐

  types of        preparations of   documents        monetary         aspects of time
  arrangement     itineraries       required         instruments used
                                    for travel       in travel

  air travel      travel            passport         cash             time zones
  arrangement     itineraries

  car rental      full itineraries  visa             debit/credit     24-hour time
  arrangement                                        cards

  hotel                             health           bank drafts
  arrangement                       certificate

                                    tax clearance    travellers'
                                    certificate      cheques
```

Making travel arrangements

There may be instances when an organization's executives need to take business trips, whether within the country or to another country, and so arrangements for such trips need to be made. Travel arrangements may be made by:

- the executive him/herself;
- a personal (office) assistant or an executive secretary;
- a Travel Department;
- a travel agency.

The Travel Department

Small companies may have one person in charge of making travel plans for employees, while a large company may have an entire Travel Department. A Travel Department is an important aspect of large organizations whose executives do a lot of travelling.

Personnel within this department will be responsible for managing travel programmes on behalf of staff members, as well as negotiating with hotels, airlines, car rental companies and other travel partners for preferred prices and discounts. They may also be responsible for coordinating the details and arrangements for conferences, meetings and other activities.

Travel agency

travel agencies ▶

Travel agencies are businesses that sell travel products to customers on behalf of airlines, shipping companies, hotels and car rentals. Travel agencies provide services not only to tourists but to business travellers too. Services offered by travel agencies include:

- preparation of travel itineraries;
- costing proposed journeys;
- making hotel reservations;
- booking cruises;
- making car rental reservations.

It may be the responsibility of the personal (office) assistant or executive secretary to deal with arrangements for the executive's travel. This may be done with the assistance of travel agencies.

ITQ1

Outline **three** duties of a travel agent.

Air travel arrangements

In order for a personal assistant to make air travel reservations for an executive, there are a number of questions that need to be asked, such as:

- which airline is preferred – if the executive is travelling within the Caribbean region it would be more practical to use regional airlines such as Caribbean Airlines;
- seating preferred – window or aisle;
- the time of day at which he/she would prefer to travel;
- the class by which he/she wishes to travel – for example First Class, Business (Executive) Class or Economy (Coach). First-Class seats may be present on domestic and international flights. First-Class service usually involves the provision of more leg room and premium meals and dedicated check-in desks. First-Class flights are, however, being phased out by some airlines as they are proving to be very costly. Some airlines have a Business or Executive Class. In many instances this is the highest class available. Airlines usually transport most passengers in Economy (Coach) Class which is the cheapest class of travel, offering the least comfort, with limited leg room

and amenities. Some airlines have renamed their economy class with names such as 'Tourist Class', 'Lovebird Economy' or 'World Traveller', to improve its image. 'Premium Economy' class varies from airline to airline, in the best cases taking the place of 'Business Class' transport;

- which airport the executive would want to depart from and arrive at – since some countries may have several airports, the one closest to where the business traveller will conduct business should be selected – for example, Jamaica has two major airports and three aerodromes;

- form of ticketing preferred – electronic tickets (or e-tickets) are becoming increasingly popular among commercial airline travellers as they are now a requirement of the International Air Transport Association (IATA). A traveller simply has to book their flight either on the internet or by telephone and is then assigned a confirmation number which will be provided at check-in. This makes the check-in process much smoother and quicker;

- does the executive wish to have the use of VIP lounges at the airport?;

- how does the executive wish to handle check-in? There are several ways in which travellers are able to check in, up to 24 hours in advance, instead of standing in long lines at the airline's desk. These include mobile check-in, web check-in and airport kiosk check-in. Mobile check-in is done by using an internet-enabled mobile device such as a cellular phone. Web check-in is done using a computer. Both the web and mobile check-in methods allow passengers, among other things, to select their seat and confirm their baggage amount. Some airports have self-service kiosks that allow passengers to check in as well as to print boarding passes and baggage tags.

An executive's personal assistant may choose to make air travel arrangements by going through a travel agent or by interfacing directly with the selected airline. Many airlines offer on-line services which include the booking of flights. This system provides quick and efficient service to its customers.

Figure 7.1 Checking in online for a flight

Figure 7.2 Air travel in the Caribbean

Car rental arrangements

Perhaps the personal assistant needs to make arrangements for ground transportation for the executive. Car rental arrangements may be made through a travel agency or directly with a car rental company. It is advisable that business travellers who wish to rent cars overseas obtain an International Driving Permit. This can be obtained from the driver's own country's driver's licence issuing authority. For example, in Jamaica, an International Driving Permit is obtained by producing a valid Jamaican driver's licence and two passport-size photographs. This service is free of charge and the permit is accepted in Commonwealth countries such as Trinidad, Bahamas and Grenada.

Special preferences of the driver must be identified – for example:

- body type of vehicle – sedan or SUV;
- left-hand or right-hand drive;
- manual or automatic transmission;
- colour of vehicle;
- GPS (Global Positioning System) or Satellite Navigation Systems.

In some cases company-owned vehicles and aeroplanes may be available for use during business travel. Reservations for use of these carriers must be made in advance to ensure their availability.

What is an International Driving Permit?

Hotel arrangements

Hotel reservations may be made by the personal assistant or by utilizing the services of a travel agent. Many hotel reservations are made by telephone or via the internet on the hotel's website. Written confirmation of these reservations is usually sent to the hotel by fax or e-mail.

Figure 7.3   Hotels

When making hotel reservations, preferences of the executive must be taken into consideration. They include:

- What is the cost? Does the executive have a loyalty card for any hotel chain?
- Type of room or suite needed – single/double occupancy or a room with a view?
- Do the rooms provide internet access or wireless internet connectivity and at what cost?
- Is the hotel all inclusive?
- How close is the hotel to meeting venues?
- How close is the hotel to the airport?
- Are there facilities such as gyms, swimming pools etc.?
- Is there 24-hour room service?

Many hotels and smaller motels cater specifically to business travellers and so provide many amenities to facilitate them, for example having computers with internet access in each room or suite.

We also need to find out the meal plans offered by the hotel chosen. These outline the rates charged for rooms and meals at a hotel. Types of meal plans include:

- **AI** – All-Inclusive: the price quoted includes the cost of the hotel room, all meals, drinks, tips and most non-motorized activities.
- **EP** – European Plan: the rate includes only the hotel room and no meals.
- **AP** – American Plan (also known as Full Board or FAP – Full American Plan): the price quoted includes hotel room and three meals per day.
- **MAP** – Modified American Plan (also known as Half Board): the rate includes hotel room plus two meals; breakfast and either lunch or dinner.
- **CP** – Continental Plan: the price quoted includes the hotel room plus a continental breakfast. All other meals attract an additional cost. Continental breakfast includes coffee, tea or juice and freshly baked products such as muffins and scones.
- **BP** – Breakfast Plan: the rate includes the cost of the room and breakfast.

There may be cases where meeting/conference rooms of hotels also need to be reserved. In order to do so, certain specific information needs to be forwarded to the hotel – for example:
- the number of meeting rooms that will be needed;
- the number of persons expected to be in attendance at each meeting;
- whether meals need to be provided, e.g. for coffee breaks or lunch;
- the provision of audio-visual equipment such as multimedia projectors.

Itineraries

The personal assistant or executive secretary may also be required to prepare an itinerary.

> DEFINITION: An **itinerary** is a list of places a traveller is to visit.

There are two types of itineraries: the travel itinerary and the full itinerary.
- The **travel itinerary** is one that is usually prepared by a travel agent and typically outlines arrival and departure times and ports.
- The **full itinerary** is more detailed, with information about the executive's meetings and other activities. The full itinerary would be prepared by the personal assistant who is more familiar with the executive's plans.

Itinerary

For:　**Elaine Palmer, Assistant Marketing Director**

From:　**January 2**　**To:　January 4, 2011**
　　　　　Trip to Fort Lauderdale, Florida

January 2, 2011
1150 hours　　ETD from Donald Sangster International Airport (MBJ) on Air Jamaica flight JM35; Executive class; Airbus 320; non-stop.

1435 hours　　ETA at Fort Lauderdale-Hollywood International Airport (FLL).

January 4, 2011
1535 hours　　ETD from Fort Lauderdale-Hollywood International Airport (FLL) on Air Jamaica Flight JM34; Executive class; Airbus 320; snack served

1615 hours　　ETA Donald Sangster International Airport (MBJ).

Figure 7.4　Travel itinerary

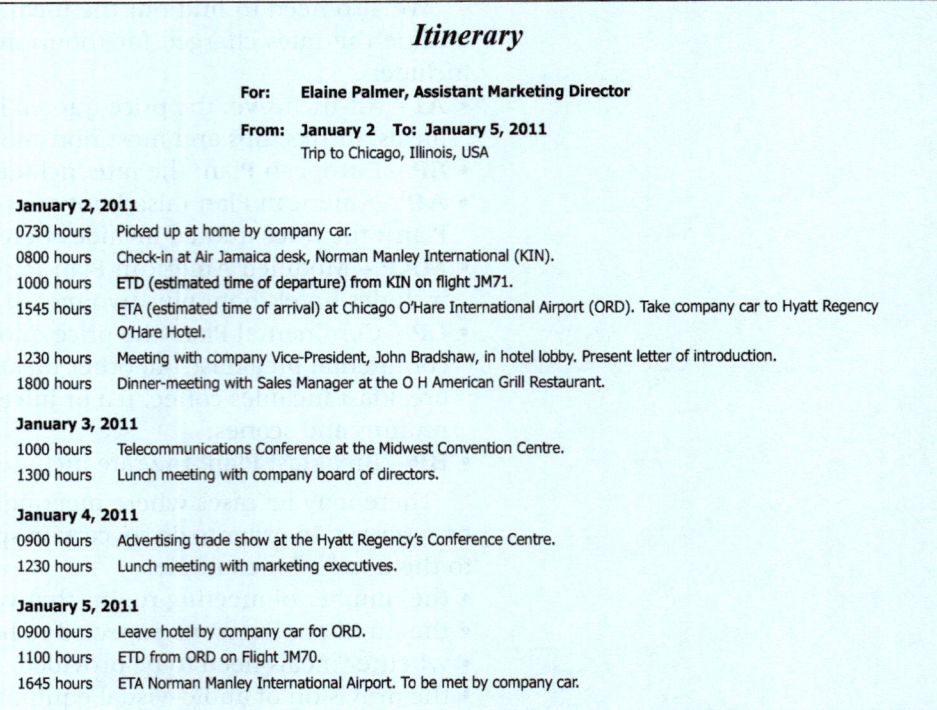

Figure 7.5 Full itinerary

ITQ3

Differentiate between a full itinerary and a travel itinerary.

Scheduling appointments

It will be the responsibility of the personal assistant to make appointments for meetings necessary while the traveller is in the foreign country. These appointments should be entered in his/her diary and placed in the travel folder. It may also be necessary to reschedule any appointments in the executive's own area that will be missed when he/she is away. As soon as it is discovered that the appointment will be missed, the client or customer should be contacted and arrangements made for a new meeting date and time.

Travel folder

Before the executive departs on his/her trip the personal assistant should organize specific materials in a folder. This will allow the executive to be able to find documents easily and efficiently when needed. Travel folders may contain:

• documents pertaining to the trip – for example a speech or presentation, either on paper or on a flash drive;
• valid passport;
• visa/entry permit;
• confirmations of travel – for example hotel/car rental reservations;
• itineraries;
• tickets or e-ticket confirmation number;
• confirmation of baggage allowances;
• certificate of vaccination;
• certificate of insurance;
• tax clearance certificate.

ITQ4

State **four** items you would expect to find in a business traveller's folder.

Time zones

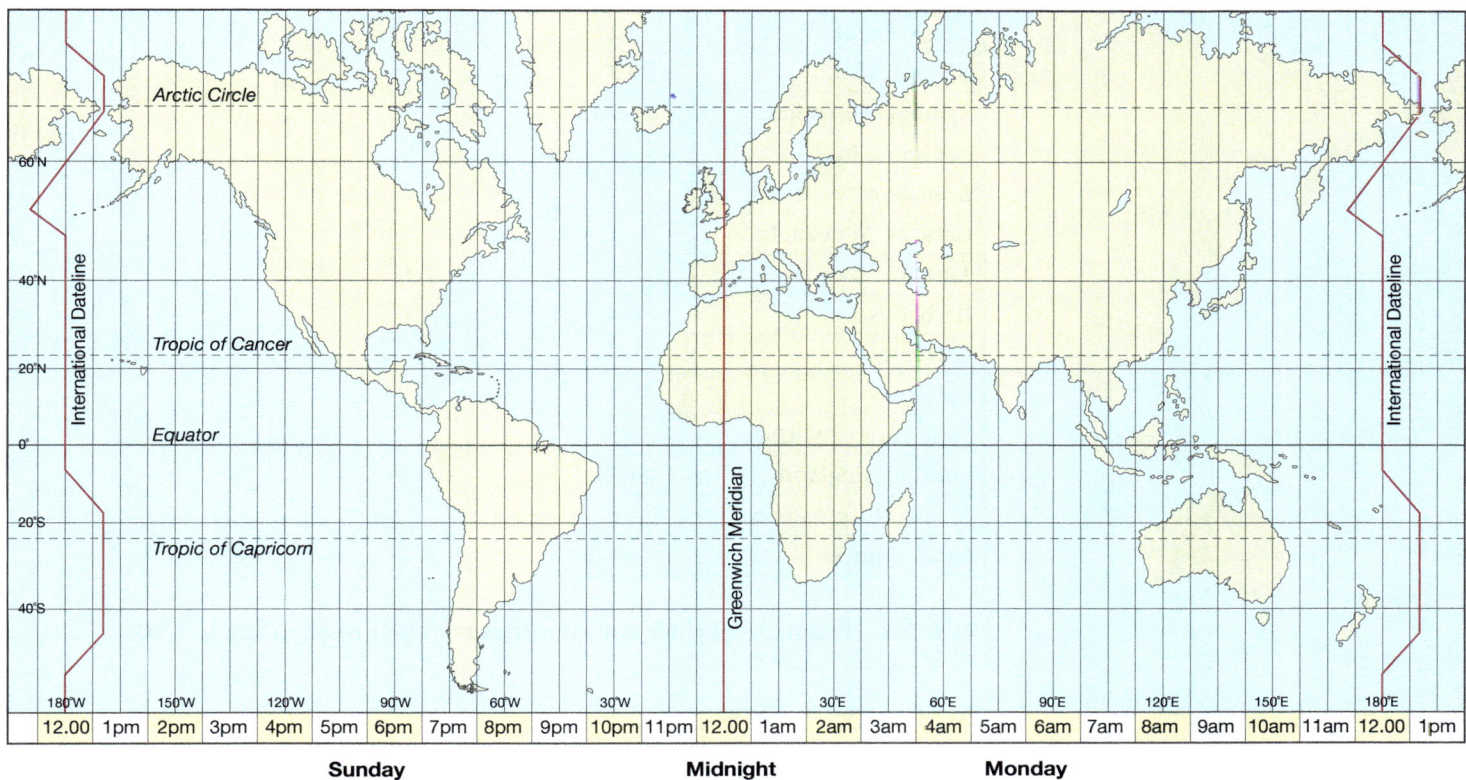

Figure 7.6 Map of time zones

Coordinated Universal Time ▶

The Coordinated Universal Time (UTC) (formerly known as Greenwich Mean Time (GMT), though the term 'GMT' is still widely used and understood) is the reference point for standard times throughout the world. The UTC allows for the synchronization of time across areas such as the internet, telephones, weather forecasts and radio stations. It was initially used to prevent confusion when referring to various local or standard time zones. For further information, see http://wwp.greenwichmeantime.co.uk/.

The UTC is important because of the increase in worldwide travel and communication. Travellers need to be clear in terms of the time of day in other parts of the world: this is primarily important when telephone calls need to be made from one country to another, making travel plans and coordinating teleconferencing and videoconferencing.

Time is usually given in relation to UTC. For example, 'Aruba UTC–4' means that Aruba is 4 hours behind UTC; 'Cairo, Egypt UTC+2' means that Cairo is 2 hours ahead of UTC.

Los Angeles, California	+9
Tokyo, Japan	+2
Cairo, Egypt	+2
Beijing, China	+8
Sydney, Australia	+10
Baghdad, Iraq	+3
Buenos Aires, Brazil	−3
Caracas, Venezuela	−4
Jamaica	−5
Barbados	−4
Grenada	−4
Bahamas	−3
New York City, USA	−5
London, England	UTC
Mexico City, Mexico	−6
Paris, France	+1

Table 7.1 Examples of cities and countries and their relationship to UTC

Facts about time zones

- The earth is divided into 24 time zones and within each time zone the same local or standard time is used.
- Each time zone is approximately 15 degrees wide, but there are variations because some time zones are bounded by country or state borders and it is usually easier to follow those borders.
- Neighbouring time zones have a one-hour time difference.

Daylight Saving or Summer Time ▶

- Some countries observe Daylight Saving Time or Summer Time, which means that local time is advanced by one hour at the beginning of spring and then returned in autumn. Daylight Saving Time is used to take advantage of the extra daylight hours. In Europe, Summer Time is observed from March to October. In Australia, Summer Time is observed from October to March or April. In most of North America, Daylight Saving Time begins in March and ends in November.
- Information on time zones can be found in reference books such as *Whitaker's Almanack* and the *World Almanac and Book of Facts*.

24-hour time

When referring to time, the International Organization for Standardization (ISO) recommends the use of 24-hour time. The 24-hour time is used in many documents such as travel itineraries, airline tickets and schedules and so knowledge of how to write it is essential.

The 24-hour time system is a way of keeping time where the day goes from midnight to midnight and is divided into 24 hours. The 24-hour clock is used in many countries and will reduce confusion experienced with the 12-hour clock. For example, if you are asked to meet someone at 6 o'clock, does that mean 6 am (in the morning) or 6 pm (in the evening)?

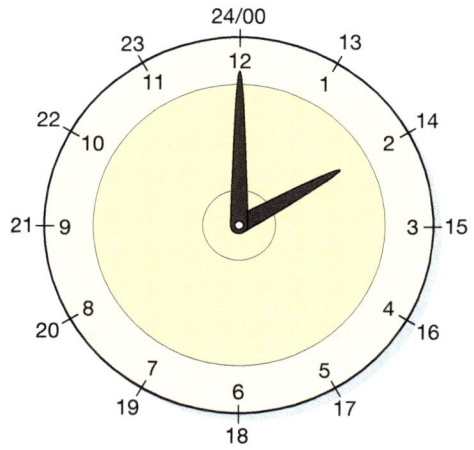

Figure 7.7 12-hour and 24-hour clocks

12-hour time

The am/pm system or 12-hour time uses a 12-hour clock where the day is divided into 12 hours from midnight to midday (am) and 12 hours from midday to midnight (pm).

24-hour time	12-hour time (AM/PM)
0000/2400	12 midnight
0100	1.00 am
0200	2.00 am
0300	3.00 am
0400	4.00 am
0500	5.00 am
0600	6.00 am
0700	7.00 am
0800	8.00 am
0900	9.00 am
1000	10.00 am
1100	11.00 am
1200	12 midday
1300	1.00 pm
1400	2.00 pm
1500	3.00 pm
1600	4.00 pm
1700	5.00 pm
1800	6.00 pm
1900	7.00 pm
2000	8.00 pm
2100	9.00 pm
2200	10.00 pm
2300	11.00 pm

Table 7.2 12-hour and 24-hour time

ITQ5

a Convert the following am times to 24-hour time:
 i 12.14 am;
 ii 5.32 am;
 iii 10.45 am;
 iv 8.20 am;
 v 11.03 am.
b Convert the following pm times to 24-hour time:
 i 6.18 pm;
 ii 10.39 pm;
 iii 2.08 pm;
 iv 12.40 pm;
 v 11.59 pm.
c Convert the following 24-hour times to am/pm time:
 i 1220 hours;
 ii 2200 hours;
 iii 0045 hours;
 iv 0218 hours;
 v 1815 hours.

ITQ6

Give your answers in 24-hour time.
a If it is 1100 hours UTC, what time is it in:
 i New York;
 ii Jamaica;
 iii Grenada;
 iv Sydney;
 v Bahamas?
b If it is 1045 hours in Jamaica, what time is it in:
 i Barbados;
 ii Bahamas;
 iii Cairo;
 iv London;
 v Mexico City?

Converting from 12-hour/am/pm time to 24-hour time

Converting from am time to 24-hour time

For the first hour of the day:
From 12 midnight to 12.59 am, subtract 12 hours.

For example: 12.10 am   0010 hours
              12.41 am   0041 hours.

NB. The use of the word 'hours' in the 24-hour time is optional, so the answer above could have been written as '0041'.

When converting other am time, the time remains the same.

For example: 11.20 am   1120 hours
              9.38 am   0938 hours.

NB. The 24-hour time should have four digits, so whenever the hours are less than ten, a zero is placed at the beginning of the time.

Converting from pm time to 24-hour time

From 12 noon to 12.59 pm, there is no change.

For example: 12.30 pm   1230 hours
              12.52 pm   1252 hours

From 1 pm to 11.59 pm, add 12 hours

For example   3.34 pm   1534 hours
              11.41 pm   2341 hours.

Travel schedules

Schedules or timetables are prepared for air, sea and land (bus, rail) travel. Timetables may be presented in booklet/journal form, however, many carriers also have schedules on their websites or other areas on the internet. They can also be obtained from travel agencies.

Airline schedules may include information such as the number of seats on a plane, the departure and arrival times and meals provided. The OAG (Official Airline Guide) manages the schedules for many airlines and produces timetables for them. A reference book, *OAG Flight Guide*, is published monthly.

Sea schedules and timetables are available from the various carriers either at their offices or on their websites. However, these schedules can also be obtained from the reference book *Cruise and Ferry Guide*, which outlines timetables and directories for cruise ships and ferries.

The *Official Railway Guide* is a timetable published bi-monthly and gives routing and shipping information for freight on US railroads.

LIAT AIRLINE

From: Antigua (ANU)[1]

To: Barbados (BGI)[2]

From – To[3]	Days[4]	Stops[5]	Departure time[6]	Arrival time[7]	Flight number[8]	Aircraft[9]	Elapsed time[10]
April 1–30, 2011	1234567	0	0920	1050	L151	DH3	1 hr 30 minutes
To: Georgetown, Guyana (GEO)							
April 1–30, 2011	1234567	1	0920	1415	L521	DH3	4 hours 55 minutes

Notes:
1 – Departure city
2 – Arrival city
3 – Period of validity of flights
4 – Days of operation, e.g. 1 – Monday, 2 – Tuesday, 3 – Wednesday …7 – Sunday
5 – Number of stops
6 – Time of departure
7 – Time of arrival (+1 means next day arrival)
8 – Flight information consisting of airline code and flight number
9 – Type of aircraft, e.g. Airbus A320, Boeing 737
10 – Total elapsed time from departure to arrival in hours and minutes

Figure 7.8 Travel schedule extract

ITQ7

The following questions relate to the travel schedule in Figure 7.8.

a On the flight from Antigua to Guyana, how many stops are made?

b How long does the flight last?

c On which days will there be flights from Antigua to Barbados?

d State the type of aircraft used.

e What is the time of departure from Antigua to Barbados?

f What is the time of arrival in Barbados?

There are certain codes that need to be known in order to interpret travel schedules. Each airline has a unique two-letter code created by the IATA (International Air Transport Association), which enables the smooth running of electronic applications relating to passenger and cargo. This abbreviation precedes the flight number.

Airline designators

Designator	Name of airline
CU	Cubana Airlines
JM	Air Jamaica
KX	Cayman Airways
YI	Air Sunshine
WM	Winair
JY	Air Turks and Caicos
LI	LIAT (Leeward Islands Air Transport) [In 2007 Caribbean Star Airlines merged with former rival LIAT Ltd and currently operates under the LIAT brand.]
BW	Caribbean Airlines
TY	Air Caraibes
AA	American Airlines
AC	Air Canada
BA	British Airways
NK	Spirit Airlines
VS	Virgin Atlantic

Table 7.3 A selection of airline designators

Airport codes

Each airport has a unique code made up of three letters.

Code	City or country	Name of airport
GCM	Georgetown, Cayman	Owen Roberts International
HAV	Havana, Cuba	Jose Marti International
TAB	Tobago	Crown Point Airport
POS	Port of Spain, Trinidad	Piarco International
BGI	Barbados	Grantley Adams International
GND	Grenada	Point Salines International
UVF	St Lucia	Hewanorra International
MBJ	Montego Bay, Jamaica	Donald Sangster International
MIA	Miami, Florida	Miami International
YYZ	Toronto, Canada	Lester B Pearson International
LGW	London, England	Gatwick Airport
LHR	London, England	Heathrow Airport
GEO	Georgetown, Guyana	Cheddi Jagan International
KIN	Kingston, Jamaica	Norman Manley International

ITQ8

Identify **two** reference books which can be used to obtain travel schedules.

Table 7.4 A selection of airport codes

Special regulations for air travel

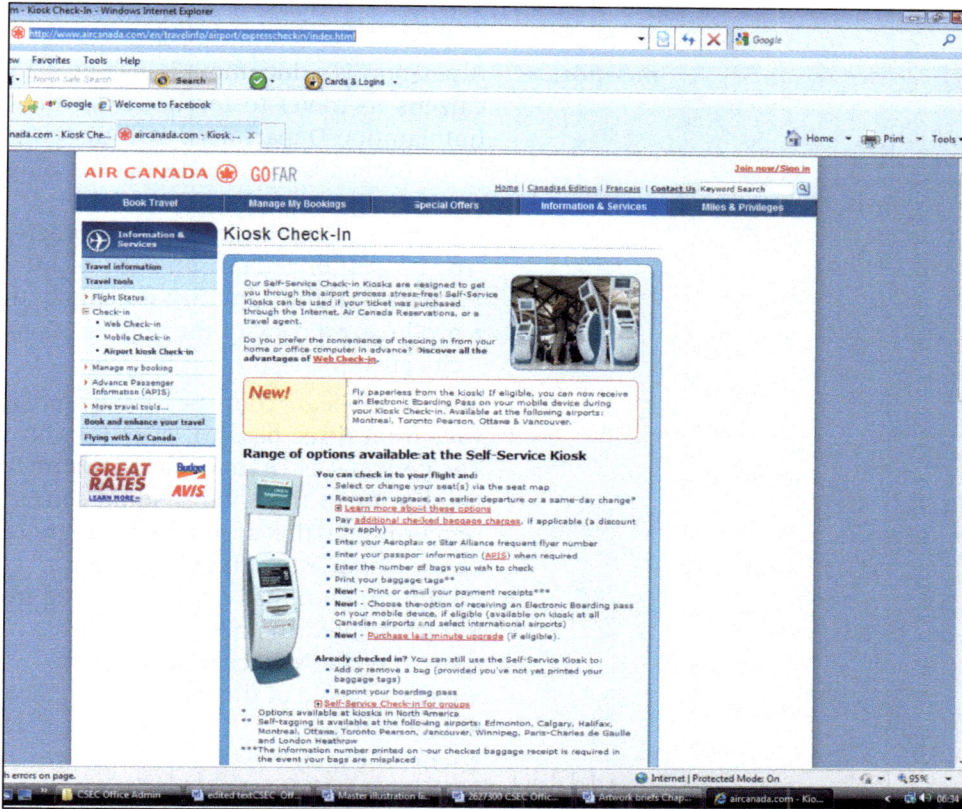

Figure 7.9 Special regulations for air travel (correct as at February 2011)

While air travel has become a routine and easy way of travelling, there are certain regulations of which travellers need to be made aware. These include:

- check-in-times for international flights vary from airline to airline, but usually fall within one to three hours before the flight time;
- carry-on baggage allowance;
- checked baggage allowance;
- excess baggage allowance;
- the amount of currency that can legally be taken into a country;
- items that may be prohibited or require special licence – for example, plants or pets;
- new security measures stipulate rules such as that any bottle of liquid in carry-on baggage should contain no more than 100 ml.

It is the responsibility of the personal assistant to find out from the various airlines or customs agencies of the country being visited about special regulations that must be adhered to. The travel agency will also be able to assist with information on airline and country regulations.

Documents required for travel

Passport

passport ▶ A passport is a document issued by a government which gives permission for its citizens to travel to foreign countries. A passport may be obtained from the Immigration Department of your country.

In Barbados the process of obtaining a passport includes the following steps:
* completing an application form;
* providing two passport-size photographs, one of which should be certified by an authorized person such as a notary public or justice of the peace who attests that the applicant is actually the individual on the photograph;
* producing a copy of the applicant's original birth certificate or proof of citizenship.

Most Caribbean countries have similar procedures, and processing times can vary from three days to several weeks. Passports are usually valid for ten years. The personal assistant needs to ensure that the executive's passport is sufficiently valid prior to the trip, as some countries require at least six months' validity remaining at the time of travel. Travellers who make frequent journeys can obtain passports with extra pages.

Information that can be obtained from a passport includes:
* the traveller's name;
* the traveller's place of birth
* place of issue of the passport;
* date of issue;
* date of expiry
* signature of the traveller;
* occupation of the traveller;
* names of countries previously visited and the duration of those visits;
* visas.

Visa

> DEFINITION: A **visa** is an endorsement made in a passport that allows the bearer to enter the country issuing it for the purpose outlined in the visa, such as travel, work or study.

visa ▶ A visa is usually in effect for a specified period of time, for example five years, after which the traveller will need to re-apply. Not all countries require visas for entry, so the personal assistant should find out beforehand if the country being visited by the executive requires a visa. Visas are usually obtained by applying to the embassy, consulate or high commission of the country to be visited. A fee may be payable and application may need to be made well before the date of travel.

Entry permit

entry permit ▶ An entry permit is an endorsement granted by an authority that denotes that an application has been examined and approved for the bearer to reside, work or study for a specific length of time after entry. Permits usually expire when a person leaves the country.

Health certificate

International travel can pose various health risks. The World Health Organization (WTO) encourages vaccination and other precautionary measures against diseases such as yellow fever and malaria.

The international certificate of vaccination is one document endorsed by the WHO, however, individual countries' vaccination cards are also accepted. Proof of vaccination is often required for travellers coming from countries with a risk of yellow fever transmission. For example, Anguilla requires a yellow fever vaccination certificate for travellers over one year of age coming from countries with such a risk. Country requirements are subject to change at any time. The personal assistant should find out whether the country being visited has any special requirements regarding vaccinations.

Tax clearance certificate

tax clearance certificate ▶

A tax clearance certificate is issued by a country's revenue or tax department to confirm that an individual departing the country has no tax liabilities. The certificate is usually shown to the customs or immigration personnel on departure.

Monetary instruments used in travel

There are a number of ways in which a business traveller can carry funds.

Cash

A popular method of carrying funds is by using cash. In order for the executive to travel with cash, the traveller or personal assistant should ascertain the legal tender of a country and what other currencies may be acceptable. For example, in Jamaica, the legal tender is the Jamaican dollar, however, the United States dollar is accepted by many local merchants.

Various countries have different regulations regarding the amount of cash that can be brought in. The personal assistant should find out the specific regulations regarding the country being visited.

Foreign currencies may be purchased by banks or other legal foreign currency trading institutions, such as cambios.

The traveller may request a travel advance of cash to pay for expenses which may be incurred during the trip, such as taxi fares. Upon return, receipts of all expenses should be produced.

Traveller's cheques

traveller's cheques ▶

Traveller's cheques are a safer way to carry funds. Sequentially numbered traveller's cheques are available in various denominations and currencies, for example US dollar or British pound sterling. Traveller's cheques may be purchased from commercial banks and a few other financial institutions for a small fee. The business traveller must purchase the cheque in person and sign each traveller's cheque at the time of acquisition, in the presence of the bank representative. When the traveller arrives in the foreign country and is ready to cash the cheque, it must be signed again in the presence of the sales agent, who will verify the two signatures, with the help of some form of identification such as a passport. Traveller's cheques may be redeemed at hotels and some restaurants.

Letter of credit

letter of credit ▶ A letter of credit allows the travelling executive to draw funds from a specific bank in the foreign country up to a predetermined amount while on trips. The letter of credit is prepared by a local bank, for a fee.

Credit cards

Travel expenses may be charged directly to the organization by using business credit cards issued to the traveller. In other cases, personal credit cards may be used, with receipts submitted to the organization for reimbursement.

Some common credit cards are Visa, MasterCard, American Express and Discover. Some credit cards are not widely accepted because of high penalties charged to merchants and customers, so it is recommended that an executive travel with more than one credit card.

Internationally accepted credit cards, for example Visa, may be used at ATMs to obtain cash advances. Some dual-currency ATMs will facilitate payment in two currencies, for example the currency of the country being visited and the US dollar.

Figure 7.10   Credit and debit cards

Debit cards

debit cards ▶ Debit cards, although similar in appearance to credit cards, do not allow the card holder to spend money he/she does not have. The debit card is linked directly to a savings or current account and so when it is used for payment the amount charged is taken from the account. Debit cards can also be used to access funds from an account through an ATM. Arrangements can also be made with the bank to use the card in other countries.

Bank drafts

bank draft ▶ A bank draft is a cheque guaranteed by a bank and made payable to the person requesting it, another bank or a third party. Bank drafts are usually issued in a foreign currency and are considered to be as good as cash. They are used in situations where a transaction involves a large sum of money or when a supplier is unwilling to accept personal cheques. The customer will request a bank draft from his bank to be made payable to the seller. The bank will either collect the cash from the customer or withdraw the amount from the customer's account to cover the cheque. The bank will then prepare a bank draft to be made payable to the supplier. The bank draft is usually prepared in return for a fee.

Summary

- Travel agency duties include costing proposed trips, making hotel reservations and booking car rental reservations.
- Travel folders may contain passports, visas, itineraries and tickets.
- Travel schedules may be prepared for air, sea and land transportation.
- Airline schedules such as the *OAG Flight Guide* provide information such as the arrival and departure times of airlines.
- Documents required for travel include passports, visas and entry permits.
- Monetary instruments used in travel include traveller's cheques, credit cards, debit cards and letters of credit.

Answers to ITQs

1 Booking cruises; making hotel reservations; preparing itineraries.

2 An International Driving Permit is a document which, when used alongside a valid licence from the traveller's home country, allows him/her to drive a motor vehicle in a foreign country.

3 The travel itinerary is usually prepared by the travel agency and includes mainly information on arrival and departure times while the full itinerary is usually prepared by the executive's personal assistant and includes information on appointments and meetings.

4 Four items found in the travel folder include: passport, itinerary, ticket and tax clearance certificate.

5 **a** **i** 0014 hours
    ii 0532 hours
    iii 1045 hours
    iv 0820 hours
    v 1103 hours.
  b **i** 1818 hours
    ii 2239 hours
    iii 1408 hours
    iv 1240 hours
    v 2359 hours.
  c **i** 12.20 pm
    ii 10.00 pm
    iii 12.45 am
    iv 2.18 am
    v 6.15 pm.

6 **a** **i** 0600 hours
    ii 0600 hours
    iii 0700 hours
    iv 2200 hours
    v 0800 hours.
  b **i** 1145 hours
    ii 1245 hours
    iii 1745 hours
    iv 1545 hours
    v 0945 hours.

7 a One.

b 4 hours 55 minutes.

c Monday, Tuesday, Wednesday, Thursday, Friday, Saturday and Sunday.

d DH3.

e 0920 hours or 9.20 am.

f 1050 hours or 10.50 am.

8 *Whitaker's Almanack* and *World Almanac and Book of Facts*.

Examination-style questions

Multiple choice questions

1 Which meal plan's price includes only the cost for the hotel room?

a All-inclusive.

b American Plan.

c European Plan.

d Continental Plan.

2 The document that outlines a list of places that a traveller wishes to visit is a/an:

a itinerary

b airline schedule

c travel folder

d passport.

3 'IATA' stands for

a International Air Transport Association.

b International Air Travel Association.

c International Air Traffic Association.

d International Airline Travel Association.

4 The main reference book on airline schedules around the world is:

a *Cruise and Ferry Guide.*

b *OAG Flight Guide.*

c *Official Railway Guide.*

d *OAG Aeroplane Guide.*

5 When making airline reservations for a traveller, the travel agent does **not** need to know which of the following?:

a airline of choice

b seating preference

c employee's job title

d class of travel.

Questions 6–10 relate to the itinerary in Figure 7.11:

March 8–10, 2011	
March 8, 2011	
0630 hours	Check-in Caribbean Airlines Desk, Piarco International Airport (POS), Trinidad.
0800 hours	ETD from Piarco International on Flight BW 414.
1235 hours	ETA at Norman Manley International, Kingston, Jamaica (KIN). Hire taxi to the Knutsford Court Hotel.
1900 hours	Cocktail reception in the hotel's ballroom.
March 9, 2011	
0900 hours	Company's AGM at the Jamaica Conference Centre.
1800 hours	Dinner-meeting with company executives in the hotel's restaurant.
March 10, 2011	
1000 hours	Check-in at Norman Manley International Airport.
1405 hours	ETD from Norman Manley International.
2035 hours	ETA at Piarco International Airport.

Figure 7.11 Itinerary for James Smart

6 What does the abbreviation 'ETA' mean?
   a European Travel Agency
   b Estimated Time of Arrival
   c Estimated Travel Agency
   d Electronic Travel Agenda.

7 How long is the flight from Trinidad to Jamaica?
   a 5 hours
   b 6 hours
   c 6 hours 30 minutes
   d 4 hours 35 minutes.

8 What is the airport code for the Piarco International Airport?
   a BGI
   b PIT
   c POS
   d KIN.

9 'BW' is the airline designator for which airline?
   a British Airways
   b Bermuda Airlines
   c Virgin Atlantic
   d Caribbean Airlines.

10 What is the airport code for Norman Manley International Airport?
   a KIN
   b MBJ
   c POS
   d BGI.

Structured questions

1 **a** State **two** reasons why it is important to prepare an itinerary for a business traveller. [2]
   b Identify **three** factors that must be considered when making hotel reservations. [3]

2 Your executive is travelling to Puerto Rico on business.
   a Outline **four** ways by which he / she can make payments in the foreign country. [4]
   b State **one** advantage or disadvantage of each way selected in **a** above. [4]

3 Prepare a full itinerary for your executive's four-day business trip to Barbados. [15]

4 Convert the following am/pm times to 24-hour time:
   • 1.17 am
   • 3.55 pm
   • 6.08 pm
   • 9.30 am
   • 12.05 pm
   • 12 midnight
   • 11.59 pm
   • 12.36 am
   • 7.19 pm
   • 2.57 pm. [10]

5 Convert the following 24-hour times to am/pm times:
- 0150 hours
- 2340 hours
- 1856 hours
- 0010 hours
- 0005 hours
- 1317 hours
- 0542 hours
- 1121 hours
- 2021 hours
- 2255 hours. [10]

6 Your business is located in Kingston, Jamaica, and your executive will be travelling to a number of overseas countries in the coming month. You are responsible for making his/her travel arrangements. Find out the local times in the following countries that he/she will be visiting, when it is 0800 hours in Kingston. Write your answers in 24-hour time.
- **a** Caracas, Venezuela
- **b** Buenos Aires, Argentina
- **c** Mexico City, Mexico
- **d** New York City, USA
- **e** Aruba. [5]

8 Human resources management

By the end of this chapter you should be able to:

- ☑ describe the role and function of the Human Resources Department;
- ☑ understand the relationship of the Human Resources Department with other departments;
- ☑ identify the duties and responsbilities of a Human Resources Clerk;
- ☑ prepare and maintain records used in a Human Resources Department;
- ☑ identify the benefits of legislation related to workers' welfare;
- ☑ describe the factors that contribute to employee turnover in an organization.

Concept map   Human resources management

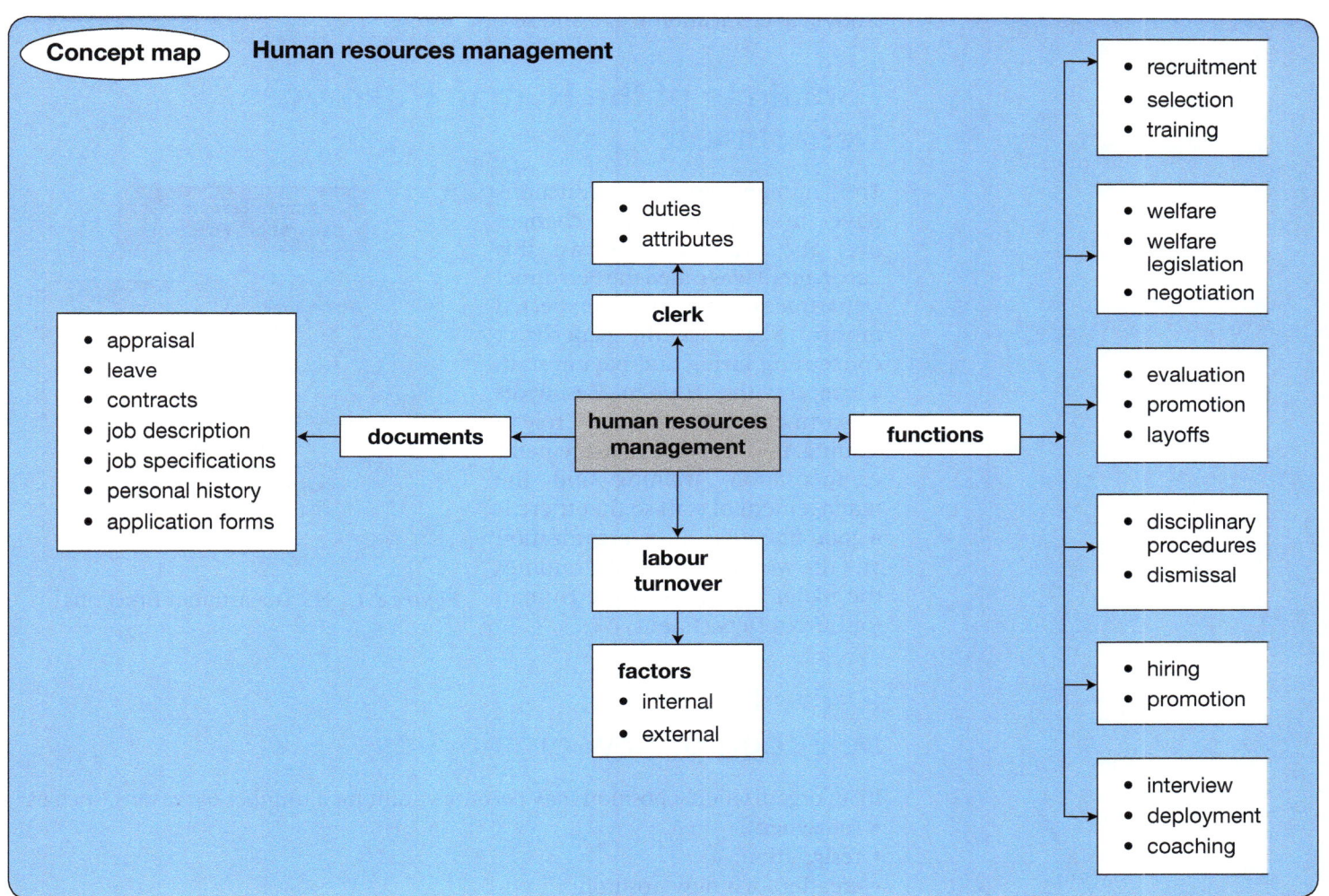

163

The Human Resources Department

human resources ▶

'Human resources' is a term used to refer to how employees are managed by organizations, or to the Personnel Department charged with that role. The main objective of the Human Resources Department is to meet the organizational needs of the company with regard to human resources. The Human Resources Department is seen as the hub of the organization, serving as a liaison between all concerned. Depending on the size of the company, the Human Resources Department might be called the Personnel Department, with a manageable workforce that can be handled by a Personnel Manager and a small staff. For larger organizations with hundreds of departments and divisions, the task is much more demanding, thus the need for a Human Resources Department.

It is important for the Human Resources Department to work closely with other departments, as they must inform the Human Resources Department of their staffing needs, including the need for temporary staff when necessary. The Human Resources Department is also responsible for the welfare of staff – for example, it processes paperwork for employees who go on maternity leave, study leave, vacation leave and so on.

Functions of the Human Resources Department

The human resources functions have undergone many changes over the years. In the past this department was called the Personnel Department and was expected mostly to manage the paperwork concerning hiring and paying staff. Currently, the Human Resources Department plays an integral role in staffing, performance management, compensation, training and the management of staff so that there is a good fit between the organization and the workers. Figure 8.1 outlines the major functions of the Human Resources Department.

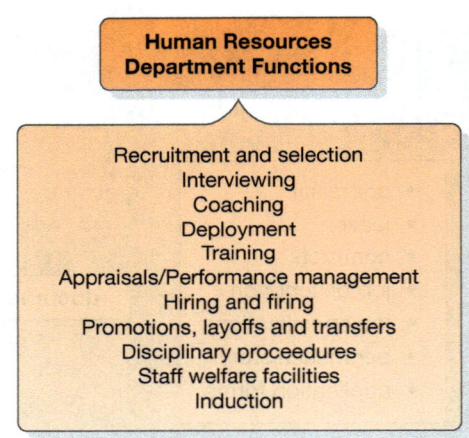

Human Resources
Department Functions

Recruitment and selection
Interviewing
Coaching
Deployment
Training
Appraisals/Performance management
Hiring and firing
Promotions, layoffs and transfers
Disciplinary proceedures
Staff welfare facilities
Induction

Figure 8.1 HR Department functions

Recruitment and selection of new employees

In an organization a position may become vacant for a number of reasons, such as:
- retirement;
- resignation;
- creation of a new position;
- dismissal;
- expansion of the organization;
- death of an employee.

ITQ1
List **three** functions of the Human Resources Department.

recruiting ▶

Recruiting the right staff to fit the job, thus fostering the achievement of the organizational objective, is an important part of an organization's human resource planning and its competitive strength. Employing suitably qualified people in the right positions in the organization can give it an edge over its competitors. Recruitment is therefore concerned with attracting, screening and selecting the number and quality of workers to fit a job who can help the organization achieve its goals and objectives. Recruitment can be time consuming as well as expensive: as a result, care must be taken so that the 'right' person is selected for the job.

Before the Human Resources Manager decides to recruit staff he/she must first decide on the following:

- the skills and personal qualities needed for the job;
- the method to be used when attracting staff;
- the method of employment (part time or full time);
- whether the post can be filled internally.

Recruitment options

When recruiting staff, the Human Resources Manager can use any of five methods:

- employment agencies;
- recruitment websites;
- headhunters;
- in-house recruitment; or
- niche agencies.

Employment agencies

employment agencies ▶
employment bureaux ▶

Employment agencies are also called employment bureaux. These agencies have offices which allow candidates to visit and where they may be tested and interviewed to determine whether they are employable. When there is a suitable job opening, qualified candidates are contacted and sent to interviews.

Candidates wishing to use this method of employment must pay a fee to the agency before any job interview. If the candidate is offered a job they will then pay, for example one week's or one month's salary to the agency, depending on the agreement made at the time of signing the contract.

Recruitment websites

More and more large organizations have turned to recruitment websites as a means of getting suitably qualified candidates to fill their job vacancies. Recruitment websites allow organizations to advertise job vacancies. Available job openings are listed and interested candidates are able to upload their *curriculum vitae* (CV) to be included in searches by interested companies. Online recruiting helps organizations to attract, test, recruit, employ and retain quality staff with the minimum administration cost.

Job board

job board ▶

A job board is an online location that provides an up-to-date listing of current job vacancies in various industries. Applicants are able to apply for employment through the job board itself. Many job boards have a variety of additional services to help job seekers manage their careers and their ongoing job search processes.

Headhunters

headhunter ▶

A headhunter is a job recruiter who specializes in finding highly skilled professionals. He/she is contracted to locate senior management to fill executive-level jobs or to recruit specialists (for example, scientists), usually when other methods of locating these workers have failed. Organizations benefit from using headhunters as they eliminate the need to advertise the position and having to go through the list of applicants when there may be no guarantee of finding a

165

suitably qualified candidate. Headhunters are paid a fee if they are able to find the right candidate for the job.

In-house recruitment

in-house recruitment ▶
referrals ▶

With in-house recruitment, recruiters may advertise job vacancies on their own websites, use internal employee referrals, work with external associations, trade groups and/or source candidates from college graduates by setting up recruitment drives.

Niche agencies

niche agency ▶

A niche agency is a type of recruitment agency that is widely accepted as part of the recruitment industry. There are many specialized firms who recruit for specific jobs. For example, an agency may recruit only teachers or nurses. Because these agencies focus on the recruitment of specific skills, they are able to produce good results. In Jamaica there are many niche agencies responsible for recruiting teachers, nurses, hotel workers and many others.

Stages in the recruitment process

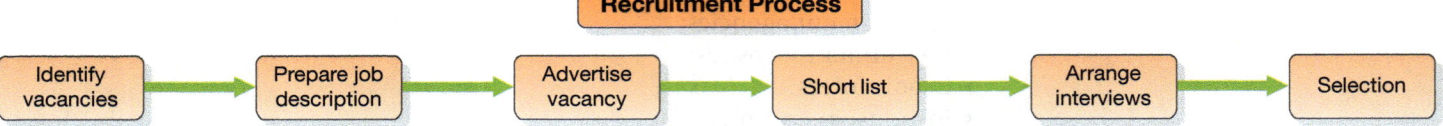

Figure 8.2 Recruitment process

Job analysis

job analysis ▶

Job analysis is the process of gathering information about the requirements and necessary skills for a job in order to create a job description.

ITQ2

Place ticks in the columns labelled 'True' or 'False' to indicate your answers to the following statements:

Items	Statements	True	False
1	When the unemployment level is high, you may have to offer increased compensation or benefits incentives to attract quality applicants, as you will be in stiff competition with other employers to attract such applicants.		
2	Many organizations use promotion from within as a motivation tool and a reward for good work or longevity with the organization.		
3	The most common method of finding qualified applicants from inside the organization is the grapevine.		

ITQ3

Place ticks in the columns labelled 'True' or 'False' to indicate your answers to the following statements:

Items	Statements	True	False
1	Even though internet recruiting may speed up the application process, it still requires trained HR staff to screen all applications and administer selection tests.		
2	In spite of all the new innovations in recruitment, newspaper ads are still the best method of generating a pool of qualified applicants.		
3	The ADA requires accommodation by employers so that a disabled applicant has equal opportunity to apply for job openings, regardless of the nature of the accommodation.		

Job description

job description ▶

A job description is a written statement that lists the duties, required qualifications, knowledge, skills and responsibilities of a position, as well as salary range – all based on a job analysis. Job descriptions also outline the person to whom the employee should report.

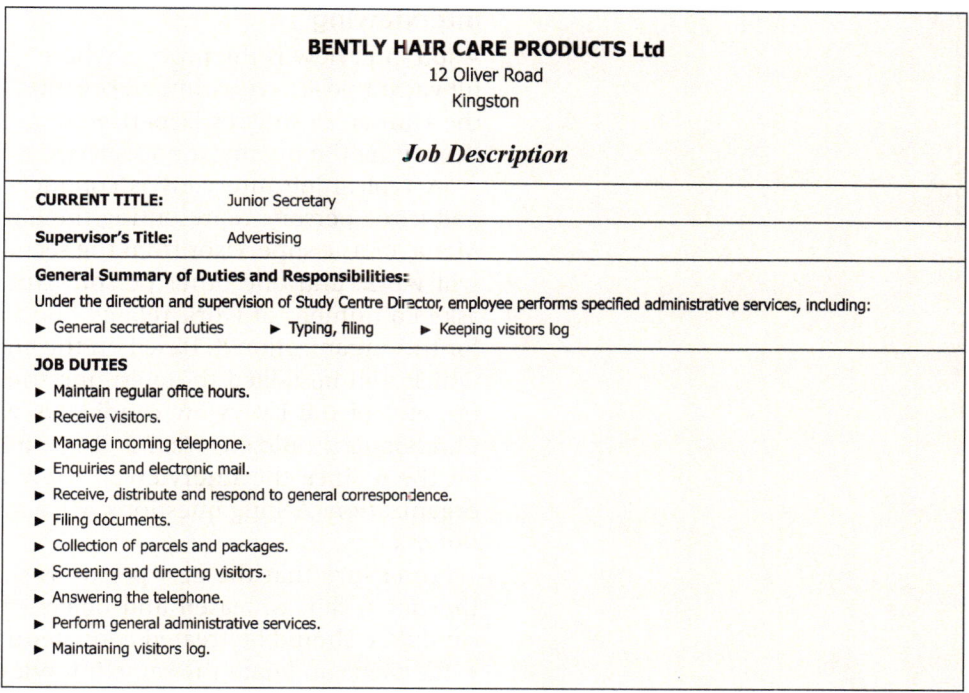

Figure 8.3 Example of a job description

ITQ4

A job description must include all of the following elements except which one?
a title;
b department;
c emergency numbers to call;
d reporting relationship.

Job advertisement

classified section ▶ Many organizations use the classified section of the newspaper; the radio; television; billboards; or magazines to advertise job vacancies. Job advertisements should be designed so that they attract the right number and quality of candidates for the job. A good ad, no matter what its size, should inform prospective candidates about the company and what it does; outline the actual job to be done (main duties); the title of the job; qualifications; and experience needed for the job; as well as how to apply.

Figure 8.4 Example of an advertisement

Short-listing suitable applicants

short-listing ▶ Short-listing applications is the process of deciding which applicants should be offered an interview and which applicants can be ruled out immediately. Short-listing must be completed based on the job specifications outlined in the job advertisement. Applicants not meeting the criteria based on the qualifications and experience required will not be called to an interview.

Interviewing

A job interview is the process whereby prospective employees are evaluated to fill vacant positions within an organization. Interviewing is a crucial function of the Human Resources Department, as the quality of the people employed can determine the organization's success or failure.

A typical job interview is conducted with the candidate and between one and three persons representing the employer, including the Human Resources Manager, the supervisor from the section or department in which the candidate will work, and one other person. During the interview the candidate will be asked a number of work-related questions, such as 'Why do you wish to work for this organization?'. Based on the answers given, candidates will score points which will be tallied to determine the most suitable candidate for the job. At the end of the interview candidates will be given a chance to ask questions. Candidates should ensure that they capitalize on this area, as it reflects positively on them since the interviewers view appropriate questions as interest in the organization. Asking questions will give a candidate an edge over those who do not ask any.

To ensure that the best person is selected for the job, interviewers must be thorough, fair, unbiased and objective. To achieve this at an interview, each candidate should be treated consistently. Therefore the interviewers should:
- ask each candidate the same interview questions;
- use follow-up questions, as appropriate;
- ask clear, concise and job-relevant questions;
- ask open-ended questions where possible, in order to give candidates the opportunity to discuss their abilities;
- not allow any discriminatory questions, such as asking about the religious background of the prospective candidate, race, age, gender or marital status.
    Here are some suitable questions for candidates to ask:
- Will I be mentored at the start of the job?
- What kinds of processes are in place to help me work collaboratively?
- What can I bring to this to help the team achieve more?
- Do team members typically eat lunch together or do they eat at their desks?

ITQ5

List **two** statutory provisions implemented by law for the protection of employees.

Local newspaper	Trade magazines
Local radio or television	Notice boards
Employment agencies	Notices at the gates of firms
Internal bulletins or memo	Internet

Table 8.1   Places where job vacancies may be advertised

Selection

Employers must select from those interviewed the most suitable applicant to fill the vacancy. At this stage all applicants who are considered may be interviewed again and / or tested, after which a selection will be made.

In selecting the successful candidate, the panel must make a decision based on the merit and eligibility of the candidates as judged by:
- content of application;
- qualifications (if required for the post);
- performance at interview;
- outcome of any selection tests.

ITQ6

Place ticks in the columns labelled 'True' or 'False' to indicate your answers to the following statements:

Items	Statements	True	False
1	As many as 40% of applicants lie about their work histories and educational backgrounds and about 20% present false credentials and licences.		
2	An interview is really a verbal test of the candidate, with no clear right or wrong answers.		
3	Selection tests are used to identify applicant skills that cannot be determined in an interview process.		
4	Unstructured interviews require candidates to give real examples of past actions and results and are based on the theory that past behaviour is a good predictor of future behaviour.		

Training

The term 'training' refers to the acquisition of knowledge, skills and competencies. Training of employees is an essential function of the Human Resources Department – as a result, training must be constant as this will help to keep employees motivated and effective in the organization. Employees who are constantly offered the latest technology to help them in their jobs will help the organization to remain competitive.

The following outlines the main types of training used by employers, which are:
- on-the-job or in-house training;
- off-the-job training; and
- induction training.

On-the-job training

on-the-job training ▶

On-the-job training, also referred to as 'in house training', is training done during normal working hours, using the actual materials the trainee will use when their training is completed. This type of training can take a number of forms, including:

mentoring ▶
buddy system ▶
- **mentoring or 'buddying'** – in a mentoring or buddy system the employer will assign an experienced employee to work with the new worker. The experienced employee (mentor) will be able to guide the new employee throughout their daily tasks and help them to overcome problems encountered on the job;
- arranging for a supervisor or another worker to guide the employee through the task so that the employee knows how the task should be performed;

shadowing ▶
- **shadowing** means allowing the employee to work alongside another employee to get a better understanding of the job to be performed;

coaching ▶
- **coaching** means that the employee will learn new skills and have the opportunity to practise the skills with the coach before using them in the workplace. An effective coach will review the employee's performance to ensure that he/she uses the newly learned skills until they become habit.

Off-the-job training

off-the-job training ▶

Off-the-job training is done away from regular working stations. Therefore, employees will not perform their regular duties but will instead use the time to attend the location set up for training. Off-the-job training may be carried out in the same building where jobs are performed or off site. It may be provided by trainers working for the same employer as the employees being trained or by an outside company hired by the employer.

Induction training

induction training ▶

Induction training is training that an employee will receive when he/she first joins an organization or begins a new role. It is designed to provide the employee with the essential skills needed to perform the job. Induction training can also include an introduction to the company ethos, values and culture so that the employee is aware of the behaviours expected of him/her.

To the employer	To the employee
• Reduce wastage of raw material	• Improved job satisfaction
• Reduce customer turnover	• Improved morale
• Reduce employee turnover	• Opportunity to develop skills and knowledge
• Increase revenue collection	• Fewer errors made
• Increase product innovation	• Increase efficiency
• Reduce grievances	• Keep employees motivation
• Reduce errors	• Reduce boredom
• Reduce equipment downtime	• Improve confidence

Table 8.2 Benefits from training

ITQ7

Match the statements in column 1 with the words or phrases in column 2, by writing the letters beside the numbers.

Items	COLUMN 1		COLUMN 2
1	When training is held off the job, workers are not distracted by	A	balance
2	Off-the-job training has the disadvantage of not allowing the workers to	B	training room
3	On-the-job training is conducted by the supervisor or work colleague, but off-the-job training is conducted by a	C	interactive role-plays
4	On-the-job training is done in the workplace, but off-the-job training is conducted in a	D	professional trainer
5	Some examples of off-the-job training are	E	practise on the job
6	There must be a good — between on-the-job and off-the-job training.	F	work responsibilities

Orientation

orientation ▶

Staff orientation, also called job-specific orientation, is the process that is used to help employees fit in quickly with their new position. A good orientation will make a significant difference in how quickly employees become productive. Orientation is usually conducted by the supervisor or manager in the section or department in which the new recruit will be working. The following are some areas that are outlined at a recruitment session:
• duties and responsibilities of the employee;
• employer's expectations of the employee;
• organizational function;
• rules and regulations of the organization;
• policies and procedures to be followed;
• training on operating equipment;
• introduction to co-workers.

Purposes of orientation

- Reduce anxiety.
- Reduce start-up costs.
- Reduce employee turnover.
- Save time for supervisor and co-workers.
- Develop realistic job expectations, positive attitudes and job satisfaction.

ITQ8

List **four** benefits of an orientation programme to a new employee.

Appraisal and evaluation of employees

appraisal ▶

An employee appraisal is a formal meeting held between the supervisor and the employee to discuss the performance of the employee over a period of time. A copy of this evaluation will be placed on the employee's file, for future use. At the next appraisal the previous appraisal will be examined to determine the level of improvement made by the employee during that period.

The appraisal may be conducted by the manager or employer but is usually carried out by the employee's immediate supervisor (if not the same person). Doing it this way is more effective as the supervisor will have a better knowledge of the employee and therefore will be able to evaluate performance with more accuracy.

Despite the fact that appraisals should be done throughout the year, it is recommended that the first staff appraisal should be done six months after the employee begins working, after which appraisals should be done yearly. Some employers stagger their appraisal periods, meaning that employees are appraised in the same month of the year they began working, while other employers will designate a specific time of the year where all appraisals will be done.

Reasons for conducting an appraisal

- To identify training needs.
- To outline clearer objectives.
- To identify employees who have potential for promotion.
- To review salaries or payment methods.
- To identify employees' strengths and weaknesses.
- To increase staff motivation.
- To facilitate the improvement of performance.

ITQ9

Job appraisal includes all of the following elements except which one?
a rotating jobs
b indicating strengths and weaknesses
c providing feedback
d determining how well an employee is performing.

How to evaluate performance

The following could be taken into consideration when evaluating employees:
- meeting deadlines for projects, paperwork, returning phone calls and attending meetings;
- number of sales, production rate (for example, invoices sent per day);
- procedural responding to complaints, giving out information and so on;
- financial profit made or ability to work to budgets;
- negative personal complaints, number of defects (for example, per day), comments made by other staff and customers;
- recognizable relations with customers, presentations, comments made by other staff and customers;
- educational background;
- experience;
- ability to use own initiative.

Staff welfare

staff welfare ▶ Staff welfare is the provision of safe working conditions and the provision of services and facilities to create efficient, healthy, loyal and satisfied workers who will contribute to the success of the organization. The purpose of providing such facilities is to make their work life better by keeping morale and motivation high and also to raise their standard of living. This will also reduce the turnover level in an organization.

Typical welfare services provided for employees include health plans, pension schemes, superannuation schemes, canteen and restroom facilities, flexible working hours and a healthy working environment.

Employers could benefit from a good welfare plan in the following ways:

- provision of better physical and mental health to workers promotes a healthy work environment
- provision of health plans and recreation facilities, for example a gym, will help in raising employees' standards of living;
- higher retention of workers.

Some typical welfare schemes:

pension scheme ▶
retirement ▶

- **Pension scheme.** Usually, the employer and employee contribute to a pension scheme and, on retirement, the employee receives a sum of money determined by the number of years for which the employee has worked for the particular organization and the weekly or monthly contribution made.

superannuation scheme ▶

- **Superannuation scheme.** A superannuation scheme is similar to a pension scheme, except that an employee can benefit from the scheme if he/she decides to terminate employment with the organization. In some superannuation schemes, an employee must complete a set number of years' service before he/she can receive any benefit.
- **Medical scheme.** This scheme is designed to assist employees with expenses incurred because of illness – for example, in Jamaica, Sagicore Health Insurance Scheme provides insurance for all teachers.

Promotion, transfers, layoffs and dismissals

As firms change, their labour requirements change too. For example, if a firm opens new branches or adds more departments or products to its business, new jobs will be created. On the other hand, if the volume of work is reduced or branches of the firm close their doors, the workforce will have to be reduced. These two factors usually influence promotion, transfers, layoffs and dismissals. Resignations, retirement and dismissals of employees can also result in the movement of employees.

Promotion

promotion ▶ Promotion is the movement of workers into a higher position within the organization. Promotion from within is good business practice, as it has been proven to help with the motivation of employees and can generate loyalty through recognition. In some organizations workers are promoted based on their competence and work dedication; others are promoted because of the length of time for which they work with the organization as management feels that this suggests loyalty which should be rewarded; while others are promoted simply because they are liked by management or because they are performing well in their current position but that alone does not determine their effectiveness at a higher level.

The employee to be promoted should be looked at as a whole. Competence and work dedication are the two main reasons for promotion, however; the focus should not be only on these. Some additional factors that should be examined before promoting employees are:

- length of service;
- attitude to present job;
- education;
- training;
- attendance/punctuality;
- dependability.

Transfers

transfer ▶ Transfer is the lateral movement of workers in the same type of position and pay range, with comparable duties and responsibilities. A staff transfer can be done at the request of the supervisor or the employee or based on organizational needs. An employee may wish to be transferred to another position because of the new opportunities available or because the new location requires less commuting. The supervisor may request the transfer because he/she identifies additional potential or talent in the employee, while the transfer may be done based on organizational changes, for example layoff of workers which leaves a shortfall of labour in critical departments. When requesting a transfer, a formal letter must be sent to the Human Resources Department.

Layoffs

layoffs ▶ Layoffs occur where employers temporarily send workers home until further notice. This usually happens when the volume of work available is less than that needed to keep the current number of workers occupied. For example, some firms operate on a seasonal basis, so in high season, for example in tourism, the number of workers will be greater while in low season the number of workers will be fewer. Therefore in low season some workers are laid off until there is a boom in the high season

Dismissals or firing

dismissal ▶ Dismissal is the releasing of an employee from his/her current job, for reason or cause. An employee's employment can be terminated at any time but the dismissal must be fair. If it is not fair, the employer may be found guilty of unfair dismissal by an Employment Tribunal.

Dismissal for reason occurs where there is:
- the need for new skills and expertise to keep up with technological changes and to keep the business competitive that workers refuse to attain, resulting in the business having to remove those workers and replace them with better-skilled workers;
- **downsize ▶** downsizing of business – with the current changes in the global economy, many organizations must downsize in order to keep their doors open. As a result, some workers will have to be relieved of their duties. This type of **redundancy ▶** dismissal is called redundancy.
- **automation ▶** automation – in automation, advanced machinery is used to carry out labour-intensive work, thereby reducing the need for workers. A business organization's failure to automate will have a negative effect on its productivity. Employers will have to dismiss some workers since the machinery purchased can do much of the work.

Dismissal for cause occurs where employees are not performing their duties. Action must be taken, as this will have a negative impact on productivity as well as other workers. At times, despite many warnings, employees refuse to follow organizational rules – for example, poor attendance and punctuality despite

173

repeated warnings; gross misconduct where the employee displays disobedience, dishonesty or negligence; and refusal to accept changes in the redesigning of their job. Under these circumstances the employee would have to be dismissed.

Statutory disciplinary procedure

disciplinary procedure ▶ There is a basic three-step dismissal and disciplinary procedure (DDP) that must be used before an employer dismisses or imposes a significant sanction on an employee such as demotion, loss of seniority or loss of pay. It applies to all types of dismissal, including conduct, capability, redundancy, retirement, expiry of a fixed-term contract, unsuccessful probation and so on.

The following steps must be followed during the disciplinary procedures:

1 Employers must set out in writing the reasons for dismissal or disciplinary actions against the employee. A copy of this must be sent to the employee, who must be invited to attend a meeting to discuss the matter, with the right to be accompanied.

2 A meeting must be convened with the employee, employer and/or union representative.

3 An appeal procedure must be established to allow employees to voice their concerns.

ITQ10

Place ticks in the columns labelled 'True' or 'False' to indicate your answers to the following statements:

Items	Statements	True	False
1	The grievance procedure is designed to encourage settlement of a dispute before reaching the arbitration phase.		
2	One of the functions of the grievance procedure is to offer the employer a chance to air its complaints about its employees.		
3	The Labor Management Relations Act permits the employer to discharge any employee engaged in union activity.		

Deployment of staff

deployment ▶ Deployment of staff is moving staff around to make use of them according to their qualifications, experience, training and abilities. Several factors should be taken into consideration when deploying staff. These are:
• specific needs of each section of the organization;
• objectives of the organization as a whole;
• experience, qualifications, abilities and interests of individual employees.

The Human Resources Clerk

Duties and responsibilities

These may be many and varied, however, the major ones are:
• collecting and short-listing job applications;
• preparing letters calling candidates for interviews;
• attending to staff welfare matters;
• maintaining personnel records database (filing and retrieving staff records);
• carrying out other functions of the Human Resources Management Office.

Attributes

- Confidentiality.
- Patience.
- Tact.

Benefits of legislation related to staff welfare

Statutory provisions for employees' protection

There are statutory provisions, established by law, which are aimed at protecting employees. The Factories Act is set up to provide for, for example, protective clothing and gear and workmen's compensation. The law requires that there are certain employment rights that must be adhered to and if organizations fail to follow the established regulations this is punishable in the courts of law.

Workplace (Health, Safety and Welfare) Regulations

These regulations cover the following:
- protective clothing and gear;
- workmen's compensation;
- workplace conditions;
- health and safety management.

Protective clothing and gear

Regulations require that:
- risks are assessed to ensure that protective equipment is suitable;
- protective clothing and gear must always be used and maintained in working order and stored properly;
- workers must be provided with information, instructions and training about protective clothing and gear.

Workplace Conditions Regulations

These apply to all workplaces and cover four broad areas:
- safety – for example falling objects; floors; ability to open and close windows;
- working environment – for example proper ventilation, lighting, etc.;
- maintenance of equipment, cleanliness and removal of waste;
- facilities – for example washrooms, restrooms and eating, changing and washing areas.

Occupational Health and Safety Management Regulations

These require that the following be carried out:
- setting up of emergency procedures (fire exits, extinguishers etc.);
- producing information which is easily understood by employees;
- employment of specialist staff who understand the law.

ITQ11
List **three** statutory provisions implemented by law for the protection of employees.

Collective bargaining

collective bargaining ▶

Collective bargaining occurs where a trade union is recognized by the employer in a workplace as having the right to negotiate about the terms and conditions of employees. Where a trade union is granted statutory recognition, it has a legal right to bargain with the employer about pay, hours and holidays.

How collective bargaining works

For collective bargaining to work, a trade union and an employer will need to agree on how the process will operate, for example:
- who will represent the workers, or a particular group of workers (known as the 'bargaining unit') in negotiations;
- which workers are included in the bargaining unit;
- when meetings will be convened;
- how failures to come to an agreement will be resolved.

Collective agreements

collective agreements ▶

In most cases, collective bargaining will lead to an agreement, for example a pay increase. These agreements are called 'collective agreements' and they often result in a change to employment terms and conditions.

ITQ12

Collective bargaining may deal with which of the following issues?
  i working hours
  ii wages
  iii working conditions
  iv job security.

  a i, ii, iii, iv
  b i, ii, iii
  c i, iii, iv
  d ii, iii, iv.

Employees' rights

- Contract of employment.
- Redundancy compensation.
- Equal opportunity for all workers.
- Time off for public duties, for example juror duties.
- Public holiday leave with pay.
- Guaranteed payment of wages.
- Detailed pay slip.
- Termination notice.
- Maternity benefits.
- Safe working environment.
- National minimum wage rate.
- Rest periods/maximum work hours.

Expectations of employee and employer

The relationship between employers and employees, whether good or bad, is very important as it could have an impact on the quality and quantity of work done and also the labour turnover rate of the organization. The expectations identified below are actual statutory rights.

Employee	Employer
1. A fair wage for the work they do	**1.** Employees should be punctual
2. To work reasonable hours	**2.** Employees should respect and care for the facility
3. To receive rest periods (holidays, etc.)	**3.** Employees should be loyal
4. To be treated with respect	**4.** Employees should be co-operative

Table 8.3 Expectations of employee and employer

Maintenance of records used in the Human Resources Department

Some of the major documents used are:
- application form;
- job specification;
- job description form;
- interview assessment form;
- contract of employment;
- staff record form;
- employee appraisal form;
- leave form.

Application form

This form is often the first record placed in an employee's file and is frequently perused when the file is in circulation. The type and amount of information requested on an application form differ from one firm to the other.

An application form should be carefully read and completed, as it is often the first impression an organization receives of a prospective employee.

APPLICATION FOR EMPLOYMENT			
PERSONAL INFORMATION **Date of Application:**			
Name: .... Last, First, Middle			
Address: .... Street, City			
Mailing Address: .... Street, City			
Telephone Number: .... Home, Mobile, **Email address:**			
How did you learn about the post?			
Position sought		**Available start date:**	
Desired pay range ($):		**Are you currently employed? Yes ☐ No ☐**	
EDUCATION	**Name and address**	**Graduate? Degree?**	**Major**
High school			
College or University			
Specialized training school			
Other education			
Please list your areas of highest proficiency, skills that may contribute to you performing in the above-mentioned post.			

Figure 8.5   Example of an application form

Note: There are many different job application forms as each company designs its own forms to make it relevant to its own needs.

177

Job specification

job specification ▶ A job specification is a document which lists the knowledge, skills, abilities and other characteristics that an individual must have in order to perform a specific job. 'Skills' are an employee's level of proficiency at performing a task. 'Ability' refers to a more general enduring capability that an employee has, while other

personality traits ▶ characteristics may be personality traits, for example one's persistence. This very explicit record should be completed, paying attention to the job description. This record is usually completed in duplicate. One copy is filed in the employee's personal data file and the other is given to the employee.

The job specification includes the following:

- job definition;
- list of all work to be performed;
- minimum education requirements;
- minimum and maximum salary range requirement.

Job description

job description ▶ A job description is an outline of the duties, tasks and responsibilities related to a job. It should form the basis of all future dealings with the person appointed to that job. This document should be revised at regular intervals.

Interview assessment form

Interview assessment forms are pre-printed forms used during an interview session to award scores to prospective candidates as they answer questions at the interview. These points are added up at the end of the interview to help determine the candidate to be selected for the job. The higher the number of

applicant ▶ points scored, the more likely the applicant is to succeed in getting the job.

Some firms give specific questions to interviewers to be asked of the interviewees and at the end of the interview a general discussion takes place, weighing the performance of each candidate. In other firms, there are no set interviewing procedures and the selection committee decides strategies at a brief meeting before the first scheduled interview. Whichever system is used, it is customary for the interviewing committee to regroup after the last interviewee has left, for the purpose of general discussion and possible selection of the successful candidate.

Contract of employment

contract of employment ▶ A contract of employment is a document given to a new employee, outlining all the terms and conditions of his/her employment. This contract may end upon the death or retirement of the employee or the resignation of the employee. There are, however, instances where the employment may be terminated because of some breach of the contract.

The contract usually shows:

remuneration ▶
- remuneration;
- welfare services and conditions;
- date of commencement of service;
- hours of work;
- vacation arrangements;
- section in which employee will be stationed;
- length of notice to be given by either party for termination of employment.

Staff record form

staff record forms ▶

Staff record forms give basic information on each employee and should be kept current. This record card contains confidential information on each employee, therefore the card must be stored in such a way that unauthorized persons cannot access it.

STAFF RECORD CARD				
SURNAME	**FIRST NAMES AND INITIALS**	**DOB**	**DEPT**	**CARD NO**
ADDRESS	**NATIONALITY**	**DATE STARTED**		
	MARITAL STATUS	**OCCUPATION**		
	No of children:	Nat Ins No:		
	TRN No:	Wages/Salary		
	Name and address of doctor	Change in Job/wages/salary		
	Date of medical examination	Job	Wage	Merit	Date
Union	**Accident/Injury/ Claims**				
Pension Scheme					
Disciplinary action/s					
Date					
Type		Date departed:			
		Reason:			
Previous employment					

Figure 8.6 Example of a staff record form

Employee appraisal form

This is a form used by managers and supervisors to measure an employee's performance over a period of time, for example one year. The information gathered on this form can be used for a number of purposes such as: determining salary increment, promotion, training needs, etc.

Leave

Leave may be granted with or without pay. The different categories of leave include:
- study leave;
- vacation leave;
- compassionate leave;
- sick leave;
- no-pay leave;
- maternity leave;
- special leave;
- duty leave.

Study leave

Study leave is granted for the purposes of studying to obtain further qualifications. An employee on study leave may be granted full pay, half pay or no pay. Some of the factors taken into consideration in granting pay are as follows:
- area of study;
- level of study;
- length of time working with firm.

Vacation leave

vacation leave ▶ Vacation leave is granted to employees who are entitled to a vacation after one year's service. In many firms the length of service of an employee and the position he/she holds determine the duration of the vacation leave.

Compassionate leave

compassionate leave ▶ Compassionate leave is granted to employees when there is a death in the employee's immediate family.

Sick leave

Sick leave is given to employees who are sick and produce a doctor's certificate stating that he/she recommends that the employee be absent from work for a specific number of days.

No-pay leave

no-pay leave ▶ No-pay leave is leaving granted to an employee at his/her request. In this case the employee is not paid for the time he/she is not at work.

Maternity leave

maternity leave ▶ Maternity leave is granted to employees who are pregnant. These employees receive full pay during the period they are off on maternity leave. The leave can vary from six weeks to three months.

Special leave

Special leave is granted to an employee in cases where he/she has to attend to an emergency or to some personal matter.

Duty leave

duty leave ▶ Duty leave is usually granted to employees so that they can undertake assignments related to their jobs or on behalf of their government. For example, firms permit their employees to attend for jury duty and to participate in conferences. An employee on duty leave receives full pay.

Labour turnover

labour turnover ▶ 'Labour turnover' or 'employee turnover' is the term used to describe the rate at which an employer gains and loses employees. High turnover can affect the productivity level, especially if skilled workers continue to leave. High labour turnover can also affect the company where recruitment is costly or where it takes several weeks to fill a vacancy. It is worth noting that some employee turnover can be beneficial to an organization, for example if a poor performer leaves and is replaced by a productive employee or an employee with new ideas and talent.

Measuring labour turnover

Most labour turnover can be measured monthly or yearly. The formula used is:

$$\frac{\text{Total number of leavers over period} \times 100}{\text{Average total number employed over period}}$$

The total figure includes all leavers – even people who left involuntarily because of dismissal, redundancy or retirement.

Factors that contribute to labour turnover

Some of the most common reasons why employees tend to leave organizations are:

Internal factors	External factors
• Low compensation/salary	• State of the economy
• Unhealthy working conditions	• Better opportunities
• Lack of career opportunities and challenges	• Better salary
• Retirement	• Competition for job placement
• Unrealistic expectations	• Lack of recognition
• Conflict with management	• Globalization
• Redundancy	• Migration

Table 8.4   Contributors to labour turnover

Advantages and disadvantages of labour turnover

Some degree of labour turnover is healthy for any organization; on the other hand, if it is too high, organizations may experience many challenges. Table 8.5 outlines some advantages and disadvantages of labour turnover.

Advantages	Disadvantages
• Allows for promotional opportunities	• Instability caused by loss of experienced staff
• May help to reduce an ageing workforce	• Costly to recruit, select and train new staff
• New ideas may enter the organization	• Loss in production levels because of replacement time

Table 8.5   Advantages and disadvantages of labour turnover

Controlling labour turnover

It is the responsibility of the Human Resources Department to increase staff morale and job satisfaction. This can be done by:
• improving working conditions;
• job enrichment;
• adequate remuneration packages;
• promoting a corporate feeling;
• facilitating promotions.

181

 **Summary**

- The Human Resources Department is responsible for managing the human resources in an organization.
- All departments must work closely with the Human Resources Department, as they must give information on staffing needs.
- The functions of the Human Resources Department include: recruitment and orientation; interviewing; performance management; training and development; and staff welfare, among others.
- Human Resources Managers are able to recruit from websites, in house, from niche agencies and by using headhunters and employment agencies.
- Job descriptions are written statements that list the duties, required qualifications, knowledge, skills and responsibilities of a position as well as the salary range.
- New as well as regular workers are usually trained on a continuous basis to help keep the organization competitive.
- Training may be done on the job or off the job.
- Induction training is designed to provide an employee with the essential skills needed to perform his/her job.
- Orientation, also called job-specific orientation training, is the process that is used to help employees fit in quickly with their new position.
- An employee appraisal is held between the supervisor and the employee, to discuss the performance of the employee over a period of time.
- Employee/staff welfare is the provision of safe working conditions and the provision of services and facilities to create efficient, healthy, loyal and satisfied workers who will contribute to the success of the organization.
- Deployment of staff means moving staff around to make use of them according to their qualifications, experience, training and abilities.
- There are statutory provisions established by law that are aimed at protecting employees. The Factories Act is set up to provide for the protection of employees – for example, rules on protective clothing and gear and on workmen's compensation.
- Collective bargaining occurs where a trade union is recognized by the employer in a workplace as having the right to negotiate about the terms and conditions of employees.
- Collective agreement results where unions represent employees and come to some terms – for example, a set salary.
- Many documents are used in the Human Resources Department, including: contract of employment, leave forms and job descriptions.
- 'Labour turnover' is the term used to describe the rate at which an employer gains and loses employees. High turnover can affect the productivity level, especially if skilled workers continue to leave. Many factors contribute to labour turnover.

Answers to

1 From the following list:
- recruitment and selection;
- interviewing;
- coaching;
- deployment;
- training;
- appraisals / performance management;
- hiring and firing;
- promotions, layoffs and transfers;
- disciplinary procedures;
- staff welfare facilities;
- induction.

2

Items	True	False
1		√
2	√	
3		√

3

Items	True	False
1		√
2		√
3		√

4 c.

5 Two statutory provisions implemented are (from the following):
- the right to be paid wages or salary;
- the right to leave;
- redundancy compensation.

6

Items	True	False
1	√	
2	√	
3	√	
		√

7

Items		COLUMN 2
1	F	work responsibilities
2	E	practice on the job
3	D	professional trainer
4	B	training room
5	C	interactive role-play
6	A	balance

8 Four benefits of an orientation programme are (from the following):
- It helps employees to be less anxious on the first day at work, as they will feel valued.
- Employees will understand the job expectation from the first day.
- Employees become more comfortable in their new environment, which will result in them adjusting to the job more quickly.
- Employees may make fewer mistakes because of the training process.
- The orientation programme will help to foster a supportive team-oriented work environment within the workplace,
- Employees will be aware of the vision and mission of the organization.
- To familiarize them with important policies and procedures.

9 a.

10

Items	True	False
1	√	
2		√
3		√

11 • Workplace (Health, Safety and Welfare) Regulations.
 • Workplace Conditions Regulations.
 • Occupational Health and Safety Management Regulations.

12 b.

Examination-style questions

Multiple choice questions

1 Human Resources Managers are in charge of:
 a hiring
 b dismissing
 c insurance (and other benefits)
 d all of the above.

2 Human Resources Managers must determine the number of employees needed for a job, and they do this by:
 a recruiting employees
 b selecting employees
 c analyzing the characteristics of a job
 d appraising employees.

3 How can an organization eliminate unneeded workers?
 a by laying them off
 b by firing them
 c by offering them early retirement
 d all of the above.

4 How can a Human Resources Manager know the specifications of a job and develop a job description?
 a by watching someone do a job
 b by reading résumés in application for a particular job
 c by interviewing a person about his/her job
 d all of the above.

5 _____ is the process managers engage in to develop a pool of qualified candidates for open positions:
 a Hiring
 b Recruitment
 c Retention
 d Selection.

6 Training focuses on:
 a teaching organizational members how to perform effectively in their current jobs
 b broadening organizational members' knowledge and skills
 c preparing organizational members to take on new responsibilities
 d none of these.

7 Which of the following provides managers with information they need to make good human resources decisions?
 a selection
 b labour relations
 c recruitment
 d performance appraisal.

8 _____ includes all of the activities managers engage in to forecast their current and future human resource needs.

   a Recruitment and selection

   b Job analysis and job design

   c Selection and job design

   d Human resource planning.

Structured questions

1 **a** Outline **three** ways in which performance appraisals of employees can be beneficial to:

     i an organization;

     ii the workers. [6]

  b List **two** statutory protections implemented by law for the protection of employees. [2]

  c List **three** sources from which job seekers can collect information about job vacancies. [3]

2 Outline the difference between job description and job specification. [4]

3 List **four** statutory rights of an employee. [2]

4 Prepare a two-column table and list **six** main responsibilities of the employee and the employer at work. [6]

5 Explain the meaning of 'collective agreement'. Who are the main participants in collective agreement? [4]

6 List **four** internal and **four** external factors that contribute to employee turnover in an organization. [4]

7 List and explain **six** functions of the Human Resources Management Office in an organization. [6]

8 Explain the following terms:

  a headhunter

  b niche agencies

  c mentoring/buddying

  d shadowing

  e coaching. [10]

9 Explain the difference between a pension scheme and a superannuation scheme. [4]

10 List **three** reasons why employers may deem it necessary to reduce the number of staff within an organization. [3]

11 List **two** advantages and **two** disadvantages of labour turnover. [4]

12 For the following concepts, select the appropriate definition below for how companies attempt to enhance job satisfaction:

job rotation, job enlargement, empowerment, participative management, teamwork

  a Expanding employee responsibilities: _____.

  b Delegating jobs to groups of employees without supervision: _____.

  c Moving employees from one department to another to have them become more well rounded: _____.

  d Giving employees input in decision making and consulting with them: _____.

  e Allowing employees to make decisions: _____. [5]

9 Accounts and financial services

By the end of this chapter you should be able to:

- ☑ describe the role and functions of the Accounts Office;
- ☑ list the duties and responsibilities of the Accounts Clerk;
- ☑ list the attributes of the Accounts Clerk;
- ☑ understand simple documents used in the Accounts Office;
- ☑ identify and explain types of financial institutions;
- ☑ outline the procedures for making and receiving different types of payment;
- ☑ interpret information on cheques;
- ☑ interpret entries in a bank statement;
- ☑ reconcile bank and cash book balances;
- ☑ prepare petty cash records;
- ☑ outline the functions of equipment used in the Accounts Office;
- ☑ list and explain resources used in the Accounts Office.

Concept map **Accounts and financial services**

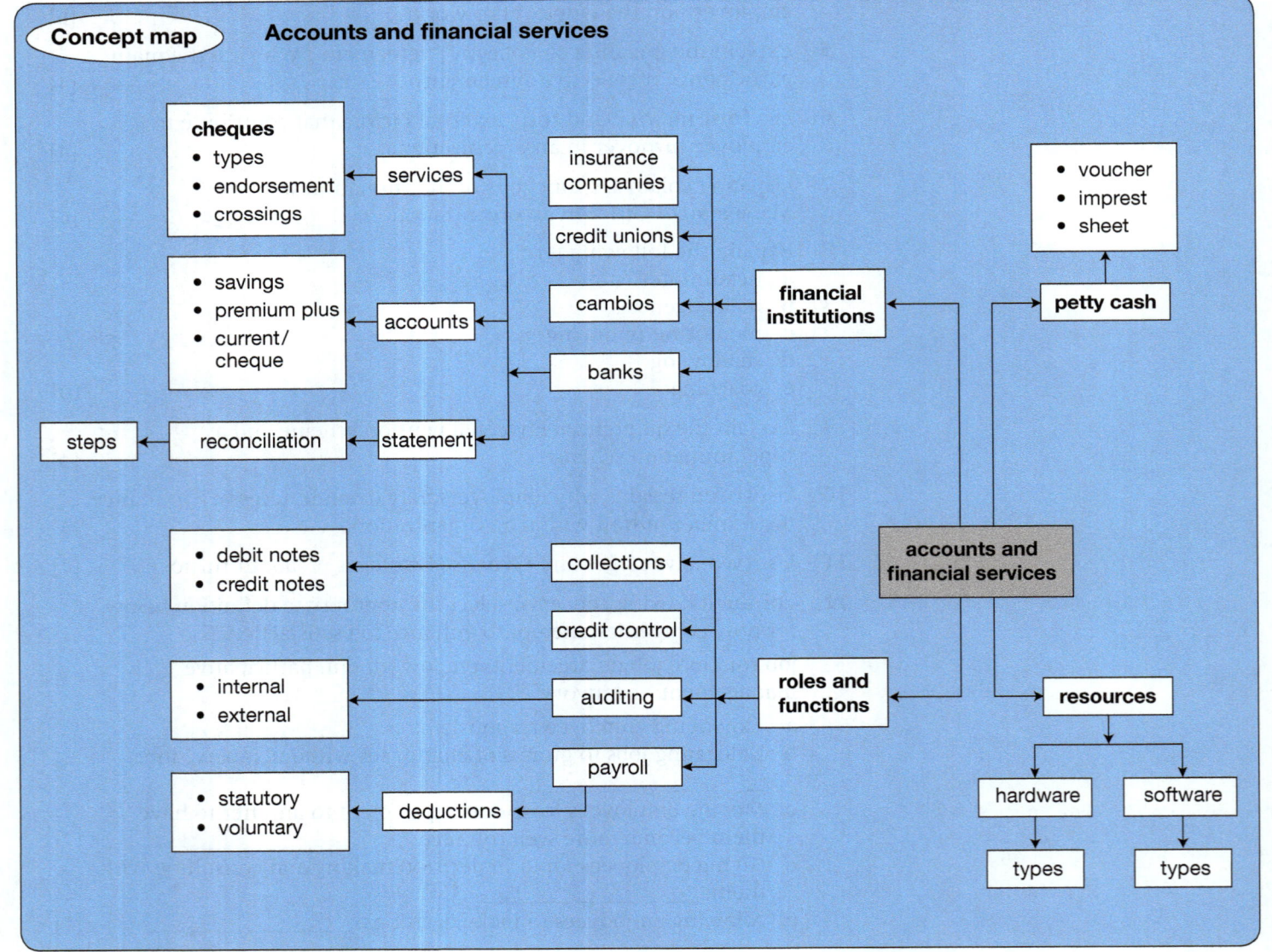

Accounts Office ▶
The Accounts Office is one of the most important offices in any business. This is because the survival of the business depends on the proper control of money going in and out of the organization. The chief accountant usually controls this office and there are usually many Accounts Clerks who work very hard to ensure that the functions are carried out efficiently.

Role and functions of the Accounts Office

The Accounts Office is responsible for the following functions:
- preparation of payroll;
- collection of accounts;
- preparation of audit;
- credit control;
- treatment of debit and credit notes;
- types of bank accounts.

ITQ1
List **three** functions of the Accounts Office.

Preparation of payroll

payroll ▶
salaries ▶
wages ▶
Payroll is the record of employee salaries and hourly wages, withholdings and deductions for all employees, for a given pay period. One of the main functions of the Accounts Office is the preparation of payroll. The person in charge is responsible for computing and preparing the employees' pay.

Several terms are used to describe the rewards paid to employees for labour services to an organization:

Salaries

Salaries are paid to persons who work on a monthly or two-weekly basis. Salaries are usually quoted on a yearly basis and payments are paid monthly or bi-weekly. Some categories of persons to whom salaries are paid are teachers, doctors, accountants and so on.

Bonus rate

bonus rate ▶
Bonus rate refers to payments or additional income paid to workers for completing more work than agreed upon. A worker earning, for example, a salary or commission may earn a bonus for outstanding work completed. For example, if a welder is required to build three window grills in an hour at a cost of $500 each but he builds four grills in the one-hour period, he will be paid $1,500 for the three grills built plus an extra amount for the fourth grill built.

Overtime

overtime ▶
Overtime is the number of hours an employee/worker works above his/her regular working hours. Normal working hours may be agreed by employer and employee, by law or be dictated by the type of work/profession. Workers are usually asked to work overtime when the demand for a company's product or service increases and the number of staff members available is low. The workers are usually paid at a higher rate for any overtime work done. For example, if the employee's normal working hours are from 8.00 am to 5.00 pm, but on a particular day he/she worked until 9.00 pm, he/she will be paid overtime for the extra four hours worked. The rates of overtime paid to workers differ from firm to firm.

Currently, overtime pay is calculated as at least one-and-a-half (1.5) times an employee's regular pay rate. For example, if an employee ordinarily earns $300 per hour, then the employee's overtime pay rate is at least $450 per hour, as shown below.

$300 per hour x 1.5 = $450 per hour

Hourly rate

hourly rate ▶

An hourly rate pay scheme is where employees are paid a set rate (before tax) for each hour that they work. They may have a set minimum number of hours, or it may change each week / month. Hourly rate paid employees are motivated to attend work as they will not be paid for the hours not worked. For example, if an employee earns $1,000 an hour, for a 26-hour work week, they will earn $26,000 before tax in that week.

Piece work

piece work ▶

Piece-rate pay is sometimes referred to as a 'payment by results' system. Piece-rate pay describes a type of employment in which workers are paid a fixed amount for each item produced or action performed. In a garment manufacturing setting, the output of piece work can be measured by the number of physical items (pieces) produced – for example, one worker may be responsible for cutting the sole of a shoe and is paid for each sole produced. Piece rate rewards workers who produce more and offers less to those who produce little. As a result, it increases efforts, as workers may be motivated to complete as many units/items as possible. Piece rate also ensures that workers who produce more are not disgruntled as they will earn more than workers who produces little and this will encourage them to continue producing.

Employees working in a service setting are paid according to the number of operations completed. For example, a telemarketer will be paid by the number of calls made or completed. Similarly, a dressmaker may be paid for each piece of garment completed.

Wages

'Wages' is another term used to describe financial compensation given to workers in exchange for the services provided by them. It must be noted that the term 'wages' refers to payment to workers (babysitters, gardeners or household helpers) and 'salary' is the term used to refer to payment given to employees (teachers, doctors, nurses).

Minimum wage

minimum wage ▶

A minimum wage is the lowest wage that employers are legally bound to pay to employees or workers for work completed. Some workers are employed full time, others part time, and some receive their payments on a weekly or monthly basis. Irrespective of the situation, they are all entitled to a salary or to wages equivalent to at least the minimum wage set by law.

Double-time overtime

double time ▶

Double time is payment for work done after normal working hours or on public holidays. For example, if a person's regular salary is $400.00 per hour, for every extra hour worked he/she would be paid $800.00, which is double the amount earned regularly.

ITQ2

Nevrene Rodney's regular work week is 40 hours per week at a regular rate of $320 per hour. She is paid overtime at 1.5 times regular rate (1.5 x regular hourly pay). Calculate her regular and overtime pay from the following table:

Day	Hours worked
Monday	8
Tuesday	12
Wednesday	9
Thursday	10
Friday	9
Saturday	4
Sunday	4
Total hours	56

CLOCK/TIME CARD

Employee's name: Andrew Ellis **Date:** Monday, April 28, 2010–12–08
Employee's no: 001 **Department:** PRODUCTION

DAY	Regular hours				Overtime		Total Hours
	IN	OUT	IN	OUT	IN	OUT	
Monday	0802	1200	1300	1700	–	–	8
Tuesday	0857	1200	1300	1703	1730	1800	8½
Wednesday	0800	1200	1300	1700	1700	2000	11
Thursday	0755	1300	1400	1700	1730	1900	10½
Friday	0758	1200	1300	1701	1730	1930	10
Saturday	–	–	–	–	0900	1400	5
TOTAL HOURS							**53**
Note: Total hours include regular and overtime hours.							

Figure 9.1   Example of a clock/time card

The hours which an employee works can be recorded on a time sheet. This can be done manually or mechanically. In this case the employee puts a card into a time clock on entering and on leaving the premises. The clock stamps the card with the time at that point. See also page 266.

Flat rate

flat rate ▶

A flat rate is used where all employees are rewarded equally for work done, regardless of their performance or seniority. For example, persons who produce 500 items per day and others who produce 300 per day will earn the same wages. This type of reward does not encourage workers to perform at their best, **incentives ▶** as there are no incentives for the ones who are high producers.

Commission

commission ▶

A pay scheme based on commission is where an employee is paid solely on performance or sales. This usually involves either a set amount per sale, a **increments of pay ▶** percentage of each sale, or set increments of pay, depending on the targets met. For example, a sales clerk works at a commission of 2.5 per cent of each sale made, and makes sales of $10,000 in a week. They would be paid $250 before tax in that week.

ITQ3
What is the difference between salary and wages?

Wages and salary deductions

Every worker or employee will have taxes and other deductions taken from their pay cheque. Employees' or workers' take-home pay will be less than their gross salary or wages. This is as a result of the different types of deductions taken from their gross pay. These deductions are both statutory or compulsory deductions (i.e. deductions required by law) that are taken from an individual's salary without his/her consent and involuntary deductions (i.e. those requested to be taken out by the employee).

Statutory/involuntary deductions

Statutory deductions are:
• National Insurance Scheme contributions;
• income tax;
• education tax;
• National Housing Trust contributions.

National Insurance Scheme

National Insurance Scheme ▶

The National Insurance Scheme (NIS) is a compulsory contributory fund contributions for which are deducted directly from employees' salary or wages. The scheme offers financial protection to workers and their families against loss of income arising from injury at work, retirement or death of the insured. Everyone working and earning a salary or wage that is documented has to pay National Insurance. The size of the employee's pay will determine how much is deducted (the more he/she earns, the more must be paid).

retirement ▶

invalidity benefit ▶

pensions ▶
funeral grant ▶

employment injury benefits ▶
orphan benefit ▶
health plan ▶

The National Insurance tax covers the following:

- retirement;
- pensions;
- funeral grant;
- invalidity benefit;
- employment injury benefits;
- orphan benefit;
- health plan.

Income tax

income tax ▶

Income tax is deducted from workers' salary or wages. The amount of income tax deducted depends on the level of income. Therefore, the more the employee earns, the more income tax is deducted form his/her wages or salary each month. Income tax is deducted from the gross pay. In Jamaica the amount deducted is 25 per cent of gross earnings.

Education tax

education tax ▶

Education tax is charged on the same basis as the contributions to the National Housing Trust. The education tax is implemented to make up for any shortfall in funds needed to run the education system efficiently.

National Housing Trust

national housing trust ▶

The National Housing Trust (NHT) is funded by a combination of personal and corporate contributions. Employers are required to deduct 2 per cent of each employee's salary along with 3 per cent of their own wage bill and remit these funds to the NHT on a monthly basis. Self-employed persons contribute 2 per cent or 3 per cent of earnings, depending on the occupational category in which they fall. Under the NHT Act, all employed persons, between the ages of 18 and 65, who are earning the minimum wage and over, must make contributions to the Trust.

ITQ4

What is the difference between voluntary and statutory deductions?

Voluntary deductions

Voluntary payroll deductions are withheld from an employee's gross pay at the instruction of the employee him/herself. Voluntary deductions pay for various benefits in which the employee has chosen to participate. Voluntary payroll deductions include the following:

life assurance premiums ▶
payments to credit unions ▶
payments to charities ▶
superannuation ▶
staff social clubs ▶
mortgage ▶

- life assurance premiums;
- payments to credit unions;
- payments to charities;
- superannuation;
- staff social clubs;
- mortgage.

Gross pay

gross pay ▶

Gross pay is the term used to describe the amount of money a person earns including allowances, overtime pay, hourly wage, commissions, bonuses and any other allowance that is paid to an employee before deductions of any type are made. For example, if an employee is paid $500 per hour for a 38-hour work week ($500 x 38) the total gross pay would be $19,000 for the week: this will the be the gross pay before any deductions are taken out.

> Regular pay + any overtime pay = GROSS PAY

ITQ5

Shane McCarthy works a regular week of 38 hours each week at a regular rate of $200 per hour. He is paid overtime at 1.5 times regular rate and he earns a bonus of $310 for the week. Calculate his gross pay from the table opposite:

Day	Hours worked
Monday	7
Tuesday	10
Wednesday	8
Thursday	9
Friday	8
Saturday	3
Sunday	4
Total hours	49

Net pay

net pay ▶

Net pay is the remaining amount after deductions from the gross pay. Deductions are both statutory and voluntary.

> Gross pay – total deductions = net pay
>
> Statutory deductions + voluntary deductions = total deductions

ITQ6

Andrea works a regular week of 38 hours each week, at a regular rate of $280 per hour. She is paid overtime at 1.5 times regular rate and she earns a bonus of $590 for the week. She pays income tax of 25 per cent of her gross salary and 2 per cent is contributed to the National Insurance Scheme. She also pays $95 towards a credit union and $50 towards a health plan. Calculate her net pay from the table opposite:

Day	Hours worked
Monday	7
Tuesday	10
Wednesday	8
Thursday	9
Friday	8
Saturday	3
Sunday	4
Total hours	49

ITQ7

How does gross pay differ from net pay?

Payroll sheet

payroll sheet ▶

Payroll sheet refers to the records – paper or electronic – and calculations that are used to work out employees' pay and deductions under the PAYE (Pay As You Earn) system. It covers all the payments make to employees, including:
- wages and salaries;
- commission and bonuses;
- overtime;

holiday pay ▶
statutory payments ▶
- holiday pay;
- statutory payments.

SMIDSBURGH MANUFACTURING

PAYROLL SHEET 2011   **Week ending 19 August**

Employees Name	Rates Regular $	Rates Overtime $	Hours Regular	Hours Overtime $	Total hours	Gross pay	Deductions Income Tax	NIS	Dues $	Deductions $	Net pay $
Peter Smith	900	1350	40	4	44	41,400	10,350	828	100	11,278.00	30,122.00
Sandra Bogle	700	1050	40	3	43	31,150	7,787.50	623	–	8,410.50	22,739.50
Susan James	600	–	40	0	40	24,000	6,000	480	150	6,630.00	17,370.00
Carla Hewitt	800	1200	38	4	42	35,200	8,800	704	210	9,714.00	25,486.00
Betty Douglas	100	60	38	0	38	38,000	9500	760	–	10,260.00	27,740.00
Henry Thomas	950	1425	38	2	40	38,950	9,737.50	779	–	10,516.50	28,433.50

Figure 9.2 Example of a payroll sheet

ITQ8

From the payroll sheet in Figure 9.2, calculate the total amount taken from employees' salaries.

Pay stub

pay stub ▶ A pay stub, pay slip, pay advice, or sometimes pay cheque stub, is a document an employee receives either as notice that the direct deposit transaction crediting his/her pay has gone through the banking system, or as part of his/her pay cheque itself. It outlines the gross income and all statutory deductions from gross pay (income tax, National Housing Trust, education tax and National Insurance Scheme) as well as voluntary deductions such as mortgage payment, insurance or loan payments.

Bright Star Motors Ltd   Earnings statement 31/12/10   No.

| DEPT. 1302 | EMP NO. 09804 | NAME John Smith | INCOME TAX Ref. | TAX CODE | N.I.S. REF B480156 | |

EARNINGS				DEDUCTIONS	
DESCRIPTION	UNITS	RATE	AMOUNT	DESCRIPTION	AMOUNT
Salary			28333.33	INCOME TAX	7668.09
Bonus			13200.00	NIS	520.83
				NHT	830.67
				EDUC. TAX	747.60
				PENSION	3632.50
				MED. FUND	1234.53
				SPORTS CLU	150.00
				SAL ADV.	8000.00

| S10 937 | S2 | S1 | 50c 1 | 20c 2 | 10c 5c | 5c | 1c | | |

YEAR-TO-DATE							NET PAY 18749.11
GROSS EARN. 339118.66	INCOME TAX 58854.95	P.T.D. 6027.69	F.R.C	DAYS WORKED	ADVANCE BALANCE	LOAN BALANCE 0.00	
N.H.T. 2530.68	PENSION 17174.18	2277.60					

Figure 9.3 Example of a pay advice

Fringe benefits

fringe benefits ▶ Fringe benefits or 'perks' (short for 'perquisites') are incentives offered to workers by employers. For example, an employer may provide an employee with lunch vouchers. Some other examples of fringe benefits are:
- transportation (commuting) benefits;
- company cars;
- medical facilities.

Collection of accounts

Collection of accounts is another important function of the Accounts Office. Some companies will set up a Collections Department or section that is responsible for collecting all outstanding payments due to the organization. If a customer should become delinquent, that is several months late on a payment for goods supplied, the supplier will place the customer's account in collection status. At that point, the supplier will write letters requesting all outstanding payment from the debtor. If payments are still not made after these letters then the supplier will instruct a debt collector to collect the amount owed.

Credit control

credit control ▶

Credit control is the process of control over payments coming into and going out of the firm. Most business organizations operate by allowing some of their customers (debtors) to be supplied with goods on credit (so that they will pay for them at a later date). Each customer taking goods on credit is usually given a credit limit based on their ability to pay their debts. To determine which customers are to be given credit and for how much, the supplier must check on the references of the buyer/customer. This could be done by contacting previous suppliers or the customer's bank for a reference. Tight credit control is important if firms are to avoid cash flow problems.

ITQ9

Why is it important to control the amount of credit given to a customer at any one time?

Preparation of audit

audit ▶

true and fair ▶

auditors ▶

An audit is a vital part of accounting. It is the independent examination of the accuracy of financial statements prepared by the relevant persons in business organizations. In accounting, financial statements are said to be true and fair when they are free of errors, hence the goal of auditing is to ensure this. An audit is performed by independent and objective person known as auditors or accountants, who will prepare and issue a report based on their findings.

Auditing may be carried out by internal auditors or external auditors. Management is responsible for internal control; as a result, it is responsible for establishing policies and processes to help the organization achieve its goals and objectives. On the other hand, external auditing is carried out by auditors who are independent of the company and who are appointed to examine the accounts and business records at the end of the financial year, to ensure that they represent a 'true and fair view' of the profits, losses, assets and liabilities of the company. The government may require an audit report for tax purposes. An audit is usually carried out once per year. Auditing may be carried out without informing the employees in the department being audited.

Auditors usually:
- assess whether or not a company or department is complying with accounting and legal rules;
- assessing the reliability of financial information;
- detecting fraud;
- make recommendations for the prevention of fraud.

The Accounts Clerk

Duties

An Accounts Clerk is responsible for helping with the efficient operation of the Accounts Office. Some of the duties performed by the Accounts Clerk include:
- posting journalized data;
- handling accounts receivable and payable;
- preparing payroll;
- billing customers;
- operating accounting equipment;
- preparing financial statements;
- providing information;
- answering incoming information;
- reconciling monthly statements;
- writing receipts and cheques;
- writing up cash book;
- filing.

Attributes

An Accounts Clerk should possess the following attributes:
- integrity;
- confidentiality;
- reliability;
- honesty.

Financial institutions

financial institutions ▶

debentures ▶

Financial institutions are those organizations involved in providing various types of financial services to customers. Some financial institutions collect funds from private and public investors and place them in financial assets such as loans, bonds, debentures, stocks, insurance, hedging investments, deposits and many other types of financial assets. Financial institutions are controlled and supervised by the rules and regulations delineated by government authorities. Some examples of financial institutions are:

banks ▶
non-banking financial institutions ▶
bureaux de change ▶
building societies ▶
credit unions ▶
insurance companies ▶

- banks;
- non-banking financial institutions;
- *bureaux de change*;
- building societies;
- credit unions;
- insurance companies.

Central bank

central bank ▶

A central bank, also called a reserve bank, is a banking institution within a specific country that is given the privilege to regulate all the currency supplies for that country. Central banks have the right to lend money to government as well as to other commercial banks when needed. Interest is charged on the loans made to borrowers. A central bank differs from regular commercial banks in that it has the exclusive rights to create the currency for that country. Central banks may be government owned and controlled or may be run under regulations that are specifically created to prevent extensive government interference.

The main functions of the central bank are to ensure that the national currency and money supply remain stable; implementation of monetary policy; controlling loan interest rates; and acting as a lender to the banking sector.

The central bank in Jamaica is called the Bank of Jamaica and is located in Kingston. The Bank of Jamaica has responsibility for the following:

- issuing coins and notes, ensuring that the currency is authentic and that there is an adequate supply to meet the demands of the public;
- formulating and implementing monetary policy – that is, the measures taken by the bank to influence the Jamaican economy by regulating the amount of money in circulation;
- ensuring that the financial system is sound and operates efficiently;
- managing the foreign reserves of the country; and
- carrying out other activities that support the implementation of monetary policy and services to the government, banks and licensed financial institutions and the general public.

Commercial banks

commercial bank ▶

A commercial bank is a type of financial institution geared more toward the lending of money to customers than towards investments. Commercial banks **deposits ▶** accept deposits to personal and corporate accounts, and then use the deposits to finance individual and business loans.

The commercial bank will extend a number of different types of loans to customers. For individuals, a commercial bank may loan funds for the purchase of personal property, such as vehicles, homes and home improvements, or to **debt instruments ▶** consolidate a number of personal debt instruments. Loans attract interest, therefore, the borrower must pay back the principal (the amount loaned) along with calculated interest.

Commercial banks also offer a wide range of savings programmes for customers, including standard savings accounts, as well as current or cheque accounts, certificates of deposit, and other savings strategies that are considered to provide a small but consistent return in exchange for doing business with the bank.

Types of loans granted by commercial banks

Secured loan

secured loan ▶
collateral ▶
A secured loan is a loan in which the borrower pledges some asset (for example, a car or property) as collateral (i.e. security) for the loan.

Mortgage loan

mortgage loan ▶
lien ▶
A mortgage loan is a very common type of loan, used to purchase property such as houses and cars. Commercial banks are given security called a lien on the title to the property. The bank keeps this until the mortgage is paid off in full. If the loan were not paid off, the bank would have the legal right to repossess the house or property and sell it, to recover the amount owed by the borrower.

Unsecured loan

unsecured loans ▶
Unsecured loans are monetary loans that require no collateral from the borrower. These loans may be available from financial institutions under many different categories, such as bank overdrafts, credit card debts or even personal loans.

ITQ10
What is the difference between a secured loan and an unsecured loan?

Investment companies

investment company ▶

An investment company is a company whose main business is holding securities of other companies purely for investment purposes. An investment company invests the money it receives from its investors and the profits or losses are shared among the investors according to the amount of money invested. The amount gained from investment is based on the performance of the securities and other assets that the investment company owns. Money may be invested in stock funds, bank funds, money market funds or index funds.

In Jamaica, names such as Cash Plus, Worldwise, Olint and Higgins-Warner are just a few investment clubs that Jamaicans are familiar with and have probably invested with. They are companies that basically use monies 'loaned' by investors to invest as they see fit. Many invest in areas such as real estate, foreign exchange and perhaps other ventures which are not made known to the investors. These ventures, however, yield high returns – enough to guarantee a minimum of 10 per cent per month.

Investment companies are regulated primarily under the Investment Company Act of 1940 and the rules and registration forms adopted under that Act. Investment companies are also subject to the Securities Act of 1933 and the Securities Exchange Act of 1934.

Credit unions

credit union ▶

A credit union is a cooperative financial institution that is owned and controlled by its members, and operated for the purpose of promoting savings within its members. Only a member of a credit union may deposit money with the credit union, or borrow money from the credit union. Credit unions provide a broader range of loan and savings products at a much cheaper cost to their members than do most banks or other institutions.

Credit unions differ from banks and other financial institutions in that the members who have accounts in the credit union are its owners and they elect their board of directors in a democratic one-person-one-vote system regardless of the amount of money invested in the credit union. Credit unions offer many of the same financial services as banks.

Bureau de change

bureau de change ▶

A *bureau de change* or currency exchange is a business, for example a cambio, where customers are able to visit and purchase currency or exchange one currency for another. The rate at which a bureau will buy currency differs from that at which it will sell it; for every currency it trades, rates for both buying and selling will be on display in the shop.

Insurance companies

risk ▶
premium ▶
policyholder ▶

Insurance is the transfer of the risk or loss from one entity to another, in exchange for a premium and can be considered a guarantee to prevent a large loss. An insurer is a company selling the insurance; an insured or policyholder is the person or entity buying the insurance.

Motor insurance companies determine a customer's premium by looking at the risks they have to shoulder to cover them. Risk factors that insurance companies take into consideration involve the vehicle and the driver. For example, female drivers and those who are more experienced will carry less risk and will therefore most probably be offered a lower car insurance premium.

Banking

bank ▶ A bank is a financial institution that provides financial services to customers. Banks allows the setting up of a number of accounts such as current/cheque accounts that allow customers to make payments via paper cheques. Banks also facilitate other payment methods such as telegraphic transfer.

Business organizations may choose to lodge their money with banks for any of the following reasons:

- large amounts of cash are safer in a bank;
- no storage space is needed on the firm's premises;
- while money is in the bank, trade can be done by using cheques and bank transfers. This is quicker and safer than carrying stocks of cash.

Services provided by banks

Banks provides a number of services to their customers – some of the main services are:

- deposit/savings account;
- current/cheque account;
- standing orders;
- direct debit facilities;
- foreign exchange facilities;
- credit transfer system;
- advice on stocks and shares;
- overdrafts;
- mortgage facilities;
- debit cards;
- bank loans;
- banker's draft facilities.

Types of bank account

A bank account is a financial record of the transactions between the customer and the bank. There are several different types of bank accounts. However, there are two basic types for managing everyday money: a savings account and a current account. Banks also offer a range of accounts designed for medium- or longer-term savings.

Savings account

savings account ▶ A savings account is one type of bank account that encourages savings from the general public. Account holders are able to make deposits and withdrawals at their convenience. Money deposited in this type of account earns interest and account holders are able to make withdrawals via the Automatic Teller Machine (ATM) facility. Each account holder is issued with a passbook, which keeps track of all the financial transactions done with the bank. A disadvantage of using this type of account is that cheques cannot be written from the account.

passbook ▶

Current account

current account ▶ A current account, also called a cheque account, is another type of bank account. This type of account allows the account holder to make purchases and pay bills without using actual cash. Customers are given paper cheques that they use as instruments for payment. Current accounts usually attract no interest on deposits, however, account holders are charged a fee by the bank for operating the account on their behalf. This type of account is often utilized by business organizations as well as by individuals who make many payments on a day-to-day basis.

cheque account ▶

Premium plus account

premium plus account ▶

A premium plus account is a first-class savings account designed to improve return for the account holder by locking and unlocking funds to enjoy higher rates of interest. This type of account allows for unrestricted access to unlocked funds, tax-free interest and free statements issued to customer once per year.

Certificate of deposit (CD)

certificate of deposit ▶

A certificate of deposit is also known as a time deposit or fixed deposit account. This type of bank account requires the account holder to deposit a certain sum of money and agree to leave the funds in the account for a fixed time period or until a set maturity date. They are different from savings accounts in that the CD has a specific, fixed term (often three months, six months, or one to five years) and, usually, a fixed interest rate. They attract a higher interest rate than other accounts. Account holders are able to withdraw funds before the maturity date, however, they will be charged a penalty.

Money market account

money market account ▶

Another type of bank account is a money market account. Higher interest is paid than that paid to savings or cheque accounts. There is usually a minimum balance to be maintained in the account before interest can be earned and there is a restriction on the number of withdrawals that can be made per month.

ITQ11

Copy the table opposite and list **three main** features for the current account, savings account, money market account and certificate of deposit account.

Current account	Savings account	Money market account	Certificate of deposit account
1.			
2.			
3.			

Payments through financial institutions

Standing order

standing order ▶

A standing order, also called a banker's order, is a written instruction given by a bank account holder to his/her bank to pay a set amount of money at regular intervals to another account. Standing orders are generally used to pay rent, mortgage, loan repayments or any fixed regular payments. Standing orders are not suitable for paying bills that may fluctuate on a monthly basis. In order to use this service the account holder must fill out a standing order form at the bank, writing in the account number, branch number, amount to be transferred and the dates on which the payments should be made. The bank will make the payments on the dates specified on the standing order form. A fee is usually charged for this service.

Direct debit

direct debit ▶

Direct debit, also referred to as direct withdrawal, is an instruction that a bank account holder gives to his/her bank to collect an amount directly from another bank account holder. Permission must first be given by the person receiving the goods or services for the seller to collect funds directly from their account. Direct debits can be used to pay insurance premiums, telephone bills or loan amounts on a monthly basis. Direct debits are similar to standing orders but are initiated by the receiver of the funds. Unlike standing orders, which require the amounts to be fixed, direct debits can be used for varying amounts; the payee can simply indicate a different amount each time payment is due.

The person whose account the funds are to be paid from must ensure that sufficient funds are in the account as they will be charge a fine should the direct debit request not be met.

ITQ12

Outline the main differences between a standing order and a direct debit.

Credit transfer

credit transfer ▶

Credit transfer is a payment order made for the purpose of transferring funds from one bank account holder (the payer) to another bank account holder (the receiver). This method of payment is commonly used by business organizations to transfer employees' wages and salaries to their accounts. In this case, all the payments to be made are listed, showing the employees' branches and code numbers, and a credit slip is made out for each one. Then one cheque is written to the bank for the total amount; the bank will then transfer the relevant amount to each account.

Overdraft

overdraft ▶

Overdraft is a borrowing arrangement with the bank to permit the withdrawal of more funds than are in the account of the holder, without having to go through the formal procedure of completing documentation for a loan. Such an arrangement simply permits a customer to overdraw on his account up to a predetermined amount.

Banker's draft facilities

banker's draft ▶

A banker's draft, also referred to as a cashier's cheque, teller's cheque, bank cheque or treasurer's cheque, is a type of cheque where the payment is guaranteed to be available by the bank it is purchased from. This cheque is purchased by the payer and sent to the payee, who presents it to their bank for payment. The bank in turn presents it to the payer's bank for reimbursement. These drafts are usually used in transactions involving large sums of money or where a trader is dealing with a wholesaler for the first time.

Credit cards

credit card ▶

credit limit ▶

A credit card is a small plastic card with a magnetic strip at the back containing pertinent information about the cardholder. This card indicates that the holder has been granted a line of credit called a credit limit. It allows the cardholder to buy goods and services and/or withdraw cash up to the credit limit allowed to him/her. The bank issuing the credit card pays the vendor and that amount is repaid by the cardholder monthly. The amount used from the card can be paid in full on the due date or can be settled in part payments. If the full amount is paid each month then no interest is charged, however, if not paid then interest is charged on the amount owing from the date of each purchase. The cardholder may have to pay an annual fee for the facility of using the card.

ITQ13

List **four** services offered by banks.

Money order

money order ▶ A money order is an instrument used to make payments of a specified sum of money to the person named on the instrument. The person paying the money will go to a Post Office, grocery store or bank and pay the amount he/she wishes to pay. A fee is charged for sending this order.

An international money order is very similar to a regular money order except that it can be used to make payments abroad. With it, a buyer can pay a supplier for goods or services if he/she is located in another country. International money orders are often issued by a buyer's bank and bought in the currency that the supplier accepts.

One of the main advantages of money orders is that they are more trusted than personal cheques as they are prepaid. Therefore, the payee is guaranteed that the money will be paid to him/her.

Postal order

postal order ▶ A postal order is a type of promissory note used for sending money through the mail to make payments. Postal orders are obtained and cashed at a Post Office. They provide a secure means of transmitting funds through the mail.

Electronic transfers

electronic funds transfer ▶ An electronic funds transfer refers to the computer-based systems used to perform financial transactions electronically. This system allows for the transfer of money from one account to another without using paper money. Transfer can be done either within the same financial institution or across multiple institutions. Note that when bills are paid online it is done using electronic payments; similarly, direct debit payments are also done using electronic transfers.

Electronic transfer allows for both electronic payments and collections. They are safe, efficient, secure and cheaper than paper cheque payments and collections.

Cheques

cheques ▶
drawer ▶
drawee ▶
payee ▶

Cheques are written orders from the owner of the cheque (drawer) to the bank (drawee) to pay on demand the sum of money stated on the cheque to a third party (the payee). Cheques may be used for settling debts and withdrawing money from banks. A cheque is generally valid for six months after the date of issue unless otherwise indicated; this varies depending on where the cheque is drawn. In Australia, for example, a cheque is valid for fifteen months. In Jamaica, it is valid for six months.

Cheques may be prepared by writing in ink or printed by a machine called a cheque-writer. This looks and is operated like a typewriter, but the type cuts into the paper of the cheque so that alterations cannot be made.

Parts of a cheque
Cheques generally contain:
- name and address of issuing bank;
- bank identifying number;
- date of issue;
- amount of currency in words and figures;
- drawer's account number;
- signature of drawer;
- cheque number;
- name of payee.

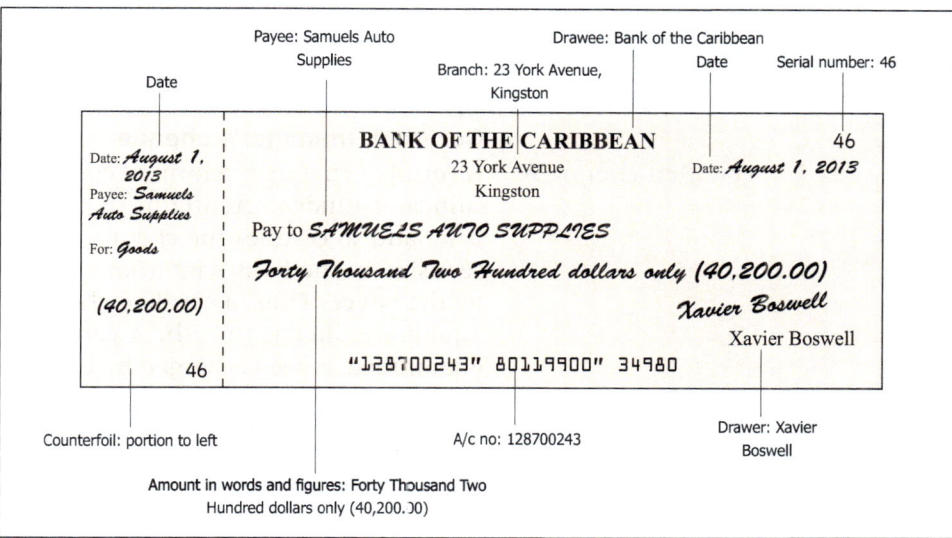

Figure 9.4 A cheque with labels showing the important elements

ITQ14
List the **three** parties to a completed cheque.

Types of cheque

Blank cheque

blank cheque ▶

A blank cheque is one that has no numerical value written in, but is already signed. Persons assigned to preparing cheques in the Accounts Office will then fill in the relevant information on the cheque.

Open cheque

open cheque ▶

An open cheque has no parallel lines drawn across the face. An open cheque can be cashed at the bank, endorsed over to another person or used as payment for good or services.

Crossed cheque

crossed cheque ▶

A crossed cheque has two parallel lines drawn across the face and this indicates that the cheque cannot be cashed over the counter of a bank. A crossed cheque may be opened by the drawer who places his/her signature between the two parallel lines.

Dishonoured cheque

dishonoured cheque ▶

A dishonoured cheque is one which has been paid over to the supplier of goods and/or services and taken it to the bank to be cashed, however, the bank indicated that the cheque could not be cashed. These cheques are known as returned deposit items (RDIs) or non-sufficient funds (NSF) cheques. Cheques may be dishonoured for any of the following reasons:

- the issuing of a stop order on a cheque;
- insufficient funds in the account;
- the drawer's account has been frozen;
- the cheque was written out more than six months ago;
- the cheque is not signed;
- the amounts in words and figures differ.

bounced ▶

rubber cheque ▶

A cheque drawn on an account with insufficient funds is said to have 'bounced' and may be called a 'rubber cheque'. Banks will typically charge customers for issuing a dishonoured cheque, and in some jurisdictions such an act is a criminal action.

Post-dated cheque

▶ **post-dated cheque**

A post-dated cheque is one written to be cashed or deposited on a future date. The bank will not accept a post-dated cheque until the date stated on it.

Certified/manager's cheque

▶ **certified cheque**

A certified cheque is a form of cheque for which the bank verifies that there are sufficient funds currently in the drawer's account to cover the amount to be paid, and so certifies the cheque at the time it is written. Those funds are then set aside in the bank's internal account until the cheque is cashed or returned by the payee. Thus, a certified cheque cannot 'bounce', and, for this reason, its liquidity is similar to cash. A certified cheque is used when payment must be guaranteed. A fee is charged by banks for preparing certified cheques.

Traveller's cheque

▶ **traveller's cheques**

Traveller's cheques are usually used by persons who are travelling and who do not wish to carry large amount of cash. They are usually bought from a bank. The cheque is signed twice: once at the time of purchase and again at the point of use. Traveller's cheques are available in various denominations, usually $20, $50 or $100.

Stale cheque

▶ **stale cheque**

A stale cheque is one written over six months ago.

Order cheque

▶ **order cheques**
▶ **endorsee**

Order cheques are payable only to the named payee or his/her endorsee, as it usually contains the wording 'Pay to the order of (name)'.

Bearer cheque

▶ **bearer cheque**

A bearer cheque is payable to anyone who is in possession of the document: this would be the case if the cheque does not state a payee, or is payable to 'bearer' or to 'cash' or 'to the order of cash'.

Counter cheque

▶ **counter cheque**

ITQ15

List **three** types of cheque.

A counter cheque is a bank cheque given to customers who have run out of paper cheques or whose cheques are not yet available. It is often left blank, and is used for the purposes of withdrawal.

Cheque crossings

▶ **crossed cheque**

ITQ16

List **three** reasons why a bank may refuse to accept a cheque.

A crossed cheque has two parallel lines drawn across its face and must be deposited into a bank account. Crossed cheques must be paid into a bank account and cannot be cashed over the counter. There are a number of cheque crossings that can be used by persons who operate a current account.

If a cheque is not crossed and the payee does not have a bank account, he/she can endorse the cheque by signing it on the back and then passing it on to someone in exchange for cash. Crossing a cheque is a means of ensuring that only the rightful holder receives payment. Even if some wrongful person manages to obtain payment, it can be traced because he/she can receive the funds only through an account with a bank.

There are two main types of crossings used on cheques. These are:
- general crossing;
- special crossing.

General crossing

▶ **general crossing**

A general crossing exists where a cheque has two parallel lines drawn across its face, without any words written in between these two lines. In general crossings the name of the banker is not mentioned.

special crossing ▶

Special crossing

A special crossing occurs where a cheque has two parallel lines written across its face, with directions written between the lines – for example 'not negotiable'. Where a cheque is crossed specially, the banker on whom it is drawn must not pay it otherwise than to the banker to whom it is crossed or to his agent for collection.

The following are some other types of crossings:

'account payee' or restrictive crossing ▶

'Account payee' or restrictive crossing

An 'account payee' or restrictive crossing can be made in both general and special crossings by adding the words 'account payee' between the two parallel lines. In this type of crossing the collecting banker is supposed to credit the amount of the cheque to the account of the named payee only.

'Not negotiable' crossing

'not negotiable' ▶

The words 'not negotiable' can be added to general as well as special crossings and a crossing with these words is known as a 'not negotiable' crossing. Its effect is that it stops the cheque from being transferred to a third party. If the cheque is transferred, the person receiving the cheque has no more claim to the money than the person who passes it on.

'A/C Sam & Hayles Printers' (for example)

This type of cheque crossing indicates that the cheque must be lodged to the bank account of the company named between the two parallel lines at the specified branch of a bank and no other branch of that bank or to any other bank.

ITQ17

What is the difference between special crossings and general crossings?

Endorsement

endorsement ▶

Endorsement refers to the signing of the back of a cheque before it is presented to a bank or other business organization for payment.

Bank statement of account

bank statement of account ▶
credits ▶
debit ▶

A bank statement of account is a document listing all payments into (credits) and payments out of (debit) an individual account over a set period of time, usually one month. It also shows the opening monthly balance as well as the monthly closing balance. This document is sent to the account holder, usually at the end of the month. Currently, many banks are sending paperless bank statements. These are online statements of all financial transactions completed on behalf of the customer. Customers are then able to check online to view their banking transactions.

The statement usually shows some or all of the following, depending on the nature of the monthly transactions done on behalf of the account holder:

Deposits	Withdrawals
interest earned	ATM withdrawals
cheque lodgement	cheque withdrawals
dishonoured cheques	bank charges or fees
direct debits	standing order payments
	credit transfers

Table 9.1 Types of transaction shown on bank statements of account

BANK STATEMENT OF ACCOUNT

FIRST LOCAL BANK

45 Parrots Boulevard

Kingston

JAMAICA

Tel: 876-905-5190   Date: June 30, 2011

To: Peter Anderson
3b Bingh Street
Kingston

DATE	DETAILS	DEBIT	CREDIT	BALANCE
June 1	Balance b/f			10,000.00
June 2	Credit transfer		2,000	12,000.00
June 10	Deposit		15,000	27,000.00
June 14	Direct debit	4,100		22,900.00
June 26	Cheque no 007	3,200		19,700.00
June 28	Standing order: loan	8,000		11,700.00

Figure 9.5 Example of a bank statement

Bank reconciliation statement

bank reconciliation ▶ Bank reconciliation is the process of comparing figures from the business accounting records with those shown on the bank statement. Whenever the bank statement is received it should be compared with the customer's records. Usually, the statement and the company's records do not show the same balance. The reasons for the discrepancy can be many and varied.

The following are some reasons why the customer's account balance and the bank statement balance may not agree:

unpresented cheques ▶
- **Unpresented cheques.** Cheques given to creditors who have not yet taken them to the bank for payment. These should be credited in the cash book.

late lodgements /
outstanding deposits ▶
- **Late lodgements / outstanding deposits.** Cheques received and lodged with the bank after the statement was prepared or the cheques were not cleared by the bank.

- **Standing orders.** These are regular payments of a fixed amount made by the bank at the customer's request. These transactions would be recorded on the bank statement but not in the customer's cash book.

- **Cash book errors.** Errors which occur when transactions are entered on the wrong side of the account or a figure is written incorrectly – for example, $37 may have been written as '$73'.

bank charges ▶
- **Bank/service charges.** Bank charges are deducted from the customer's account by the bank for completing transactions on the customer's behalf.

credit transfer ▶
- **Credit transfers.** A credit push or bank credit transfer is a method whereby the buyer instructs his/her bank to send funds to the seller. The transfer can be initiated online, via the telephone or in person.

interest paid / received ▶
- **Interest paid / received.** At times, the account holder is paid interest directly into his/her account by the bank. The bank may deduct interest from the account holder, depending on the agreement.

After the reasons for the difference in balances have been noted, adjustments must be made. The items which appear in the bank statement but not in the cash book should be recorded in the updated cash book and the items in the cash book but not on the bank statement should be used to prepare the bank reconciliation statement.

Steps in reconciling bank statement

The following steps should be followed when reconciling the bank statement with the cash book:

1 Compare the cash book entries with the bank statement entries and note the unknown items.
2 Compare the bank statement entries with the cash book and note the unknown items.
3 Update the cash book with the items from the bank statement which were unknown.
bank reconciliation statement ▶ 4 Prepare the bank reconciliation statement using the items from the cash book.

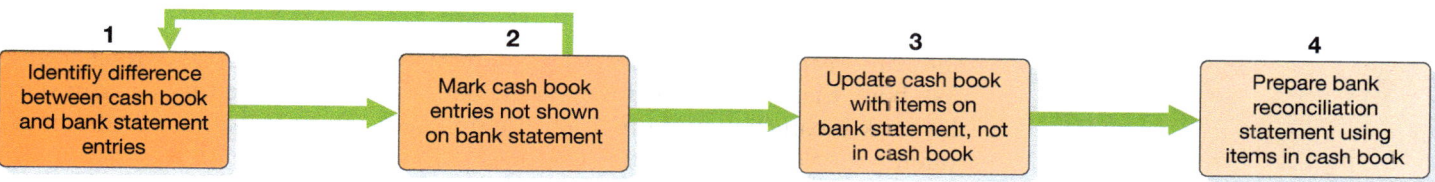

Figure 9.6 Bank reconciliation steps

Figures 9.7 and 9.8 are extracts from the cash book and the bank statement for Trendy Fashion Manufacturing Company for the month of June 2011. Note that on examination of the two documents the items found on one account and not the other were highlighted. These were found after following steps 1 and 2 outlined above.

Date	Details	Folio	Amount	Date	Details	Folio	Amount
2011 June 1	Balance	B/f	6 200	June 1	Premium Carpeting		3,600
June 6	D. Dallas		6 000	June 3	Z. Vassel		850
June 12	R. Kelly		4 000	June 14	D. Mullings		700
June 25	Sales		1 500	June 18	ABC Co. Ltd		1 050
June 29	Y. Henry		1 100	June 26	A. Alli		500
June 30	G. James		1 300	June 26	Printry Plus		650
				June 27	F. Gayle		460
				June 28	Sandy Styles		1 300

Figure 9.7 Cash book for Trendy Fashion (bank columns only)

Date	Details	Debit	Credit	Balance
June 1	Balance			6 200
June 7	D Dallas		6 000	12 200
June 10	Z Vassel	850		11 350
June 14	D Mullings	700		10 650
June 14	Lodgement		1 500	12 150
June 16	Share interest		1 000	13 150
June 25	Lodgments		1 100	14 250
June 27	Standing order – Insurance	3 260		10 990
June 27	A Alli	500		10 490
June 28	Premium Carpeting	3 600		6 890
June 30	Bank charges	110	6 780	
June 30	Credit transfer		290	7 070

Figure 9.8 Bank statement for Trendy Fashion

The updated cash book is prepared after identifying the items in the bank statement that were not included in the cash book. See Figure 9.9.

Date	Details	Folio	Amount	Date	Details	Folio	Amount
2011 June 1	Balance	B/f	10 990	June 1	Standing order		3,260
June 16	Interest		1 000	June 30	Bank charges		110
June 30	Cedit transfer		290	June 30	Bal.	c/d	8 910
			12 280				12 280
June	Bal.	B/d	8 910				

Figure 9.9 Updated cash book for Trendy Fashion

The bank reconciliation statement is prepared after identifying the items in the cash book that were not included in the bank statement. Note that you can start the bank reconciliation with either the updated cash book balance or the bank statement balance. The methods are done in for you in Figures 9.10 and 9.11.

	$	$
Balance as per updated cash book		8 910
Add: unpresented cheques	1 050	
	650	
	460	
	1 000	3 460
		12 370
Less: late lodgements	4 000	
	1 300	5 300
Balance as per bank statement		7 070

Figure 9.10 Bank reconciliation statement as at June 30, 2011 (Method 1)

	$	$
Balance as per bank statement		7 070
Add: late lodgements	4 000	
	1 300	5 300
		12 730
Less: unpresented cheques	1 050	
	650	
	460	
	1 300	3 460
Balance as per bank statement		8 910

Figure 9.11 Bank reconciliation statement as at June 30, 2011 (Method 2)

ITQ18

The following data is available for Trendy Fashion for October 2011:
- book balance, October 31: $5,575;
- outstanding cheques: $584;
- deposits in transit: $2,500;
- service charges: $75;
- interest revenue: $25.
  i What is the adjusted cash book balance on October 31, 2011 for Trendy Fashion, based on the above data?
  ii Prepare the adjusted cash book and bank reconciliation statement.

Petty cash

petty cash ▶ Petty cash is a small amount of funds used for small cash payments. This fund is set up to cover payments so small that it would be costly to prepare cheques for them. The petty cash duties are usually given to a junior clerk who is responsible for disbursing the funds according to the rules of the company.

The imprest system

imprest system ▶ Petty cash is controlled by an imprest system. The person in charge of the imprest is called a petty cashier. He/she is given an amount to operate the petty cash and this amount is called the imprest or float. The float is given for a **float ▶** specific period, for example weekly, monthly or even quarterly. Monies are paid **petty cash voucher ▶** out from the float when an authorization form (petty cash voucher) is presented with a valid signature.

petty cash book ▶ In a petty cash book, the analysis columns (which are headed according to requirements) enable petty cash in any class of item to be determined at a glance. Additionally, when the total is added to the sum of money in the cash box (the balance); it should represent the starting sum. Once checked, the chief cashier should reimburse the expenses and in this way re-establish the initial imprest.

The petty cash book consists of two sides: on one side payments into the account are recorded and on the other side payments out of the account. Any payment made must be recorded twice: once in the total column and again in the analysis column. There is also a 'petty cash voucher number' column for recording the number on the petty cash voucher. See Figure 9.12.

PETTY CASH BOOK

Credit	Date	Details	Voucher #	Total	Postage	Travel	Stationery	Cleaning
110	Apr. 30	Bal. b/f						
90	May 1	Cash						
	May 1	Stamps	1	20.00	20.00			
	May 4	Bus fare	2	15.00		15.00		
	May 5	Pens	3	10.00			10.00	
	May 14	Soap	4	6.00				6.00
	May 18	Aerogramme	5	20.00	20.00			
	May 20	Petrol	6	50.00		50.00		
	May 22	Bond paper	7	16.00			16.00	
	May 27	Broom	8	19.00				19.00
				156.00	40.00	65.00	26.00	25.00
	May 31	Bal c/d		44.00				
200.00				200.00				
44.00	June 1	Bal b/d						
156.00		Cash replenish						
200.00								

Figure 9.12   A completed petty cash book page

Petty cash vouchers

Payments are authorized on petty cash vouchers. These vouchers are normally issued before the person in charge of the petty cash book pays out any money. The petty cash vouchers are used as the source documents for preparing the petty cash book. See Figure 9.13.

PETTY CASH VOUCHER

Folio _____   Date: _____

For what required	AMOUNT	
	$	C

Signature: _____

Passed by: _____

Figure 9.13   Example of a petty cash voucher

ITQ19

Based on the following petty cash information, prepare a petty cash sheet showing the entry for October 1, 2011 when a $300 cheque was written to establish the petty cash fund. During the month, the following vouchers were written for cash taken from the petty cash fund:

Oct 1	Postage expense	$11.00
4	Miscellaneous expense	$16.00
7	John Smith – bus fare	$36.00
10	Telephone expense	$45.00
15	Charity contribution expense	$30.00
28	Writing paper	$39.00.

Hardware resources

hardware resources ▶ Hardware resources are the peripheral devices and the assignable, addressable bus paths that allow those devices and system processors to communicate with each other.

Calculator

calculators ▶ Modern electronic calculators are small, digital and usually inexpensive devices to perform the basic operations of arithmetic. In addition to general-purpose calculators, there are some designed for specific markets. For example, there are scientific calculators that focus on operations slightly more complex than those specific to arithmetic, such as trigonometric and statistical calculations; others have the ability to do computer algebra.

Adding machine

adding machine ▶ An adding machine is a type of calculator, usually specialized for bookkeeping calculations. Adding machines have now largely been phased out in favour of personal computers.

Computer

computer ▶ A computer is a programmable machine that receives input, stores and manipulates data, and provides output in a useful format. The ability to store and execute lists of instructions called programs makes computers extremely versatile, distinguishing them from calculators. There are many types of computers, ranging from notebooks to a supercomputers, and they are all able to perform the same computational tasks, given enough time and storage capacity.

Computers needs software applications in order for them to perform tasks: some of these applications are word processing, spreadsheets, databases, web browsers and e-mail. In the past, personal computer users had to write programs to operate the machines: today's users have access to a wide range of commercial and non-commercial software which is easy to use.

Printer

printer ▶
peripheral ▶
hard copy ▶
USB cable ▶

In computing, a printer is a peripheral which produces a hard copy, i.e. a readable text and/or graphics of documents stored in electronic form, usually on physical print media such as paper or transparencies. Many printers are attached to a computer by a printer cable or, in most newer printers, a USB cable which serves as a document source.

memory sticks ▶
memory cards ▶
digital cameras ▶

Some modern printers can directly interface to electronic media such as memory sticks or memory cards or to image-capture devices such as digital cameras and scanners; some printers are combined with scanners and/or fax machines in a single unit and can also function as photocopiers. Some printers, called 'multifunction printers' or 'all-in-one printers', include printing, scanning and copying as well as other features.

Scanner

scanner ▶

A scanner is a device that scans images, printed text, handwriting or an object, and converts it to a digital image. Common types found in offices are variations of desktop (or flatbed) scanner ▶ the desktop (or flatbed) scanner where the document is placed on a glass hand-held scanners ▶ window for scanning. Hand-held scanners, where the device is moved by hand, have evolved from text scanning 'wands' to 3D scanners used for industrial design, reverse engineering, test and measurement, gaming and other applications.

Photocopier

photocopier ▶

xerography ▶

A photocopier, also referred to as a 'copier', is a machine that makes multiple paper copies of documents and other visual images quickly and cheaply. Most current photocopiers use a technology called xerography – a dry process using heat. Photocopying is widely used in business, education and government.

Software resources

software resources ▶

The following software resources are commonly used:

Accounting packages

accounting package ▶

An accounting package is a software application that records and processes accounting transactions within functional modules such as accounts payable, accounts receivable, payroll and trial balance.

An accounting package is a useful tool, however, users must have an accounting background or a consultant may have to be hired to set up the system. Many types of accounting packages may be utilized by companies. Some of the most common ones are:

QuickBooks

QuickBooks by Intuit ▶

QuickBooks by Intuit is seen as the market leader in entry-level accounting software. It is specifically intended for small businesses without much accounting experience, and is relatively easy to get up and running. On the other hand, it is not as customizable as an application such as Peachtree, so users who want to set up their books or reports in a particular way may find it limiting.

Peachtree

Peachtree by Sage ▶

Peachtree by Sage is another type of accounting software that allows the setting up of reports and accounting charts as they are required. The Peachtree accounting package assumes that users have basic accounting experience.

Fund ware

Fund ware by Kintera ▶

Fund ware by Kintera is a more robust accounting package and is specifically geared towards non-profit and government organizations. It includes functionality for managing activities, projects, and grants, cost centres, contracts and investments.

**Summary**

- The functions of the Accounts Office are: preparation of payroll; credit control; collection of accounts; treatment of debit and credit notes; preparation of audit.
- Payroll is used to calculate the net pay of workers.
- Many terms are used to describe the payment for work done by workers, such as: 'bonus rate', 'piece rate', 'flat rate', 'commission', 'wages' and 'salary', among others.
- Statutory and voluntary deductions are taken from workers' pay.
- Statutory deductions are compulsory deductions required by law to be taken from an employee's pay.
- Voluntary deductions are those that workers request be taken from their pay.
- Gross pay includes regular pay as well as any overtime earned by the employee, i.e. it is the pay amount before any deductions are made.
- Net pay is the amount remaining after taken out all deductions.
- Auditing is the checking of the accounting documents of an organization to ensure that all records are correct and up to date.

- The most common types of electronic transfer are those from Automatic Teller Machines and direct deposits.
- Some of the many ways in which funds can be transferred are: bank draft, bank money order and electronic transfer
- There are many types of financial institution, which collect and invest funds on behalf of private as well as public investors.
- Financial institutions include: banks, building societies, credit unions and insurance companies.
- A bank is a financial institution that provides financial services to customers.
- Some services offered by banks are: savings and current accounts, standing order facilities, credit transfers and direct debits.
- A cheque is an order in writing, addressed to a bank, to pay on demand a specific sum of money to the named payee.
- Many types of cheques are used by banks.
- A statement of account is sent to each current account holder at the end of each month, showing all the transactions done on his/her behalf by the bank.
- The statement of account is used by the account holder to update the cash book and reconcile the bank statement.
- A petty cash fund is used to pay for small cash payments, such as postage stamps, petrol and bus fares.

Answers to 

1 **i.** Preparation of payroll.
   ii. Credit control.
   iii Collection and payment of accounts.

2 Any hours worked over 40 in a week are overtime hours. Nevrene worked 16 overtime hours (56 − 40 = 16). Nevrene's pay for the week is calculated as follows:

Regular pay: 40 x $320	= $12,800
Overtime pay:16 x $480	= $7,680
Total pay:	$ 20,480

3 Salary is usually paid on a monthly basis (calculated yearly, then divided by 12) and is usually paid to civil servants such as teachers, policemen etc., while wages are usually paid weekly or bi-weekly and are usually paid to workers such as waiters, babysitters, cleaners etc.

4 Voluntary deductions are taken from an employee's salary on the instruction of the employee – for example, payment for staff dues or life insurance premiums. Statutory deductions are taken from an employee's salary without his/her specific consent and are deductions required by law, such as income tax or education tax.

5 Any hours worked over 38 in a week are overtime hours. Shane worked 11 overtime hours (49 − 38 = 11). Shane's gross pay for the week is calculated as follows:

Regular pay: 38 x $200	= $7,600
Overtime pay:11 x $300	= $3,300
Bonus pay	= $310
GROSS PAY:	$ 11,210

6

	Regular pay: 38 x $280	= $10,640
	Overtime pay:11 x $340	= $3,740
	Bonus pay	= $590
	GROSS PAY:	**$ 14,970**
DEDUCTIONS		
Income tax	3,742.50	
NIS	299.40	
Credit union	95.00	
Health plan	50.00	
Less: Total deductions		4,186.90
NET PAY		10,783.10

7 Pay is the payment made by the employer to an employee for the services rendered by the employee. Gross pay is the total salary including the standard deductions which include bonuses, commissions and all other allowances. For example, if a person, before joining an organization, is told that his/her salary would be $87,000, then this is his/her gross pay or salary.

Net pay, on the other hand, is the salary after all the deductions have been made. Net pay is the salary in hand. So, a person with a gross salary of $87,000 may receive a net pay of $55,000, after all the deductions have been made.

8 11,278.00 + 8,410.50 + 6,630 + 9,714.00 + 10,260.00 + 10,516.50 = $56,809.

9 The amount of credit given to customers must be controlled, as giving too much credit may result in a company experiencing cash flow problems. Remember that credit is a two-way function. Your suppliers give credit to you and you give credit to your customers. If your customers do not pay on time, you may have difficulty in paying your suppliers on time. Also, controlling the amount of credit will reduce the risk of bad debts.

10 A secured loan/debt is one in which the creditor maintains a security interest in an item or piece of personal property such as a house or an automobile. With secured loans/debts, if the debtor falls behind on payments, the lender can repossess the property that originally secured the debt.

An unsecured loan/debt is one in which the debtor borrows from a creditor to obtain goods or services on credit in exchange for a promise to repay the debt. The primary difference between secured and unsecured debt is that unsecured debt does not require the borrower to present collateral but secured loans require collaterals.

11

Main features of current, savings, money market and certificate of deposit accounts			
Current account	**Savings account**	**Money market account**	**Certificate of deposit account**
Receive money	Interest is paid on deposits	Interest is paid on this account	Fixed interest rate
Allows for the payment of bills	A debit card is given by the bank	Minimum balance should be maintained in account	Easy withdrawal of funds
The bank will issue a cash card	Allows for bills payment	Restrictions on the number of withdrawals per month.	Funds must be deposited for a fixed time

12 Standing order:
- A standing order requires the customer's bank to send the money.
- A standing order might be used to pay a fixed amount.
- With a standing order, customers need to give their bank new instructions each time a change is needed.

Direct debit:
- A direct debit requires the beneficiary to claim the money.
- A direct debit is more likely to be used to make payments the amount of which can vary from time to time.
- When the payment amount changes, the beneficiary can claim the new amount automatically.

13
- Standing order facility.
- Mortgage facilities.
- Credit transfer system.
- Current account.

14
- Drawer.
- Payee.
- Drawee.

15
- Crossed cheques.
- Certified cheques.
- Dishonoured cheques.

16
- A cheque written out for a future date.
- The cheque may be stale, i.e. if six months have passed.
- There may be a correction on the cheque which was not initialled by the writer of the cheque.

17 Crossed cheques are those, the payment of which is not made over the counter. There are two types of crossing: general crossings and special crossings. In general crossings, two transverse parallel lines are drawn across the face of the cheque, with or without the words '& Co', 'not negotiable' etc. but not including the name of a bank. In the case of special crossings, two transverse parallel lines are drawn across the face of the cheque with the name of the bank.

18 Adjusted cash book balance is $5,525.

Examination-style questions

Multiple choice questions

1 A stale cheque is one which was written over how long ago?:
   a three months
   b six months
   c nine months
   d twelve months.

2 For which of the following reasons might a time/clock card be used?
   a To calculate salaries for workers.
   b To show the time required to complete a job.
   c To calculate monthly salaries for workers.
   d To calculate the number of hours needed to complete a job.

3 The original petty cash float was $90.00. $40.00 remains in the till at the end of the period. The new imprest is to be increased by $21.00. How much is needed to replenish the petty cash?
   a $50.00
   b $51.00
   c $61.00
   d $71.00.

4 The drawee of a cheque is the:
   a person who receives the cheque
   b person who writes the cheque
   c bank on which the cheque is drawn
   d person who sold the cheque.

5 Cancelled cheques that are sent with a bank statement are those which:
   a the bank dishonoured
   b the bank exchanged for cash
   c are more than four months old
   d the account holder lodged in their account.

6 A bank statement is defined as a document:
   a listing all payments into and out of an individual account
   b listing all small cash payments
   c indicating an overdraft
   d listing the balance of the business cash account.

7 Which of the following would be included on a bank statement from a bank?
   a Unpresented cheques.
   b Dishonoured cheques.
   c Petty cash payments.
   d Invoices.

8 Polish Jewellery Company provides the following information about the month end. Use the information to show the correct bank reconciliation figure.

Ending cash per bank statement	$1,367
Ending cash per company records	7,383
Monthly bank service charge	25
Deposits in transit at month end	8,345
Outstanding cheques at month end	2,399
Customer cheque returned NSF	45

The correct ending cash balance at the bank is:
   a $4,914
   b $7,268
   c $7,313
   d $7,383.

Structured questions

1   List **three** functions of the Accounts Office. [3]

2   With the exception of wages or salaries, outline **four** terms which could be used to refer to rewards earned for work done. [4]

3   Explain the difference between wages and salaries, giving **two** examples of persons who are paid each. [4]

4   List and explain the statutory deductions taken from employees' salaries.

5   List **three** fringe benefits which may be offered to employees. [3]

6   List **four** duties which should be performed by an Accounts Clerk. [4]

7   A bank offers a number of services to customers. List and explain **four** such services offered. [8]

8   List and explain **four** types of cheque. [4]

9   There a number of ways in which payments may be made by bank customers. List, with brief explanation, **three** such methods other than cheques. [6]

10 Explain the meaning of 'cheque crossings', giving two examples. [3]

11 Give **three** reasons why a bank may refuse to accept a cheque. [3]

12 The petty cashier for your company is absent from work because of illness. You are asked to take over the petty cash duties until she returns to work. On March 1 you inspect the petty cash till and observe a balance of $142.00, a petty cash voucher book which begins at number 14, and an envelope marked 'petty cash reimbursement' which amounts to $158.00. During the month you make the following transactions:

July	1	Paid for postage	$30.00
	9	Purchased Cello tape	$22.70
	12	Purchased *Daily Gleaner*	$50.00
	18	Paid for bus fare	$40.00
	25	Purchased bond paper	$35.10
	27	Purchased stamps	$20.00
	30	Purchased soap	$15.50

Draft a petty cash form and enter the above transaction, balance the petty cash book and restore the imprest as at August 1, 2010, increasing the original imprest by $20.00. [8]

13 Mrs Trudy James works at Delmar Lumber Co Ltd. She is paid a regular rate of $350.00 per hour for the 40-hour work week and time and a half for the next three hours. After that, she is paid double time for all other hours. Note that the regular starting time (Monday to Friday) is 8.00 am. She is allowed a five-minute grace period without deduction.

Use Mrs James' clock card in Figure 9.14 to calculate:
a the total hours worked; [4]
b her regular and overtime earnings; [4]
c her gross pay. [3]

CLOCK/TIME CARD

Employee's name: ___Mrs Trudy James___ Date: ___November 11, 2011___
Employee's no: ___1234___ Department: Production

DAY	Regular hours				Overtime		Total Hours
	IN	OUT	IN	OUT	IN	OUT	
Monday	0755	1200	1300	1700	1730	2000	
Tuesday	0804	1200	1300	1705	1700	1730	
Wednesday	0800	1200	1300	1700	1730	1930	
Thursday	0805	1300	1400	1730	–	–	
Friday	0757	1200	1300	1701	1730	1930	
Saturday	–	–	–	–	1000	1400	
TOTAL HOURS							

Note: Total hours include regular and overtime hours.

Regular time _____   Overtime _____

Gross pay $ _____

Figure 9.14 Clock/time card

14 O Dallas, Z Emanuel, M Smith, U Pitters and L Harvey all work at ABC Co Ltd. Each worker works a regular work week of 38 hours, at a rate of $420.00 per hour. However, T Thomas, C Harris and P Reynolds each work 44, 46 and 47 hours respectively at a rate of 1½ times regular rate.

NOTE:
a All workers except D Bromfield and P Reynolds pay union dues of $120.00.
b All workers pay income tax of 25%, National Insurance of 2%, National Housing Trust of 2% and education tax of 1.5%.
c Thomas and Harris pay Blue Cross costs of $250.00.

Draft a payroll sheet and calculate the payroll for the above employees. [10]

15 Briefly explain the following terms:
a dishonoured cheque
b bank charges
c credit transfer
d direct debit. [8]

16 **a** List the procedures to be followed before preparing a bank reconciliation statement. [6]

b Figures 9.15 and 9.16 show the cash book and bank statement respectively for Material Plus Co Ltd for August 31, 2011.

Date	Details	Folio	Amount	Date	Details	Folio	Amount
2011 Aug. 1	Balance	B/f	8 100	June 1	V Nelson		500
Aug. 3	Peter Lucas		5 300	Aug. 4	Materials & More		300
Aug. 6	Trevor Miller		2 000	Aug. 11	Fagan Ray		540
Aug. 16	Sales		3 500	Aug. 14	Jay's Garments		2 900
Aug. 20	George Lee		4 700	Aug. 19	Sandra Henry		750
Aug. 31	Lenna Smith		3 050	Aug. 22	Perfect Wear Ltd		290
				Aug. 25	Y Willis		880
				Aug. 27	Andrew Collins		1 900
				Aug. 31	Balance		18 590
			26 650				26 650
	Balance	B/d	18 590				

Figure 9.15 Cash book for Material Plus (bank columns only)

MATERIAL PLUS COMPANY

Date	Details	Debit	Credit	Balance
Aug 1	Balance			8 100
Aug 4	Peter Lucas		5 300	13 400
Aug 4	Material & More	300		13 100
Aug 13	Fagan Ray	540		12 560
Aug 14	Trevor Miller		2 000	14 560
Aug 20	Lodgments		4 700	19 260
Aug 24	Standing order – insurance	1 790		17 470
Aug 26	Perfect Wear Ltd	290		17 180
Aug 30	Bank charges	365		16 815
June 30	Trader's credit		945	17 760

Figure 9.16 Bank statement for Material Plus

You are required to prepare:

i the revised cash book for Material Plus Co Ltd; [5]

ii a statement to reconcile the revised cashbook with the bank statement. [4]

10 Procurement and inventory management

By the end of this chapter you should be able to:

- ☑ identify the functions of the Procurement Office;
- ☑ define terminology and abbreviations used in purchasing;
- ☑ state the duties of the Purchasing Clerk;
- ☑ outline purchasing procedure;
- ☑ prepare documents used in purchasing;
- ☑ identify the different types of stock;
- ☑ explain the importance of inventory management;
- ☑ describe the types of stocktaking/inventory;
- ☑ maintain stock records;
- ☑ calculate the value of closing stock.

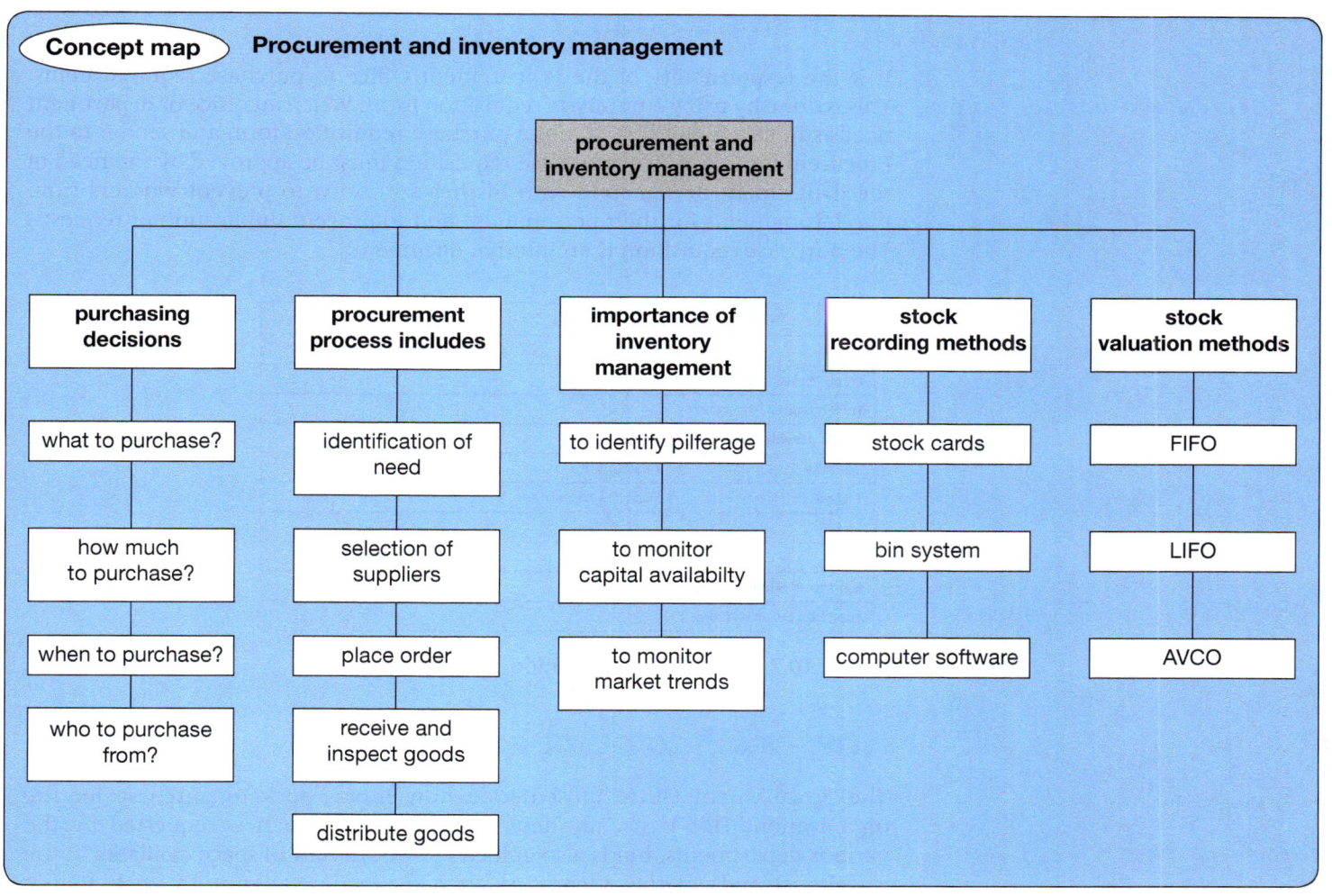

Concept map Procurement and inventory management

procurement and inventory management

purchasing decisions	procurement process includes	importance of inventory management	stock recording methods	stock valuation methods
what to purchase?	identification of need	to identify pilferage	stock cards	FIFO
how much to purchase?	selection of suppliers	to monitor capital availabilty	bin system	LIFO
when to purchase?	place order	to monitor market trends	computer software	AVCO
who to purchase from?	receive and inspect goods			
	distribute goods			

Procurement functions

Procurement involves sourcing and obtaining goods, such as raw materials and equipment, and services necessary to carry on the productive activities of a business. The process of procurement in an organization may be **centralized** ▶ or **decentralized** ▶.

When procurement is decentralized in an organization it means that each department will handle its own purchasing needs. If procurement is centralized, it means that one department, the Procurement Office, will be responsible for taking care of the purchasing needs of the entire organization.

Benefits of having a centralized purchasing system include:
- the ability to employ specialized personnel who are trained or have experience in purchasing;
- having uniformed purchasing standards;
- receiving larger trade discounts;
- making possible an efficient record-keeping system.

The head of the Procurement Office may be known as the Chief Buyer, the Purchasing Director or the Chief Procurement Officer. This individual is accountable to the upper-level managers. The Chief Buyer will have a number of important purchasing decisions to make, such as what to purchase; how much to purchase; when to purchase; and who to purchase from.

What to purchase?

purchase requisition form ▶

It is the responsibility of the Procurement Office to purchase required items. This is done by using a purchase requisition form. When an office or department needs supplies it will first fill out a purchase requisition form and send it to the Procurement Office. The purchase requisition must be approved by the head of the department or someone with his/her authority, to prevent workers from purchasing items for their personal use and to prevent duplication of requests. The purchase requisition is an internal document.

PURCHASE REQUISITION		Requisition # : 123
Bell & Co Ltd		**Date:** April 1, 2009
From: Marketing Department		
To: Procurement Department		
Please provide the following items:		
Quantity	**Description**	
3 reams	Photocopy paper	
Suggested Suppliers: Paper & More Ltd		
Approved by: Lorna Brown		

Figure 10.1 A purchase requisition

How much to purchase?

The Procurement Office must decide how much stock to purchase for the organization. This is usually determined by how much is requested by the various departments, but is also guided by the amount of space available in the warehouse and whether there is an already adequate amount in stock. Before the Procurement Office makes orders from external companies, an officer will usually check the warehouse to see whether the item is already in stock. The Purchasing Officers may also want to purchase goods in bulk, to take advantage of trade discounts.

When to purchase?

The Procurement Office also needs to make decisions relating to when it should buy. In many cases it will choose to buy the goods 'as soon as possible' (ASAP), depending on how urgently they are needed. However, other factors could guide this decision – for example, if there is an anticipated price fall the buyers may delay purchase, if they can, in order to benefit from the reduced cost.

The availability of the goods will also play a role in determining when to purchase. Some items may be available only at certain times of the year, so the Procurement Office will have to wait to make the purchase. For example, mangoes are seasonal fruits and are usually available in abundance only during summer months in the Caribbean.

Who to purchase from?

The Procurement Office needs to decide which supplier it will use to obtain the goods. This decision can be based on a number of factors, such as the cost of the goods, which can be obtained from the price lists or catalogue of prospective suppliers. It is usual for the Purchasing Clerk to maintain an index of suppliers, which is a list of suppliers of various goods and services and their contact information.

The choice of supplier can also be based on the quality of goods or services provided, as well as the reputation of the firm. Other factors include special benefits or incentives that may be offered, such as the provision of delivery services, discounts or credit facilities.

It is important for the Procurement Office to identify reliable sources of supply, and to establish good relationships with them, so that if the company finds that it needs emergency stock, the supplier would be willing to assist.

Liaising with other departments and offices

In order to carry out its various functions, the Procurement Department needs to maintain relationships with a number of departments, including the following:

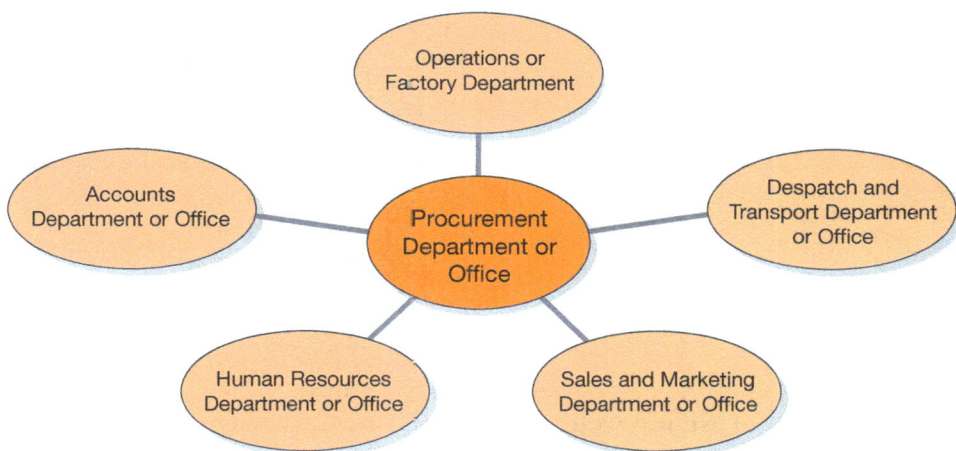

Figure 10.2 Relationship between the Procurement Department and other departments in the business

Operations or Factory Department

Operations or Factory Department ▶

The Procurement Department needs to liaise with the Operations or Factory Department in order to purchase the necessary raw materials, supplies and equipment needed to carry out the production process in an effective and efficient manner.

Human Resources Department

Human Resources Department ▶

The Procurement Department will need to liaise with the Human Resources Department whenever there are vacancies within the Procurement Department that need to be filled. The Human Resources Department will also deal with training and appraisal of the Procurement Department staff as well as dealing with aspects of general staff welfare.

Accounts Department

Accounts Department ▶

It is important for the Procurement Department to establish a close relationship with the Accounts Department, as it is the Accounts Department that is responsible for all the financial allocations in the business. It is ultimately the Accounts Department that will be responsible for paying the bills for all the purchases made by the Procurement Department. The Accounts Department will also be responsible for paying the wages and salaries of the workers in the Procurement Department.

Sales and Marketing Department

Sales and Marketing Department ▶

The Procurement Department needs to liaise with the Sales and Marketing Department in order to provide all the supplies and equipment needed to carry on the day-to-day operations of the department.

Despatch and Transport Department

Despatch and Transport Department ▶

ITQ1
State **three** departments with which the Procurement Office must liaise, and explain why.

There needs to be a close relationship between the Procurement Department and the Despatch and Transport Department as it may be necessary for this department to transport the goods purchased by the Procurement Department to the business's warehouse. The Procurement Department will also be responsible for purchasing equipment and supplies necessary for the operations of the Despatch and Transport Department.

Terminology and abbreviations used in purchasing

It will become necessary for individuals in the Procurement Department to become familiar with certain terms and abbreviations which may appear on various purchasing documents. The following are the more common abbreviations:

free on board ▶
- f.o.b. – free on board (sometimes referred to as 'freight on board') is a shipping term which means that the selling price includes the cost of the goods plus transportation and delivery to a specific location, usually on board a ship;

cost and freight ▶
- c.f. – cost and freight (also 'CFR' or 'C&F') – this means that the price quoted includes the cost of the goods as well as transportation charges;

cost, insurance and freight ▶
- c.i.f. – cost, insurance and freight – this is a trade term which indicates that the selling price quoted includes the cost of the product and insurance as well as other transportation charges to a named port of destination;

ex-works ▶ • ex-works (sometimes referred to as 'excluding works', 'ex factory' or 'EXW') – means that the selling price quoted includes only the cost of the goods: the buyer will be responsible for arranging insurance, transportation and other related expenses;

cash with order ▶ • c.w.o. – cash with order (also 'cash in advance' (CIA) or 'cash advance order' (CAO)) – this is a payment method in which an order is not processed until the full payment is received in advance. The buyer pays when ordering;

cash on delivery ▶ • c.o.d.– cash on delivery – this is when the payment for goods/services is made at the time of delivery. The payment methods include cash, cheques, credit cards, debit cards or money orders;

errors and omissions excepted ▶ • e. & o. e. – errors and omissions excepted – this abbreviation is usually placed on documents to indicate that the person who prepared the document reserves the right to correct any errors or omissions on it;

trade discount ▶ • trade discount – this is the rate by which the retail price of goods is reduced when sold to a reseller;

quantity discount ▶ • quantity discount – this can also be defined as a reduction in price given for bulk purchasing;

cash discount ▶ • cash discount – this is a reduction in price given to encourage prompt payment of bills. Examples of cash discount terms are:
  • 2/20 – this means that if the buyer pays his bill within 20 days of the date on the invoice he will receive a 2 per cent discount;
  • n/30 – this means that if the buyer waits until 30 days after the invoice date he has to pay the full price;

special discounts ▶ • special discounts – these are reductions in prices given for various reasons, such as being a regular customer.

ITQ2
What is the difference between a quantity discount and a cash discount?

ITQ3
The following prices for a product were quoted by four suppliers. Which quote is the best deal?
• Supplier A $24 ex works;
• Supplier B $20 c.f.;
• Supplier C $20 ex works;
• Supplier D $21 c.i.f.

ITQ4
A seller quotes a selling price of $15 000 for a machine. He offers dealers a trade discount of 30 per cent. The seller also offers a sales discount of 2/10, n/20. What is the total or net cost of the machine to a dealer, if it is paid for within ten days of purchase?

The Purchasing Clerk

Duties

The Purchasing Clerk has a number of very important tasks to carry out in order to aid the procurement or purchasing process. These include:
• assisting in processing purchase requisitions – he/she may have to check the purchase requisitions received to ensure that they are properly completed and signed;
• receiving deliveries – he/she will be required to receive deliveries on behalf of the firm and inspect them for damage. If all is in order he/she will forward the goods to the appropriate department;
• maintaining inventory records – he/she may need to update documents such as stock cards;
• preparing and verifying the accuracy of purchase orders;
• maintaining a database of suppliers – which will include a list of various suppliers of goods and services and their catalogues or price lists;
• keeping track of the orders and updating the requesting department accordingly;
• making sure that what was ordered is delivered on time and meets the requesting department's specifications;
• performing clerical duties such as answering the telephone and filing purchasing records.

Attributes

- Resourcefulness.
- Good judgement.
- Tact.
- Good negotiation skills.
- Initiative.
- Honesty.
- Creativity.
- Integrity.
- Attention to detail.

Steps in the procurement process

1 The first step in the process would be to identify a suitable supplier. This can be done by searching through the index of suppliers, checking directories or getting recommendations from trade associations. An enquiry note could be sent to a prospective supplier. This will seek to find out the availability of the goods, their prices and any other terms, such as discounts available.

catalogue ▶

2 In response to an enquiry note, the potential seller may submit a catalogue, a price list or a quotation. A catalogue is a document, usually in a booklet or magazine format, containing information about the products available, terms of delivery and prices. The catalogue is usually illustrated with pictures of the items for sale. Some firms will place the prices of the items on a separate price list in order to allow the catalogue to be in circulation for a longer period of time.

invitation to tender ▶

3 In some cases a competitive quotation is required and so an invitation to tender may be used. Invitations to tender may be issued to pre-selected suppliers or to the public at large, especially through newspaper advertisements. Interested suppliers will respond with a tender or bid to provide the particular good or service. It will then be left to the purchasing team to decide on the best bidder, who may not necessarily be the cheapest.

4 Invitations to tender are usually used in public procurement, in which government bodies buy goods and services. However, many private firms also use this method as a way of identifying possible suppliers.

5 When the purchasing team has selected the most suitable supplier, a purchase order is then prepared and sent to them. In many instances when a supplier has received an order they will send an acknowledgement of order to the buyer as evidence that they have received the order.

6 When the goods arrive the Purchasing Clerk may be required to prepare a goods received note (see page 118) to ensure that they match the specifications ordered and then distribute them to the department that raised the purchase order. If there is a problem with the goods, this should be reported to the Procurement Officer for action.

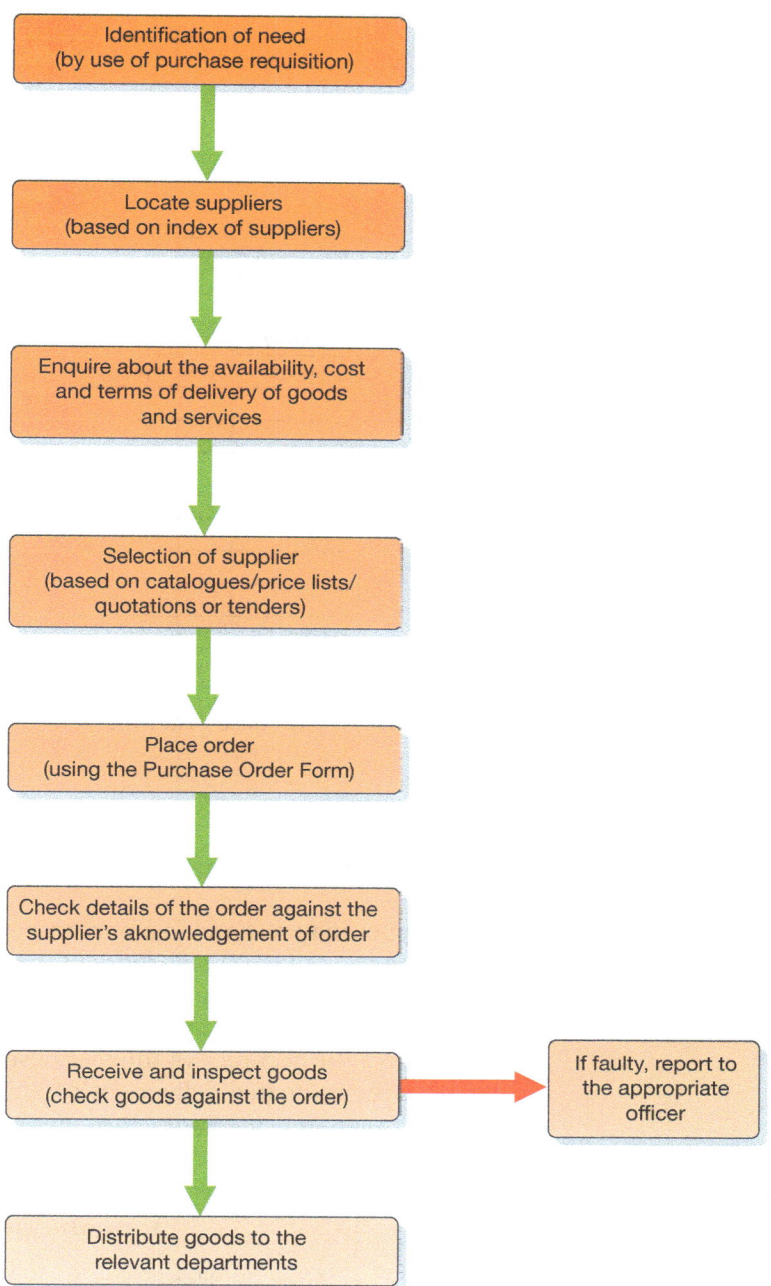

Figure 10.3 Purchasing procedures flowchart

Purchase order form

purchase order ▶ The purchase order is a written request to a seller to provide certain goods at a specific price. The order form is prepared by the Procurement Office and sent to the supplier. This form is usually approved by the head of department or someone with his/her authority.

ITQ5

Assume that you are Jean Simms, a clerk in the Purchasing Department of ABC Insurance Ltd, located at 2 Main St, Port of Spain, Trinidad. Prepare a purchase order for the following items, to be sourced at City Bookshop, 25 Main St, Port of Spain:

- 5 dozen Paperstik pens (black) @ $25 each;
- 10 boxes of file jackets @ $45 per box;
- 2 dozen boxes of standard staples @ $5 per box.

PURCHASE ORDER

Order # : 532

Bell & Co Ltd
2 Bent Ave
St Ann
Jamaica
823-1580/820-9854 (fax)

To: Paper & More Ltd
1 Collins Ave
Kingston

Date: April 5, 2011

Quantity	Description	Unit Price ($)	Total Price ($)
50 reams	Everbrite photocopy paper	520	26 000
	TOTAL		26 000

Prepared by: Boris Brown

Approved by: M Bent

Figure 10.4 Purchase order form

Acknowledgement of order

A supplier may respond to a purchase order by sending an acknowledgement of order to the buyer. The purpose of the acknowledgement of order is to:

- verify receipt of the purchase order;
- thank the buyer for his patronage;
- confirm the accuracy of the purchase order;
- state the estimated delivery or completion date.

The acknowledgement is usually sent by facsimile or e-mail.

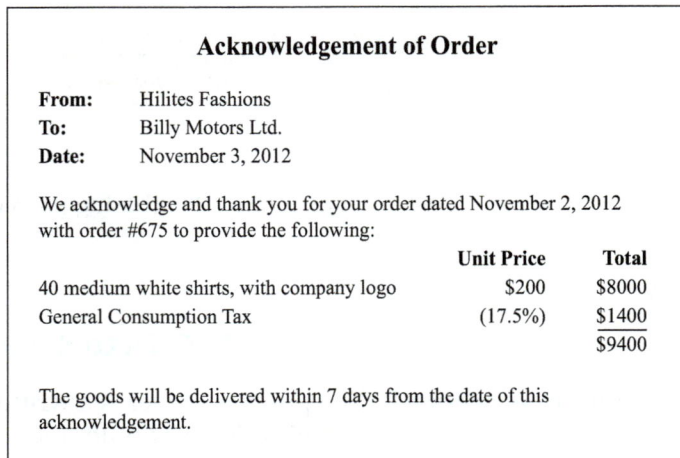

Acknowledgement of Order

From: Hilites Fashions
To: Billy Motors Ltd.
Date: November 3, 2012

We acknowledge and thank you for your order dated November 2, 2012 with order #675 to provide the following:

	Unit Price	Total
40 medium white shirts, with company logo	$200	$8000
General Consumption Tax	(17.5%)	$1400
		$9400

The goods will be delivered within 7 days from the date of this acknowledgement.

Figure 10.5 Acknowledgement of order

E-commerce

e-commerce ▶

The role of e-commerce (electronic commerce) is now growing rapidly because of the widespread use of the internet. 'E-commerce' refers to business activities that involve the exchange of information and funds across the internet. It basically involves buying and selling online. Many online retail stores accept payment in the form of credit cards, debit cards and e-cheques. E-cheques (electronic cheques) perform the same functions as regular cheques but have added safety features such as digital signatures to facilitate their online use. Online companies such as PayPal and Google Checkout provide online banking services where users are able to pay safely and quickly for goods and services purchased on the internet.

e-cheques ▶

Many purchasers will consider making purchases online because of the following **advantages**:

- The cost is sometimes less since there is reduced human interaction and paperwork.
- The reduction in cost may also be as a result of goods moving directly from the producer to the consumer, thus eliminating the middlemen.
- Online purchasing usually includes programmed checks to eliminates errors.
- Purchases can be made at any time of the day, 24/7.

    Drawbacks of e-commerce include:

- credit card fraud – sometimes customers' personal information is obtained and used illegally by others;
- websites may be fake or contain viruses or spyware. When verifying the authenticity of a website or webpage, look for the following:
    - 'https' at the beginning of the URL (universal resource locator) address (for example 'https://www.cxc.org');

"https' means 'hypertext transfer protocol secure'

Figure 10.6 'https' and the lock symbol on a website page

- the lock symbol – a yellow padlock icon that indicates that a website is secure;
- the VeriSign symbol – this guarantees that a web page is secure;
- goods may be lost in transit;
- pilferage may occur;
- wrong items may be delivered.

Figure 10.7 The VeriSign symbol

Stock

stock ▶
inventory ▶

'Stock' or 'inventory' refers to the goods and materials kept by an organization in a warehouse or storeroom. Stock is important as it is a current asset and so adds to the value of a business.

Types of stock are:

- raw materials and components;
- work-in-progress – unfinished goods;
- finished goods;
- consumable stock – stock purchased for use in the business;
- stock-in-trade – stock purchased for resale.

Stock control

stock control ▶

Stock control involves the storing and handling of goods. The primary goal of stock control is to minimize the cost of holding stocks while ensuring that there is adequate material for production to continue and to be able to meet customer demand.

Businesses need to maintain **adequate** stock levels; there should not be too much stock or too little.

Some of the drawbacks of keeping **little (or no)** stock are:

- the firm might run out of stock and not have enough raw materials and components to maintain production, though some businesses are able to arrange that suppliers deliver on a regular schedule so that goods arrive exactly when they are needed;
- the firm might lose customers because of missed orders.

However, keeping small amounts of stock might suit a firm if these items are perishable or if replenishing stock is quick and easy.

The disadvantages of keeping **too much** stock include:

- goods might deteriorate – for example, perishable goods such as fruits and vegetables;
- higher storage fees and insurance costs;
- higher security costs to prevent theft from warehouse/storeroom;
- stock may become obsolete or go out of fashion;
- capital that could be spent otherwise may be tied up in cash;
- stock will take up space n the warehouse.

However, keeping a lot of stock may suit a business whose sales are difficult to predict.

To prevent the problems of overstocking or understocking, maximum, minimum and re-order levels need to be set:

- **Minimum stock level** – this is the lowest amount of stock that should be held. Going below the minimum stock level will mean that the firm runs the risk of running out of stock needed for production or of losing customers because of its inability to meet demand.
- **Maximum stock level** – this is the largest amount of stock to be kept in the organization: keeping more than this amount means that the warehouse may become overcrowded.

Minimum and maximum stock levels are decided on based on factors such as:

- the type of product – if it is perishable or if it is very large – for example, a truck;
- the amount of storage space available;
- the amount of funds available to purchase stock;
- delivery charges that will be applied by suppliers.

re-order level ▶

The **re-order level** can also be maintained. It is the level of stock at which a further replenishment order should be placed. When selecting a re-order level, the lead time must also be considered. The lead time is that period of time between when goods are ordered and when they are delivered. With modern computer systems keeping track of stock use, this may be an automatic process.

The importance of stock control

- To monitor trends in the marketplace – stock control allows organizations to identify those items that are selling quickly and those that are not. It will allow the organization to assess which goods it should order more or less of, based on the demand in the market.
- To keep track of available storage space – having an efficient stock control system allows a business to identify when goods are sold and to see how much storage space is available to accommodate additional stock.
- To monitor the availability of capital – if proper stock control measures are in place it will allow the business to maintain a suitable level of stock and to prevent much-needed cash from being tied up in stock
- To ascertain items that are overstocked or understocked – properly monitoring the stock will allow the organization to identify both, and finding the right balance will enhance the level of productivity and efficiency. Having adequate stock levels will also improve customer relations as well as maintain a positive company image.

pilferage ▶
- To identify pilferage – efficient and accurate stock control measures allow a business to identify theft of stock quickly.

> **DEFINITION: Pilferage** – the theft of a small quantity of stock.

Stock recording

stock requisition form ▶ Requests by various departments for items from the warehouse or storeroom are usually prepared on a stock requisition form. The form is usually approved by the head of the requesting department.

STOCK REQUISITION		Requisition # : 59
Bell & Co Ltd		**Date:** November 12, 2011
From: Human Resources Department		
To: Warehouse		
Please provide the following items:		
Quantity	**Description**	
100	Photocopy paper	
Approved by: Vincent Plummer, Head of Department		

Figure 10.8　Stock requisition form

stock / bin cards ▶ Stock / bin cards may be used to monitor additions to and withdrawals from stock. It will show how much stock is left in the storeroom. The stock card is usually kept in the same location as the item.

The stock card will indicate the maximum and minimum stock levels, as well as the re-order level. When stock is purchased, details such as the invoice number of the transaction and the name of the supplier are included. When stock is withdrawn from the warehouse, details such as the requisition number and the name of the department requesting the goods are included as well. After each transaction, the balance remaining is calculated.

Without stock records it would be impossible to maintain adequate stock necessary for the efficient operation of a business.

STOCK CARD					
Item: Receipt books				**Item No.:** RB23	
Maximum stock level: 50					
Minimum stock level: 6					
Re-order level: 10					
Stock location: Row 2, shelf 3					
Date	Details	Receipts	Issues	Balance	
2010					
28 Feb	Balance b/f	-	-	5	
3 March	Salesman Bookstore Invoice # 6012	40	-	45	
5 March	Sales Department Requisition # 301	-	5	40	
17 March	Accounts Department Requisition # 421	-	10	30	
21 March	Reception Desk Requisition # 318	-	1	29	

Figure 10.9   Stock card

Bin system

The bin system may also be used to control stock. There are two types:
- one-bin system;
- two-bin system.

One-bin system

one-bin system ▶ In the one-bin system a bin or storage container is filled with stock. When the stock has reached a pre-determined re-order level, more stock is ordered to fill the bin once again. For example, a petrol station operator will check the level of the fuel inside the tank to decide when to re-order fuel and how much to order.

Two-bin system

two-bin system ▶ In the two-bin system two bins or containers are utilized. Both are filled with stock and when one is empty the second one is used while the first one is restocked. For example, a restaurant operator would ensure that she has two cylinders of gas. Whenever one is finished the other will be used while the empty cylinder is being replenished.

Computerized stock recording

The process of stock control is usually computerized in medium-sized and large organizations. However, even small firms are now able to take advantage of the benefits of computerized inventory systems because of reductions in the cost of the technology. Computerized stock control operates on the same principles as a manual system, however, information is usually easier to retrieve.

Benefits of the computerized inventory system include:
- stock valuation can be done quickly and accurately;
- it allows fast-selling items to be identified quickly and in some cases re-ordered automatically;
- it checks how well stock is moving and is able to identify slow-selling items, thereby prevent a build-up of unwanted stock;
- information can be used to predict seasonal fluctuations;
- it processes and prepares purchase orders.

barcodes ▶
RFID ▶ Computerized systems include the use of barcodes (or Universal Product Codes – UPCs) and RFID (radio frequency identification).

Barcodes consist of a series of parallel, adjacent bars and spaces. They are a cheap, simple and accurate way of encoding and reading information by using economical barcode readers. When products fitted with barcodes are scanned, using the point-of-sale system at a cash desk, it automatically updates the database showing one less of that particular item in stock. This allows the business to know how much of an item is in stock at any time. This system can also automatically alert the business when the re-order level has been reached so that it can replenish its stock before it runs out.

ISBN 978-0-230-02948-4

Figure 10.10   A barcode

RFID (radio frequency identification) comes in a variety of shapes and sizes and is placed on products in tags. It consists of a micro-chip with an antenna that uses radio waves to send information to a database. Its primary purpose is to identify and track inventory and to prevent over- and understocking.

The primary advantage of RFID over barcode technology is that it does not require contact or line of sight for communication.

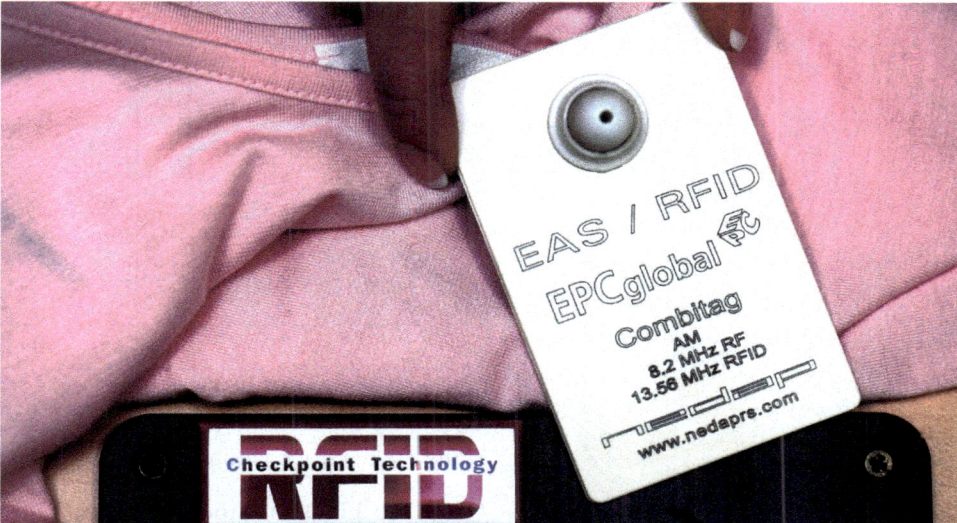

Figure 10.11 An RFID tag

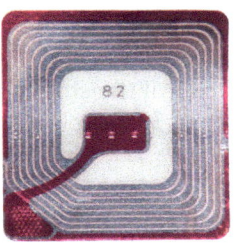

Figure 10.12 An RFID chip

Other types of stock control software include:
• Atrex[12] – inventory control and point-of-sale system;
• Soft Trader – inventory management;
• Mamut – point-of-sale system;
• Pastel My Business – inventory control and purchases.

Stock valuation

Stock valuation is necessary mainly in order to ascertain closing stock figures for the final accounts such as the balance sheet. The three primary methods of valuing stock are:
• FIFO (First In First Out);
• LIFO (Last In First Out);
• AVCO (Average Cost)

It should be noted that these methods are for accounting calculations and do not necessarily mean that the stock is physically handled on a FIFO or LIFO or on an AVCO basis.

FIFO method ▶ In the FIFO method of stock valuation, it is assumed that the first set of stock bought will be the first set of stock to be sold or used in the business. For instance, at a restaurant, perishable stock, such as fruits and vegetables, are handled on a First In First Out basis. Therefore the finished product (in this case, the meals) will always be fresh because the raw materials are used or sold in the order in which they are received.

Use the information in Table 10.1 to calculate the value of closing stock:

Purchases		Sales	
2010		2010	
January	15 items @ $20 each	April	10 items for $30 each
March	15 items @ $23 each	October	30 items for $40 each
August	20 items @ $28 each		

Table 10.1 Stock valuation information

Date	Received	Issued	Stock after each transaction		
2010					
January	15@20	–	15@20	300	300
March	15@23	–	15@20	300	
			15@23	345	645
April	–	10@20	5@20	100	
			15@23	345	445
August	20@28	–	5@20	100	
			15@23	345	
			20@28	560	1005
October	–	5@20			
		15@23			
		10@28	10@28	280	

The value of closing stock using the FIFO method is $280.

Table 10.2 Stock valuation (FIFO method)

LIFO method ▶

In the LIFO method of stock valuation it is assumed that the most recent stock received will be the first set of stock to be sold or used in the business. This method can be used in periods of rising prices, where all the stock is sold at the current price. For example, a gas station gets a delivery of gas on Monday at $50 per litre and on Thursday another delivery is made at $55 per litre. All the stock, including that received on Monday, will be sold at the current rate of $55 per litre plus mark-up.

Date	Received	Issued	Stock after each transaction		
2010					
January	15@20	–	15@20	300	300
March	15@23	–	15@20	300	
			15@23	345	645
April	–	10@23	15@20	300	
			5@23	115	415
August	20@28	–	15@20	300	
			5@23	115	
			20@28	560	975
October	–	20@28			
		5@23			
		5@20	10@20	200	

The value of closing stock using the LIFO method is $200.

Table 10.3 Stock valuation (LIFO method)

AVCO method ▶

In the AVCO method stock is calculated at the average cost for the period, by dividing the total cost of material by the number of units to find average cost. The AVCO method is more reliable in periods of price fluctuations because it shows an average price and so tends to balance out any fluctuations.

Date	Received	Issued	Average cost per item ($)	No of items	Total value of items ($)
2010					
January	15@20	–	20	15	300
March	15@23	–	21.501	30	645
April	–	10@21.50			
21.50	20	430			
August	20@28	–	24.752	40	990
October	–	30@24.75	24.75	10	247.50

Table 10.4   Stock valuation (AVCO method)

The value of closing stock using the AVCO method is $247.50

1 – (15 x 20) + (15 x 23)/30
   300 + 345 = 645 /30 = 21.50
2 – (20 x 21.50) + (20 x 28)/ 40
   430 + 560 = 990 /40 = 24.75

Types of stocktaking / inventory

There are two methods of stocktaking / inventory:
- periodic stocktaking/inventory;
- perpetual stocktaking/inventory.

periodic stocktaking ▶ **Periodic** stocktaking is usually carried out at the end of a firm's financial year, to ascertain purchases and stock figures for the final accounts – for example, the balance sheet. It involves finding out how much stock is at hand at a given date. In order to carry out periodic stocktaking some stores have to be closed for a day or two and this could mean a loss in productive activity.

perpetual or continuous stocktaking ▶ **Perpetual** or **continuous** stocktaking means that after each stock movement (purchase or sale) the balance on hand is calculated. This system allows businesses to respond accurately to customers' queries regarding the availability of goods. It also allows for effective stock control as it minimizes the risk of running out of stock.

 ITQ6

What is the principal difference between the perpetual inventory system and the periodic inventory system?

Many retail and manufacturing firms who traditionally used the periodic stocktaking method now find it more advantageous to utilize the perpetual stocktaking method. One primary reason for this is that they also use barcode technology to update their stock as items are sold and so the stocktaking process becomes simple and automatic.

 **Summary**

- The process of procurement in an organization may be centralized or decentralized.
- Benefits of centralized purchasing include having uniformed purchasing standards and receiving large discounts.
- Purchase requisition forms are used by various departments to request stock from the Purchasing Department.
- Factors influencing the choice of suppliers include the quality of goods or services, the reputation of the firm and the cost of the goods.
- Duties of the Purchasing Clerk include assisting in processing requisitions and preparing purchase orders
- The purchase order form is used to request items from suppliers.

- E-commerce involves carrying out online business activities such as exchanging information and funds.
- An advantage of e-commerce is that it is cheaper because of reduced costs to the seller.
- 'Stock control' refers to the storing and handling of goods, to ensure that there are enough to carry out production and meet demand.
- Stock control includes monitoring trends in the marketplace and detecting pilferage.
- The three main methods of stock valuation are: FIFO, LIFO and AVCO.
- There are two types of stocktaking methods: periodic stocktaking and perpetual stocktaking

Answers to ITQs

1
- Sales and Marketing Department – to obtain equipment and supplies needed.
- Despatch and Transport Department – to transport goods purchased as well as to obtain equipment and supplies needed.
- Human Resources Department – to staff the Procurement Department and attend to the welfare of staff.

2 A quantity discount is given when customers buy large quantities of goods, while a cash discount is given to encourage prompt settlement of bills.

3 Supplier D – $21 c.i.f.

4 $10 290.

5

PURCHASE ORDER			
			Order # : 532
ABC Insurance Ltd			
2 Main St			
Port of Spain			
Trinidad			
To: City Bookshop			
25 Main St			
Kingston			
Trinidad			**Date:**
Quantity	**Description**	**Unit Price ($)**	**Total Price ($)**
5 dozen	Paperstik pens (black)	25	1 500
10 boxes	File jackets	45 per box	450
2 dozen boxes	Standard staples	5 per box	120
		TOTAL	2 070
Prepared by: Jean Simms			
Approved by: Purchasing Manager			

6 The perpetual inventory system carries out stocktaking usually once per year, while periodic inventory is a continuous updating of stock.

Examination-style questions

Multiple choice questions

1   The type of stock that consists of incomplete goods is known as:
    a   consumables
    b   work-in-progress
    c   finished goods
    d   raw materials.

2   Which document is used to record the movement of stock from the storeroom?
    a   Order form.
    b   Stock requisition.
    c   Stock card.
    d   Catalogue.

3   The point at which stock should be replenished is known as the:
    a   re-order level
    b   minimum stock level
    c   maximum stock level
    d   requisition level.

4   The type of discount which is offered to encourage prompt payment of bills is known as:
    a   trade discount
    b   quantity discount
    c   special discount
    d   cash discount.

5   Which of the following documents is an example of an internal document?
    a   Purchase requisition.
    b   Enquiry note.
    c   Quotation.
    d   Price list.

6   The continuous stocktaking system, where the stock balance is calculated after each transaction, is known as:
    a   periodic inventory
    b   perpetual inventory
    c   stock control
    d   inventory control.

7   An illustrated price list is known as a/an:
    a   catalogue
    b   tender
    c   enquiry note
    d   quotation.

8   The term 'ex-works' means the price quoted includes:
    a   delivery
    b   only the cost of the goods
    c   insurance and transportation
    d   the cost of goods plus insurance.

9   The following are basic steps in the procurement process:
    i   place order;
    ii   selection of supplier;
    iii payment of invoice;
    iv   process purchase requisition.

Place them in the correct sequence in which they should be carried out:

a iv, ii, i, iii;

b iv, i, ii, iii;

c ii, i, iv, iii;

d ii, i, iii, iv.

10 Which factors influence the choice of a supplier?

i   Quality of goods supplied.

ii Reputation of the firm.

iii Provision of delivery services.

iv Amount of storage space available.

a i and ii only;

b i, ii and iii only;

c i and iv only;

d i, ii and iv only.

Structured questions

1 The following information shows the purchases and sales of radios at Brownstone Ltd:

Bought		Sold	
January	12 radios @ $20 each	July	25 radios for $30 each
April	20 radios @ $23 each	November	20 radios for $35 each
September	35 radios @ $24.50 each		

Use the information above to calculate the value of closing stock, using:

a LIFO method of stock valuation;   [10]

b FIFO method of stock valuation.   [10]

2 Using the format provided on page 228, prepare the stock card to show the following information and display the closing balance.

• Item: photocopy paper.

• Item #: PP1.

• Minimum stock level: 4 reams.

• Maximum stock level: 40 reams.

• Re-order level: 15 reams.

2009	
30 April	**Balance in stock – 10 reams**
2 May	Issued to Marketing Department – 5 reams Requisition #11
15 May	Stock received from Paper & More Ltd – 30 reams Invoice #513
20 May	Issued to Accounts Department – 8 reams Requisition #21

[10]

3 Assume that you are Jamie Smith, an Accounting Clerk at G Redcam & Co Ltd. Your manager, Sam Lee, has asked you to do the following task.

Prepare a purchase requisition form for the following items to be purchased from United Office Sales:
- 8 boxes DL window envelopes;
- 3 dozen HP 96A toner cartridges – black;
- 5 reams A4 copy paper. [5]

4 Explain the meaning of the following purchasing abbreviations:
a f.o.b.
b c.i.f.
c e. & o.e.
d c.o.d.
e ex-works. [5]

5 Differentiate between the following terms:
a a catalogue and a price list
b an order form and a purchase requisition form
c a trade discount and a quantity discount. [3]

6 **a** Identify **three** duties of a Purchasing Clerk. [3]
b State **three** reasons why inventory management is important to a business. [3]
c Outline **three** factors that must be considered when ordering goods. [3]

7 You are the Purchasing Clerk at Drake's Stationery. Use the information below to calculate the value of inventory, using:
a FIFO method of stock valuation; [10]
b LIFO method of stock valuation. [10]

Record of transactions

For period January–March, 2011

RECEIPTS/PURCHASES		ISSUES	
Reams of A4 paper		Reams of A4 paper	
2011		2011	
January 5	10 @ $30	February 21	5
February 17	5 @ $32	March 25	2
March 21	2 @ $35	April 30	3
April 10	2 @ $50	–	–

8 Assume that you are Christie Allen, the Purchasing Office Clerk at P & J Hardware Ltd. Prepare the purchase order for the following stationery items, to be obtained from Office Mart, 2 Church Street, Port of Spain, Trinidad:
- 2 dozen manila file folders @ $250 per dozen;
- 1 dozen file jackets @ $15 each;
- 3 reams A4 copy paper @ $240 per ream. [5]

11 Sales, marketing and customer service

By the end of this chapter you should be able to:

- ☑ explain the functions of the Sales Office;
- ☑ identify the duties of the Sales Clerk;
- ☑ explain the functions of the Marketing Office;
- ☑ outline the duties of a Marketing Clerk;
- ☑ explain the functions of the Customer Service Department;
- ☑ identify the duties of Customer Service Representatives;
- ☑ describe the functions of the equipment in the Sales and Marketing Office;
- ☑ prepare documents used in the Sales and Marketing Offices;
- ☑ calculate various types of discount.

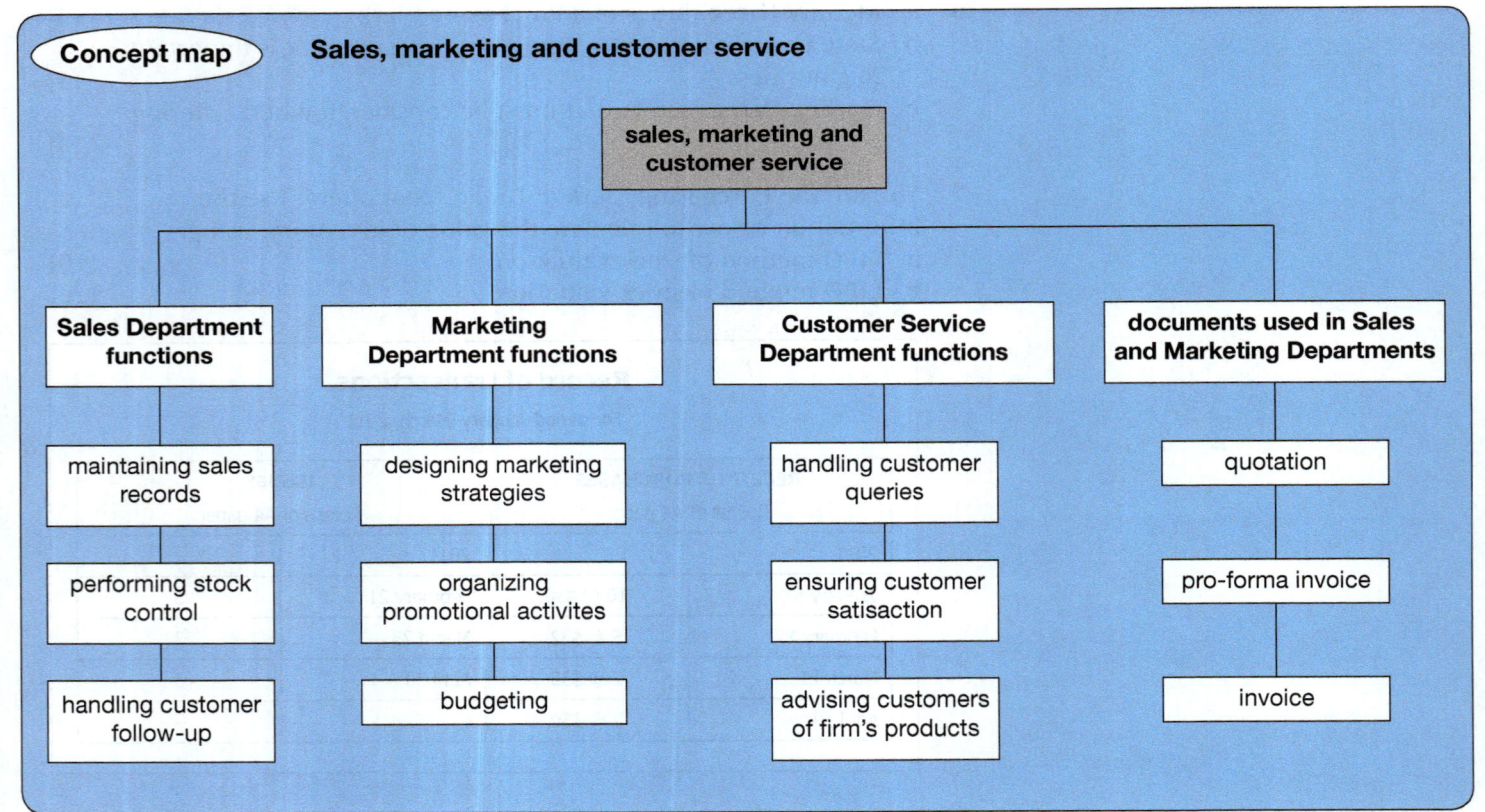

Concept map Sales, marketing and customer service

sales, marketing and customer service

Sales Department functions	Marketing Department functions	Customer Service Department functions	documents used in Sales and Marketing Departments
maintaining sales records	designing marketing strategies	handling customer queries	quotation
performing stock control	organizing promotional activites	ensuring customer satisaction	pro-forma invoice
handling customer follow-up	budgeting	advising customers of firm's products	invoice

Functions of the Sales and Marketing Offices

The Sales and Marketing Offices are often thought to carry out the same functions. However, while both offices are interrelated and often rely on each other to get the job done, they are also different.

marketing ▶ Marketing involves identifying a customer's needs and finding ways to create demand for the company's products or services. Sales involves fulfilling the demand created by the Marketing Office.

Both Sales and Marketing Offices must work together in order to create efficiency in a business. Poor marketing will lead to poor sales which will then lead to losses for the business.

Some large organizations will have separate Sales and Marketing Departments, while smaller businesses may merge the functions into one office. Regardless of the size of the organization, the functions carried out by the Sales and Marketing Offices are essential to the success of every business.

Sales Office ▶ The Sales Office is perhaps one of the most important departments of any business. This is so because it is the sales team's responsibility to sell the goods and services that generate income and profit for the firm, which will determine the firm's success or failure.

The organization of the Sales Office will usually depend on factors such as the size of the company and the nature of the business. Some large organizations will divide the sales task into different geographical regions of a country – for example, Sales Manager (Southern Region) and Sales Manager (Northern Region). This will allow the sales team to focus on increasing sales in specific locations.

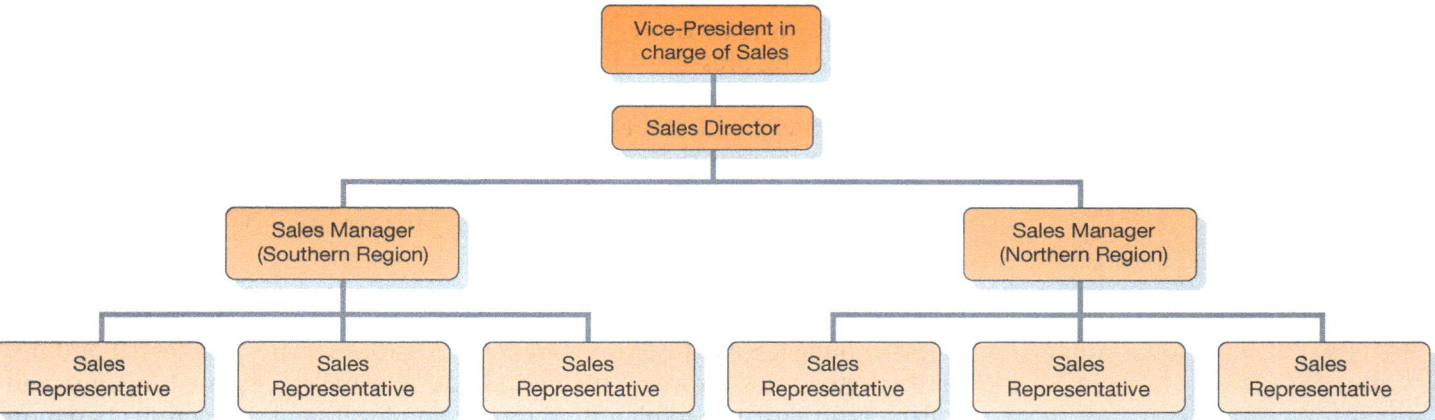

Figure 11.1 Organizational chart of a typical Sales Office, based on geographical regions

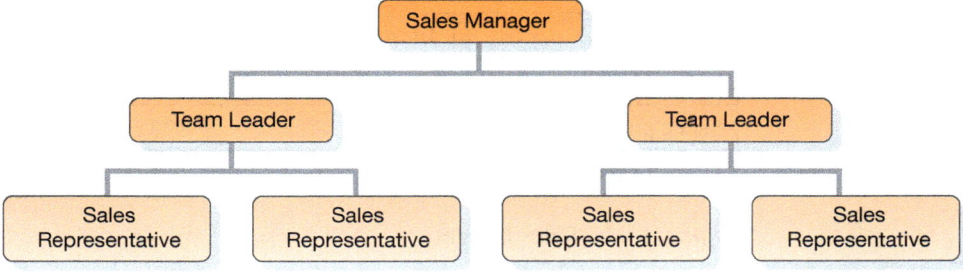

Figure 11.2 Chart showing the structure of the Sales Office in a small business

237

Sales Office functions

The Sales Office carries out a number of important functions that affect the efficiency of the organization, including the following:

Maintaining sales records

There are a number of records that are kept by the Sales Office. They include:
- price lists – an outline of the prices of the goods and services available for sale;
- sales receipts – records of orders sent to customers;
- sales call log – an outline of telephone conversations with existing customers or prospective customers;
- commission summary – a document used to calculate the commission payable to Sales Representatives during a certain period;
- sales summary card – this document provides information on the sale of a product or service – it details the amounts sold, the amounts ordered and the amounts received.

Monitoring stock control

The ideal situation exists when all stock produced or bought is sold. This requires good stock control, which is the procedure involved in maintaining the ideal amount of items in stock. However, there may be cases of overstocking (surplus stock) caused by overproduction. There may, however, be cases when organizations will deliberately overstock items, usually in anticipation of an increase in seasonal demand – for example, increasing stock of decorations at Christmas. In such cases it will be the Sales Office's responsibility to apply aggressive selling pressure to ensure that the items in stock are sold and that a profit is made.

On the other hand, there may be instances when there is understocking of goods and so there is not enough stock to meet customers' needs. In this case the Sales Office may have to withdraw its sales efforts to allow the factory to catch up with the orders or push the factory to increase production.

Budgeting

sales budget ▶ The sales budget is a critical component in the success of any business. It outlines the expected sales for a specific period and is usually presented in units and dollars. Firms are able to plan their production levels and their profits based on the sales budget.

Sales Budget
For Supreme Beverages Ltd

	1st Quarter	2nd Quarter	3rd Quarter	4th Quarter
Budgeted sales (cases)	10,000	20,000	33,000	
Selling price per case	$30	$30	$30	$30
Estimated total sales	$300,000	$600,000	$840,000	$990,000

Figure 11.3 Sales budget

Engaging in customer follow-up

It is important that the company tries to attract and retain its customers by developing a meaningful long-term relationship with them. Customers who are happy and satisfied will be loyal and not purchase from competitors; they will also spread the word, increasing the firm's goodwill.

goodwill ▶

> DEFINITION: **Goodwill** is an intangible asset which represents a firm's image, reputation and the good name that the business has developed over a period of time.

ITQ1
State **two** ways in which employees can improve their company's goodwill.

This relationship exists even after the customer has purchased the good or service. Ways of increasing customer loyalty include:

• greeting the customer by name;
• satisfying their needs – for example, providing a 24-hour helpline;
• following the adage that 'the customer is always right', whenever there is a problem with the product or service;
• providing after-sales service – this includes all the support services provided after the sale of the goods or services, such as installation and assembly, maintenance or repair and technical assistance.

It is necessary that the sales team be adequately motivated and properly trained in order to carry out their tasks effectively.

Liaising with other departments

The Sales Office must liaise with a number of other offices within the organization, such as the Accounts Office, the Human Resources Office, the Purchasing Office and the Production Office, where these exist.

Accounts Office ▶

The Sales Office must liaise with the Accounts Office regarding all financial aspects of the office. The Accounts Office will be responsible for:

• paying the wages and salaries of the Sales Office;
• approving budget allocations;
• processing invoices and ensuring that monies owed are collected.

Operations Office ▶

If the firm manufactures its own goods, the Sales Office will also need to have a close relationship with the Operations Office. This relationship is necessary, as it is the Sales Office that will determine the type and quantity of goods that should be offered. This is done based on sales forecasts and feedback from customers in the target market.

Procurement Office ▶

The Sales Office will also establish close links with the Procurement Office. This is necessary as it is the Procurement Office that will be responsible for sourcing necessary supplies and equipment for the Sales Office. In cases where the firm resells goods, the Procurement Office will need to purchase stock for resale.

Human Resources Office ▶

ITQ2
Identify **three** departments that the Sales Office has to liaise with and explain why the link is necessary.

The Sales Office must liaise with the Human Resources Office. The Human Resources Office is responsible for satisfying the staffing needs of the Sales Office, as well as other departments in the firm. The Sales Office will also train employees, carry out assessments and deal with the general welfare of the Sales Office staff.

The Sales Clerk

Duties

Typical duties of a Sales Clerk include the following:

- providing information to customers about products and prices;
- taking orders from existing customers and securing new customers;
- cashiering – processing payments received from customers;
- **sales report sheets ▶** preparing sales documents such as quotations, invoices and sales report sheets; sales report sheets are used to show the number of items sold by each Sales Representative during a specific period;
- carrying out clerical duties such as answering the telephone;
- **merchandising ▶** merchandising comprises activities which include setting up displays and ensuring that stock is properly displayed at strategic locations on store shelves, in order to attract customers' attention and increase sales. Merchandising also covers ensuring that the product is attractive to consumers and can be found easily by shoppers – for example, placing breakfast cereals on low shelves in the line of sight of children, who will encourage their parents to buy them. Another aspect of merchandising covers ensuring that the goods are displayed at the right time – for example, Christmas lights and decorations are usually prominently displayed on store shelves in the weeks leading up to Christmas;
- creating and maintaining a good relationship with customers;
- filing sales documents in an efficient way so they can be retrieved easily;
- **mailing lists ▶** maintaining mailing lists of existing and prospective customers.

> DEFINITION: **Mailing lists** are the names, addresses, contact numbers and e-mail addresses of individuals and businesses to whom advertising material is sent.

ITQ3

List **four duties** of a Sales Clerk.

Attributes

A good Sales Clerk will:

- be loyal and trustworthy;
- be patient;
- have a tidy and professional appearance;
- be a quick learner;
- be an accurate typist;
- have strong computer skills;
- have strong social skills;
- have good negotiation skills;
- have excellent communication skills;
- have great team spirit.

Figure 11.4   A Sales Clerk at work

The Marketing Office

The Marketing Office is an important component of any organization. Businesses or firms which market their products or services are more likely to survive in the harsh business climate and be profitable.

market research ▶

market ▶

The Marketing Office, led by the Marketing Manager, will be responsible for carrying out market research. The Marketing Office will research customers' needs in order to develop products and strategies geared towards satisfying these needs. The researchers will try to find out the type of customers in the market, based on factors such as age, income, occupation and preferences.

> DEFINITION: **Market research** is the process of gathering, recording and analyzing data related to specific marketing problems.

The Marketing Office will also want to research the market conditions and the firm's competitors. This will include finding out information about the competitors' products and assessing their level of sales and profits, as well as the strategies that are used.

The Marketing Office must also carefully monitor trends in the marketplace in order to determine when new products should be introduced or when new marketing strategies should be employed.

The job of marketing the firm's product or service rests not only with the workers in the Marketing Department but with all the employees in the organization. Employees can assist the marketing goal by ensuring that all potential and actual customers who come through their doors leave as happy and satisfied customers.

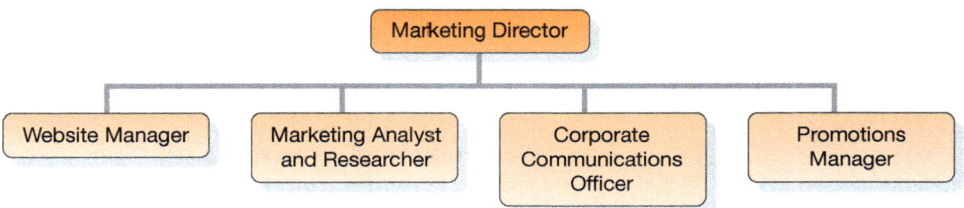

Figure 11.5 A typical Marketing Office structure

Functions of the Marketing Office

Planning marketing strategies

marketing strategy ▶

A marketing strategy is a plan of the firm's marketing efforts for a specific product or all its products. When developing a marketing strategy, marketing executives must:
1 define the target market – the target market includes those persons to whom the company aims to sell its products or services. When describing the target market, marketing personnel need to examine certain features of the consumers, such as:
   • age;
   • gender;
   • occupation;
   • income level;

241

2 analyze the market – marketers need to understand their markets in terms of:
- the size of the market and how fast it is growing;
- the competitors – who they are, how many and how their product compares with the firm's;
- the substitutes – these are goods that could be used to replace the firm's good;

3 information on the market can be obtained from doing market research or visiting agencies such as Chambers of Commerce or other statistical bodies – for example, in Jamaica, there is the Statistical Institute of Jamaica (STATIN). Information can also be found online from websites such as Allbusiness.com, which provide profiles on companies and their markets;

marketing mix ▶ **4** define the marketing mix – after the target market has been defined and the market analyzed, marketers are now able to create a marketing mix. The marketing mix outlines components of the marketing plan for a product or group of products. The marketing mix is usually referred to as the '4 Ps' – product, price, place and promotion:

- **Product or service** – this looks at the physical product being sold. Marketers need to create unique products and ensure that they meet the needs of the target market. Marketers also need to examine whether the product is properly packaged so that it is protected, but it should also be user friendly and attractive. The product should also be properly labelled. Various countries have specific regulations in terms of the type of information that is placed on product labels – for example, the ingredients, the name of the manufacturer and the expiry date.

- **Price** – when setting the price of the product, marketers must ensure that it covers the cost of production in order for the firm to make a profit. For example, if a product costs $10 to manufacture, in order to make a profit the price should be set higher than $10 – at, say, $12.50. The price should also be competitive: it should be close to the price that competitors charge. For example – if all the competitors price their products between $15 and $18, and the firm's product is priced at $35, it will be difficult to get the firm's products sold.

- Examples of pricing strategies used include:
  - penetration pricing – this includes pricing the products at a very low level in order to take over the market share. When this is achieved, the price is increased;
  - price skimming – this is where the price of the good is initially high, usually when the firm is introducing a new, highly anticipated product which consumers are willing to purchase at a high price. Once competitors begin entering the market, the price will gradually be reduced.

- **Place** – when looking at this in the marketing mix, it refers to how the goods are distributed on their way to the consumers. In determining how to distribute the goods, marketers must find out how members of the target market usually shop. Do they shop online or at a wholesale or retail outlet? These questions will guide where the marketers will place the products. Examples of distribution channels include:

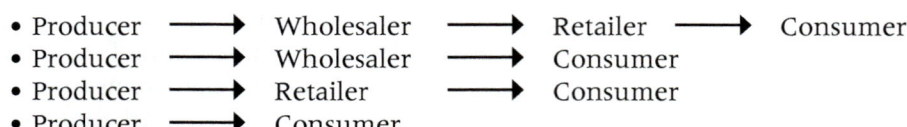

- Producer ⟶ Wholesaler ⟶ Retailer ⟶ Consumer
- Producer ⟶ Wholesaler ⟶ Consumer
- Producer ⟶ Retailer ⟶ Consumer
- Producer ⟶ Consumer

It is also necessary to find the fastest, cheapest and most efficient way to transport the goods to the customer. Examples of transportation methods include air, sea, river, canal and land. See Figure 11.6.

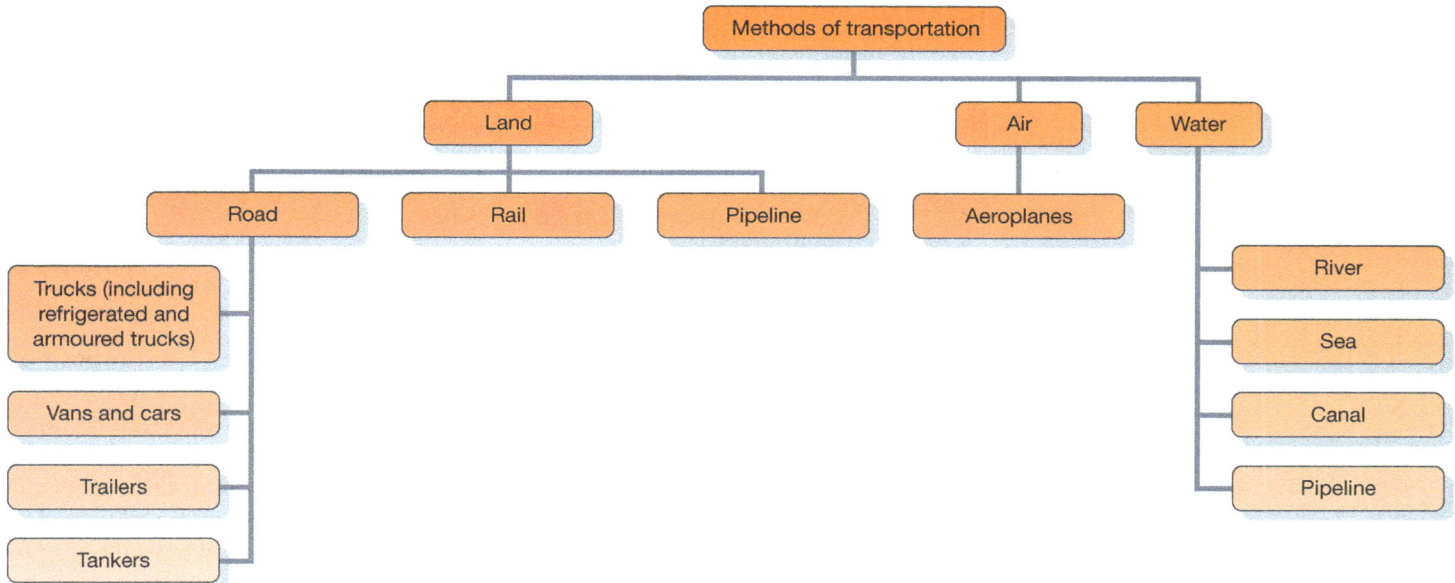

Figure 11.6   Methods of transportation

Promotion

In order to choose the right promotion techniques, marketers need to find out the kinds of advertising media to which the target customer pays attention – for example, does the target customer watch a lot of television or mostly read the newspaper? This information will give the marketers an idea of where to place information about the firm's products or services.

Budgeting

The primary aim of the marketing budget is to allow the marketing and company executives to be able to control the expenses that will be incurred.

Items	Quarters			
	1	2	3	4
Advertising	$500 000	$550 000	$500 000	$600 000
Catalogues	$200 000	$200 000	$230 000	$230 000
Promotions	$500 000	$550 000	$550 000	$560 000
Training	$150 000	$150 000	$150 000	$150 000
Other	$200 000	$200 000	$200 000	$200 000
Total	$1 550 000	$1 650 000	$1 630 000	$1 740 000

Table 11.1   An example of a marketing budget

Organizing promotional activities

Promotional activities include the ways in which the firm informs customers and potential customers about the products and services which are available. They also encourage the customers to make the purchase. Promotional activities include:

- advertising;
- sales promotion;
- personal selling; and
- publicity.

Advertising

This is a sales technique that is usually long term in nature. The purpose of advertisements is to arouse the interests of potential customers with original and innovative presentations. Advertisements are presented through various advertising media such as cinemas, magazines, billboards, newspapers, the internet and television. It is usually wise to choose media that will reach most of the potential customers – for example, when selling perfume for women, advertisements would be best placed in magazines which target female readers. The cost will also be a factor as some media, such as television, are typically expensive.

Figure 11.7   Advertisement billboards

Sales promotions

These are certain incentives or activities used to improve sales and product awareness. They may be short term or continuous in nature and are usually used in conjunction with advertising. Sales promotion activities include:

- coupons – which, when redeemed, can give a lower price;
- contests – which usually require customers to purchase the product in order to enter;
- trade shows – sometimes put on by groups such as a Chamber of Commerce, in order to highlight certain businesses. The company can display its products and carry out demonstrations for prospective customers;
- samples – a way of introducing a product by, in some cases, attaching the sample to a more popular product;
- discounts or 'sale' events – this involves price reductions on specific products or services;
- free gifts and speciality items – for example, pens, diaries with the company's name on them, etc.

Personal selling

Personal selling is direct, face-to-face communication where sales personnel try to persuade a potential customer to purchase goods or services. It may involve having a sales team visiting various locations or having personal telephone conversations in an effort to increase sales. The concept of 'cold calling' involves making an unsolicited telephone call to a prospective client or customer and telling them about the product or service. Many Sales Representatives are hesitant to make cold calls because of the fear of rejection. However, they must be persistent and carefully plan what to say to the prospective customer. For example, when the prospective customer answers the telephone, they should not ask 'Can I interest you in my company's microwaves?', as this will give the prospective customer the chance to say 'No' to the question. Instead, the best approach is to be direct and state the purpose of the call – for example, 'Good afternoon, my name is Molly Blake of Island Appliances and I would like to introduce you to our newest line of microwaves'.

Personal selling will also involve the regular Sales Clerk in a store who is able to give advice and provide information about a particular product or service to a potential customer.

Publicity or public relations

Publicity involves maintaining a positive image in the public's eye. The role of Public Relations Representatives includes:

- creating goodwill through special programmes and community events – for example, donating money to a children's home;
- monitoring various media for any negative public comments or public scrutiny about the company or its products or services – for example, if a disgruntled employee tells the media about industrial disputes within the firm;
- managing crises that could damage the company's reputation or have legal or financial repercussions – for example, if MG Chemicals is found to have accidentally disposed of toxic waste in a nearby river, the management of the company must react immediately to the crisis by creating a united front and admitting the truth to the public – that it was an accident. They can also present their track record of environmental friendliness and put forward immediate strategies for minimizing the environmental impact on the community;
- having a representative from the firm give a speech (for example, at a Rotary or Kiwanis Club meeting) or writing articles in the local newspaper is also a good way to put the firm in the public eye in a positive way.

Liaising with advertising agencies

advertising agency ▶

There may be cases where an advertising agency or a marketing agency is hired by the firm to carry out some of its marketing functions. With hundreds of new products entering the market every year, it is important for the organization to have a competitive advantage if it is to remain viable. Advertising or marketing agencies may be able to give the organization the edge that it needs to stay afloat in today's competitive market place.

> DEFINITION: An **advertising agency** is a firm that creates attractive advertising campaigns aimed at presenting its clients' companies in a positive way.

Advertising or marketing agencies services include:

- conducting market research;
- carrying out sales promotion;
- creating television commercials, radio, jingles and print advertisements.

Based on the goals of the organization, the advertising agency will gear its marketing campaign to suit the organization's specific goals which may include:

- introducing a new product to the marketplace;
- increasing sales;
- attracting new customers and keeping old customers.

Publishing

In some organizations the task of publishing may be passed over to an advertising agency. However, some Marketing Offices will do their own publishing. Examples of items that are sometimes published by the Marketing Office include:

- company brochures;
- fliers;
- catalogues.

 ITQ4
Describe **two** examples of promotional activities.

The Marketing Office Clerk

Duties

- Preparing press releases. Certain websites are dedicated to helping firms to distribute their press releases to the media. One such website is MassmediaDistribution.com.

press release ▶

> DEFINITION: A **press release** is an official announcement sent to members of the media for publication.

- Maintaining mailing lists of existing and potential customers.
- Assisting with promotional activities – for example, carrying out demonstrations of how the product works at a trade show.
- Organizing travel – the clerk may be required to make travel arrangements for the sales and marketing teams, who may be required to visit various locations across the country or region to promote and sell the goods and services.
- Preparing purchase requisitions to obtain supplies needed in the Marketing Office.
- Carrying out clerical duties such as handling enquiries and receiving and distributing mail.

Attributes

- Good analytical skills.
- High level of creativity.
- Good negotiation skills.
- Excellent communication and interpersonal skills.
- Knowledge of computers and programs used for developing documents such as brochures and fliers.

The Customer Service Department

The Customer Service Department or Customer Care Department acts as a link between customers and the companies who manufacture the goods or provide the services they use.

Figure 11.8 Relationship between customers, the Customer Service Department and the company

Customer service agents or representatives usually interface with customers in a face-to-face setting; however, the interaction may also be over the telephone, by electronic mail or by faxing. Using the post has become rare. Customer Service Representatives are usually equipped with a computer in order to access customers' accounts or other company documents easily and in order to deal with queries in an efficient manner.

While most Customer Service Representatives work within the company premises, there are some firms whose Customer Service functions are outsourced to independent call centres sometimes located in a separate country from where the firm they represent is located.

Most calls to Customer Service Representatives are recorded and managers will often listen to them to ensure that the representatives are providing efficient and quality service to customers.

Functions of the Customer Service Department

Handling customer queries

Queries from customers may range from very simple, routine questions which can be answered easily by Customer Service Representatives – for example 'What time does the store close?' – to more complex questions which require research. If the Customer Service Representative is unable to answer the customer's query the call will be forwarded to someone who will be better able to assist. Some Customer Service Departments have pre-coded answers to frequently asked questions (FAQs).

Dealing with customer complaints

Customer complaints must be dealt with in accordance with the company's policy. All valid complaints should be recorded and in some cases the Customer Service Representative may have the authority to rectify problems or to offer solutions.

When dealing with customer complaints it is important that the following guidelines be observed:

- the staff should be helpful, courteous, tactful and professional;
- accept responsibility if the company is at fault and offer sincere apologies;
- offer solutions to fix the problem so that it does not re-occur;
- offer compensation, if appropriate – for example, offering a free meal at a restaurant;
- thank the customer for his / her patience and request their future business.

Dealing effectively with customers' complaints is a good way to develop customer loyalty and a positive image for the organization.

Providing information on the company's products or services

The Customer Service Department will be responsible for providing information on the company's products and services in order to help customers make informed purchasing decisions. Customers may also be given:

- information on new product offerings as well as any special promotions being offered;
- technical assistance and information on how to use a product;
- advice on what to do in the event of misuse of the product.

Ensuring customer satisfaction

Customer satisfaction will be achieved if all the other tasks are carried out in an effective and efficient manner. Customers whose complaints are handled satisfactorily and whose queries have been adequately addressed are likely to become satisfied and loyal customers.

Customer Service Managers and other staff members should seek constant feedback from customers to find how satisfied they are. This is important, as many dissatisfied customers do not complain about poor service but simply take their business elsewhere. The Customer Service Department will need to gather information on customers' satisfaction with the business in terms of, for example, the product quality, the helpfulness of staff and the cleanliness of the store. Information can be gathered using methods such as:

- interviews – where managers or other staff members conduct face-to face or telephone interviews to get information on their level of satisfaction;
- questionnaires – these may be in the form of comment forms available in the store or online.

Feedback from customers will help to identify the firm's areas of weakness, so that they may improve their levels of customer service and, ultimately, customer satisfaction.

Riverside Restaurant **To Our Customers**			
We care about your opinion. Giving us feedback helps us to improve our service to you.			
Date visited: _____			
Service was prompt and friendly	Excellent	Average	Poor
Food quality	Excellent	Average	Poor
Food appearance	Excellent	Average	Poor
Cleanliness of the dining area	Excellent	Average	Poor
Cleanliness of the restroom	Excellent	Average	Poor
Would you return?	Yes ☐ No ☐		
Would you recommend our restaurant to a friend?	Yes ☐ No ☐		
Thank you			

Figure 11.9 Example of a comment card from a restaurant

The Customer Service Representative

Duties

- Dealing with customer enquiries.
- Identifying, researching and solving customer issues.
- Providing customers with product and service information.
- Transferring calls to appropriate staff members.
- Accepting customers' orders.
- Tracking the status of a customer's order.
- Keeping customers informed of delays or early deliveries.
- Coordinating with other departments to resolve customers' queries.

Attributes

In order to carry out these duties, the Customer Service Representative must possess the following:

- patience;
- tact;
- diplomacy;
- reliability;
- enthusiasm;
- excellent communication skills;
- excellent problem-solving skills.

Equipment used in the Sales and Marketing Offices

Computer

The computer has become such an indispensable piece of equipment that it is present in possibly all departments in an organization. The computer will assist workers in the sales and marketing staff to carry out a number of activities, including:

- word processing – preparing letters, reports, memoranda and other forms of written communication;
- storing information on existing and prospective customers;
- facilitating certain software used in sales (for example, Top Sales – which manages documents and customer contact lists) and marketing (for example, Ezy Invoice – which efficiently generates documents such as invoices).

Digital duplicator

Digital duplicators are able to handle a large volume of copying. This would be useful in the Marketing Office to copy catalogues, brochures and fliers. The digital duplicator is able to produce high-quality output at speeds of up to 180 pages per minute. Many duplicators are equipped with computer connectivity. Digital duplicators are also able to copy in colour and some are equipped with scanners.

Facsimile machine

facsimile machine ▶

The facsimile machine is a piece of digital technology that has become commonplace in most offices. Fax machines are an expedient way of sending and receiving documents, as they save time and money. Some features of the modern facsimile machine are its ability to scan, copy and print documents. The fax machine is also fairly mobile.

The most recent development in facsimile technology is the advent of the online fax. Online services can send electronic fax correspondence and alert users to incoming faxes. Online fax services such as Fax Zero, Pam Fax and e Fax allow users to send and receive faxes without having to own a fax machine. It also eliminates the cost of installing an additional phone line and the cost of paper. The transmission of documents is now mostly done through electronic mail (e-mail) via the internet.

Figure 11.10   A fax machine

Answering machine

◀ **answering machines** ▶

With the evolution of the digital age, answering machines have been replaced by voicemail or other devices. Voicemail refers to a computerized system which allows callers to leave messages. These messages will be accessed by calling the telephone service provider's network. An answering machine plugs into a telephone or is a part of it and usually has a cassette or digital memory to retain messages. The owner records a greeting that is played when the answering machine answers a phone call.

Features of the answering machine

- It is a one-time purchase and does not require monthly fees or subscription, unlike voicemail.
- It cannot record without power.
- The number of messages the answering machine can hold is limited; most machines can store up to 25 minutes' worth of messages.
- The owner can remotely check messages by calling their phone number and/or entering a code.

Figure 11.11   An answering machine

Multimedia projector

◀ **multimedia projectors** ▶

Multimedia projectors are now commonplace in conference rooms for business presentations. They may be used to enhance the quality of the presentation by adding video, music and graphics. Teleconference software can also be used and run through the projector so that other persons in various locations can participate in the presentation.

Interactive whiteboard

◀ **interactive whiteboard** ▶

An interactive whiteboard is a touch-sensitive screen. It is connected to a computer and digital projector as a display and touch screen. The projector transmits images onto the screen and the presenter is able to use special pens or his/her finger to manipulate the objects on the screen.

Figure 11.12   An interactive whiteboard

Photocopier

photocopier ▶

The photocopier is a standard piece of office equipment. Modern photocopiers are seen as multifunctional devices that can scan, print, sort, staple and send or receive faxes.

Features of the photocopier

- Some photocopiers are able to connect to personal computers and scan and print documents via a USB (Universal Serial Bus) port which is a socket on a computer that allows a number of external devices to be connected to it.
- Some photocopiers are equipped with security devices which prevent unauthorized use.
- Many photocopiers are able to monitor the usage of the machine – for example, identifying the number of copies made by a particular department for the day.
- An average-speed copier can make 45–60 copies per minute, while a high-speed copier can make in excess of 100 copies per minute.
- Copiers come in black and white or colour. Colour copiers tend to be more expensive and have a slower copy speed than black and white copiers.
- Many copiers are able to reduce the size of the copies being made.

Figure 11.13   A photocopier

Scanner

scanner ▶

The scanner is used to transfer printed material, such as photos and drawings, into a computer as digital files.

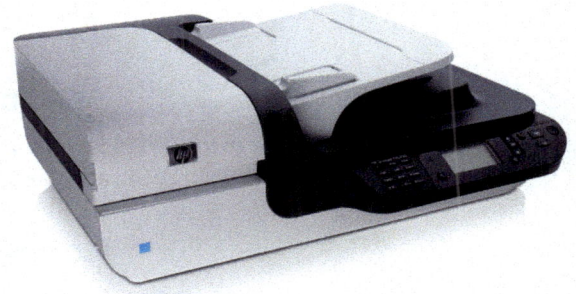

Figure 11.14   A scanner

Offset lithograph printer

offset lithograph printer ▶

The offset lithograph printer makes duplicates of a document by a process known as offset lithography. This means that an image is transferred to another surface and from that surface to the paper. Offset lithography is used in high-volume printing – for example, newspapers, magazines, catalogues and brochures. One major advantage of this method is that it makes high-quality documents cheaply. The offset lithograph printer may be present in a large Marketing Office that carries out the task of publishing its own documents.

Types of discount

discount ▶

A discount is a reduction in the selling price of a good or service. Discounts that can be given by sellers include trade discount, cash discount, quantity discount and special discount.

Trade discount

trade discounts ▶ Trade discounts are reductions in price given to traders or resellers. This reduction is given so that the resellers are able to maintain a healthy profit margin. The discount will vary so that resellers who purchase larger quantities will receive larger discounts.

Cash discount

cash discounts ▶ Cash discounts are reductions in price given to customers to encourage them to settle their bills within a stipulated period or for payments by cash instead of credit cards. Examples of cash discount terms are:
- 5/20 – this means that if the buyer settles his bill within 20 days he will receive a 5 per cent discount;
- n/30 – this means that if the buyer waits until 30 days after the date of the invoice he will pay the full price.

Quantity discount

quantity discounts ▶ Quantity discounts are reductions in price offered by a seller to a buyer for purchasing large quantities of goods. The greater the quantity purchased, the larger the discount. An example of how the discounts would be applied is shown in Table 11.2:

Quantity purchased	Discount offered
50–100 bags of cement	10%
101–200 bags of cement	15%
201 bags of cement and over	20%

Table 11.2 Quantity discount rates

Special discounts

special discounts ▶ Special discounts are reductions in price given for various reasons such as being a loyal and regular customer.

Goods on consignment

goods on consignment ▶ Selling goods on consignment is also known as consignment sale or guaranteed sale. Sale of goods on consignment is a trade agreement where the seller (consignor) provides goods to the buyer or reseller (consignee), who pays for them when the goods are sold. The seller will remain the owner of the goods until they are paid for and any unsold goods will be returned.

Goods sold on consignment include canned and bottled beverages and newspapers.

Advantages	Disadvantages
1. the seller is able to gain exposure for his product in retail outlets	1. the seller has no control over the placement of the goods on the reseller's shelves
2. the reseller is able to stock goods in their store without spending their own money to purchase them	2. even though the goods are on the reseller's shelves the seller does not receive payments until the goods are sold.

Table 11.3 Advantages and disadvantages of consignment sale

Documents used in the Sales and Marketing Offices

There are a number of documents that flow between a buyer and a seller when purchases are to be made. The potential purchaser will want to find out about the types of products available and the terms at which they are sold. The purchaser will therefore send an enquiry note to the seller to obtain details of the products. The enquiry is also sometimes made in response to an advertisement or other promotional activity.

enquiry note ▶

Quotation

quotation ▶

The potential seller may respond to an enquiry note by sending a quotation. A quotation is a document sent from a seller to a prospective buyer, outlining the price and description of goods or services offered. The quotation may be in the form of a letter or a pre-printed form or it may even be done verbally. Information on the quotation will also include any terms of the sale – for example, whether any warranties are provided.

If the buyer decides to make the purchase, a purchase order will be sent to the seller. The seller, through the Sales Office, will then prepare an invoice.

Quotation #719

ABC Office Equipment

15 Main Street

Castries

St Lucia

758-754-9085

Attention: CSP Services
9 Park Avenue
Castries, St Lucia
758-974-1465

Date: January 15, 2011

Thank you for the opportunity to quote.

Quantity	Description of Product	Unit Price	Total
1	Malcolm Photocopier XTZ153	24 650.00	24 650.00
		Sub-total	24 650.00
		GCT	4 313.75
		Grand Total	28 963.75

– GCT Sales Tax of 17.5% is applied to all products
– Quotation is valid for 3 days
– Quotation is based on information available at time of preparation

---

Figure 11.15   Example of a quotation

Invoice

invoice ▶

An invoice is a bill prepared by the seller and sent to the buyer to show how much money is owed. The invoice outlines the quantity of goods sold, the cost of the goods, the terms of the trade – for example whether discounts are offered and the due date for payment.

ITQ5

The following items were bought on credit by Nations Insurance Ltd from Mega Market Ltd:

- 25 reams Copy-Rite letter-size paper @ $555 each;
- 15 reams Copy-Rite legal-size paper @ $623 each.

Terms: quantity discount offered at 10%. If the invoice is settled within 10 days, the customer will receive a 5% discount, otherwise net. Payment due in 30 days.

a Prepare an invoice dated April 23, 2012 to show the transaction.

b How much will Nations Insurance Ltd pay if the account is settled within 10 days?

c How much will Nations Insurance Ltd pay if the bill is settled after 10 days?

INVOICE

INVOICE # : 3681

Brown's Hardware
St Ann
Jamaica
658-4571/854-6230 (fax)

Your order #135
GCT Registration # 0136–2482

To:	The Education Centre 1 Main St. St Ann Jamaica	Date:	January 3, 2011
		Due date:	February 2, 2011
		Terms:	5/20, n/30

Quantity	Description	Unit Price ($)	Total Price ($)
100 bags	Carib cement	650	65 000.00
1 ton	½ inch steel	90 000	90 000.00
			155 000.00
		Less: quantity discount 15%	23 250.00
			131 750.00
		Add: General Consumption Tax (GCT) 17.5%	23 056.25
		TOTAL	154 806.25

Figure 11.16   Example of an invoice

Several copies of the invoice are prepared:
- the customer usually receives the original;
- the Sales Office keeps a copy;
- the Accounts Office will receive a copy;

advice note ▶
- a copy will sometimes be used as an advice note. The advice note is sent ahead of the goods to inform the buyer that they are on their way;

delivery note ▶
- a copy will also be used as the delivery note. In many cases two copies are made. The delivery note will be carried by the delivery truck driver when the goods are being delivered. The signature of the buyer will be requested as evidence that the goods have been delivered. The buyer will then retain one copy of the delivery note and the driver will retain the other copy.

In many modern offices invoices are prepared using computer software such as Express Invoice, IBiz and Intuit QuickBooks.

electronic invoicing ▶
Recent years have seen the advent of electronic invoicing which is the delivery of invoices electronically over the internet via e-mails sent directly to the customer. This is facilitated by a system known as EIPP (Electronic Invoicing Presentment and Payment)

The benefits of EIPP include:
- the reduction of costs;
- reduction in paperwork;
- processing time is significantly reduced;
- delivery of the invoice is secure and immediate.

Pro-forma invoice

pro-forma invoice ▶

Another document sometimes prepared by the Sales Office is the pro-forma invoice. This looks just like a regular invoice, with the exception of the name. It is an estimated invoice sent by a seller to a buyer when:

- payment is requested in advance, especially in cases where the buyer is not known to the seller;
- the potential buyer wants to have an idea of exactly how much money he would have to pay for the items.

PRO-FORMA INVOICE

Pro-forma INVOICE # : 3681

Tool's Hardware
Main St
Port-of-Spain
Trinidad
1110-4521/210-9785 (fax)

VAT Registration # 9874

To:	The Eden Restaurant	**Date:** January 3, 2011
	2 Bailey Close	
	Port-of-Spain	
	Trinidad	
Terms:	5/20, n/30	

Quantity	Description	Unit Price ($)	Total Price ($)
3	Metal front doors	400	1200
		TOTAL	1200

Figure 11.17 Example of a pro-forma invoice

**Summary**

- The organization of the Sales Office depends on factors such as the size of the company and the nature of its business.
- The functions of the Sales Office include monitoring stock control, budgeting and engaging in customer follow-up.
- The Sales Office is required to liaise with the Accounts, Purchasing, Production and Human Resources Offices.
- Duties of the Sales Clerk include: preparing and filing sales documents, taking orders from customers and merchandising.
- The Marketing Office is responsible for monitoring trends in the marketplace and carrying out market research.
- Functions of the Marketing Office include budgeting, organizing promotional activities and liaising with advertising entities.
- Duties of a Marketing Office Clerk include preparing press releases, maintaining mailing lists and organizing travel.
- Functions of the Customer Service Department include responding to customer enquiries and solving customer complaints.
- Equipment used in the Sales and Marketing Offices includes facsimile machines, photocopiers and multimedia projectors.
- Types of discounts include: cash, trade, quantity and special discounts.
- Documentation prepared by the Sales Office includes: quotations, invoices and pro-forma invoices.

Answers to

1 By being professional and satisfying customers' needs.

2 Sales Office needs to liaise with:
   - Accounts Department – to pay Sales staff wages and to process invoices;
   - Procurement Department – to purchase supplies, equipment and stock needed to run the department efficiently;
   - Human Resources Department – to recruit workers when vacancies arise and to deal with staff welfare.

3 Duties of a Sales Clerk:
   - preparing sales documents;
   - merchandising;
   - maintaining mailing lists;
   - providing information to customers.

4 Examples of promotional activities:
   - advertising – long-term sales technique usually presented through media such as television and magazines;
   - sales promotion – short-term and long-term incentives including contests and free gifts.

5 a

	INVOICE			
				INVOICE # :
	Mega Market Ltd			
Your orfer #				
GCT Registration #				
To: Nations Insurance Ltd.		**Date:**	January 3, 2011	
		Due date:	May 23, 2011	
		Terms:	5/10, n/30	
		10% quality discount		
Quantity	**Description**	**Unit Price ($)**		**Total Price ($)**
25 reams	Copy-Rite letter size paper		555	13 875.00
15 reams	Copy-Rite legal size paper		623	9 345.00
				23 322.00
		Les quantity discount 10%		2 322.00
		TOTAL		20 898.00

b. $19,853.10

c. $20,898

Examination-style questions

Multiple choice questions

1 Ensuring that stock is properly displayed on store shelves is an example of
   a market research
   b merchandising
   c advertising
   d sales promotion.

2 The following are examples of sales promotion techniques, **except**:
   a trade shows
   b advertisements
   c free gifts
   d contests.

3 An official announcement sent to the media for publication is referred to as:

    a sales promotion

    b television commercials

    c press release

    d advertising.

4 Which machine is best suited to duplicating 5000 copies of a document?

    a Facsimile machine.

    b Photocopier.

    c Scanner.

    d Offset litho printer.

5 The type of discount given by a firm to encourage prompt payment is called:

    a special discount

    b trade discount

    c cash discount

    d bulk discount.

6 Which document is prepared when payment is required in advance?

    a Invoice.

    b Quotation.

    c Enquiry note.

    d Pro-forma invoice.

7 Which document is a statement of the price of a good or service?

    a Invoice.

    b Quotation.

    c Discount.

    d Enquiry.

8 Face-to-face promotional presentation to potential buyers is known as:

    a sales promotion

    b advertising

    c public relations

    d personal selling.

9 In Figure 11.16, if the Education Centre settles its bill on January 15, how much will it pay?

    a $155 000

    b $147 065.94

    c $131 750

    d $154 806.25.

10 If the Education Centre settles its bill on February 1, how much will it pay?

    a $155 000

    b $147 065.94

    c $131 750

    d $154 806.25.

Structured questions

1 Computer World is a wholesale supplier of computer accessories and supplies. On March 3, 2011, In Town Office Supplies ordered 15 standard keyboards @ $700 each.

   Computer World provides a trade discount of 5 per cent for purchases between $10 000 and $20 000. Computer World also offers a cash discount of 3 per cent per cent if the bill is settled within 20 days of invoice. The full amount is due 30 days from the invoice date.

   a Prepare the invoice dated March 3, 2011, to show the above transactions. [10]
   b If the bill is paid on March 10, 2011, how much will In Town Office Supplies pay? [1]
   c How much would In Town Office Supplies be expected to pay if the bill is settled on April 15, 2011? [1]

2 You have recently been employed as a Sales Clerk in a large retail store.
   a Outline **four** duties that you will be expected to perform. [4]
   b State **four** attributes that you will need to possess in order to be successful at your job. [4]
   c Identify **three** pieces of equipment that you will use as a part of your job. [3]

3 Create a newspaper or billboard advertisement for a motor vehicle of your choice. [10]

4 a Outline **three** functions of the Sales Office. [3]
   b Differentiate between the following:
      • trade discount and cash discount;
      • advertisements and sales promotions;
      • invoice and pro-forma invoice. [6]
   c Describe the following sales records:
      • price lists;
      • sales call log;
      • sales summary card;
      • commission summary;
      • sales report sheet. [10]

5 a Identify **three** types of transportation. [3]
   b State the methods of transportation most suited for transporting the following goods:
      • fresh cows' milk from Arima, Trinidad, to Chaguanas, Trinidad;
      • gasoline from Petrojam Refinery in Kingston, Jamaica, to Montego Bay, Jamaica;
      • bananas from Belize to the United Kingdom. [3]

6 You work in the Marketing Department of Caribbean Beverages Ltd. Help your marketing team by creating four promotional activities for the company's new energy drink, 'Samson'. [10]

7 a Outline **three** functions of the Customer Service Department. [3]
   b State **three** duties of a Customer Service Representative. [3]
   c Identify **two** advantages and **two** disadvantages of consignment sale. [4]

12 Operations, Despatch and Transport Offices

By the end of this chapter you should be able to:

- ☑ explain the functions of the Operations Office;
- ☑ discuss the importance of the Operations Office;
- ☑ identify the three main methods of production;
- ☑ state the duties of the Operations Office Clerk;
- ☑ prepare documents used in the Operations Office;
- ☑ discuss the importance of the Despatch and Transport Offices;
- ☑ state the duties of the Clerk in the Despatch and Transport Offices;
- ☑ prepare documents used in the Despatch and Transport Offices.

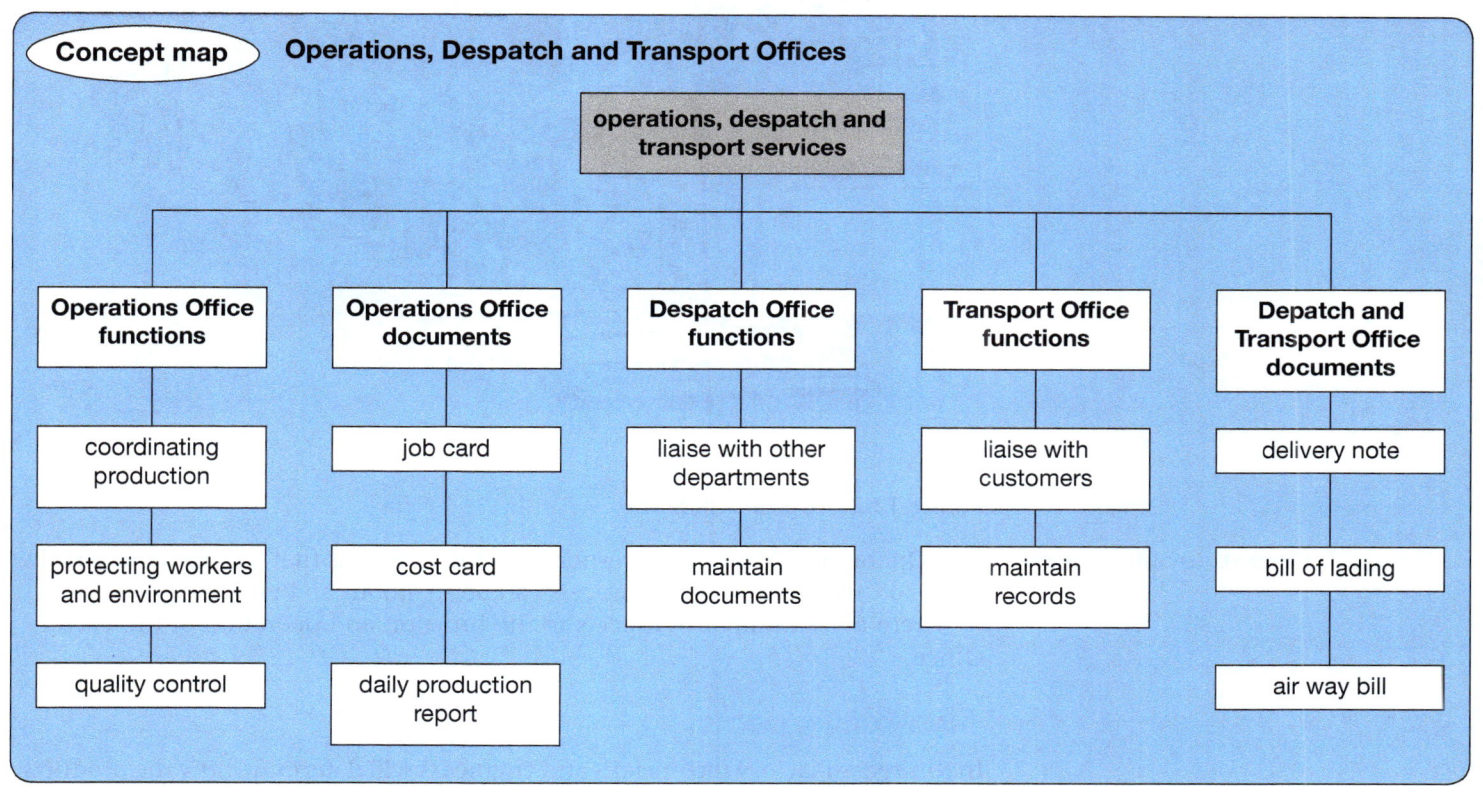

Concept map — Operations, Despatch and Transport Offices

Functions of the Operations Office

Operations Office ▶ The Operations Office, also known as the Production Department, Factory Office or Works Control Office, is headed by an Operations Manager, a Production Manager or a Works Manager.

An Operations Department is that functional area of a business in charge of carrying out the production process. The production process involves converting raw materials into finished products.

| Input (Raw materials) | → | Production process | → | Output (Finished goods) |

Figure 12.1 Flowchart production process

Figure 12.2 A production line

Operations Manager ▶ The Operations Manager is responsible for ensuring that all elements are in place so that the production process can be a smooth and efficient one.

There are a number of aspects to the function and operation of the Factory Office.

Technical aspects

In this regard factory technicians and engineers will determine how the products will be constructed or assembled. They will also assess what types of equipment will be needed to carry out the job. The quality and specifications of the raw materials required will also be taken into consideration.

Planning

production planning ▶ Production planning is essential to ensuring that all the components are organized in a structured way. This involves estimating how long the production process will take and ensuring that all raw materials and other inputs needed are on hand to ensure that everything is done within a reasonably cost-efficient timeframe.

Monitoring

The Operations Manager will monitor the progress of production to make sure all plans are being adhered to and inspect the product to ensure that it conforms to pre-determined specifications.

Protecting workers and the environment

One important function of the Operations Office is to ensure that the workers, especially those on the factory floor, are protected while carrying out their duties. In this regard factories are governed by certain regulations and laws such as:

- the Factories Act (1983) – Barbados;
- the Occupational Health and Safety Act (2004) – Trinidad and Tobago;
- the Factories Act (1943) – Jamaica.

These laws generally cover the health, welfare and safety of persons employed in factories. They may include issues such as the presence of fire escapes and exits, as well as adequate lighting and the use of protective clothing.

It is also the responsibility of the Operations Office to ensure that the environment is not adversely affected by emissions from the factory. There are laws and regulations in various territories which seek to ensure that the environment is protected – for example the Clean Air Act (1964) in Jamaica, which seeks to control air pollution in the country.

ITQ1
Why is planning an important function of the Factory Office?

ITQ2
Explain the term 'technical aspect' in relation to the Production Department.

ITQ3
State **two** laws which govern the operation of factories in the Caribbean.

Functions of the Factory Office

Ensuring quality control

quality control ▶

It is essential that the Factory Office carries out quality control and quality assurance in the production process in order to ensure efficiency and maintain reliability of the company's products and services.

> DEFINITION: **Quality control** is the process designed to ensure that the goods and services provided by the organization adhere to pre-determined standards.

Persons such as quality assurance specialists are usually employed to manage the task of ensuring quality control. The primary job of these specialists is to ensure that the finished products are of a pre-determined standard. To achieve this objective the quality assurance specialists:

- test and inspect the products at various stages during the production process
- Test the raw materials, tools and equipment used
- Test the finished goods to evaluate the product's performance under various conditions.

Any problems found are carefully documented and strategies are developed to prevent a re-occurrence.

It is also necessary for the quality control personnel to liaise with local quality standards bodies such as:

- Bureau of Standards Jamaica (BSJ) – Jamaica;
- Barbados National Standards Institution – Barbados.

These institutions monitor the quality of goods produced and traded in the country.

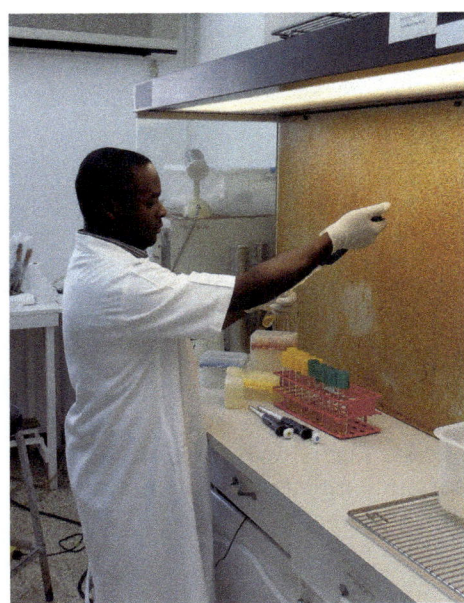
Figure 12.3 A quality control technician at work

Maintaining factory records

It is important that the Operations Office maintains proper records. The Operations Office Clerk may be responsible for raising, distributing and filing these records which may include daily production reports and shift rosters.

Costing of finished products

It is essential that the Operations Office, under the guidance of the Operations Manager, does cost estimates for producing varying quantities of goods and by using different methods. The types of costs to be borne in mind are:

direct costs ▶
- direct costs – these are costs which are directly related to the production process and are sometimes referred to as variable costs, because they vary depending on the amount of output in the factory. These costs include raw material and labour costs;

indirect or fixed costs ▶
- indirect or fixed costs – these costs are not directly related to the manufacturing process and tend to remain the same regardless of the output from the factory. These costs include rent and administrative salaries;

overhead costs ▶
- overhead costs – these are certain costs that are allocated to the factory on a proportional basis and usually represent a percentage of the entire cost. They include lighting and heating.

The main purpose of costing products is to evaluate whether a profit or loss will be made.

Liaising with other departments

The Operations Office must liaise with a number of different departments to ensure that the business achieves its goals.

Figure 12.4 Liaison of the Operations Office and other departments

Human Resources or Personnel Office

Human Resources Office ▶
The Operations Office should establish a relationship with the Human Resources Office to ensure that any vacancies within the factory are filled. The Human Resources Office will also assist the Operations Managers with the training and appraisal of the production workforce to ensure that efficiency is maintained in the production process.

Marketing Office

Marketing Office ▶
It is important for the Operations Office and the Marketing Office to work together in a cohesive way. It is the Marketing Office that will be working closely with customers and obtaining feedback on the requirements and changes in the market. This information will help to guide the decisions of the Operations Office.

Sales Office

Sales Office ▶

The Sales Office will receive the orders from customer and will ultimately determine what and how much is to be produced. Any verification that the Operations Office needs to make regarding the job will also be done through the Sales Office. The Sales Office will also liaise with Operations Office regarding complaints made about faulty goods.

Maintenance Office

Maintenance Office ▶

If the Maintenance Office is not already under the auspices of the Operations Office, it is important to maintain a relationship with the staff there. It will be the responsibility of the Maintenance Office to repair and maintain the factory's equipment.

Accounts Office

Accounts Office ▶

The Operations Office should liaise with the Accounts Office primarily since it is the Accounts Office that is responsible for all the financial dealings of the factory. It is this department that is responsible for:
- the payment of wages and salaries;
- making estimates and budgetary allocations for the materials, equipment and supplies required by the Factory Office;
- seeing to the cost efficiency of the entire organization by ensuring that the income generated exceeds the production costs.

Purchasing Office

Purchasing Office ▶

The Operations Office should maintain close relations with the Purchasing Office. This is so because it is the Purchasing Office that will procure all raw materials, equipment and other supplies needed for the Operations Office to operate efficiently. These requests need to be made well in advance so that workers and equipment are not left idle because of raw materials not arriving on time.

Despatch and Transport Office

Despatch and Transport Office ▶

A close relationship is necessary between the Operations Office and the Despatch and Transport Office, as it is the Despatch and Transport Office that will be responsible for delivering the finished goods from the Factory Office to the consumer. In some cases the Transport Office may also be required to deliver raw materials to the factory.

ITQ4

In what ways is the human resources function important to effective production?

Technology in production

automation ▶
computer-aided design (CAD) ▶
computer-aided manufacture (CAM) ▶

There are many technological aspects involved in the production process, including the automation of activities and the use of computer-aided design (CAD) and computer-aided manufacture (CAM). These measures usually help the firm to lower its costs by improving product levels and the quality of the final product.

> DEFINITION: **Automation** is the use of electronic or mechanical techniques to carry out a task.

> DEFINITION: **Computer-aided manufacture** is the use of computers and software programs in the management of the production process.

> DEFINITION: **Computer-aided design** is the use of software programs to develop three-dimensional (3D) designs. This allows engineers to experiment with the design without incurring high costs or delays.

Many robots and machines used in CAM are useful when the tasks to be carried out are repetitive or dangerous to humans' health – for example, working in a radioactive environment.

Figure 12.5   A robot on a car assembly line

Methods of production

There are three main methods of production that can be used to carry out the productive process:
- job production;
- batch production;
- flow production.

Figure 12.6   An example of flow production

Job production/one-line production

job production ▶ In job production, the factory will focus on completing one job or order at a time. There are some factories that specialize in this method of production where they provide customized products to customers based on their specifications – for example, custom-made boats or pianos. This method of production is usually very labour intensive and expensive, as it requires highly skilled labour.

Batch production

batch production ▶ Batch production occurs when groups of similar items are produced in batches – for example, a bakery bakes batches of doughnuts, buns and muffins.

Flow/mass production/continuous flow production

flow/mass production ▶ Flow/mass production is used to provide a large number of identical items – for example, computers and sodas, to a mass market. The items move from one stage of production to another in a continuous flow, usually on an assembly line. This method of production is highly capital intensive, resulting in a low cost per unit.

ITQ5
Differentiate between job production and flow production.

Duties of the Factory Office Clerk

Factory Office Clerk ▶ The Factory Office Clerk will be required to carry out a number of important functions to aid the efficiency of the department. These include:
- performing clerical duties such as answering the telephone and filing factory office records;
- **shift rosters ▶** • preparing shift rosters – shift rosters or shift rotas are prepared when staff work on shift duties. They are work schedules which cover periods of up to 24 hours. Shift roster software automatically schedules employees and makes the task easier and quicker than manual scheduling, especially in cases where there is a large number of employees. Examples of shift software are Rostermatic and Freelancer;

Employee No.	Employee Name	Monday	Tuesday	Wednesday	Thursday	Friday	Saturday	Sunday
1	S Allen	6 am–2 pm	6 am–2 pm	Day Off	Day Off	2 pm–10 pm	2 pm–10 pm	2 pm–10 pm
2	J Bromwell	6 am–2 pm	6 am–2 pm	2 pm–10 pm	2 pm–10 pm	Day Off	Day Off	6 am–2 pm
3	F Green	Day Off	Day Off	2 pm–10 pm	2 pm–10 pm	6 am–2 pm	6 am–2 pm	6 am–2 pm
4	A Plummer	2 pm–10 pm	2 pm–10 pm	Day Off	Day Off	2 pm–10 pm	6 am–2 pm	2 pm–10 pm
5	K Waite	2 pm–10 pm	2 pm–10 pm	6 am–2 pm	6 am–2 pm	6 am–2 pm	Day Off	Day Off

Figure 12.7 Example of a shift roster

• completing time cards – time cards / clock cards record the number of hours that an employee has worked. The time card is essential as it will enable the Accounts Department to calculate the wages of the hourly paid workers in the Operations Office. It is filled out by the employee, but in many instances it is inserted into a time-recording machine which stamps the current time on it. There is, however, computer software that allow workers to clock in and out via the company's computer network. The computer system will later generate daily or weekly reports for each employee. Examples of time recording software include timeQplus and Hour Guard;

Figure 12.8 A time clock

TIME CARD

Employee name: Janet Smith   **Employee Number:** 364
Period: December 6–12, 2010

Day	Time In 1	Time Out 1	Time In 2	Time Out 2	Total hours
Monday	0900	1300	1400	1700	7
Tuesday	0900	1700	–	–	8
Wednesday	0900	1300	1400	1700	7
Thursday	0900	1300	1400	1700	7
Friday	1000	1400	1430	1700	6.5
Saturday (overtime)	–	–	1000	1700	7
					42.5

Regular hours @ $50 per hour
35.5 hours @ $50 = $1775

Overtime hours @ $75 per hour
7 hours @ $75 = $535

Gross wages = $1775 + $525 = $2300

Figure 12.9 Example of a time card

• preparing daily production reports – these are essential documents that enable the Operations Manager to be able to monitor the amount of production that is done in the factory each day;

Daily Production Report

Date: November 3, 2011

Production number	Customer name	Description of product	Quantity	Time taken	No. of items completed	No. of items spoilt or wasted
3	Kings High School	Black long sleeve blouses (large)	100	6 hours	100	

Remarks:

Prepared by: Jamaal Nembhard, Operations Clerk

Approved by: Victor Fiddler, Operations Manager

Figure 12.10 Example of a daily production report

• completing other forms found in the Operations Office, such as job cards, job cost cards, cost analysis cards and master production schedules.

Documents used in the Operations Office

Master Production Schedule (MPS)/Planning Master/Master Schedule

This is one of the most important documents used in the Operations Office. The MPS guides the productive activity of the company, including staffing and inventory. It outlines what is to be made, when it is to be made, what it is to be made with and by whom. The Master Production Schedule is essential as it helps to avoid shortage and inefficient allocation of resources. The Master Production Schedule is usually computerized which enhances the speed at which the document is prepared, as well as its accuracy, especially for complex production processes.

True Art Ltd

Planning Master

For week ending September 7, 2011

Item to be produced	Quantity required	Workers required	Materials/stock required	Machines and other tools required	Estimated time to complete job	Actual time taken to complete job	Comments
White T-shirts	100	Cutters Stitchers Packers	200 yds white cotton 20 reels white thread	Sewing machines	4 days	3 days	Job finished ahead of schedule

Figure 12.11 Example of a Master Production Schedule

Production order

Production Order ▶

The production order initiates the production process and is usually authorized by the Operations Manager.

PRODUCTION ORDER
Order #: 25
Date: 5 September 2009
Customer Name: AJ's Wholesale
Production Description: Banana chips
Number of Items: 500 packets
Scheduled Completion Date: 6 September 2009
Special Instructions:
Actual Date Completed:
Prepared By: Janet Smith, Clerk
Authorized by: Elizabeth Headley, Factory Office Manager

Figure 12.12 Example of a production order

Job card

job card ▶ The job card, sometimes referred to as the 'job ticket', outlines the description of the job to be done, and the related labour and materials needed for it to be carried out. The job card usually accompanies each job through the various stages of the production process.

JOB CARD		
Date:	6 September 2009	
Customer Name:	AJ's Wholesale	**Job Card #:** 12
Description of Job:	Banana chips	
No. of items:	500 packets	
Materials Used		**Quantity**
#1. bananas		500 lbs.
#2. vegetable oil		10 gallons
#3. seasonings		20 lbs
Labour Employed		**Rate of Pay**
#1. 2 peelers		$200 per hour
#2. 2 cutters		$200 per hour
#3. 2 fry cooks		$250 per h our
Time Taken: 8 hours		
Inspected By: James Austin, Quality Control Inspector		
Approved By: Elizabeth Headley, Operations Office Manager		

Figure 12.13 Example of a job card

Cost card/job cost card

cost card ▶ The cost card outlines the actual or budgeted costs associated with the production process. It includes fixed and variable costs. It will also include the overhead costs such as lighting which are allocated to the various departments on a proportional basis.

The main purpose of job costing is to ascertain the cost per unit in order to determine whether a profit or loss will be made.

COST CARD		
Customer's Name: AJ's Wholesale	**Job No:** 12	
Description of Job: Banana chips		
Quantity: 500 packets	**Time Taken:** 8 hours	
Materials Required	**Budgeted Cost**	**Actual Cost (JA$)**
#1. 500 lbs bananas	70 000.00	70 000.00
#2. 10 gallons vegetable oil	2 500.00	2 500.00
#3. 20 lbs seasonings	2 000.00	2 000.00
Total Cost of Materials	**74 500.00**	**74 500.00**
Labour Required		
#1. 2 peelers	3 200.00	3 200.00
#2. 2 cutters	3 200.00	3 200.00
#3. 2 fry cooks	4 000.00	4 000.00
Total Cost of Labour	**10 400.00**	**10 400.00**
Overhead Costs (5%)	4 245.00	4 245.00
Total Cost of Job	89 145.00	89 145.00
Cost per unit	178.29	178.29
Prepared By: Janet Smith, Clerk		

Figure 12.14 Example of a cost card

Cost analysis card/cost summary sheet

cost analysis card /
cost summary sheet ▶

The cost analysis card/cost summary sheet is used to provide information necessary for internal planning and control. It can be used to analyze the costs of different goods that are produced or simply to assess the cost of each section within the Factory Office.

Cost Summary Sheet						
Product	Materials and Supplies	Labour	Rent and Overheads	Total Cost	No. of items produced	Cost per unit
A	2000	3000	3000	8000	800	10
B	3000	4500	3000	10500	1500	7
C	3000	5000	4000	12000	2000	6

Figure 12.15 A cost summary for three products

Accident report form

accident report form ▶

The accident report form is to be completed whenever there are accidents or injury in the Operations Office. An accident must be reported as soon as it occurs. The form may be completed by the injured employee or on his/her behalf by a colleague or his/her supervisor

Accident Report Form
Accident no.
Name of employee:
Date of accident: Time of accident:
Description of accident:
What medical action was taken?:
Form completed by:
Statement(s) of eyewitness(es)
Signature(s) or eyewitness(es) _____ Date _____
Operations Manager _____

Figure 12.16 Example of an accident report form

Progress chart

progress chart ▶

The progress chart is used to illustrate the level of completion of a job or task. It allows employees to be updated on the development of the job, as well as allowing project supervisors to determine whether the job is moving on schedule and will be delivered to the customer on time. Progress chasers may be employed to monitor the progress of a job at different stages of the manufacturing process. Project management software can be purchased to assist in planning and managing complex projects.

Arc Manufacturing Co Ltd					Date: September 3, 2011	
Progress Chart						
Project Supervisor:	V. Lee					
Project:	Dining table set					
Task/Job	**Start date**	**Actual/proposed completion date**	**Duration**	**Days complete**	**Days remaining**	**%age completion**
Dining table set	September 1	September 4	4 days	3 days	1 day	75%

Figure 12.17   Example of a progress chart

Functions of the Despatch Office

The primary role of the Despatch and Transport Offices is to make arrangements for the goods manufactured by the Operations Office to be distributed in a safe, timely and efficient manner to the wholesalers, retailers and customers.

It may be necessary for the Despatch Office to keep a database of various courier service companies and air and sea transport agents. The database will include the name of the company, their contact numbers, address, e-mail address and a description of the type of service they offer.

Another key responsibility of the Despatch Office is to prepare the products for despatch by ensuring that they are properly packaged. The type of package used

Figure 12.18   A Despatch Office Clerk at work

will usually depend on factors such as the nature of the product (for example, perishable or non-perishable) and the distance it will have to be transported. Types of packaging may include:

• crates and insulated boxes;
• strong containers that can be tightly sealed;
• loading onto pallets and shrink-wrapping for easy movement.

Shipping regulations also determine specific markings and labelling that need to appear on crates and containers in order to ensure proper handling. These rules include:

- ensuring that letters used to make markings are waterproof and permanent;
- labels must be legible and accurate and in many cases should be in the language of the country the consignment is going to;
- properly labelling hazardous materials – for example, 'Explosives' or 'Flammable Liquids';
- **handling marks ▶** using handling marks, as applicable. Handling marks give specific instructions on how the goods should be handled. Examples of handling marks are shown in Figure 12.19;
- stating clearly the weight or number of packages.

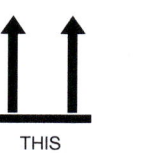      

THIS WAY UP   KEEP DRY   KEEP AWAY FROM HEAT   CENTRE OF GRAVITY   FRAGILE   NO HOOKS   SLING HERE

Figure 12.19 Handling marks

Duties of the Despatch Office Clerk

The Despatch Clerk, sometimes referred to as the Logistics Clerk, is responsible for carrying out a number of tasks in the Despatch Office, including the following:

- preparation of documents for despatched goods. These documents include the delivery note and the advice note;
- maintaining a database of external transport agents such as courier services and transport contractors;
- ensuring that certain statutory regulations are adhered to. This could include adhering to certain safety regulations, especially in large Despatch Offices where the use of cranes and other machines is common;
- scheduling deliveries;
- resolving customers' issues and ensuring that deliveries are made in a timely manner;
- packing products;
- checking that packages sent out include the correct goods that were ordered by customers;
- liaising with other departments, such as the Sales, Factory and Purchasing Offices.

Functions of the Transport Office

The delivery of finished goods may be done by using the firm's own vehicles or outside transport. If the firm's own vehicles are used, the Transport Manager should ensure that they are properly maintained and serviced. Vehicle documentation such as insurance and motor vehicle registration must always be valid. In Jamaica, the Inland Revenue Department currently has a system in place whereby it calls customers to remind them when their motor vehicle documents renewals and registrations are due.

The Transport Office may have to source outside carriers if it does not own its own vehicles. This may be advantageous to the company as it will not incur costs relating to purchasing and maintaining the vehicles.

Some contract carriers will also allow the Transport Office to mark and paint the vehicles as though they were the property of the organization. Other examples of outside carriers are shipping lines and airlines.

Many firms use state-of-the-art motor vehicle tracking systems to monitor their fleets of vehicles to ensure the greatest efficiency in the delivery of customers' goods.

Type of transport	Advantages	Disadvantages
Own	Complete control	High maintenance costs
Hired	Cheaper – no capital investment to buy vehicles	Less control of fleet
Public	Cheaper – no capital investment to buy vehicles	May be unreliable

Table 12.1   Advantages and disadvantages of transport types

Duties of the Transport Office Clerk

- Handle enquiries from customers regarding the status of their freight.
- Handling complaints from customers.
- Communicate with drivers and delivery men.
- Maintaining transport documents such as delivery schedules and destination sheets.

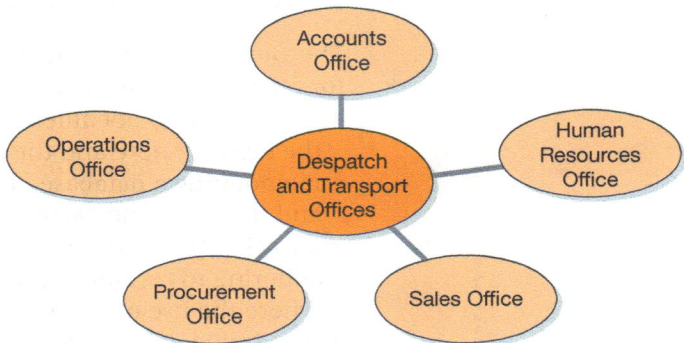

Figure 12.20   Relationship between the Despatch and Transport Offices and other departments

Liaising with other departments

The Despatch and Transport Offices must liaise with the following departments:

Accounts Office

The Accounts Office will be responsible for paying the wages and salaries of workers in the Despatch and Transport Offices.

Human Resources Office

The Human Resources Office will be responsible for:
- training the workers;
- recruiting workers to fill vacancies in the Despatch and Transport Offices;
- dealing with all aspects of staff welfare.

Operations Office

The Operations Office will manufacture the goods that will be handed over to the Despatch and Transport Offices to be passed on to customers.

Procurement Office

The Procurement Office will be responsible for purchasing supplies, equipment, motor vehicles and motor vehicle parts needed to run the Despatch and Transport Offices effectively.

Sales Office

The Despatch and Transport Offices will need to maintain contact with the Sales Office in order to:
• verify orders from customers;
• confirm addresses of customers.

Documents used in the Despatch and Transport Offices

Destination sheet

destination sheet ▶

The destination sheet is used by Transport Offices that make their own deliveries and need to manage a large fleet of vehicles. The destination sheet is usually prepared daily and assigns each vehicle and driver to a specific route. Information on the destination includes:
• the driver's name;
• the contents of the delivery;
• the destination.
The destination sheet is an internal document used by personnel within the transport office to organize the fleet of vehicles.

Destination Sheet					
Vehicle #	**Name of Driver**	**Recipient's name**	**Destination**	**Contents**	**Mileage**
Panel van # 9678	Leighton Summer	Pansy Clark	35 Rose Avenue, St Ann	1 television set	3

Figure 12.21   Example of a destination sheet

Delivery schedule

delivery schedule ▶

The delivery schedule is given to each driver at the beginning of each day to outline all the deliveries that he/she will be expected to make.

Delivery Schedule	
Vehicle #: Panel van #9678	
Driver: Leighton Summer	
Recipient's name	**Address**
Pansy Clarke	35 Rose Avenue, St Ann
Jane Simmons	20 Pineapple Drive, St Ann

Figure 12.22   Example of a delivery schedule

Delivery note

delivery note ▶

The delivery note contains the quantity, description and sometimes the cost of the goods being delivered. The driver of the delivery vehicle will obtain the buyer's signature on a copy of the delivery note and return it to the seller as evidence of delivery of the goods. The delivery note is usually a copy of the invoice that was prepared for the customer.

Delivery notes are usually used when the company is using its own vehicles to deliver the goods. If the company is hiring an outside carrier to transport the goods, a consignment note will be prepared. The consignment note serves as a contract between the sender (the consignor) and the outside carrier, to deliver goods (the consignment) to a buyer (the consignee). The consignment note, when signed by the carrier, acts as a receipt for the goods to be delivered. When the buyer's signature is obtained on the consignment note as evidence of delivery, a copy is usually sent to the consignor.

Advice note

advice note ▶ Also known as an advice of shipment, the advice note is sent from the seller to the buyer to informing them that the goods ordered are on their way. The advice note may also be accompanied by a copy of the invoice and a bill of lading.

ADVICE NOTE

Bell & Co Ltd
1 High Way
St Ann
Jamaica
876-321-2118

Advice Note No. 453　　　　　　　**Date:** January 8, 2012

To:　New England School　　　　　　**Order no:** 643
　　　27 Steele Place
　　　Trelawny
　　　Jamaica

Quantity	Description	Unit Price ($)	Amount ($)
20	White T-shirts (size – small)	100	2000
20	White T-shirts	150	3000
		Sub-total	5000
		VAT (10%)	500
		Total	5500

The above items will be delivered on March 30, 2012 and will be delivered by FedEx

Figure 12.23　Example of an advice note

Bill of lading

bill of lading ▶ The bill of lading is presented to the shipper from the carrier or its representative, as evidence of a contract to carry the goods from the port of embarkation to the port of destination. The bill also acts as a receipt of the transaction and serves as

consignment ▶ a title or proof of ownership of the consignment.

Information contained in the bill of lading includes:
• the list of goods being transported;
• the number of packages;
• the name of the vessel /carrier;
• dates of arrival and departure;
• names of consignor and consignee;
• names of ports of departure and destination.

DEFINITION: **Consignment** is a shipment of goods sent from a consignor (seller) to a consignee (buyer).

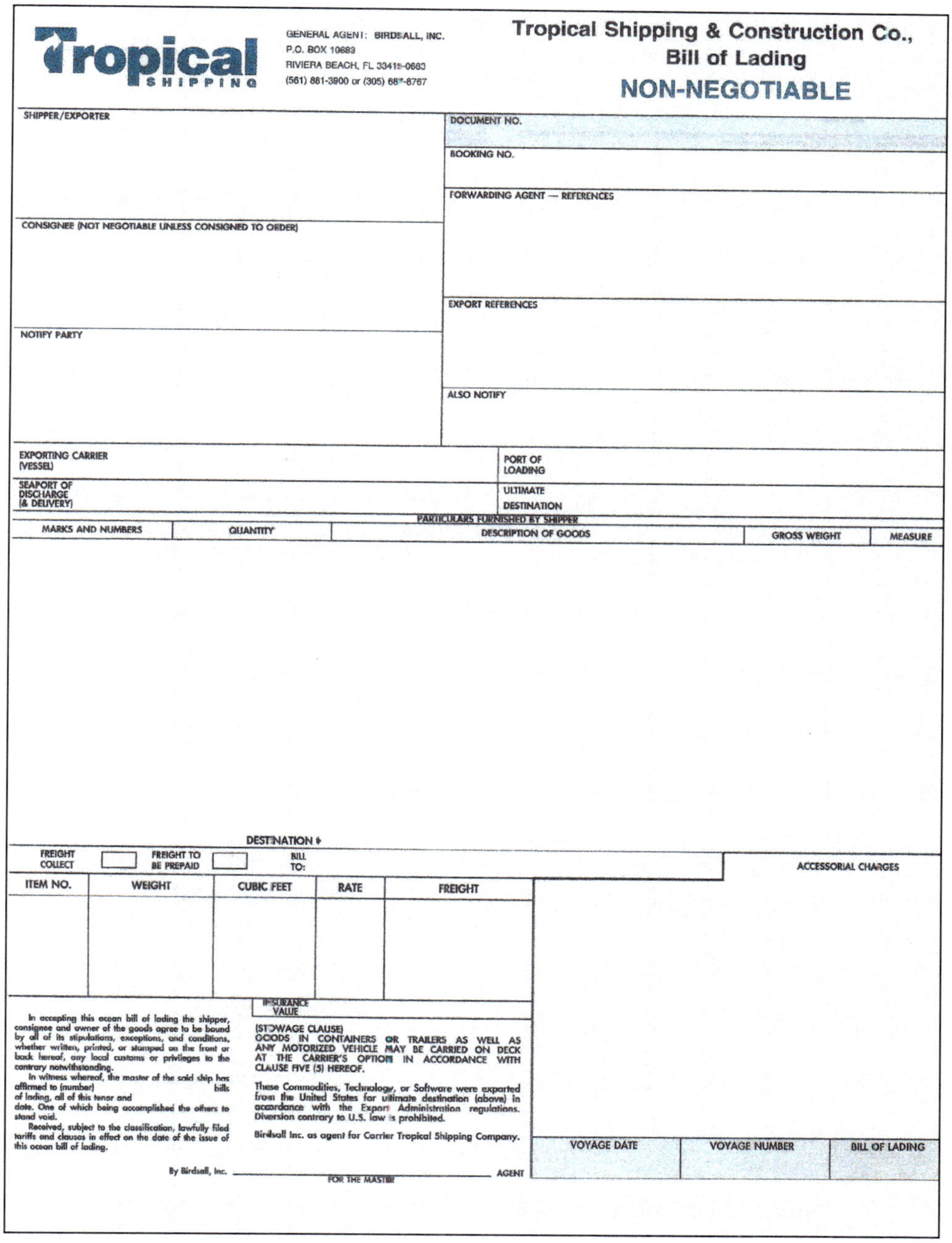

Figure 12.24   A bill of lading

Air waybill

air waybill ▶

This document is also known as an air waybill of lading or an air consignment note. It is used when the consignment is being transported by air. The air waybill represents a contract of carriage and a receipt for the consignment; however, it does not serve as proof of ownership.

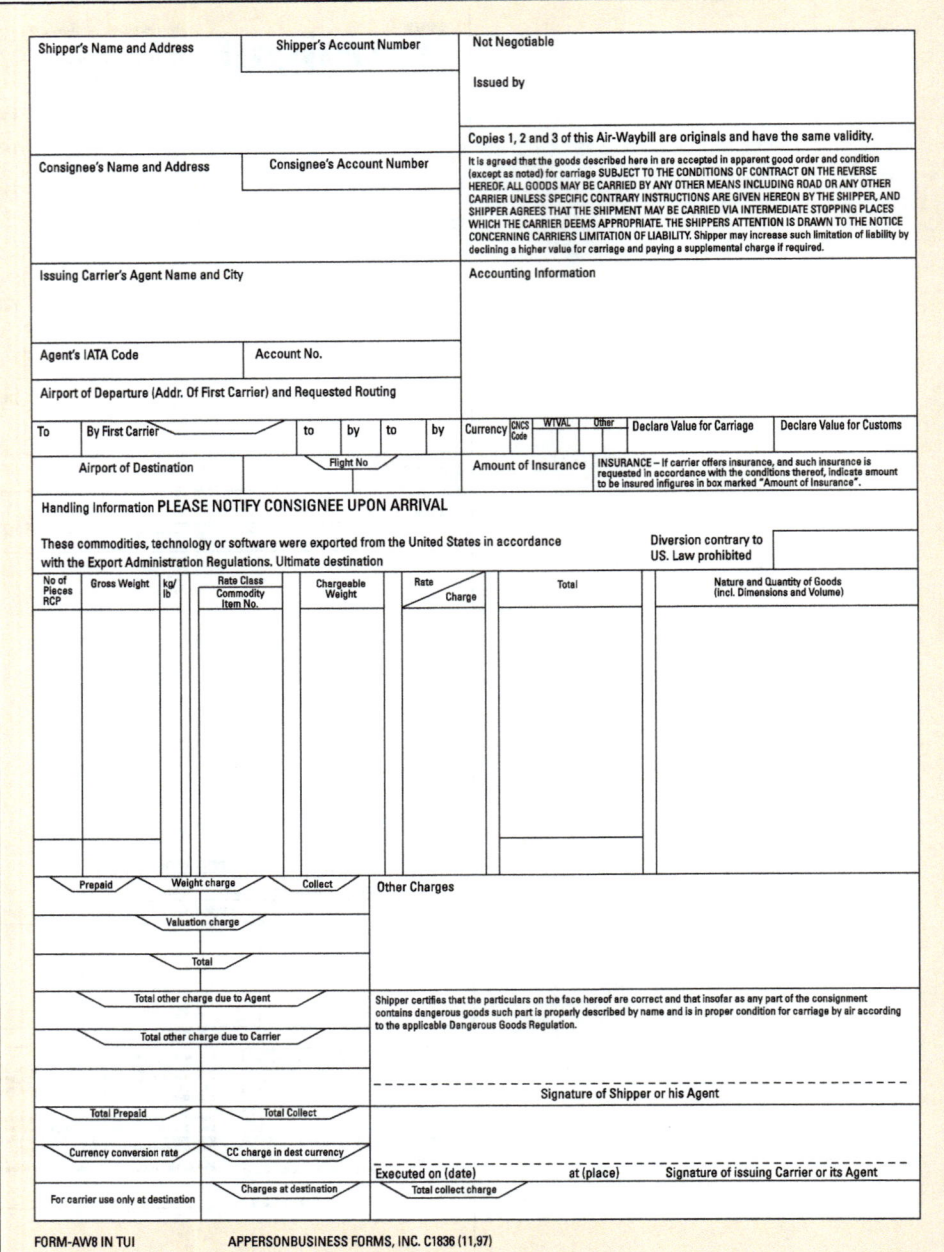

Figure 12.25   An air waybill

Manifest

manifest ▶

The manifest is a document which gives a summary of all cargo placed on a ship or other vehicle. It will show a list of all bills of lading (or airway bills, in the case of air travel) for each journey. It is usual for a copy of the manifest to be kept in a safe place so that in the event that the ship is destroyed there will be evidence of the cargo that it contained.

Customs entry form

customs entry form ▶

The customs entry form will be completed by an importer to declare information on the goods being brought into a country. The customs officer will assess the goods and levy the appropriate customs duty.

Insurance certificate

insurance certificate ►
pilferage ►

The insurance certificate represents a policy that was taken out to cover the loss or damage to the cargo during transportation. Coverage can also be taken out against delay and pilferage.

> DEFINITION: **Pilferage** is the theft of a small amount of goods.

Depending on the agreement, either the buyer or the seller may be responsible for taking out the insurance coverage. An example of a type of policy that could be bought is the marine cargo insurance which covers the loss of or damage to goods at sea.

Import and export licences

import and export licences ►

Import and export licences are documents issued by the government, authorizing the importation and exportation of certain goods. Governments may issue these licences in order to protect the environment or the economic stability of the nation. Examples of items requiring import licence in Jamaica are milk, sugar and gases such as hydrogen.

Items that require an export licence before they can be exported from Barbados include live goats and tortoise shells.

Import and export licences can be obtained from the Trade Board in Jamaica and the Department of Commerce and Consumer Affairs in Barbados.

Certificate of origin

certificate of origin ►

The certificate of origin is an international trade document that is used to verify the country that the goods are shipped from. This may be required because of established free trade areas and varying customs duty fees across the world. Some countries have also placed bans on goods coming from certain countries as well as imposing quotas which limit the amount of goods that can be imported.

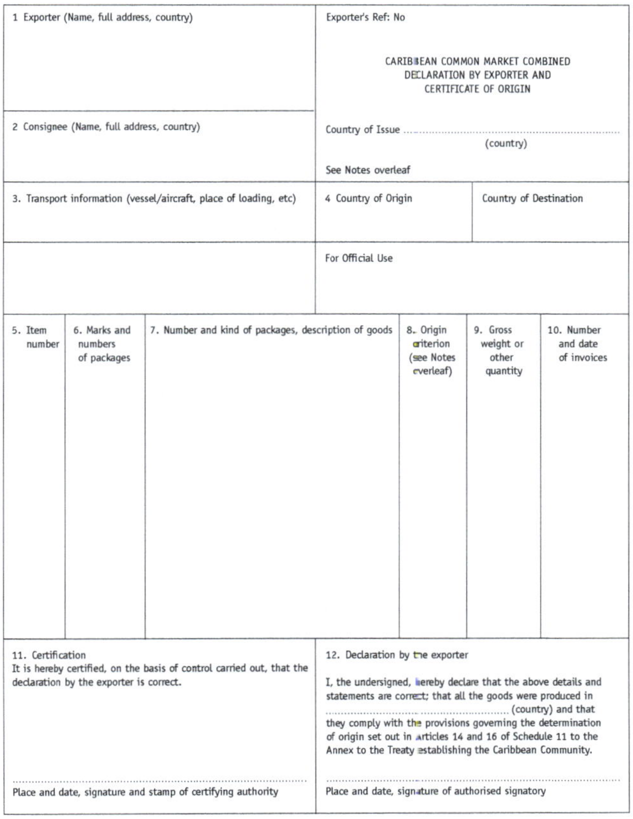

1 Exporter (Name, full address, country)

Exporter's Ref: No

CARIBBEAN COMMON MARKET COMBINED DECLARATION BY EXPORTER AND CERTIFICATE OF ORIGIN

2 Consignee (Name, full address, country)

Country of Issue .... (country)

See Notes overleaf

3. Transport information (vessel/aircraft, place of loading, etc)

4 Country of Origin

Country of Destination

For Official Use

5. Item number	6. Marks and numbers of packages	7. Number and kind of packages, description of goods	8. Origin criterion (see Notes overleaf)	9. Gross weight or other quantity	10. Number and date of invoices

11. Certification
It is hereby certified, on the basis of control carried out, that the declaration by the exporter is correct.

....
Place and date, signature and stamp of certifying authority

12. Declaration by the exporter

I, the undersigned, hereby declare that the above details and statements are correct; that all the goods were produced in .... (country) and that they comply with the provisions governing the determination of origin set out in articles 14 and 16 of Schedule 11 to the Annex to the Treaty establishing the Caribbean Community.

....
Place and date, signature of authorised signatory

Figure 12.26 A certificate of origin

Freight note

Also referred to as 'freight notation', freight notes are simply words or phrases that appear on certain documents, such as invoices, to tell who will pay or has paid for the freight and where. Examples of such notation are 'freight prepaid' and 'freight payable at destination'.

Summary

- The Operations Office is the functional area responsible for carrying out the production process.
- One responsibility of the Operations Office is the costing of finished goods.
- The Operations Office should liaise with departments such as the Human Resources Office, the Marketing Office and the Purchasing Office.
- The three main methods of production are: job production, batch production and flow production.
- Documents used in the Operations Office include: the production order, the job card and the cost card.
- Duties of a Clerk in the Despatch and Transport Office include maintaining a database of couriers and liaising with other departments.
- Documents used in the Despatch and Transport Department include: the air waybill, the bill of lading and the certificate of origin.

Answers to  ITQs

1 Planning is necessary to ensure that there are adequate raw materials, labour and equipment to do the job.

2 Technical aspects look at how the product will be created and the types of equipment and quality of raw materials that will be used.

3 The Factories Act (1943) (Jamaica) and the Occupational Health and Safety Act (2004) (Trinidad and Tobago).

4 The Human Resources function will ensure that production staff are adequately trained to carry out their tasks and are comfortable in their work environment.

5 Job production deals with completing one job order at a time while flow production is the production of large amounts of items on an assembly line.

Examination-style questions

Multiple choice questions

1 Which method of production focuses on completing one job/order at a time?
   a Job production.
   b Batch production.
   c Flow production.
   d Continuous production.

2 Which document is used to monitor the amount of production done in the factory each day?
   a Planning master.
   b Job card.
   c Daily production report.
   d Cost card.

3 Which Factory Office document guides the productive activity of the business?
   a Planning master.
   b Job card.
   c Daily production report.
   d Cost card.

4   Which one of the following is an example of a fixed cost?
   a   Lighting.
   b   Heating.
   c   Raw materials.
   d   Rent.

5   The purpose of which document is to ascertain the cost per unit of production?
   a   Planning master.
   b   Job card.
   c   Daily production report.
   d   Cost card.

6   Which document serves as a title or proof of ownership of a consignment?
   a   advice note
   b   certificate of origin
   c   bill of lading
   d   air waybill.

7   Which document is used when goods are being transported by air?
   a   advice note
   b   certificate of origin
   c   bill of lading
   d   air waybill.

8   A consignment is:
   a   the name of the seller
   b   the name of the vessel
   c   a shipment of goods
   d   a seller of goods.

9   Which document lists all bills of lading?
   a   customs entry form
   b   manifest
   c   export licence
   d   certificate of insurance.

10   Which document is used to declare information on goods being imported?
   a   customs entry form
   b   manifest
   c   export licence
   d   certificate of insurance.

Structured questions

1   Differentiate clearly between:
   a   bill of lading and air waybill;
   b   consignor and consignee;
   c   computer-aided manufacturing (CAM) and computer-aided design (CAD);
   d   delivery note and consignment note.   [4]

2   Identify **three** departments that the Despatch and Transport Office must liaise with and explain why the link is necessary.   [6]

3 Assume that you are Ann Williams, a clerk in the Factory Office. You are required to prepare job card #5 for 600 size 14 white shirts. The requirements are:

Materials
200 yards white cotton
6 dozen reels white thread
Labour
4 cutters @ $300 per day
4 stitchers @ $300 per day
2 packers @ $150 per day.

The job is expected to take 5 days. The manager, Mr Bryce, must approve the job.

a Prepare the job card to record the above information. [10]
b Calculate the labour cost per shirt. [1]

4 The cost card in Figure 12.27 was prepared by the Operations Clerk at JG Fashions:

JG Fashions	
COST CARD	
Description of Job: V-neck T-shirts, white	**Job no:** 9
Quantity: 500	**Time taken:** 40 hours
Materials required	**Cost**
#1 250 metres cotton	1200
#2 30 reels white thread	50
#3 500 collars	250
Total cost of materials	**1500**
Labour required	
# 1 machinist	800
# 2 packers	200
Total cost of labour	**1000**
Overhead costs (10%)	
Total cost of job	
Cost per unit	
Prepared by:	

Figure 12.27 JG Fashion cost card

a Complete the cost card by calculating:
- the overhead costs; [1]
- the total cost of the job; [1]
- the cost per unit. [1]

b If JG Fashions plans to sell the shirts for $9 each, calculate how much profit or loss will be made. [1]

5 Identify **four** duties of a Clerk in the Operations Office. [4]

6 Use the following information to prepare the cost card for your customer, New Town Electronic Systems, who ordered three tables.

Materials:
Wood $800
Glue $50
Varnish $100
Labour: $700

Overheads calculated at 20 per cent of total cost.
The job took four days to complete. [10]

13 Guidelines for preparing the School-Based Assessment

School-Based Assessment (SBA) ▶ The School-Based Assessment (SBA) is an important component of the Office Administration examination. The project is marked out of 50 but it accounts for 25 per cent of your overall examination score.

The SBA allows students to develop their research skills by carrying out an investigation into a real or virtual office.

The SBA topics are pre-determined by the Caribbean Examinations Council (CXC) each year and will be given to you by your teacher. In the coming years the topics are:
- 2012: Communication and Factory & Office Accounts;
- 2013: Office Orientation and Purchasing & Stock Control;
- 2014: Records & Information Management and Sales Office;
- 2015: Human Resources and Travel;
- 2016: Orientation and Recruitment & Factory Office.

The project

While you may work in groups, each student must each produce a unique and individual project. The project should be written in Standard English, following the rules of proper syntax, spelling and punctuation.

The SBA project is divided into three sections:
- Criterion 1 – Preparation   14 marks
- Criterion 2 – Gathering data   13 marks
- Criterion 3 – Presentation   23 marks.

Criterion 1 – Preparation

Title

You should select an appropriate title based on the topics given by your teacher. The title should be related to the syllabus and should be researchable. You should identify an organization large enough for you to be able to obtain the information you need easily. Then identify a specific department within the organization.

It is a good idea is to begin your topic with probing words such as 'An investigation into … '.

An example would be 'An investigation into the methods of classification used in the Records Department and how it impacts on the efficiency of the organization'.

Aims

You will need to outline two aims for your project. These aims are necessary to guide the research process. They should be directly related to your topic. The aims should begin with verbs such as 'to compare', 'to examine' and 'to identify': for example, 'The researcher hopes to examine which method of filing is in use'.

Functions

You will need to identify two functions of the department in which you are carrying out your study. For example:

'Two functions of the Human Resources Department are:

1   preparing job specifications,
2   selecting and recruiting suitably qualified persons.'

Correspondence

In this piece of correspondence you are seeking permission from the organization to conduct your project in its working area. The letter should explain what you are trying to achieve and what you would like to do while there. For example, you might want permission to ask questions of particular employees or to observe them at work. Here is an example of a suitable letter:

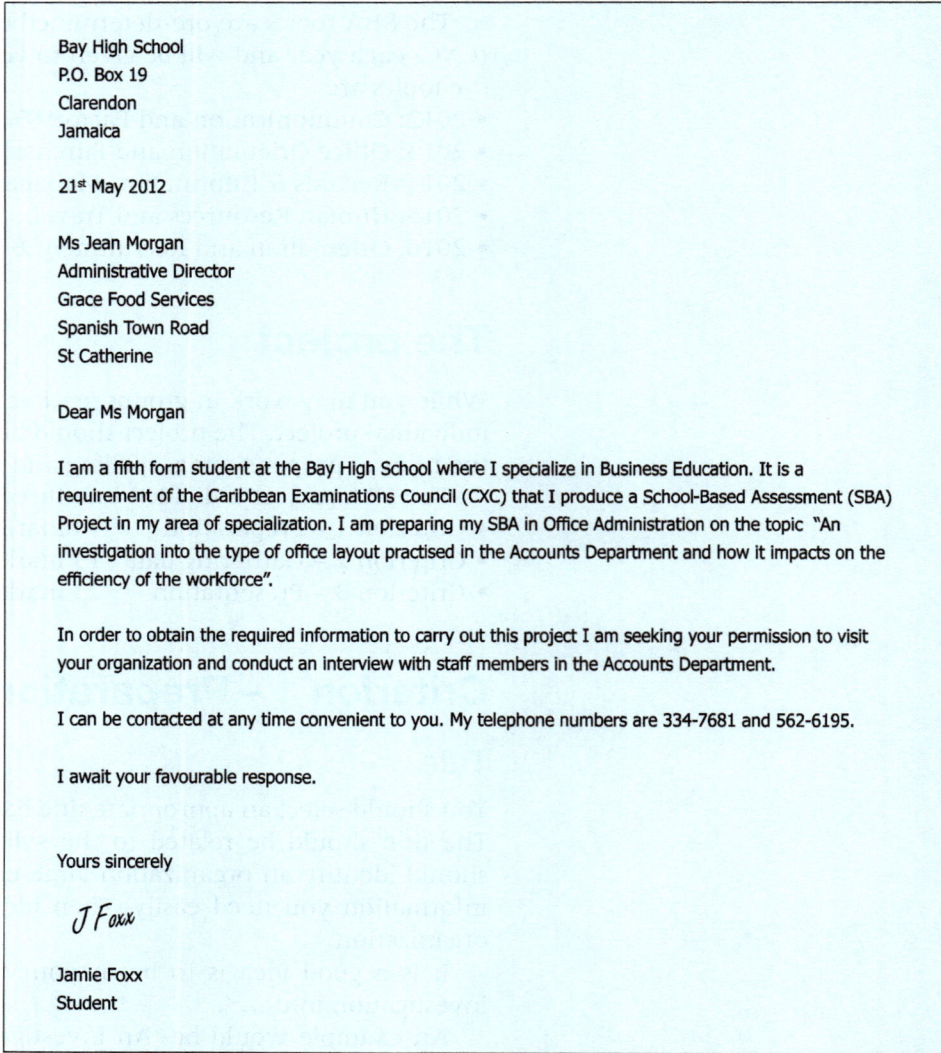

Bay High School
P.O. Box 19
Clarendon
Jamaica

21st May 2012

Ms Jean Morgan
Administrative Director
Grace Food Services
Spanish Town Road
St Catherine

Dear Ms Morgan

I am a fifth form student at the Bay High School where I specialize in Business Education. It is a requirement of the Caribbean Examinations Council (CXC) that I produce a School-Based Assessment (SBA) Project in my area of specialization. I am preparing my SBA in Office Administration on the topic "An investigation into the type of office layout practised in the Accounts Department and how it impacts on the efficiency of the workforce".

In order to obtain the required information to carry out this project I am seeking your permission to visit your organization and conduct an interview with staff members in the Accounts Department.

I can be contacted at any time convenient to you. My telephone numbers are 334-7681 and 562-6195.

I await your favourable response.

Yours sincerely

J Foxx

Jamie Foxx
Student

Figure 13.1   Example of a suitable letter

The letter should follow proper business letter-writing patterns such as matching salutation and complimentary close, as well as using a proper layout. You must ensure that there are no spelling or grammatical errors. The letter must be signed!

Business forms

Copies of business forms relevant to the department being studied must also be provided. An example of a completed document (an invoice) can be found in Chapter 11 at page 254.

Office equipment

It is also important that you demonstrate knowledge of office equipment and its functions, so you will prepare a table similar to the one in Figure 13.5.

Date	Equipment used	Purpose of equipment	Suitability for task
October 31, 2011	Computer	To research and store information; To type final draft of project	Gathers information in an efficient way and produces formatted copies of documents
October 31, 2011	Photocopier	To make single or multiple copies of documents	Provides accurate copies in colour if necessary

Figure 13.5 Example table of office equipment

Acknowledge your sources

At the end of your project you must acknowledge your sources by preparing a Bibliography / References / Sources of Information List.

Persons list

Date	Name	Job title	Place interviewed
May 1	Brown, Cathy	Human Resources Clerk	Interviewed in the Conference Room

Figure 13.6 Example of a persons list

Publications list

The information should be listed in the following forms:

Books

Trenfield-Newsome, A and Wright, C (2011). Office Administration for CSEC Examinations. London: Macmillan

Newspapers

Collinder, Avia (July 25, 2010). Building a business on business machines. The Sunday Gleaner, p C2

Internet / electronic sources

Lake, Laura (May 3, 2010). 'Marketing versus advertising: What's the difference?' Retrieved from http://marketing.about.com/cs/ advertisingamarketvsad.htm

Figure 13.7 Example of an entry from a publications list

Answers to multiple choice questions

Chapter 1									
1. a	2. d	3. b	4. c	5. a	6. d	7. b	8. c	9. a	10. c

Chapter 2								
1. b	2. c	3. b	4. c	5. a	6. b	7. b	8. c	9. a

Chapter 3								
1. d	2. a	3. c	4. b	5. a	6. b	7. b	8. a	9. d

Chapter 4									
1. a	2. a	3. c	4. a	5. c	6. a	7. a	8. a	9. a	10. a

Chapter 5									
1. d	2. b	3. a	4. b	5. d	6. c	7. c	8. a	9. b	10. a

Chapter 6						
1. a	2. b	3. d	4. c	5. c	6. a	7. a

Chapter 7									
1. c	2. a	3. a	4. b	5. c	6. b	7. d	8. c	9. d	10. a

Chapter 8							
1. d	2. c	3. d	4. a	5. b	6. b	7. d	8. d

Chapter 9							
1. b	2. a	3. d	4. a	5. b	6. a	7. b	8. c

Chapter 10									
1. b	2. b	3. a	4. d	5. a	6. b	7. a	8. b	9. a	10. b

Chapter 11									
1. b	2. b	3. c	4. d	5. c	6. d	7. b	8. d	9. b	10. d

Chapter 12									
1. a	2. c	3. a	4. d	5. d	6. c	7. d	8. c	9. b	10. a

Index

Where more than one page reference is given, the **bold** number indicates the more detailed reference.

Criterion 2 – Gathering data

Methodology

You can gather data from primary sources or secondary sources:

primary sources ▶
- Primary sources include data you collect yourself, for example through questionnaires, interviews and observation.

secondary sources ▶
- Secondary sources include data that has already been prepared for you, for example newspaper or magazine articles, information in textbooks or found on the internet.

A statement outlining the data-gathering instruments such as questionnaires, surveys and interviews must be presented in the project. Samples of these instruments that you are going to use must also be provided. You are also expected to explain why you chose the instrument you did.

Some examples of advantages of the two main methods are shown in Table 13.1.

Data collection instruments	Advantages
1 Questionnaire	1. Cheaper than face-to-face interview. 2. Easy to analyze the data. 3. A quick way to collect information.
2 Interview	1. Suitable for complex topics. 2. The interviewer is able to probe responses from the interviewee. 3. Helpful if the respondent has reading difficulties.

Table 13.1   Advantages of data collection methods

When preparing your interview schedule or questionnaire, it is important to ensure that you use properly structured questions that relate to the topic and to your aims. Questions will be either open-ended or close-ended.

close-ended questions ▶
Close-ended questions limit the choices given to the respondent. Examples of such questions are:

1   Which records management classification system is used in your office?
   a   alphabetical ☐
   b   geographical ☐
   c   subject ☐
   d   numerical ☐
   e chronological ☐
2   Do you use accounting software?
   Yes ☐   No ☐

open-ended questions ▶
Open-ended questions allow the person asking the question to gain more information from the respondent. For example: 'What are the duties of the receptionist in your organization?'.

observation checklist ▶
Another way of obtaining primary data is by using an observation checklist. This will outline items or events in the organization that you wish to observe.

In this methodology section you should explain how the data-gathering instrument was used. For example: 'The Records Management Supervisor was interviewed in her office on March 20, 2010'.

Observation Checklist

1.   Entry/Exit Signs ☐
2.   Fire Extinguisher ☐
3.   'Slippery when wet' Sign ☐

Figure 13.2   Extract from an observation checklist

Questions asked of office personnel

You need to list five questions that were asked of employees in the organization. These questions should be related to the aims previously identified. Questions from the questionnaire or interview schedule may be used.

Schedule of activities

This table should list at least ten activities involved in carrying out the project. Your comments should begin with the start of the project and end when the project is presented to the teacher. For example, you might begin like this:

Dates	Activities	Comments
September 9, 2011	Formulated topic and identified firm to conduct study	Showed topic to teacher for approval and submitted firm's name.
September 12, 2011	Went back to teacher to confirm topic and make corrections where necessary	Teacher approved topic and instructed me to draft permission letter to firm
September 14, 2011	Drafted permission letter	Teacher corrected letter and returned draft for correction.

Figure 13.3   Extract from a schedule of activities

Regulations and policies

In this section you will need to state:
- one **piece of legislation** governing the organization that you visited. Remember that a piece of legislation is a law – for example, the Factories Act of 1943. You should also state how you became aware of this law – for example, that you were told about it by the Human Resources Manager;
- one **health and safety practice** that you observed while carrying out your research – for example, you saw that there was a fire extinguisher on a wall;
- one **staff rule** with which you had to comply while carrying out your project – for example: 'One staff rule I had to obey was to turn off my cellular phone'.

Criterion 3 – Presentation

Your report should be between 1000 and 1200 words (2½ to 3 pages) in length.

You should state the type of office being investigated and complete a journal showing at least three activities carried out there in a typical day.

> ### August 7, 2011
>
> Today I observed a receptionist greeting a visitor. She welcomed the visitor to the organization and enquired whether the visitor had an appointment. The visitor did have an appointment which the receptionist confirmed by checking the appointments book. The visitor was offered a seat whilst the receptionist informed a staff member of the visitor's arrival.

Figure 13.4   Example of a journal entry

You must outline ways in which you think that the office can be more efficient – for example, by recommending that the furniture available for staff members be more ergonomically designed, to increase the workers' efficiency.